NEGIMA!

27

Ken Akamatsu

TRANSLATED AND ADAPTED BY
Alethea Nibley and Athena Nibley

LETTERING AND RETOUCH BY
Steve Palmer

BALLANTINE BOOKS • NEW YORK

Negima! volume 27 is a work of fiction. Names, characters, places, and incidents are the products of the author's imagination or are used fictitiously. Any resemblance to actual events, locales, or persons, living or dead, is entirely coincidental.

A Del Rey Manga/Kodansha Trade Paperback Original

Published in the United States by Del Rey, an imprint of The Random House Publishing Group, a division of Random House, Inc., New York.

Publication rights arranged through Kodansha Ltd.

First published in Japan in 2009 by Kodansha Ltd., Tokyo

ISBN 978-0-345-52159-0

Printed in the United States of America

www.delreymanga.com

9 8 7 6 5 4 3 2 1

Translators/adapters: Alethea Nibley and Athena Nibley
Lettering and retouch: Steve Palmer

Honorifics Explained

Throughout the Del Rey Manga books, you will find Japanese honorifics left intact in the translations. For those not familiar with how the Japanese use honorifics and, more important, how they differ from American honorifics, we present this brief overview.

Politeness has always been a critical facet of Japanese culture. Ever since the feudal era, when Japan was a highly stratified society, use of honorifics—which can be defined as polite speech that indicates relationship or status—has played an essential role in the Japanese language. When addressing someone in Japanese, an honorific usually takes the form of a suffix attached to one's name (example: "Asuna-san"), is used as a title at the end of one's name, or appears in place of the name itself (example: "Negi-sensei," or simply "Sensei!").

Honorifics can be expressions of respect or endearment. In the context of manga and anime, honorifics give insight into the nature of the relationship between characters. Many English translations leave out these important honorifics and therefore distort the feel of the original Japanese. Because Japanese honorifics contain nuances that English honorifics lack, it is our policy at Del Rey not to translate them. Here, instead, is a guide to some of the honorifics you may encounter in Del Rey Manga.

-san: This is the most common honorific and is equivalent to Mr., Miss, Ms., or Mrs. It is the all-purpose honorific and can be used in any situation where politeness is required.

-sama: This is one level higher than "-san" and is used to confer great respect.

-dono: This comes from the word "tono," which means "lord." It is an even higher level than "-sama" and confers utmost respect.

-kun: This suffix is used at the end of boys' names to express familiarity or endearment. It is also sometimes used by men

among friends, or when addressing someone younger or of a lower station.

-chan: This is used to express endearment, mostly toward girls. It is also used for little boys, pets, and even among lovers. It gives a sense of childish cuteness.

Bōzu: This is an informal way to refer to a boy, similar to the English terms "kid" and "squirt."

Sempai/Senpai: This title suggests that the addressee is one's senior in a group or organization. It is most often used in a school setting, where underclassmen refer to their upperclassmen as "sempai." It can also be used in the workplace, such as when a newer employee addresses an employee who has seniority in the company.

Kohai: This is the opposite of "sempai" and is used toward underclassmen in school or newcomers in the workplace. It connotes that the addressee is of a lower station.

Sensei: Literally meaning "one who has come before," this title is used for teachers, doctors, or masters of any profession or art.

Anesan (or *nesan*): A generic term for a girl, usually older, that means "sister."

Ojōsama: A way of referring to the daughter or sister of someone with high political or social status.

-[blank]: This is usually forgotten in these lists, but it is perhaps the most significant difference between Japanese and English. The lack of honorific means that the speaker has permission to address the person in a very intimate way. Usually, only family, spouses, or very close friends have this kind of permission. Known as *yobisute,* it can be gratifying when someone who has earned the intimacy starts to call one by one's name without an honorific. But when that intimacy hasn't been earned, it can be very insulting.

A Word from the Author

Sorry to have kept you waiting. I present *Negima!* volume 27!
Shockingly, this entire volume is dedicated to the battle with Rakan!! A superbattle, fitting of a shounen manga, unfolds over nine chapters. It created a huge sensation in *Shonen Magazine*, too.
Negi's pactio card and artifact, which you could say are a special bonus for this battle only, drive his master Rakan up against a wall with their terrifying abilities.

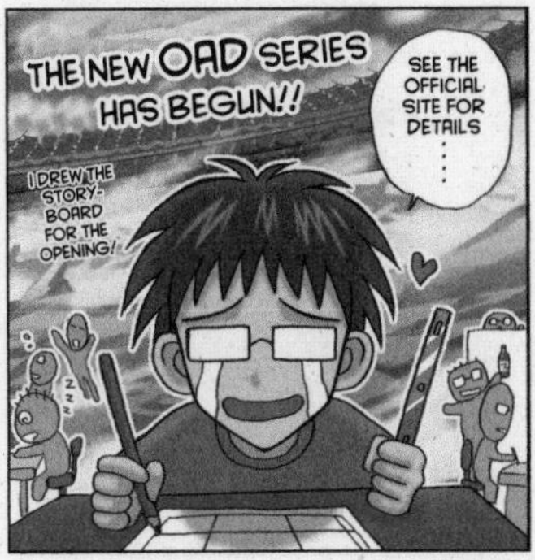
THE NEW OAD SERIES HAS BEGUN!!
SEE THE OFFICIAL SITE FOR DETAILS
...
I DREW THE STORY-BOARD FOR THE OPENING!

Negi or Rakan—who will come out the victor!?
...Incidentally, as a side effect of the battle, this time the classmates don't show up at all. m(_ _)m, Many apologies to their fans. They appear a lot in the next volume, so those of you who read for the classmates, please don't abandon me! (^^;)

Ken Akamatsu
www.ailove.net

27

魔法先生ネギま!

MAGISTER NEGI MAGI

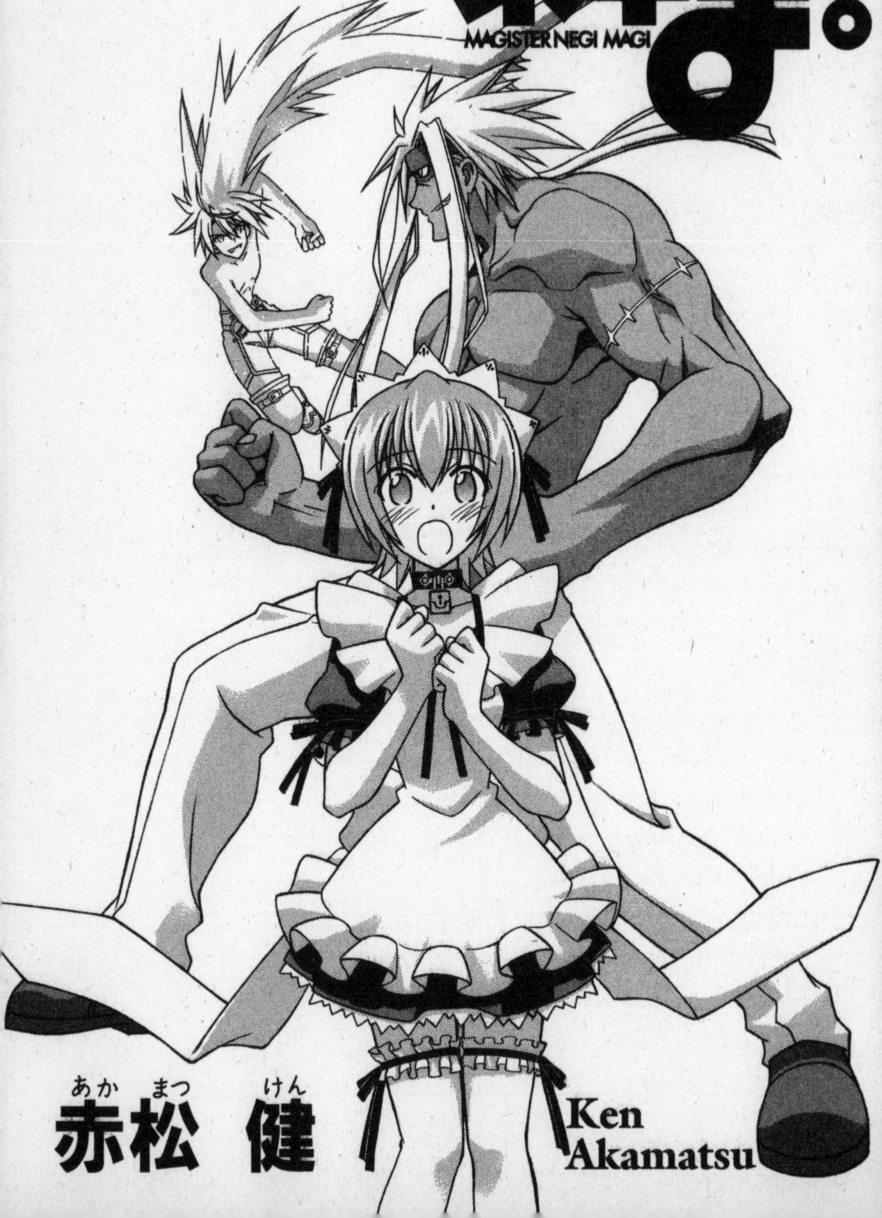

赤松 健

Ken Akamatsu

CONTENTS

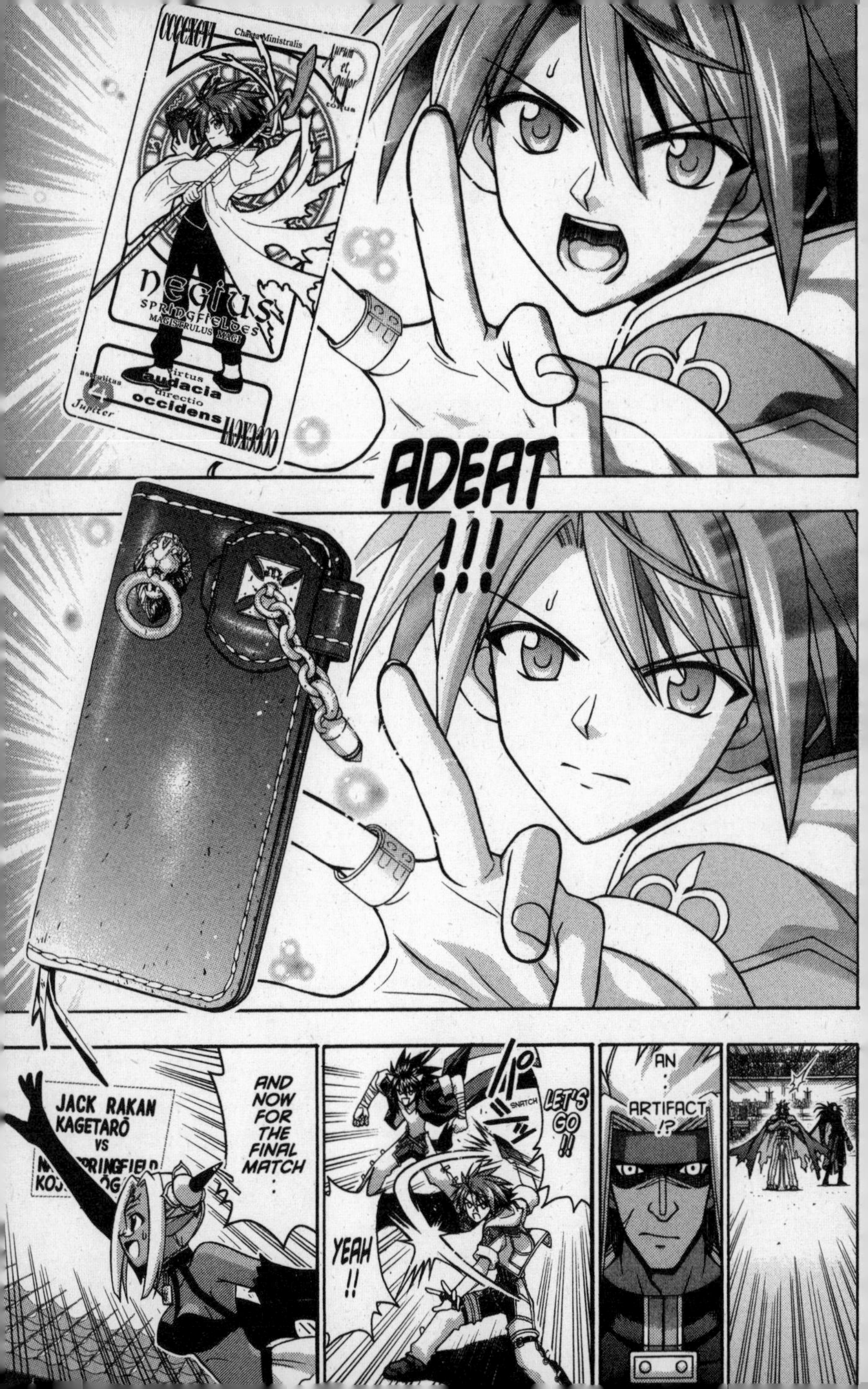

Chartae Ministralis
Negius
Springfieldes
Magistrulus Magi
virtus
audacia
directio
occidens
Jupiter
ADEAT!!!
AN... ARTIFACT!?
LET'S GO!!
SNATCH
YEAH!!
AND NOW FOR THE FINAL MATCH...
JACK RAKAN
KAGETARŌ
VS

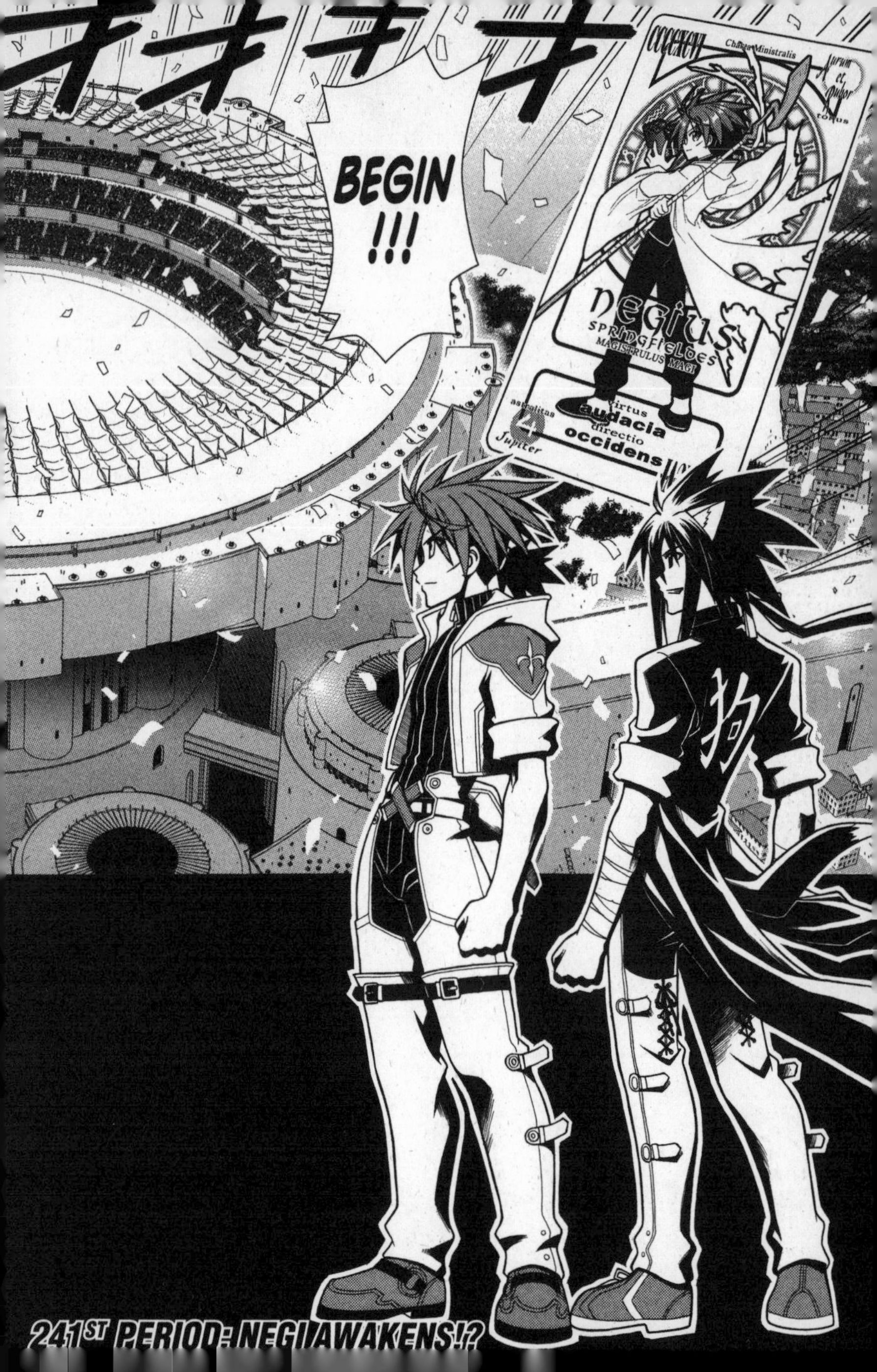

オオオオ
BEGIN !!!
negius springfieldes
MAGISTRULUS MAGI
virtus audacia
directio occidens
astralitas
4
Jupiter
241ST PERIOD: NEGI AWAKENS!?

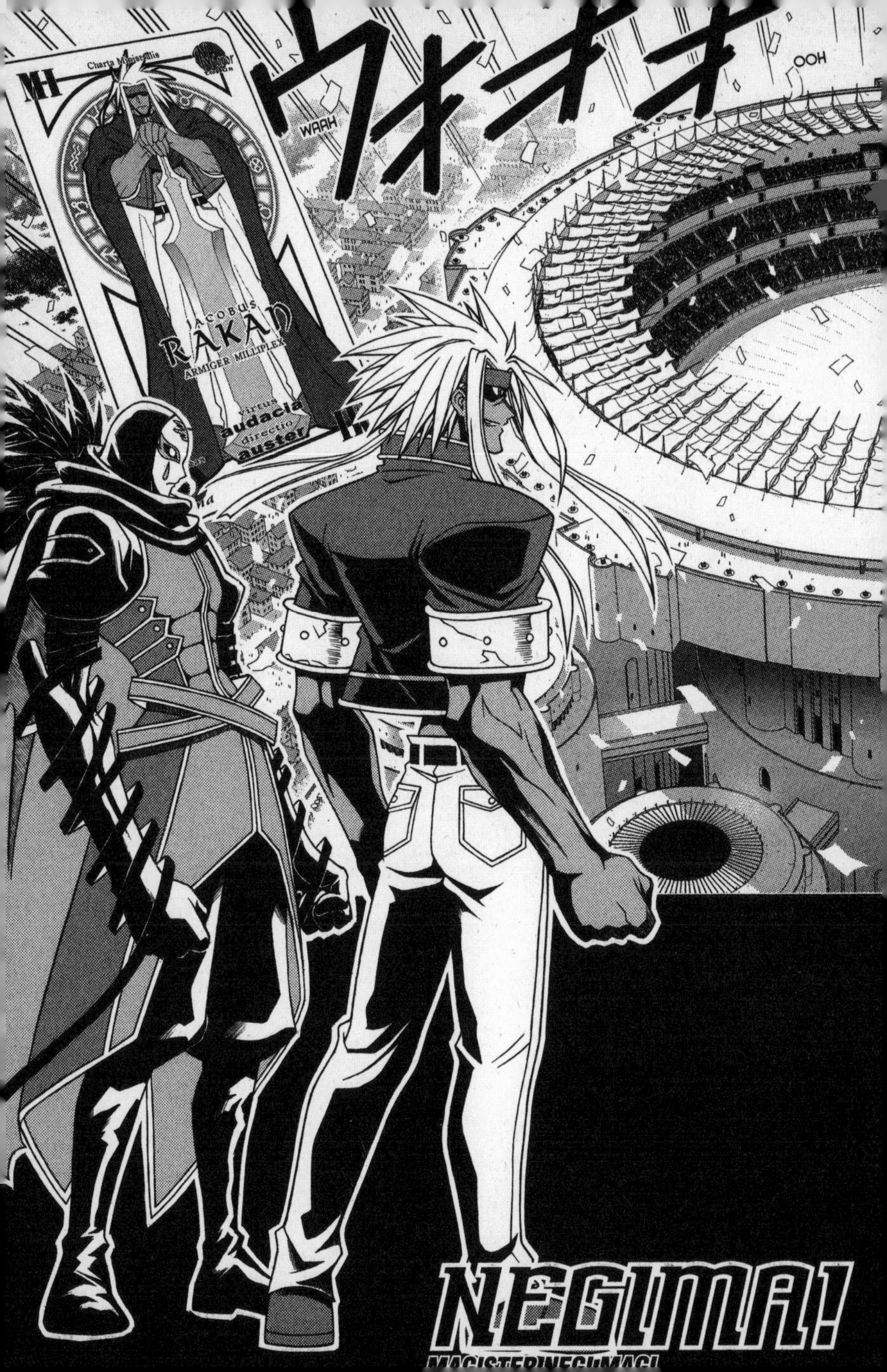
ウォオオ
OOH
WAAH
Charta Magistralis
JACOBUS
RAKAN
ARMIGER MILLIPLEX
virtus
audacia
directio
auster
NEGIMA!

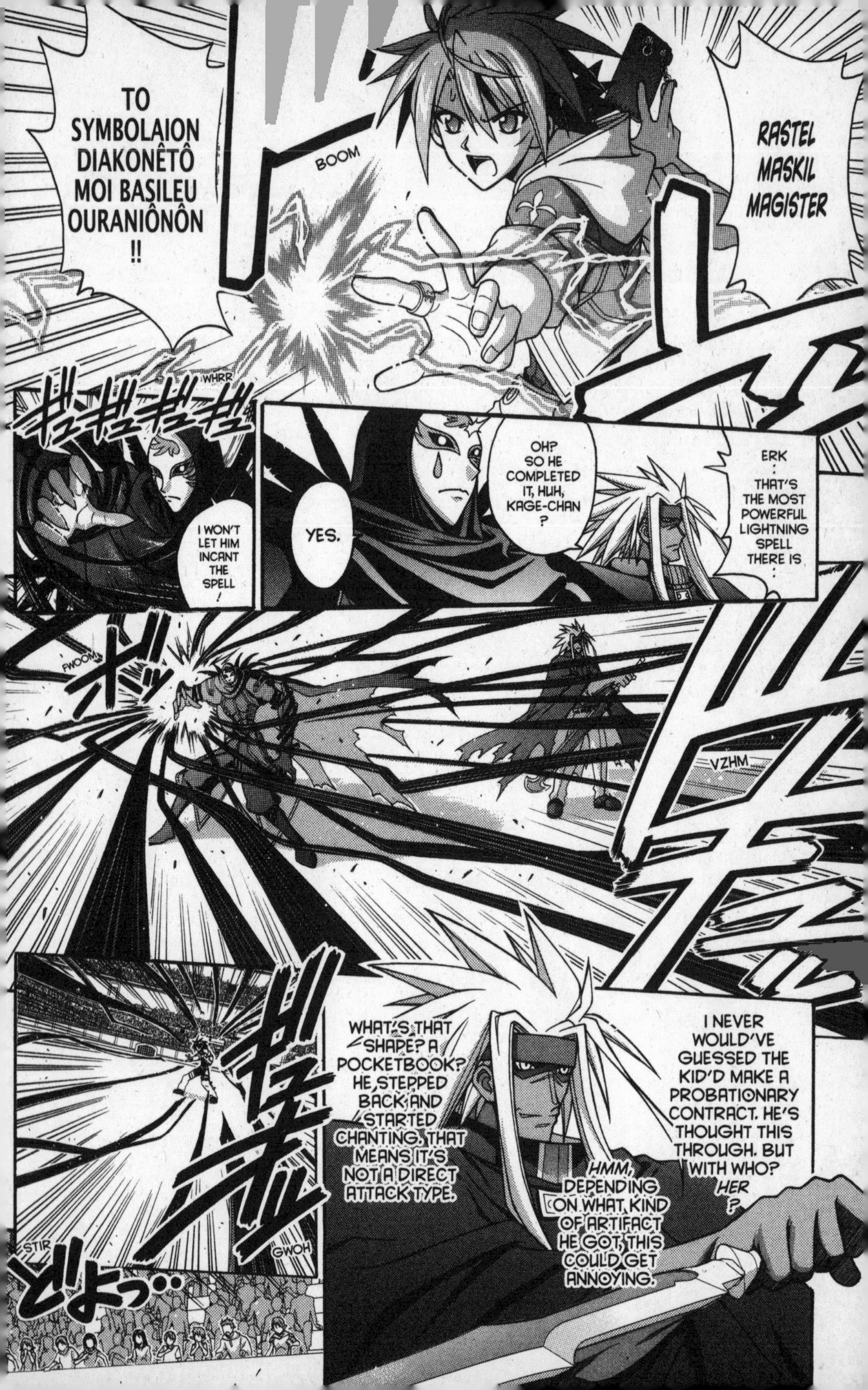
RASTEL MASKIL MAGISTER
BOOM
TO SYMBOLAION DIAKONÊTÔ MOI BASILEU OURANIÔNÔN !!
ERK : THAT'S THE MOST POWERFUL LIGHTNING SPELL THERE IS :
OH? SO HE COMPLETED IT, HUH, KAGE-CHAN ?
YES.
WHRR
I WON'T LET HIM INCANT THE SPELL !
VZHM
FWOOM
I NEVER WOULD'VE GUESSED THE KID'D MAKE A PROBATIONARY CONTRACT. HE'S THOUGHT THIS THROUGH. BUT WITH WHO?
HER ?
HMM, DEPENDING ON WHAT KIND OF ARTIFACT HE GOT, THIS COULD GET ANNOYING.
WHAT'S THAT SHAPE? A POCKETBOOK? HE STEPPED BACK AND STARTED CHANTING. THAT MEANS IT'S NOT A DIRECT ATTACK TYPE.
GWOH
STIR

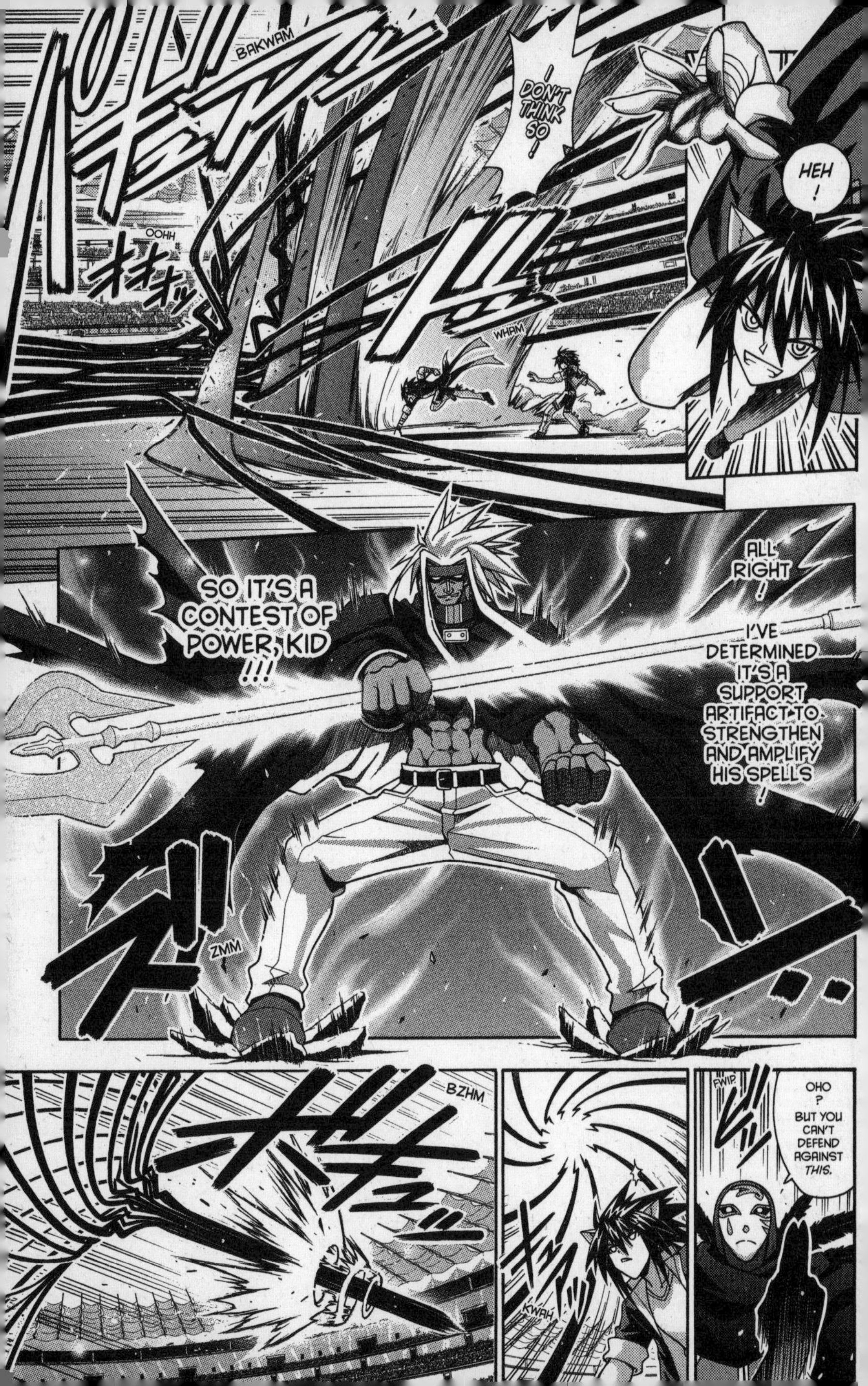
HEH!
I DON'T THINK SO!
BAKWAM
OOHH
WHAM
ALL RIGHT!
I'VE DETERMINED IT'S A SUPPORT ARTIFACT TO STRENGTHEN AND AMPLIFY HIS SPELLS!
SO IT'S A CONTEST OF POWER, KID!!!
ZMM
OHO?
BUT YOU CAN'T DEFEND AGAINST *THIS*.
FWIP
KWAH
BZHM

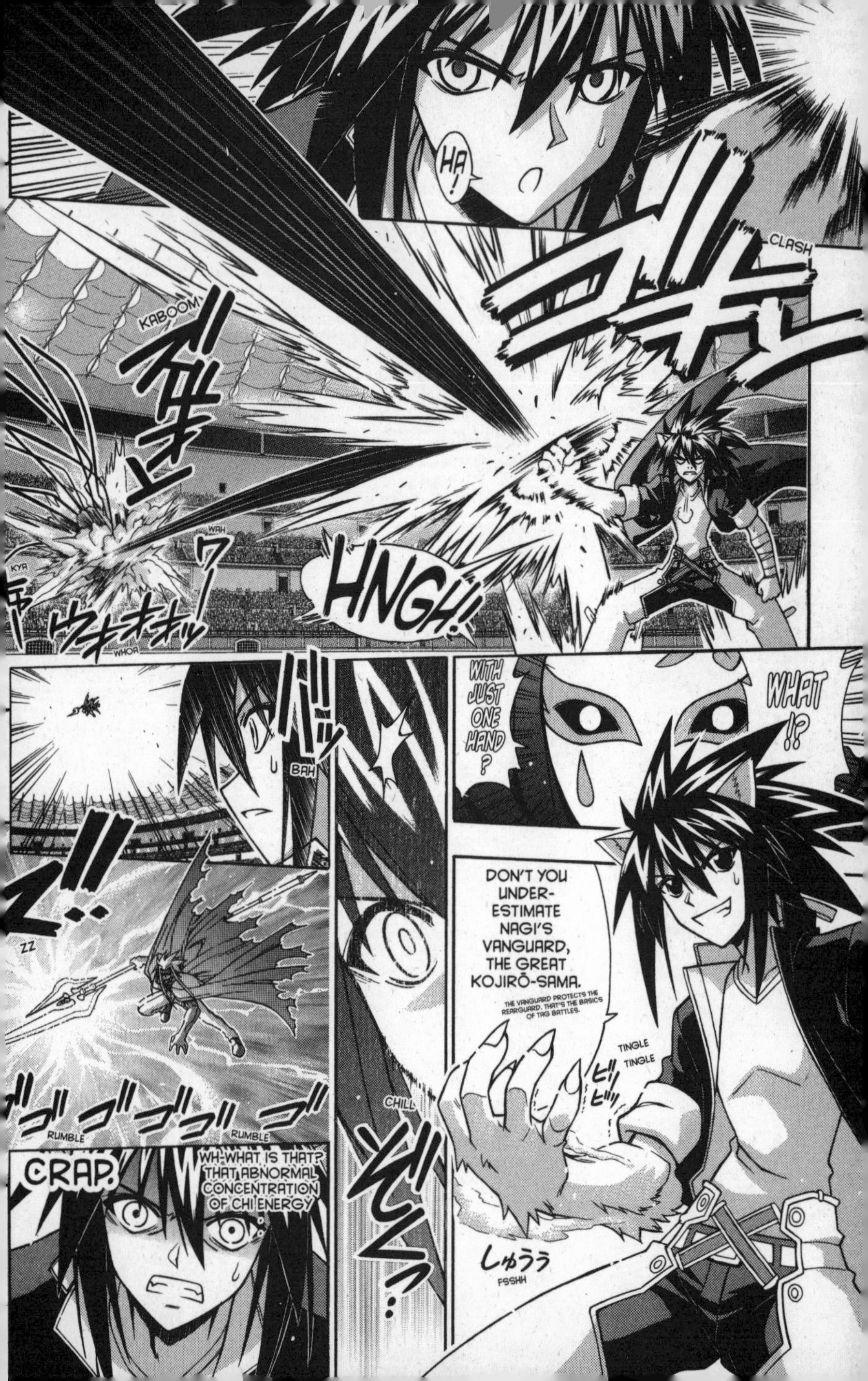
HA!
CLASH
HNGH!
KABOOM
WAH
KYA
WHOA
WHAT!?
WITH JUST ONE HAND?
DON'T YOU UNDER-ESTIMATE NAGI'S VANGUARD, THE GREAT KOJIRŌ-SAMA.
THE VANGUARD PROTECTS THE REARGUARD. THAT'S THE BASICS OF TAG BATTLES.
TINGLE TINGLE
CHILL
しゅううう
FSSHH
BAH
ZZ
RUMBLE
RUMBLE
CRAP.
WH-WHAT IS THAT? THAT ABNORMAL CONCENTRATION OF CHI ENERGY

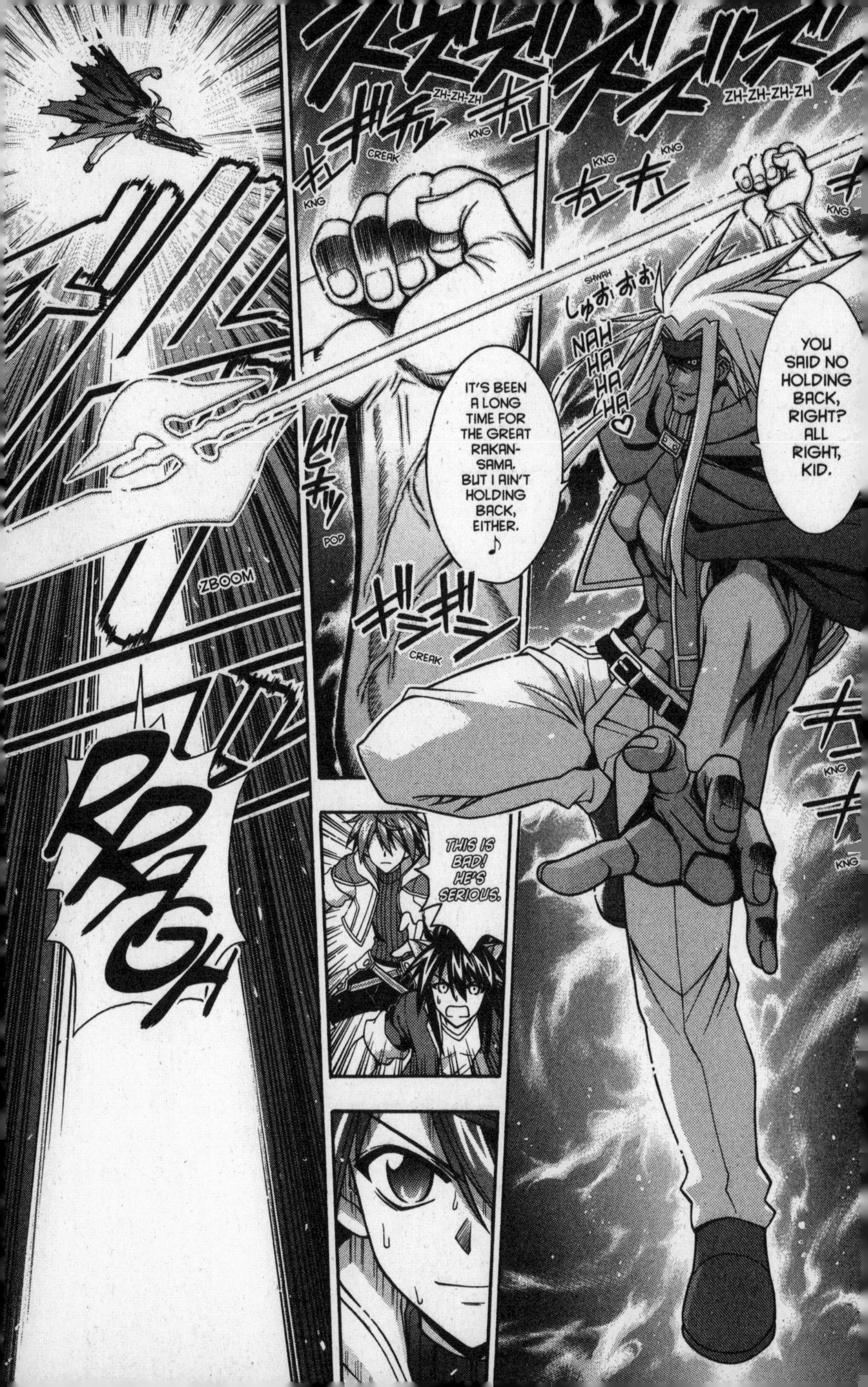
ZH-ZH-ZH-ZH
KNG
KNG
KNG
SHWAH
しゅおおお
NAH HA HA HA HA ♡
YOU SAID NO HOLDING BACK, RIGHT? ALL RIGHT, KID.
KNG
KNG
ZH-ZH-ZH
KNG
CREAK
KNG
POP
IT'S BEEN A LONG TIME FOR THE GREAT RAKAN-SAMA. BUT I AIN'T HOLDING BACK, EITHER. ♪
CREAK
THIS IS BAD! HE'S SERIOUS.
ZBOOM
RRAGH

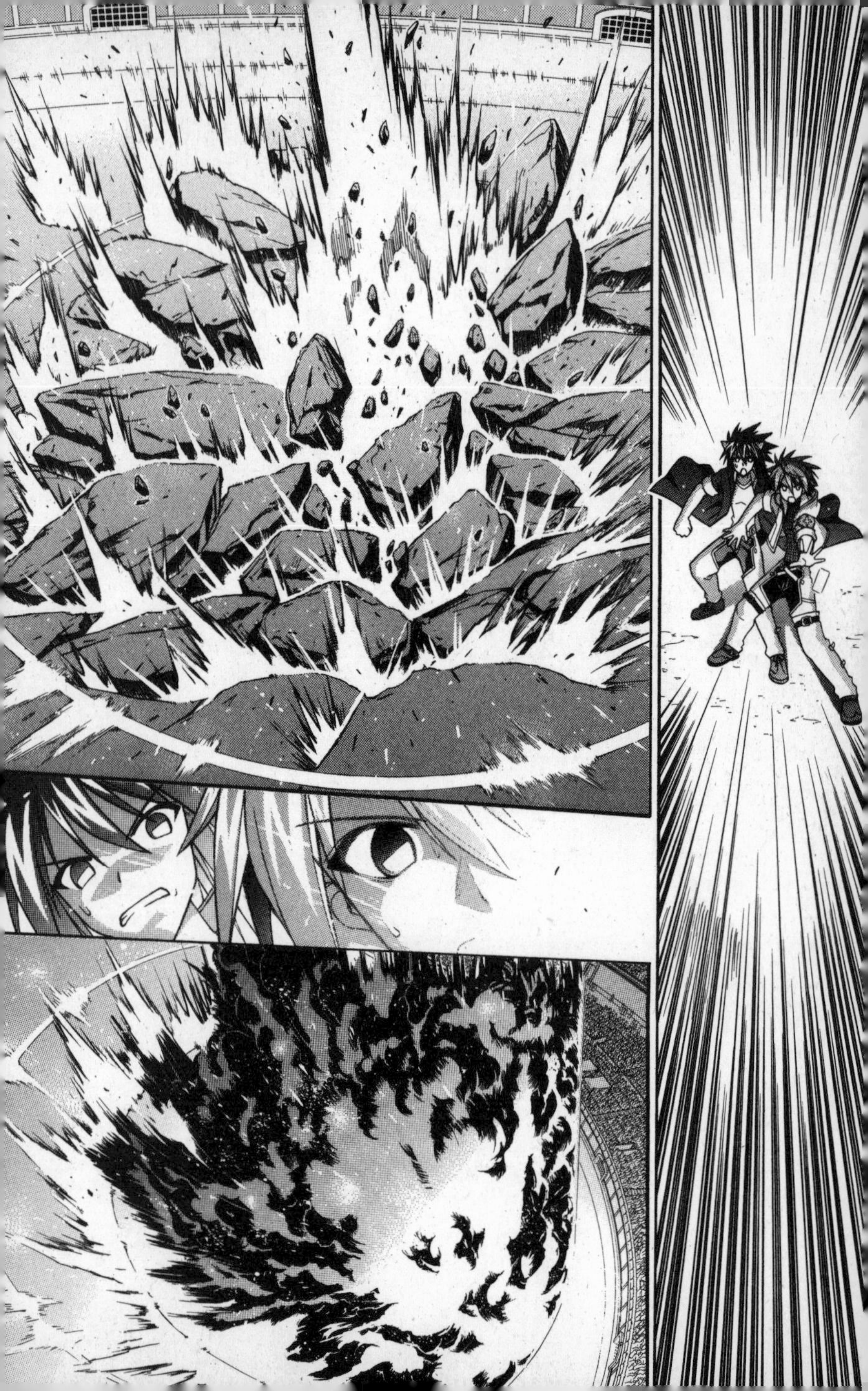

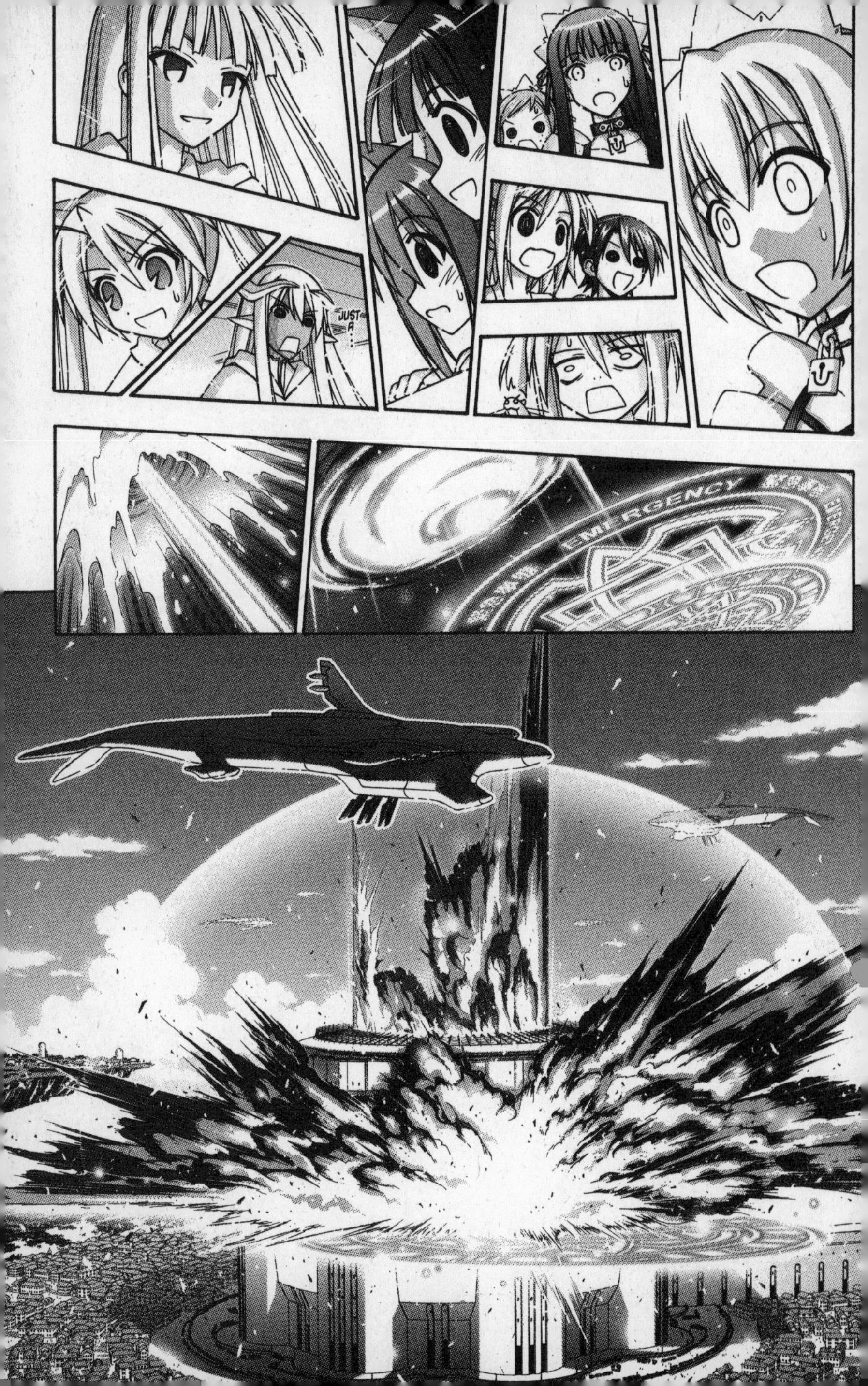
JUST A...
EMERGENCY

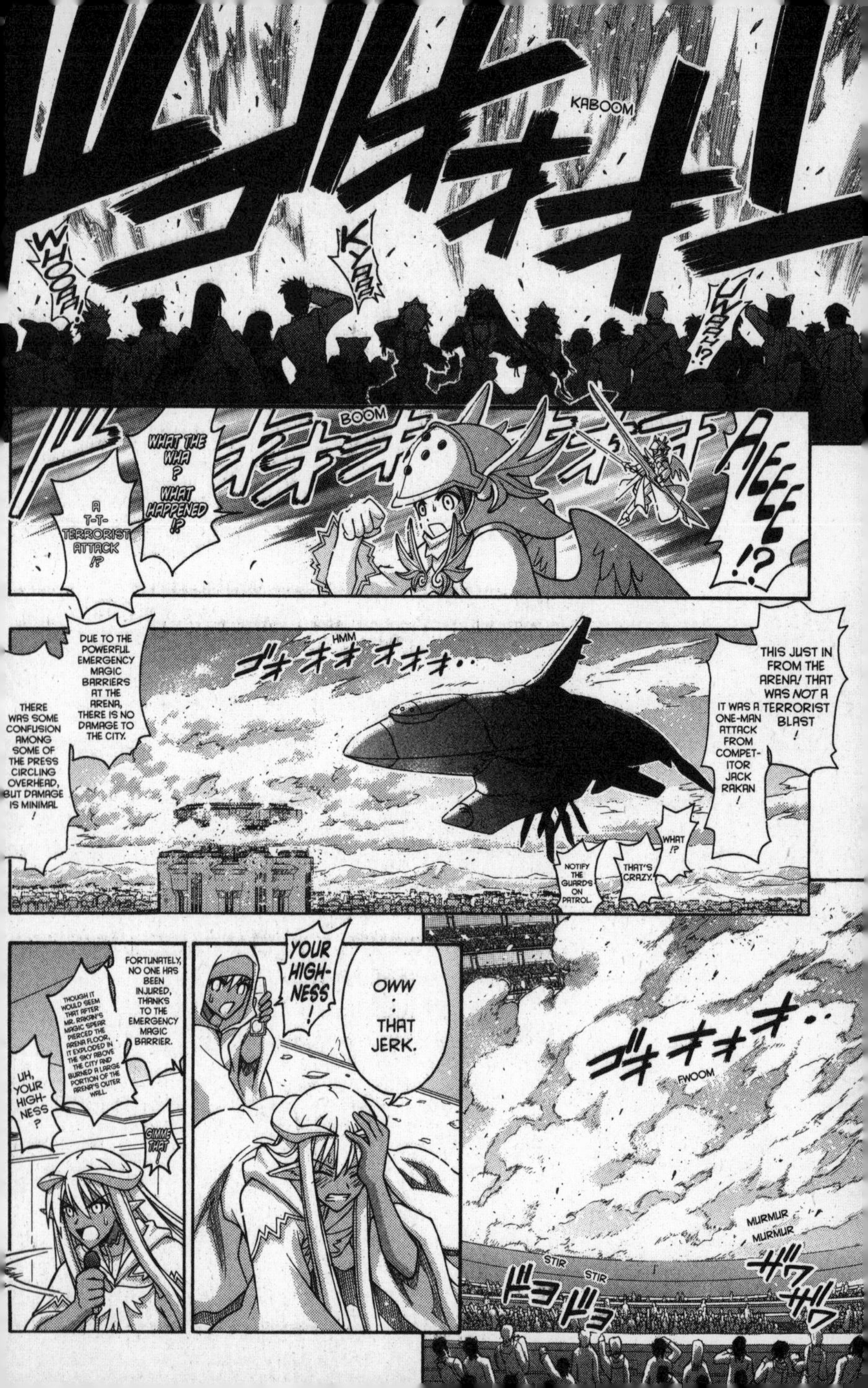
KABOOM
UWAAH!?
KYAA
WHOOM!
AEEE!?
BOOM
WHAT THE WHA? WHAT HAPPENED!?
A T-T-TERRORIST ATTACK!?
THIS JUST IN FROM THE ARENA! THAT WAS *NOT* A TERRORIST BLAST!
IT WAS A ONE-MAN ATTACK FROM COMPETITOR JACK RAKAN!
WHAT!?
THAT'S CRAZY.
NOTIFY THE GUARDS ON PATROL.
HMM
DUE TO THE POWERFUL EMERGENCY MAGIC BARRIERS AT THE ARENA, THERE IS NO DAMAGE TO THE CITY.
THERE WAS SOME CONFUSION AMONG SOME OF THE PRESS CIRCLING OVERHEAD, BUT DAMAGE IS MINIMAL!
FWOOM
MURMUR
MURMUR
STIR
STIR
YOUR HIGHNESS!
OWW... THAT JERK.
FORTUNATELY, NO ONE HAS BEEN INJURED, THANKS TO THE EMERGENCY MAGIC BARRIER.
THOUGH IT WOULD SEEM THAT AFTER MR. RAKAN'S MAGIC SPEAR PIERCED THE ARENA FLOOR, IT EXPLODED IN THE SKY ABOVE THE CITY AND BURNED A LARGE PORTION OF THE ARENA'S OUTER WALL.
UH, YOUR HIGHNESS?
GIMME THAT!

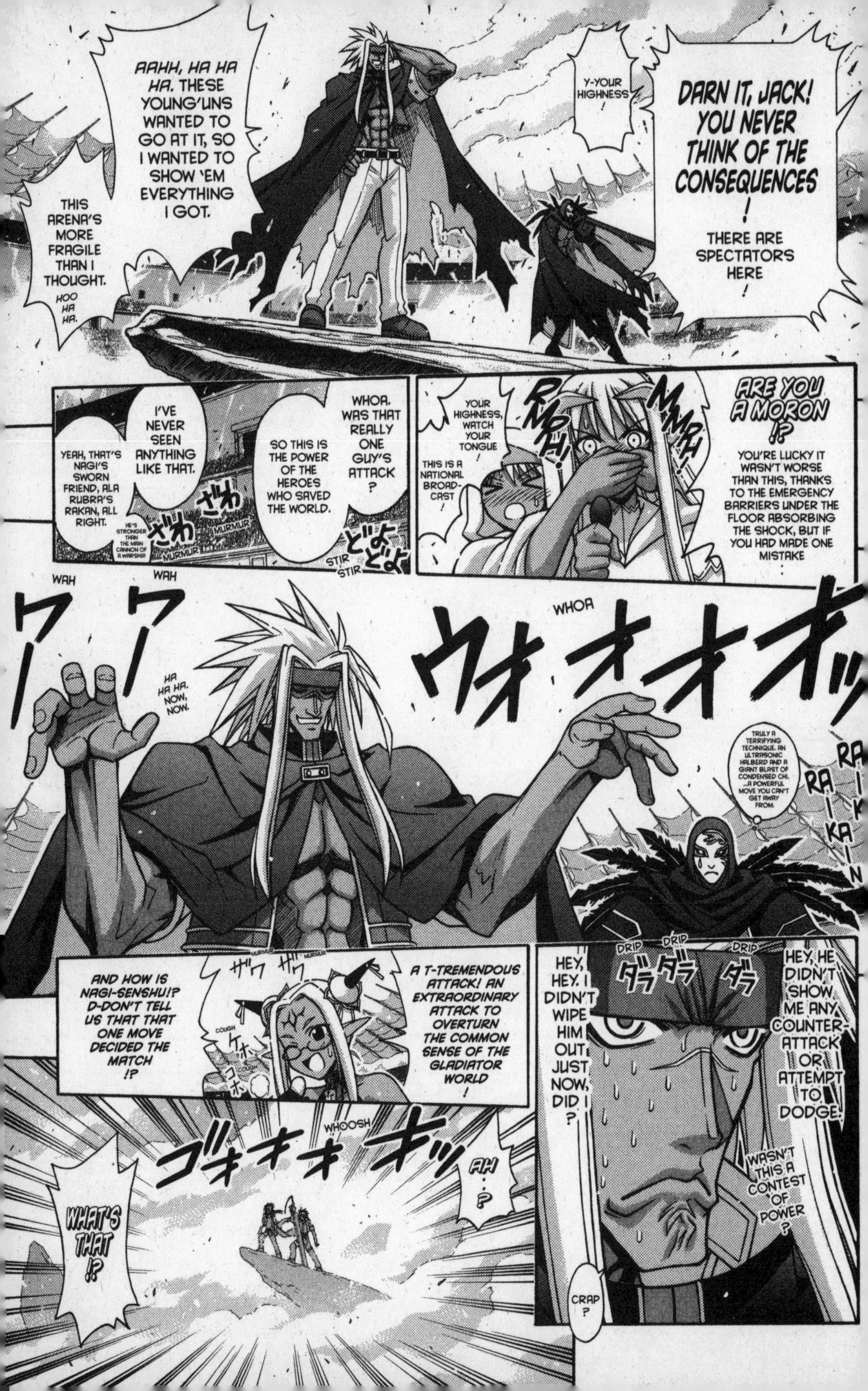
DARN IT, JACK! YOU NEVER THINK OF THE CONSEQUENCES!
THERE ARE SPECTATORS HERE!
Y-YOUR HIGHNESS!
AAHH, HA HA HA. THESE YOUNG'UNS WANTED TO GO AT IT, SO I WANTED TO SHOW 'EM EVERYTHING I GOT.
THIS ARENA'S MORE FRAGILE THAN I THOUGHT.
HOO HA HA.
ARE YOU A MORON!?
YOU'RE LUCKY IT WASN'T WORSE THAN THIS, THANKS TO THE EMERGENCY BARRIERS UNDER THE FLOOR ABSORBING THE SHOCK, BUT IF YOU HAD MADE ONE MISTAKE
MMMPH!
RMPH!
YOUR HIGHNESS, WATCH YOUR TONGUE!
THIS IS A NATIONAL BROADCAST!
WHOA. WAS THAT REALLY ONE GUY'S ATTACK?
SO THIS IS THE POWER OF THE HEROES WHO SAVED THE WORLD.
I'VE NEVER SEEN ANYTHING LIKE THAT.
YEAH, THAT'S NAGI'S SWORN FRIEND, ALA RUBRA'S RAKAN, ALL RIGHT.
HE'S STRONGER THAN THE MAIN CANNON OF A WARSHIP
ざわ ざわ MURMUR MURMUR
どよ どよ STIR STIR
RA-KAN RA-KAN
TRULY A TERRIFYING TECHNIQUE. AN ULTRASONIC HALBERD AND A GIANT BLAST OF CONDENSED CHI. ...A POWERFUL MOVE YOU CAN'T GET AWAY FROM.
ウォオオオッ WHOA
HA HA HA. NOW, NOW.
ワーアー WAH WAH
HEY, HE DIDN'T SHOW ME ANY COUNTER-ATTACK OR ATTEMPT TO DODGE!
ダラ ダラ ダラ DRIP DRIP DRIP
HEY, HEY. I DIDN'T WIPE HIM OUT JUST NOW, DID I?
WASN'T THIS A CONTEST OF POWER?
CRAP?
A T-TREMENDOUS ATTACK! AN EXTRAORDINARY ATTACK TO OVERTURN THE COMMON SENSE OF THE GLADIATOR WORLD!
ザワ ザワ MURMUR MURMUR
AND HOW IS NAGI-SENSHU!? D-DON'T TELL US THAT THAT ONE MOVE DECIDED THE MATCH!?
ケホ コホ COUGH COUGH
AH...?
ゴオオオオッ WHOOSH
WHAT'S THAT!?

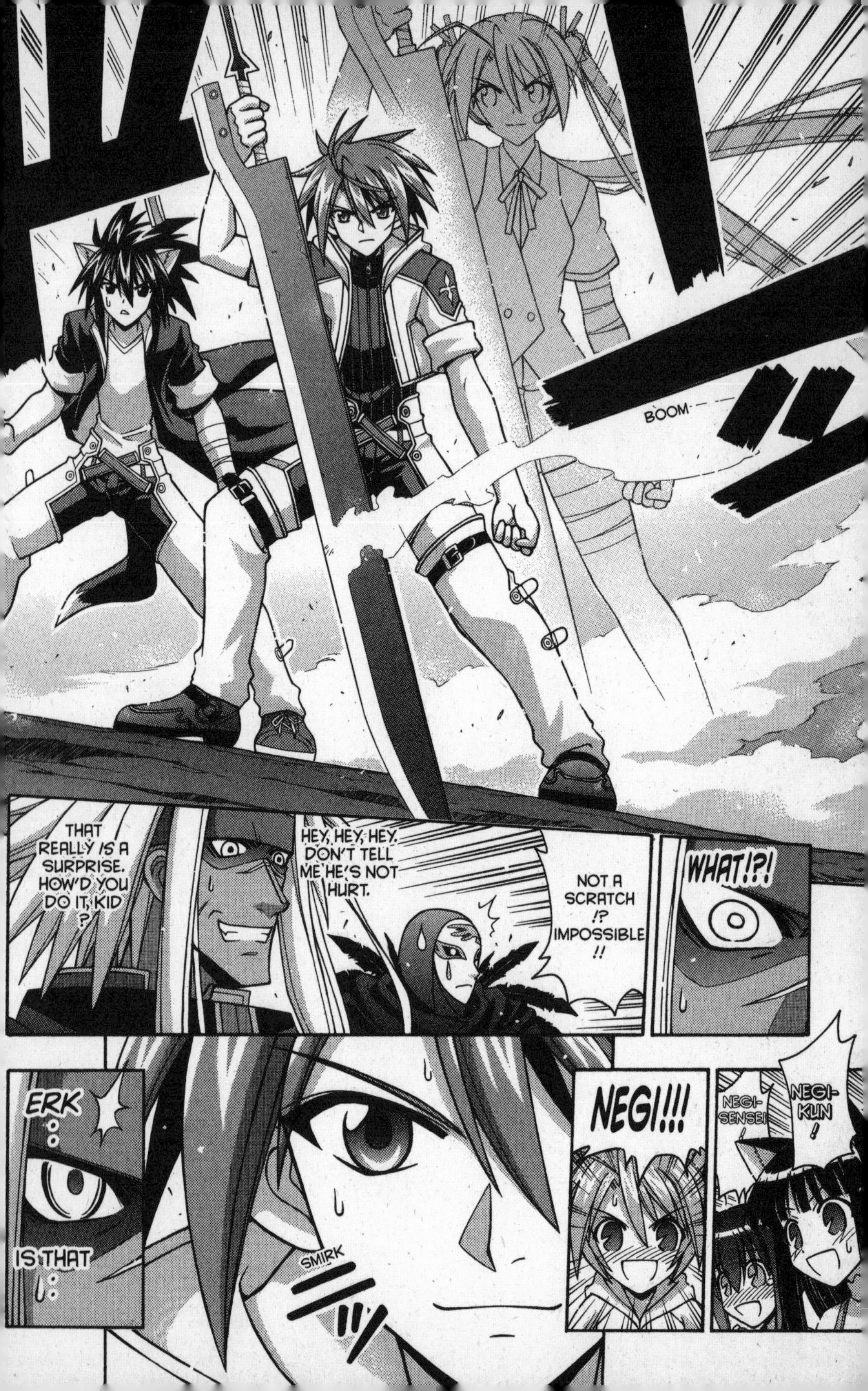
BOOM
WHAT!?!
NOT A SCRATCH!? IMPOSSIBLE!!
HEY, HEY, HEY. DON'T TELL ME HE'S NOT HURT.
THAT REALLY IS A SURPRISE. HOW'D YOU DO IT, KID?
NEGI-KUN!
NEGI-SENSEI!
NEGI!!!
SMIRK
ERK...
IS THAT...

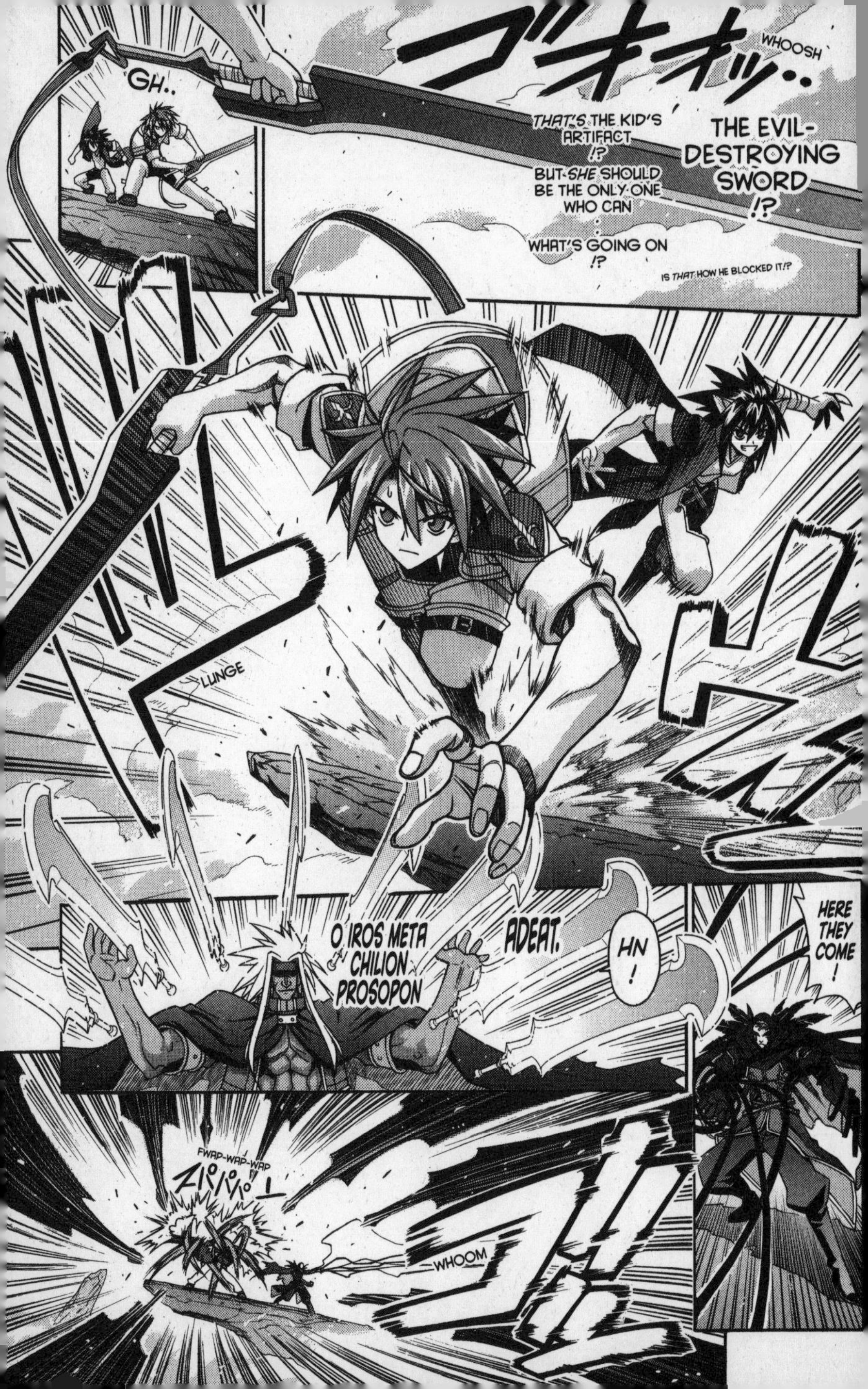
ゴオオッ・・
WHOOSH
THE EVIL-DESTROYING SWORD !?
THAT'S THE KID'S ARTIFACT !?
BUT SHE SHOULD BE THE ONLY ONE WHO CAN . . .
WHAT'S GOING ON !?
IS THAT HOW HE BLOCKED IT!?
GH..
LUNGE
HERE THEY COME !
HN !
ADEAT.
O IROS META CHILION PROSOPON
FWAP-WAP-WAP
スパパパッ
WHOOM

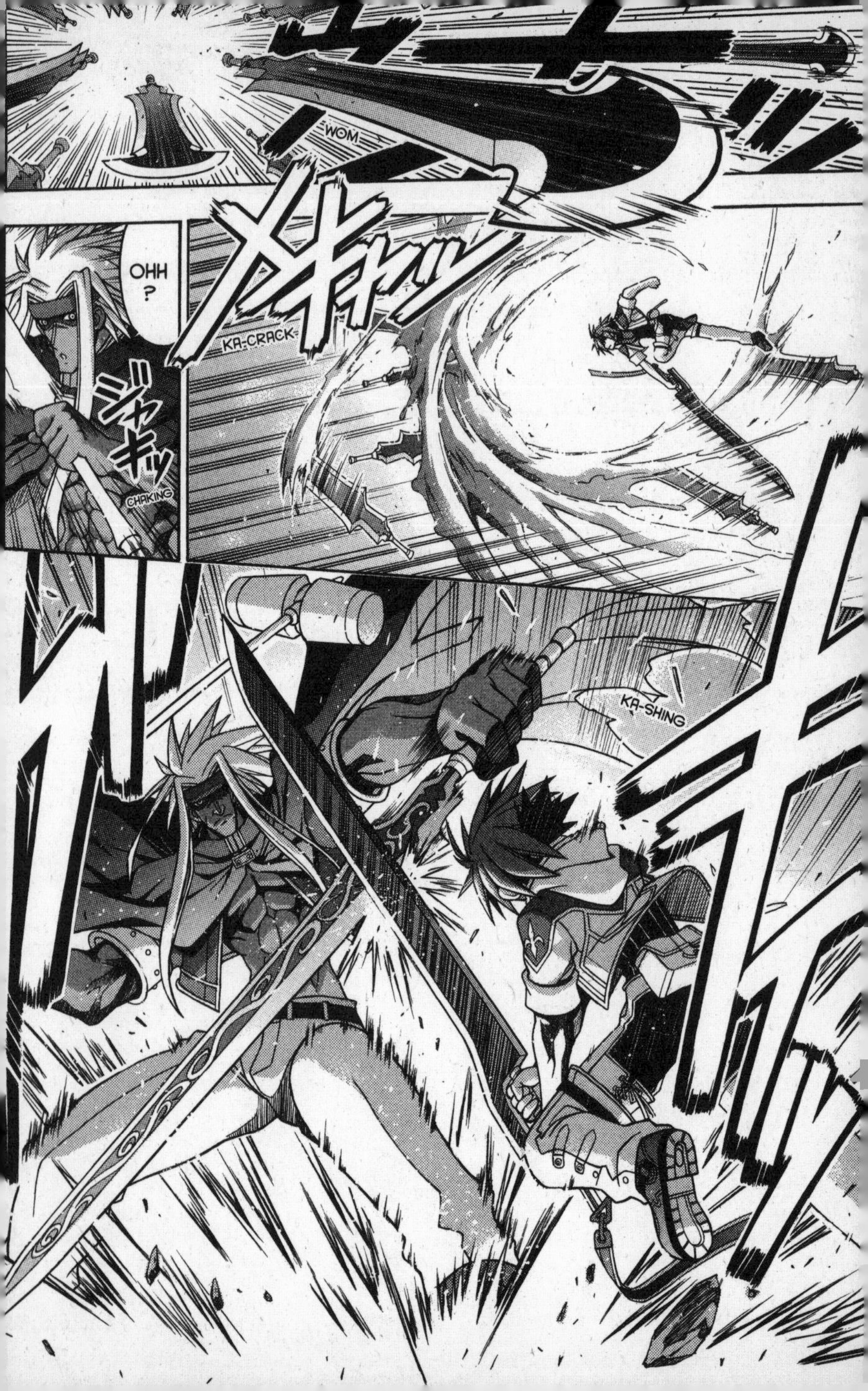
WOM
KA-CRACK
OHH ?
ジャキッ
CHAKING
KA-SHING

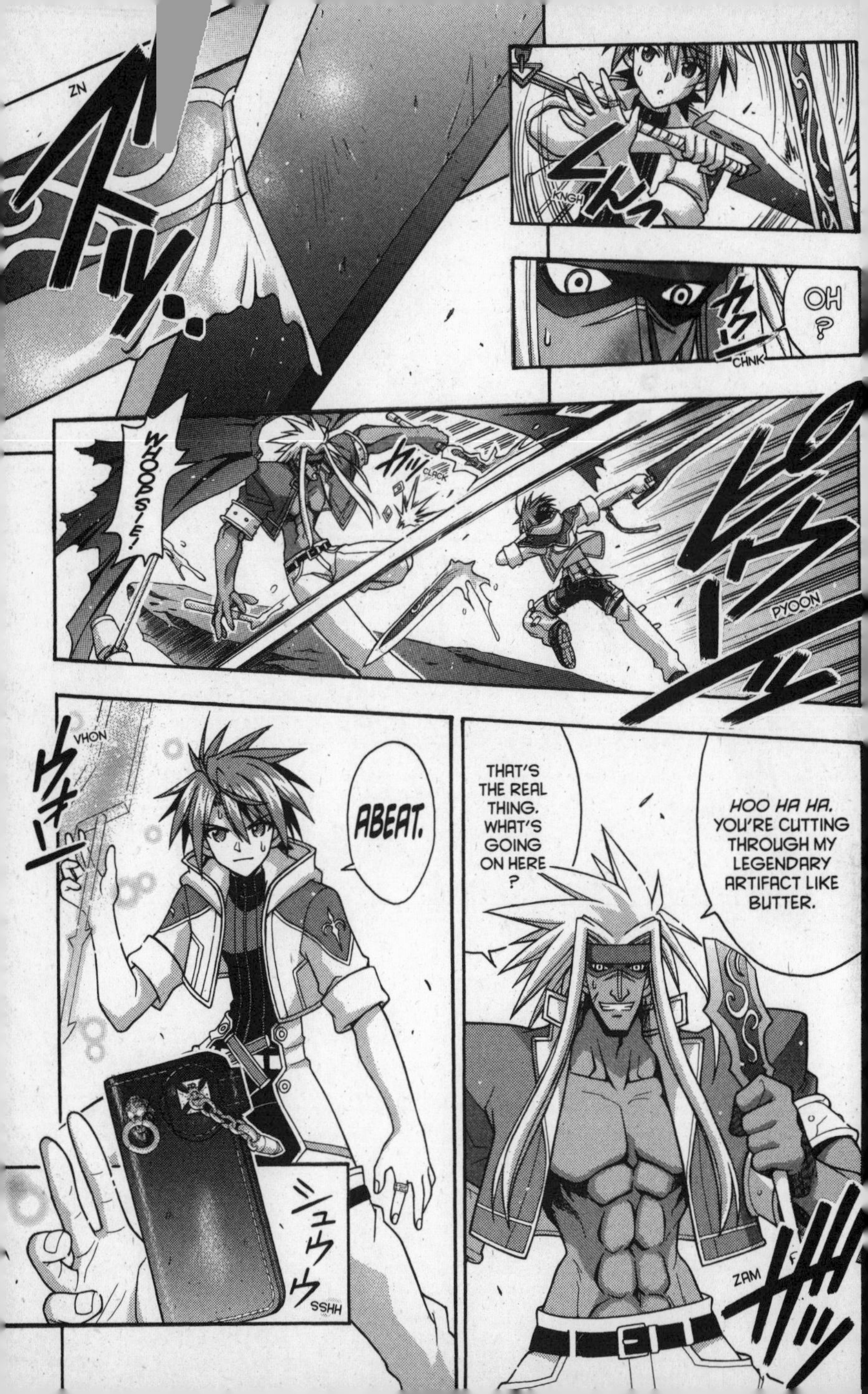
KNGH
OH?
CHNK
ZN
PYOON
CLACK
WHOOPSIE!
HOO HA HA. YOU'RE CUTTING THROUGH MY LEGENDARY ARTIFACT LIKE BUTTER.
THAT'S THE REAL THING. WHAT'S GOING ON HERE?
ZAM
VHON
ABEAT.
SSHH

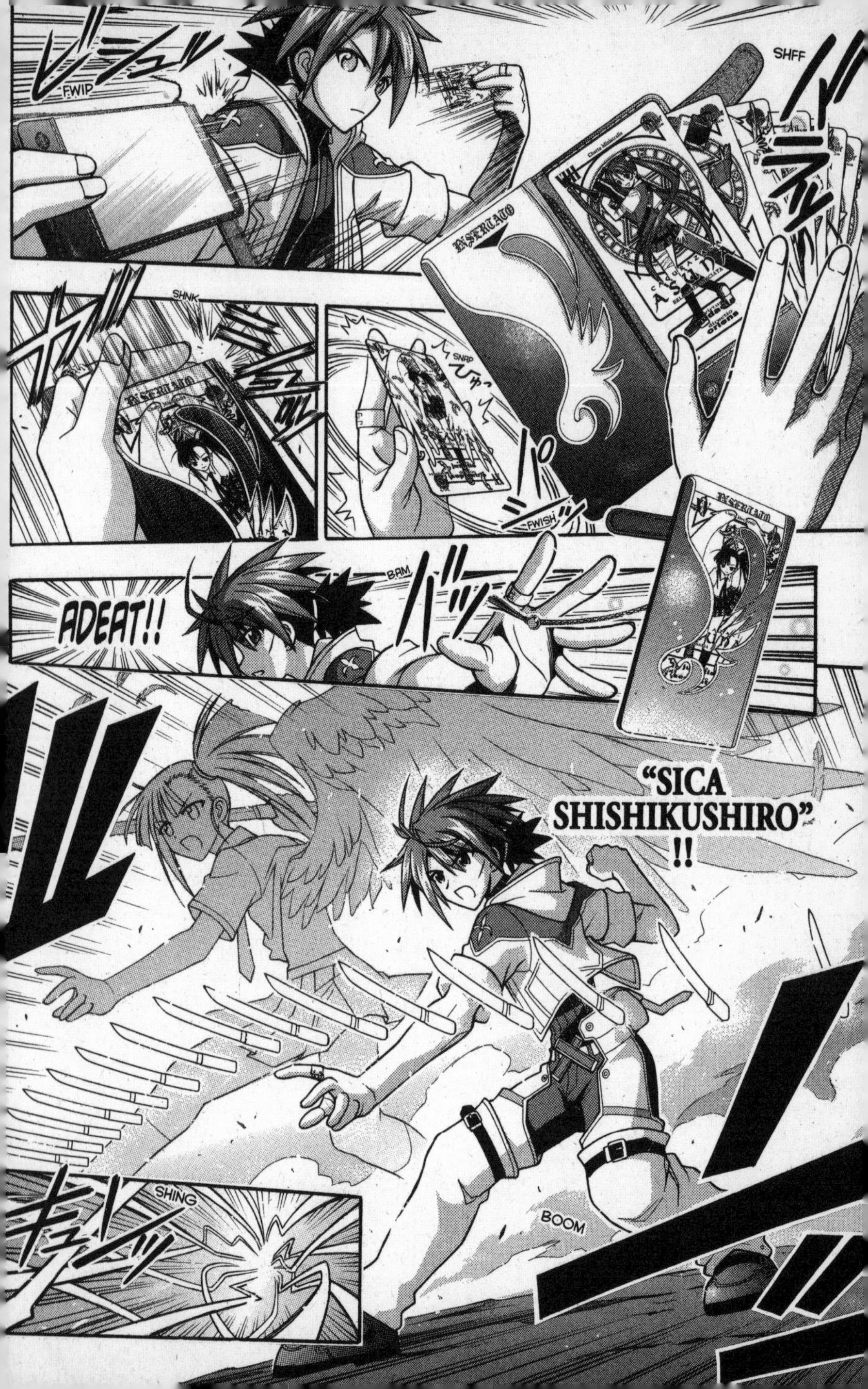
SHFF
FWIP
SNAP
FWISH
SHNK
BAM
ADEAT!!
"SICA SHISHIKUSHIRO"!!
BOOM
SHING

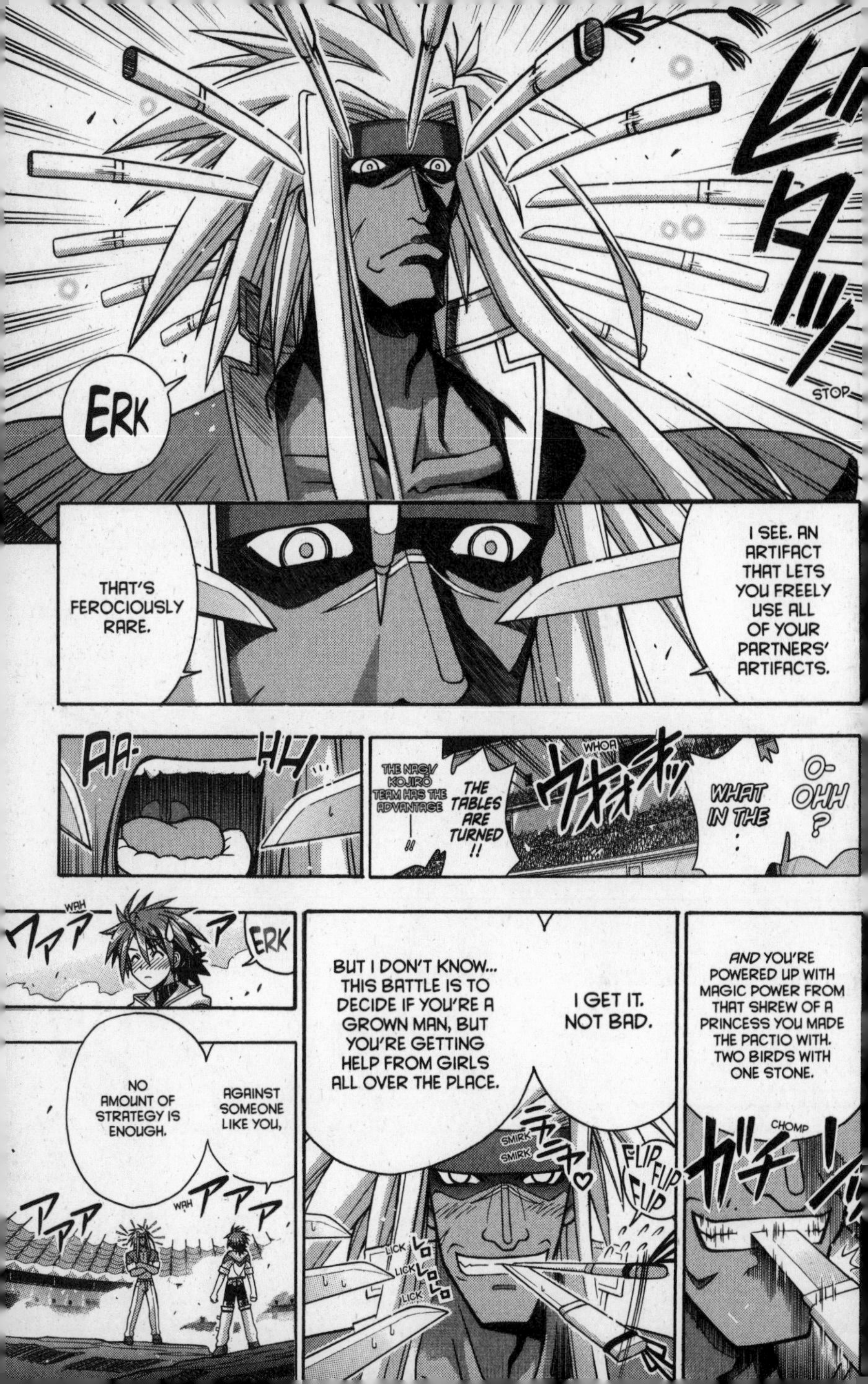
ビタッ
STOP
ERK
I SEE. AN ARTIFACT THAT LETS YOU FREELY USE ALL OF YOUR PARTNERS' ARTIFACTS.
THAT'S FEROCIOUSLY RARE.
O-OHH?
WHAT IN THE...
ウォォォッ
WHOA
THE TABLES ARE TURNED!!
THE NAGI/KOJIRŌ TEAM HAS THE ADVANTAGE—!!
AA-HH
AND YOU'RE POWERED UP WITH MAGIC POWER FROM THAT SHREW OF A PRINCESS YOU MADE THE PACTIO WITH. TWO BIRDS WITH ONE STONE.
ガチッ
CHOMP
I GET IT. NOT BAD.
BUT I DON'T KNOW... THIS BATTLE IS TO DECIDE IF YOU'RE A GROWN MAN, BUT YOU'RE GETTING HELP FROM GIRLS ALL OVER THE PLACE.
ニヤニヤ
SMIRK SMIRK
FLIP FLIP FLIP
LICK LICK LICK
ワァァァ
WAH
ERK
AGAINST SOMEONE LIKE YOU,
NO AMOUNT OF STRATEGY IS ENOUGH.
アアア
WAH

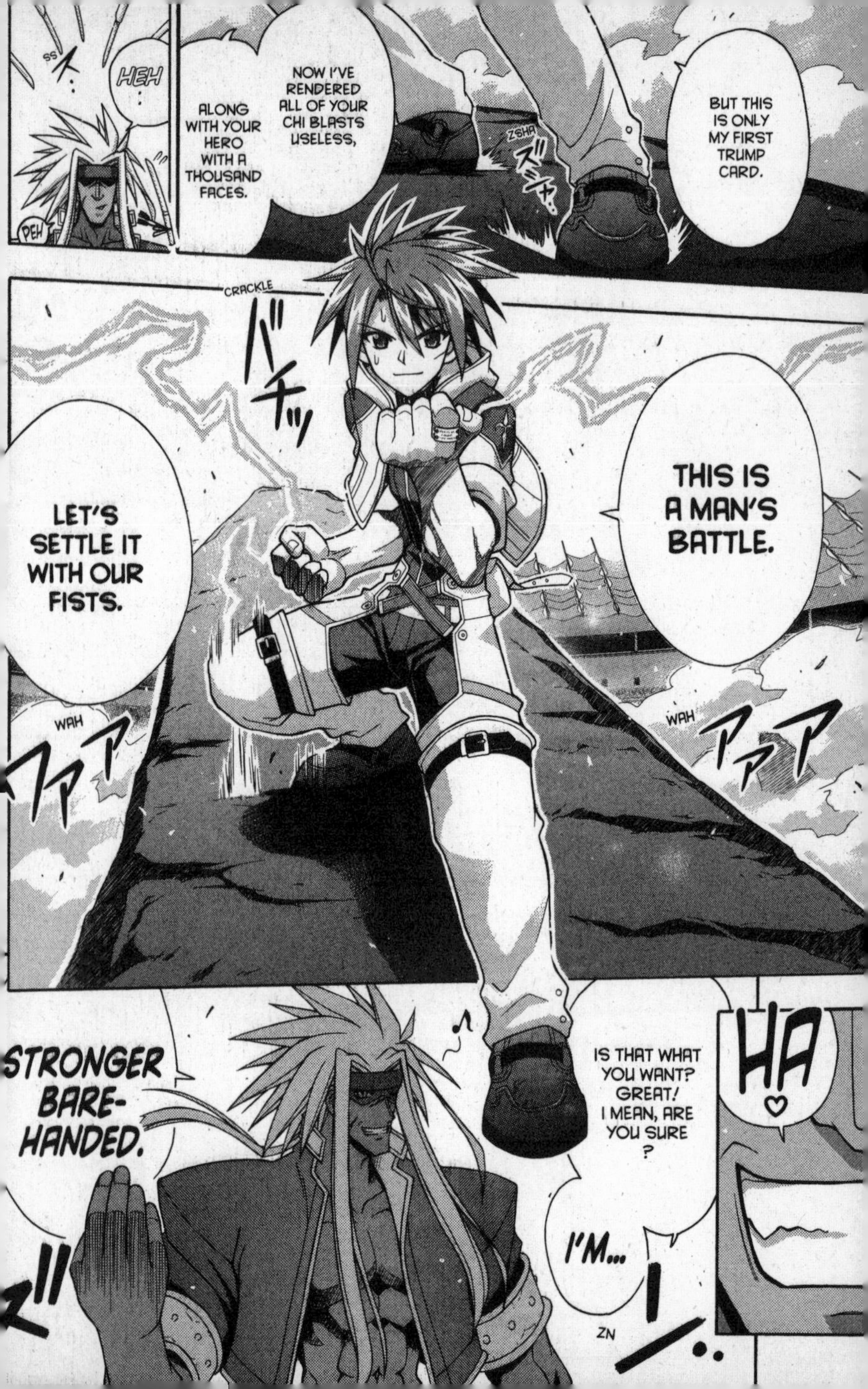
ZSHA
BUT THIS IS ONLY MY FIRST TRUMP CARD.
NOW I'VE RENDERED ALL OF YOUR CHI BLASTS USELESS,
ALONG WITH YOUR HERO WITH A THOUSAND FACES.
HEH
SS
PEH
CRACKLE
THIS IS A MAN'S BATTLE.
LET'S SETTLE IT WITH OUR FISTS.
WAH
WAH
HA ♥
IS THAT WHAT YOU WANT? GREAT! I MEAN, ARE YOU SURE?
I'M...
STRONGER BARE-HANDED.
ZN

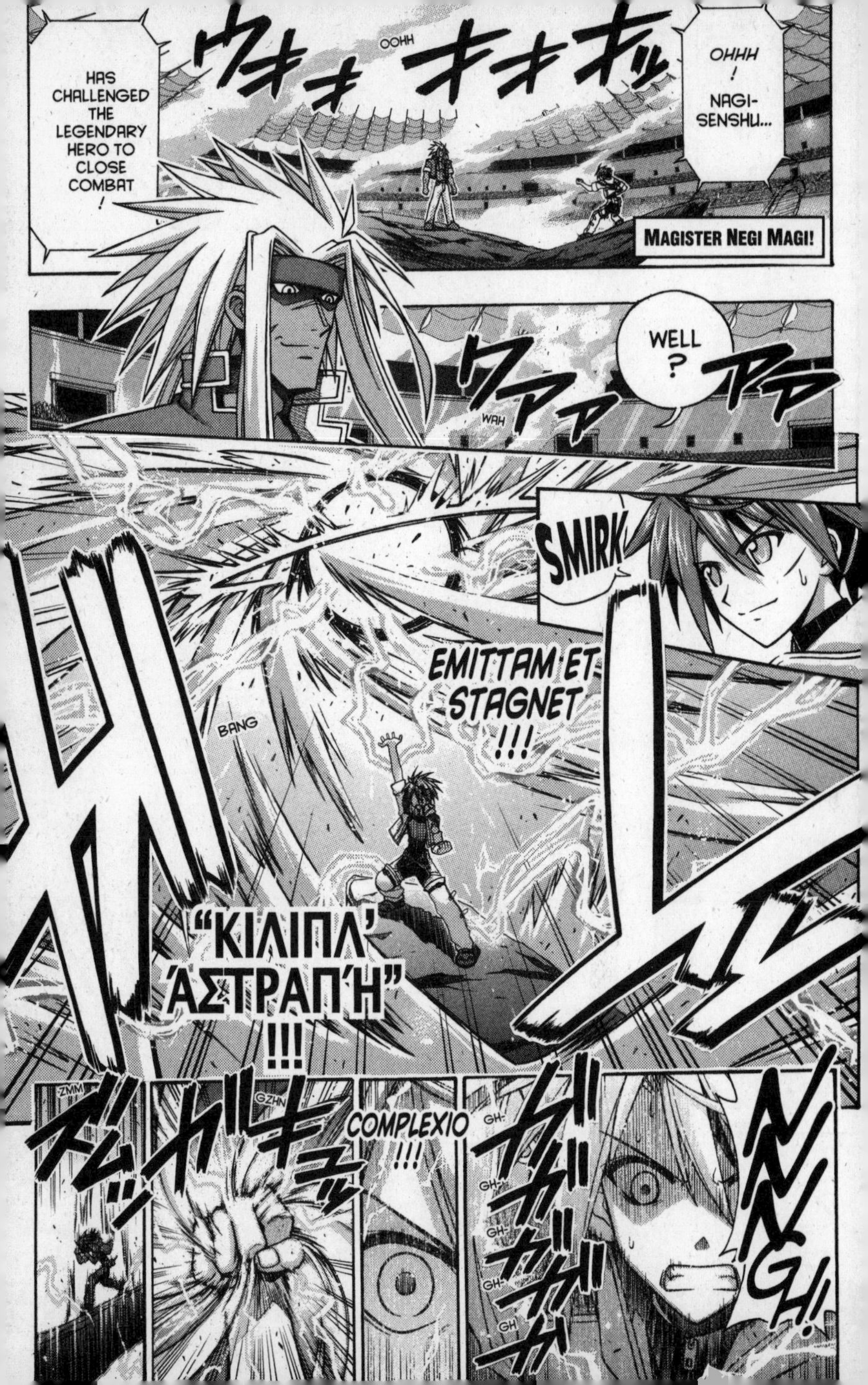
OHHH! NAGI-SENSHU...
OOHH
HAS CHALLENGED THE LEGENDARY HERO TO CLOSE COMBAT!
MAGISTER NEGI MAGI!
WELL?
WAH
SMIRK
EMITTAM ET STAGNET!!!
BANG
“ΚΙΛΙΠΛ’ ΆΣΤΡΑΠΉ” !!!
NNNGH!!
GH- GH- GH- GH- GH
COMPLEXIO!!!
GZHN
ZMM

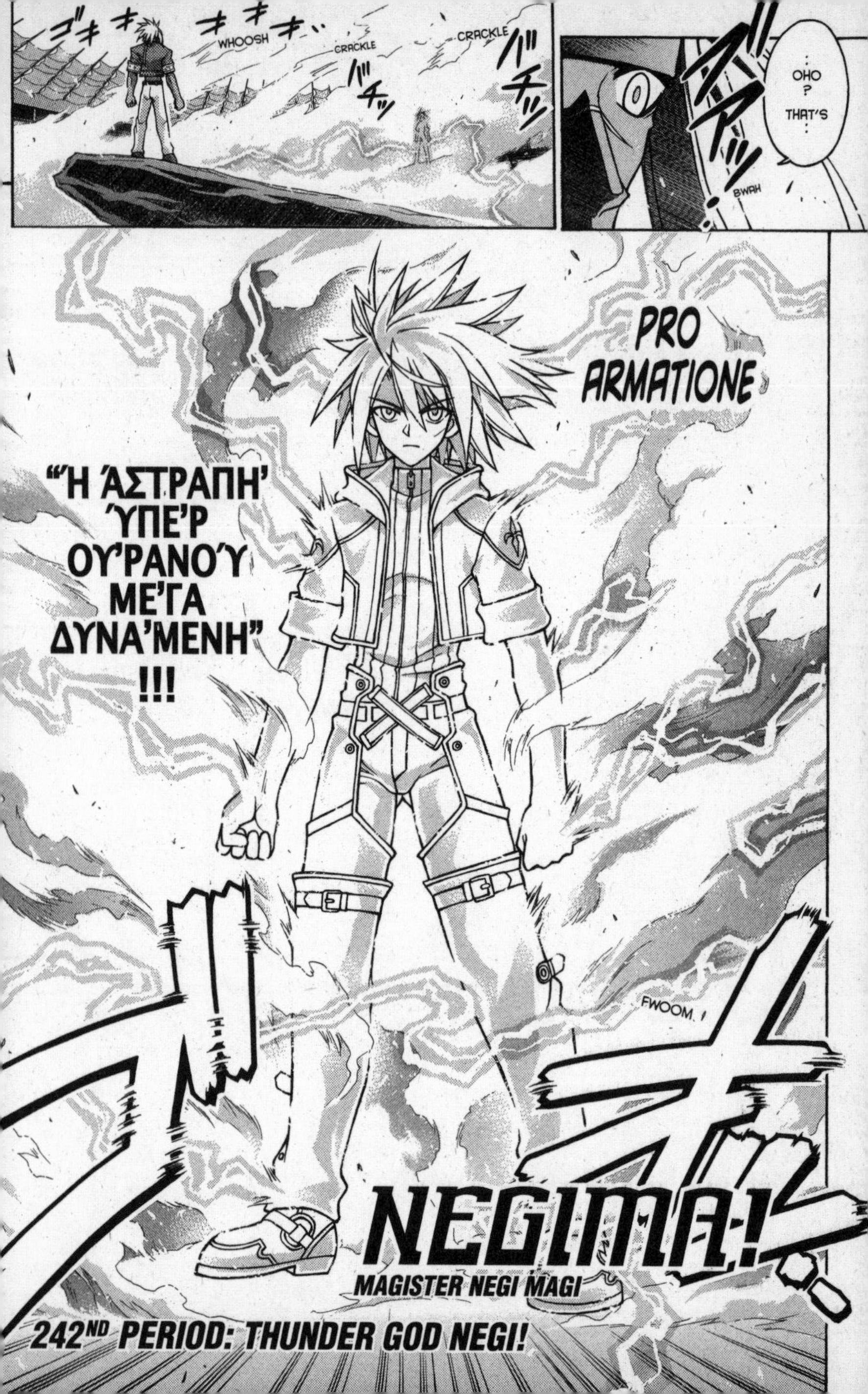
OHO? THAT'S...
BWAH
WHOOSH
CRACKLE
CRACKLE
PRO ARMATIONE
"Ή ΆΣΤΡΑΠΗ' ΎΠΕ'Ρ ΟΥ'ΡΑΝΟ'Υ ΜΕ'ΓΑ ΔΥΝΑ'ΜΕΝΗ"!!!
FWOOM
NEGIMA!
MAGISTER NEGI MAGI
242ND PERIOD: THUNDER GOD NEGI!

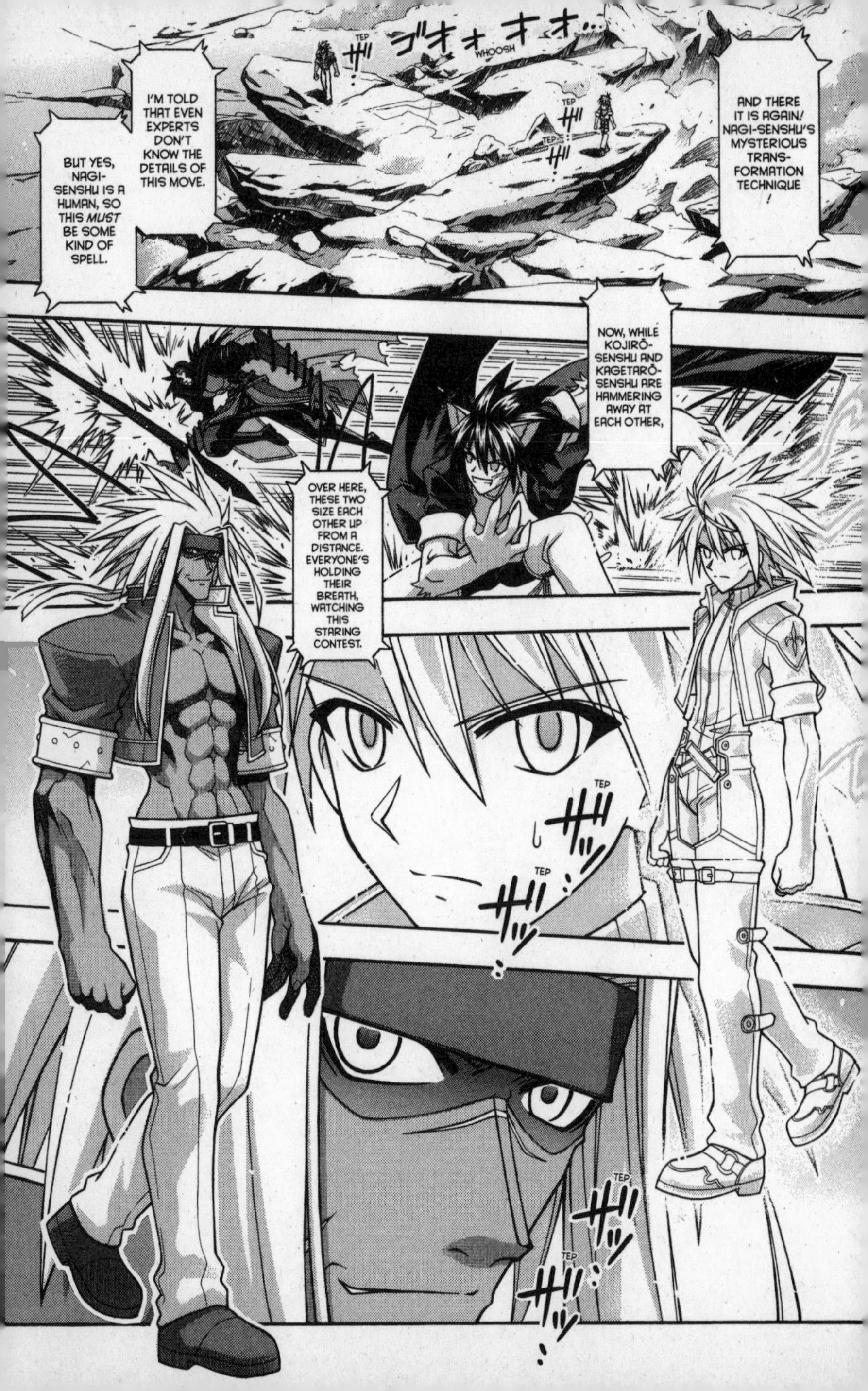
AND THERE IT IS AGAIN! NAGI-SENSHU'S MYSTERIOUS TRANS-FORMATION TECHNIQUE!
ゴォォオオ… WHOOSH
ザ TEP
ザ TEP
ザ TEP
I'M TOLD THAT EVEN EXPERTS DON'T KNOW THE DETAILS OF THIS MOVE.
BUT YES, NAGI-SENSHU IS A HUMAN, SO THIS *MUST* BE SOME KIND OF SPELL.
NOW, WHILE KOJIRŌ-SENSHU AND KAGETARŌ-SENSHU ARE HAMMERING AWAY AT EACH OTHER,
OVER HERE, THESE TWO SIZE EACH OTHER UP FROM A DISTANCE. EVERYONE'S HOLDING THEIR BREATH, WATCHING THIS STARING CONTEST.
ザッ TEP
ザッ TEP
ザッ TEP
ザッ TEP

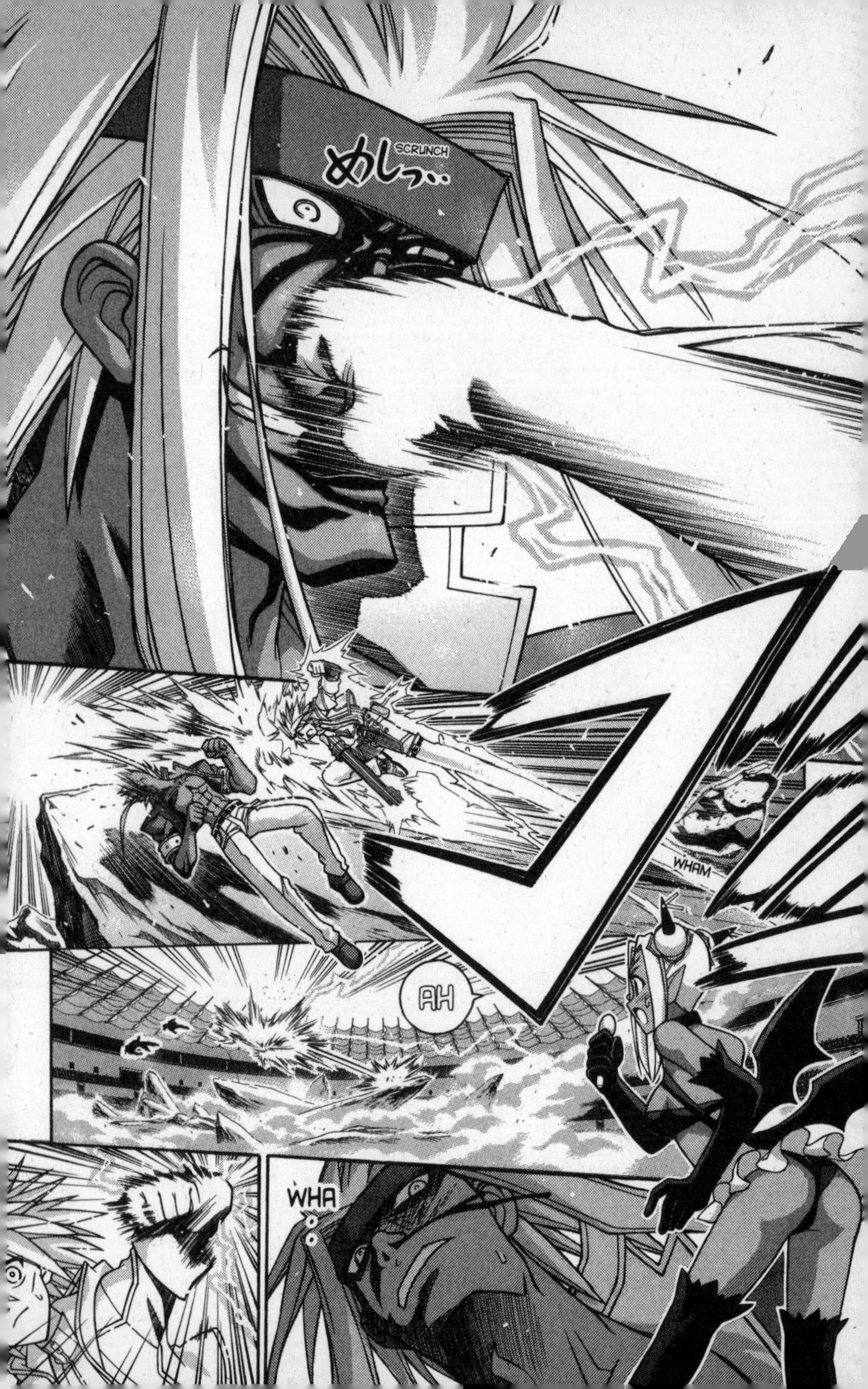

めしっ…
SCRUNCH
WHAM
AH
WHA...

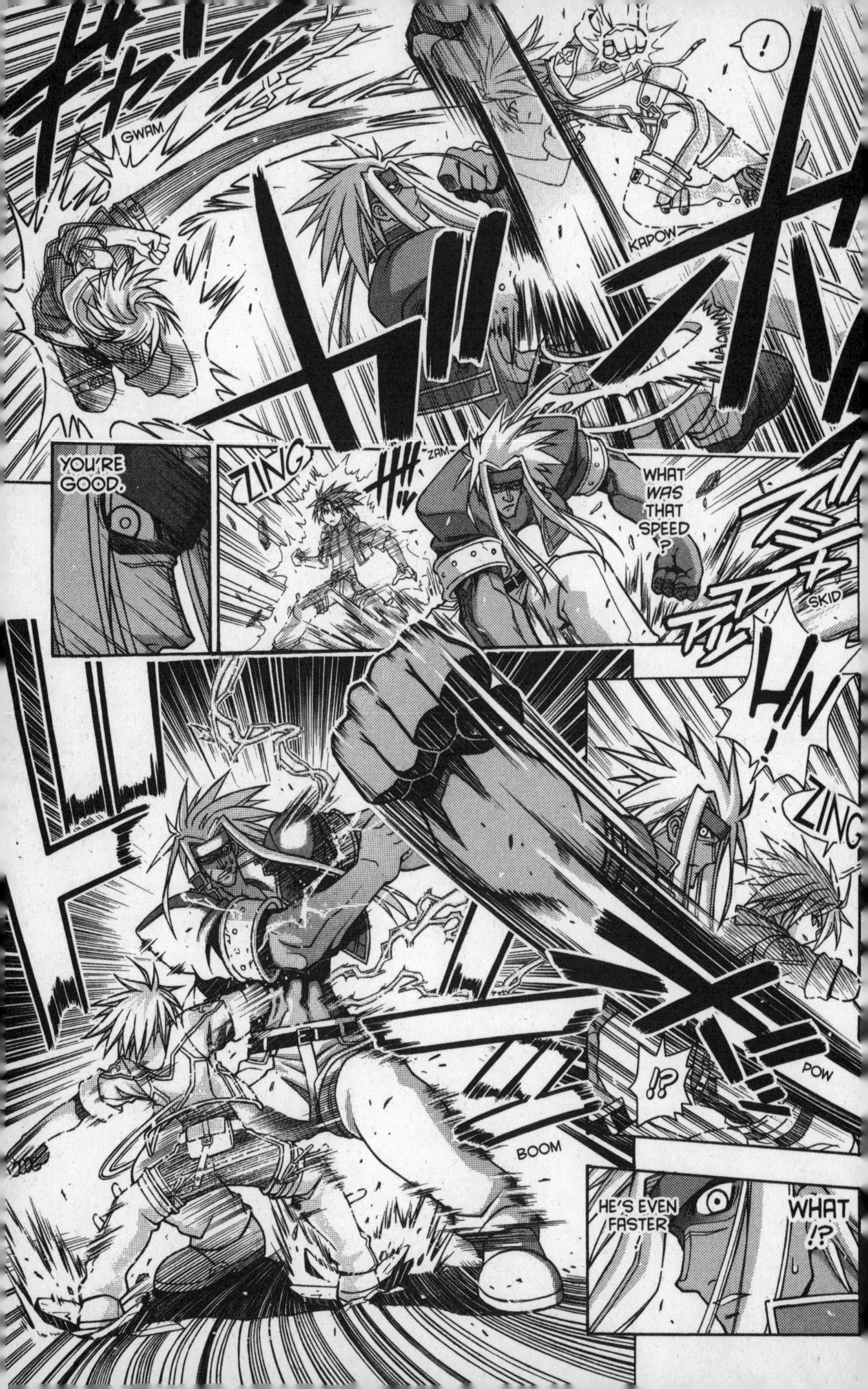
!
KAPOW
GWAM
SKID
WHAT WAS THAT SPEED?
ZAM
ZING
YOU'RE GOOD.
ZING
HN!
POW
!?
BOOM
WHAT!?
HE'S EVEN FASTER

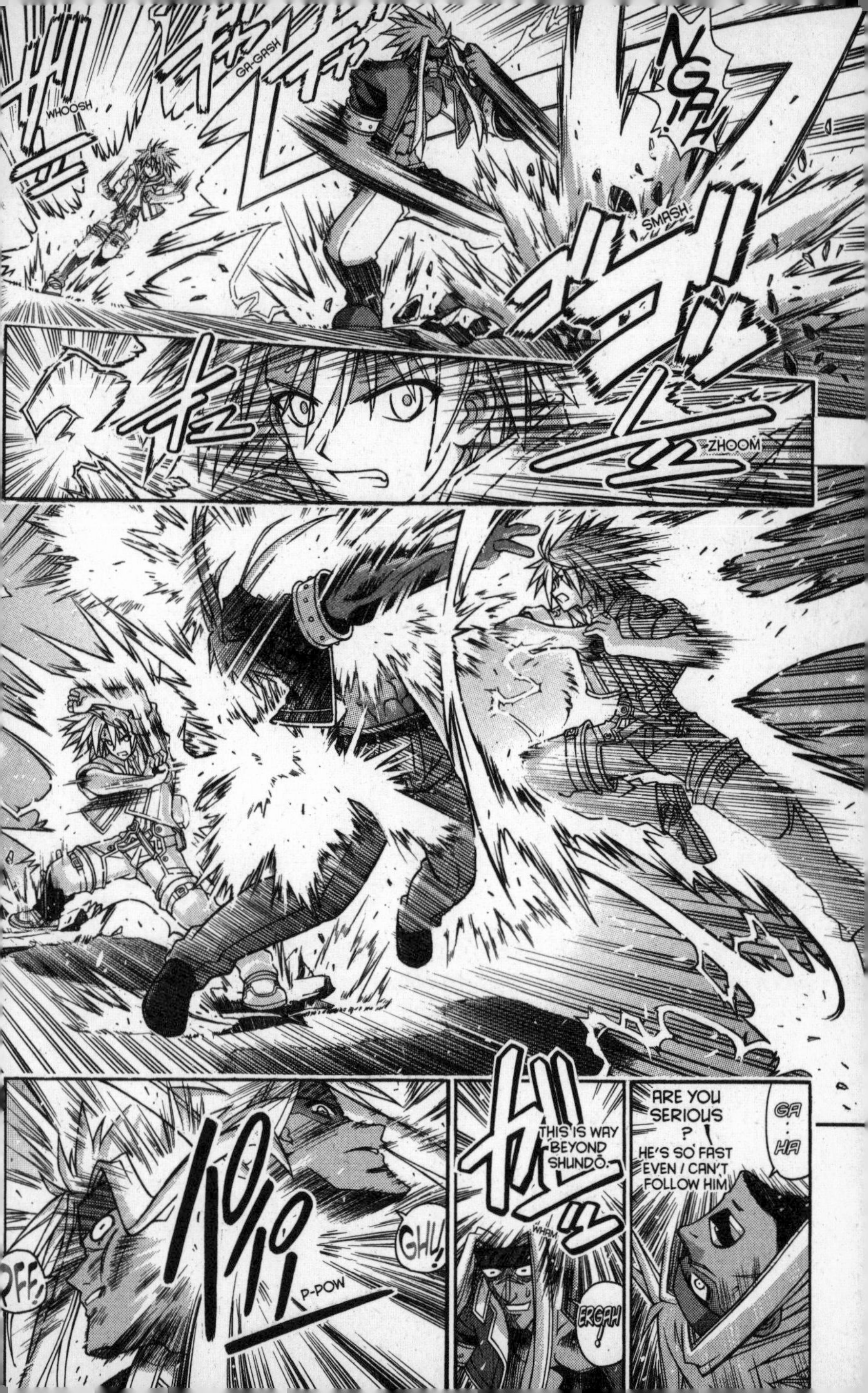
NGAH!
SMASH
GA-GASH
WHOOSH
ZHOOM
GA... HA
ARE YOU SERIOUS?!
HE'S SO FAST EVEN I CAN'T FOLLOW HIM
THIS IS WAY BEYOND SHUNDŌ.
WHAM
ERGAH!
GHU!
P-POW
PFF!

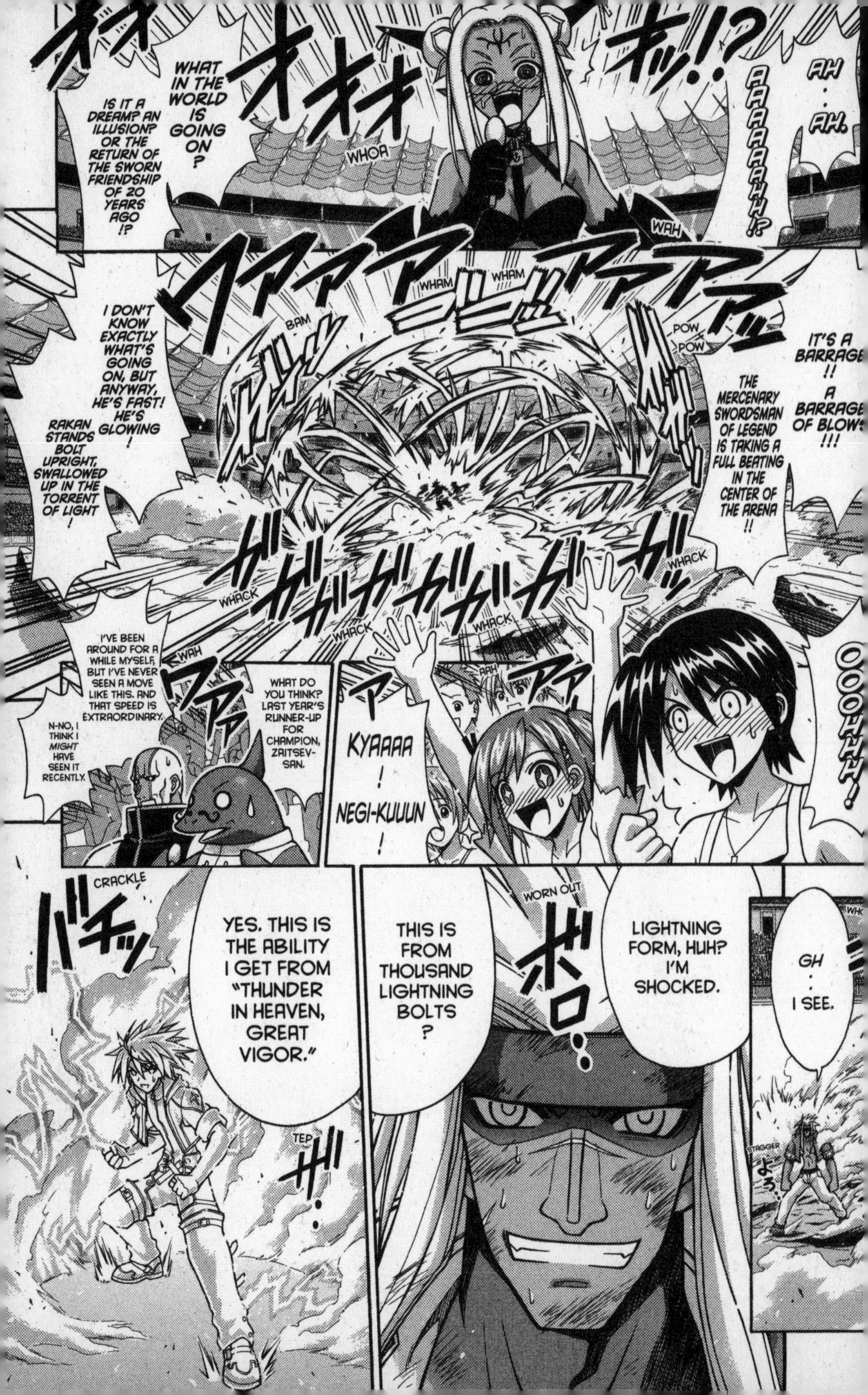
AH . . . AH.
AAAAAAAAAAAH!?
WHAT IN THE WORLD IS GOING ON?
IS IT A DREAM? AN ILLUSION? OR THE RETURN OF THE SWORN FRIENDSHIP OF 20 YEARS AGO!?
WHOA
WAH
IT'S A BARRAGE!! A BARRAGE OF BLOWS!!!
THE MERCENARY SWORDSMAN OF LEGEND IS TAKING A FULL BEATING IN THE CENTER OF THE ARENA!!
POW
POW
WHAM
WHAM
BAM
I DON'T KNOW EXACTLY WHAT'S GOING ON, BUT ANYWAY, HE'S FAST! HE'S GLOWING!
RAKAN STANDS BOLT UPRIGHT, SWALLOWED UP IN THE TORRENT OF LIGHT!
WHACK
WHACK
WHACK
WHACK
OOOOHHH!
RAH
KYAAAA! NEGI-KUUUN!
WHAT DO YOU THINK? LAST YEAR'S RUNNER-UP FOR CHAMPION, ZAITSEV-SAN.
I'VE BEEN AROUND FOR A WHILE MYSELF, BUT I'VE NEVER SEEN A MOVE LIKE THIS. AND THAT SPEED IS EXTRAORDINARY.
WAH
N-NO, I THINK I MIGHT HAVE SEEN IT RECENTLY.
GH . . . I SEE.
STAGGER
LIGHTNING FORM, HUH? I'M SHOCKED.
WORN OUT
THIS IS FROM THOUSAND LIGHTNING BOLTS?
YES. THIS IS THE ABILITY I GET FROM "THUNDER IN HEAVEN, GREAT VIGOR."
TEP
CRACKLE

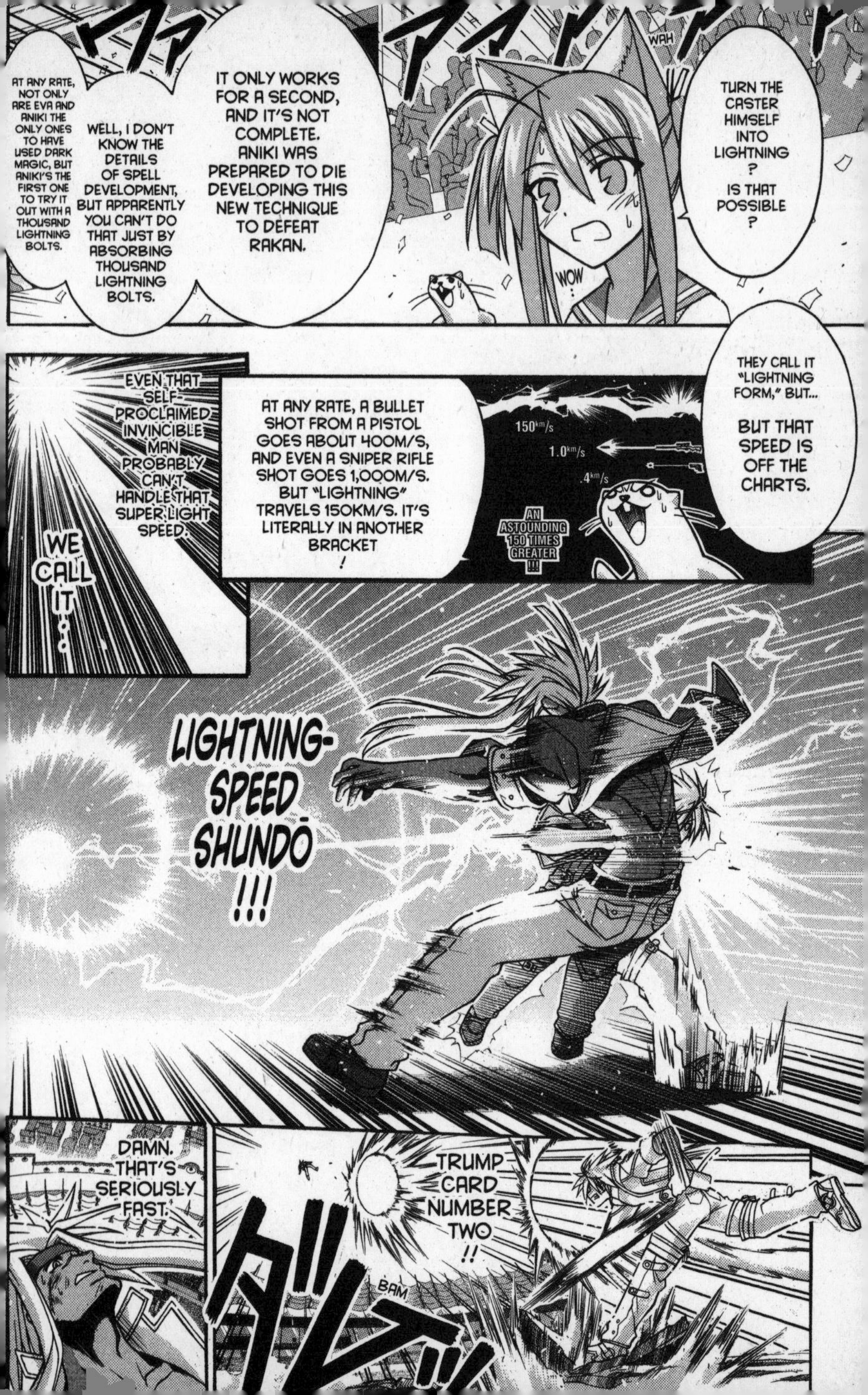
WAH
TURN THE CASTER HIMSELF INTO LIGHTNING? IS THAT POSSIBLE?
WOW
IT ONLY WORKS FOR A SECOND, AND IT'S NOT COMPLETE. ANIKI WAS PREPARED TO DIE DEVELOPING THIS NEW TECHNIQUE TO DEFEAT RAKAN.
WELL, I DON'T KNOW THE DETAILS OF SPELL DEVELOPMENT, BUT APPARENTLY YOU CAN'T DO THAT JUST BY ABSORBING THOUSAND LIGHTNING BOLTS.
AT ANY RATE, NOT ONLY ARE EVA AND ANIKI THE ONLY ONES TO HAVE USED DARK MAGIC, BUT ANIKI'S THE FIRST ONE TO TRY IT OUT WITH A THOUSAND LIGHTNING BOLTS.
THEY CALL IT "LIGHTNING FORM," BUT...
BUT THAT SPEED IS OFF THE CHARTS.
150km/s
1.0km/s
.4km/s
AN ASTOUNDING 150 TIMES GREATER!!!
AT ANY RATE, A BULLET SHOT FROM A PISTOL GOES ABOUT 400M/S, AND EVEN A SNIPER RIFLE SHOT GOES 1,000M/S. BUT "LIGHTNING" TRAVELS 150KM/S. IT'S LITERALLY IN ANOTHER BRACKET!
EVEN THAT SELF-PROCLAIMED INVINCIBLE MAN PROBABLY CAN'T HANDLE THAT SUPER LIGHT SPEED.
WE CALL IT...
LIGHTNING-SPEED SHUNDŌ!!!
TRUMP CARD NUMBER TWO!!
BAM
DAMN. THAT'S SERIOUSLY FAST.

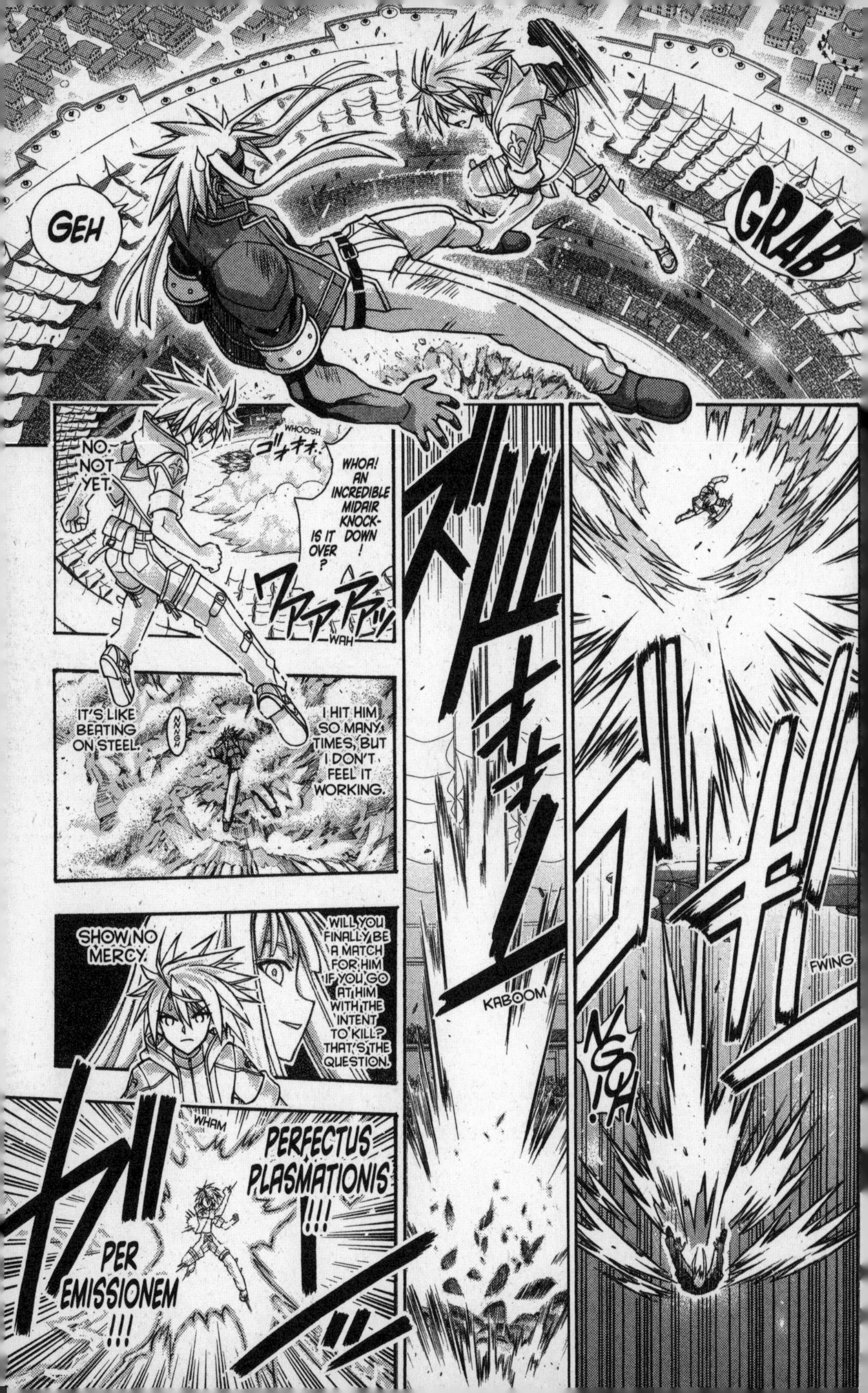
GRAB
GEH
FWING
NGOH!
KABOOM
WHOOSH
WHOA! AN INCREDIBLE MIDAIR KNOCK-DOWN!
IS IT OVER?
NO. NOT YET.
WAH
I HIT HIM SO MANY TIMES, BUT I DON'T FEEL IT WORKING.
NNGH
IT'S LIKE BEATING ON STEEL.
WILL YOU FINALLY BE A MATCH FOR HIM IF YOU GO AT HIM WITH THE INTENT TO KILL? THAT'S THE QUESTION.
SHOW NO MERCY.
PERFECTUS PLASMATIONIS!!!
WHAM
PER EMISSIONEM!!!

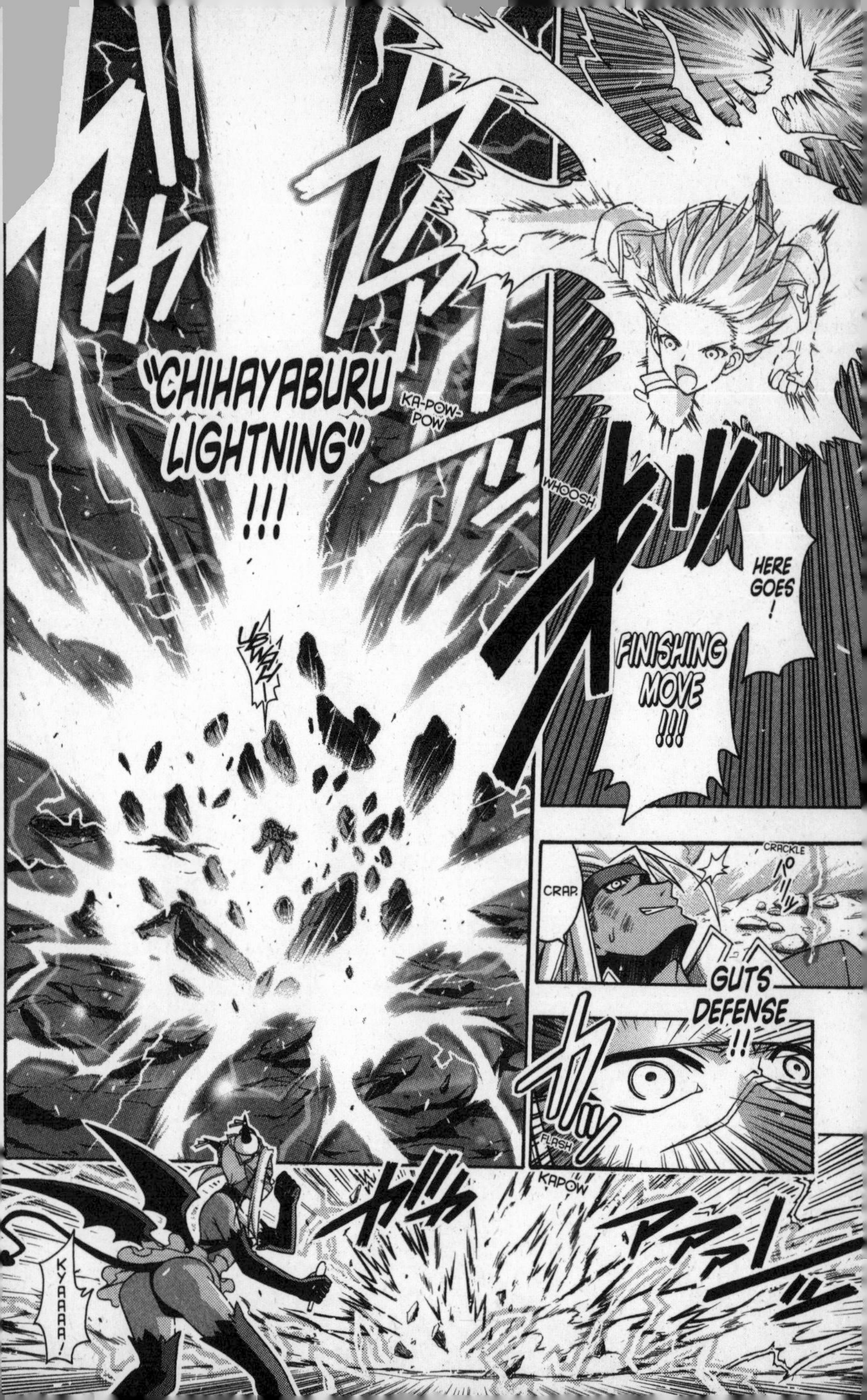
HERE GOES!
FINISHING MOVE!!!
WHOOSH
CRACKLE
CRAP.
GUTS DEFENSE!!
FLASH
"CHIHAYABURU LIGHTNING"!!!
KA-POW-POW
KAPOW
KYAAAA!

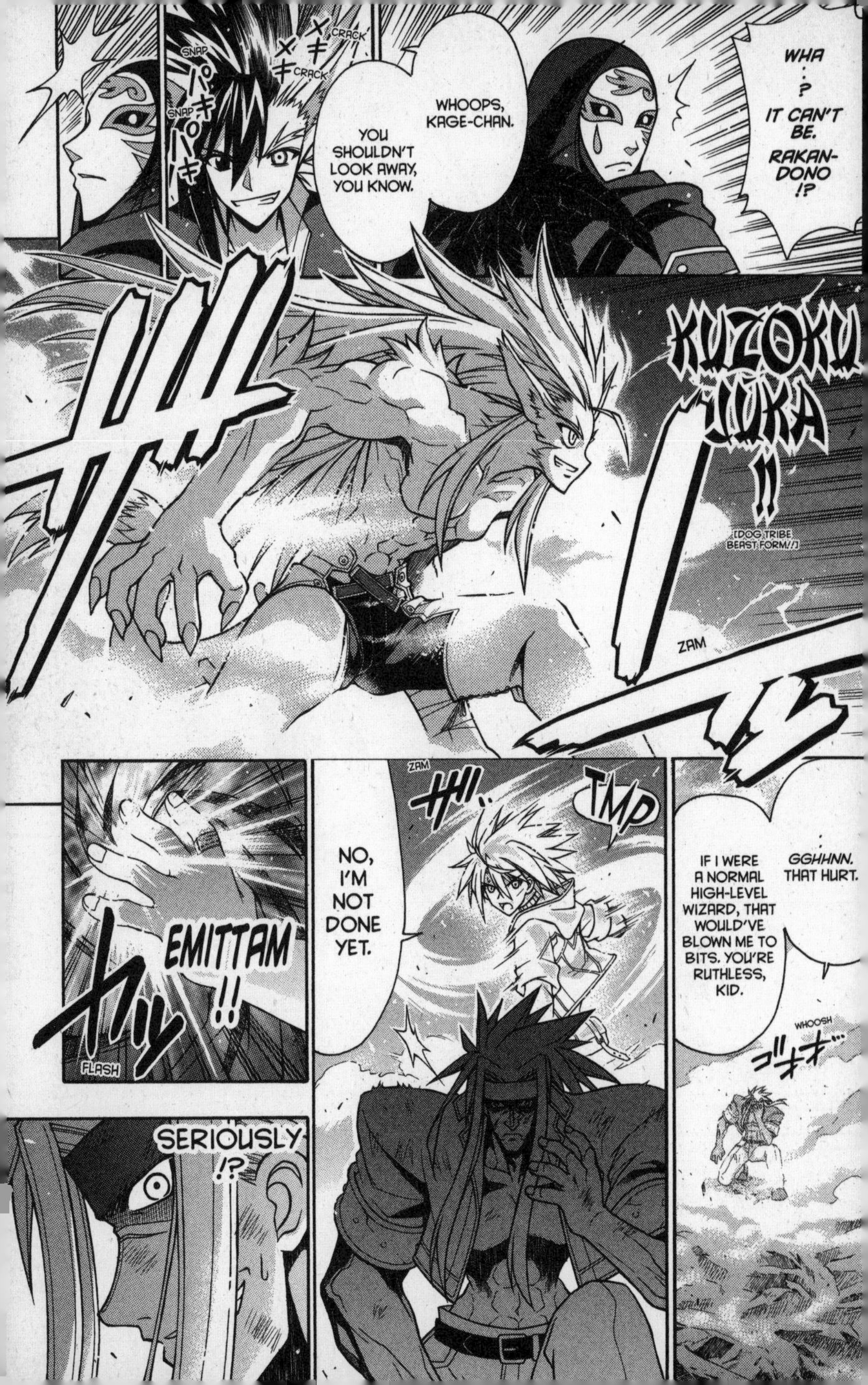

WHA . . ? IT CAN'T BE. RAKAN-DONO !?
WHOOPS, KAGE-CHAN.
YOU SHOULDN'T LOOK AWAY, YOU KNOW.
CRACK
CRACK
SNAP
SNAP
KUZOKU JUKA !!
[DOG TRIBE BEAST FORM!!]
ZAM
GGHHNN. THAT HURT.
IF I WERE A NORMAL HIGH-LEVEL WIZARD, THAT WOULD'VE BLOWN ME TO BITS. YOU'RE RUTHLESS, KID.
WHOOSH
ZAM
TMP
NO, I'M NOT DONE YET.
EMITTAM !!
FLASH
SERIOUSLY !?

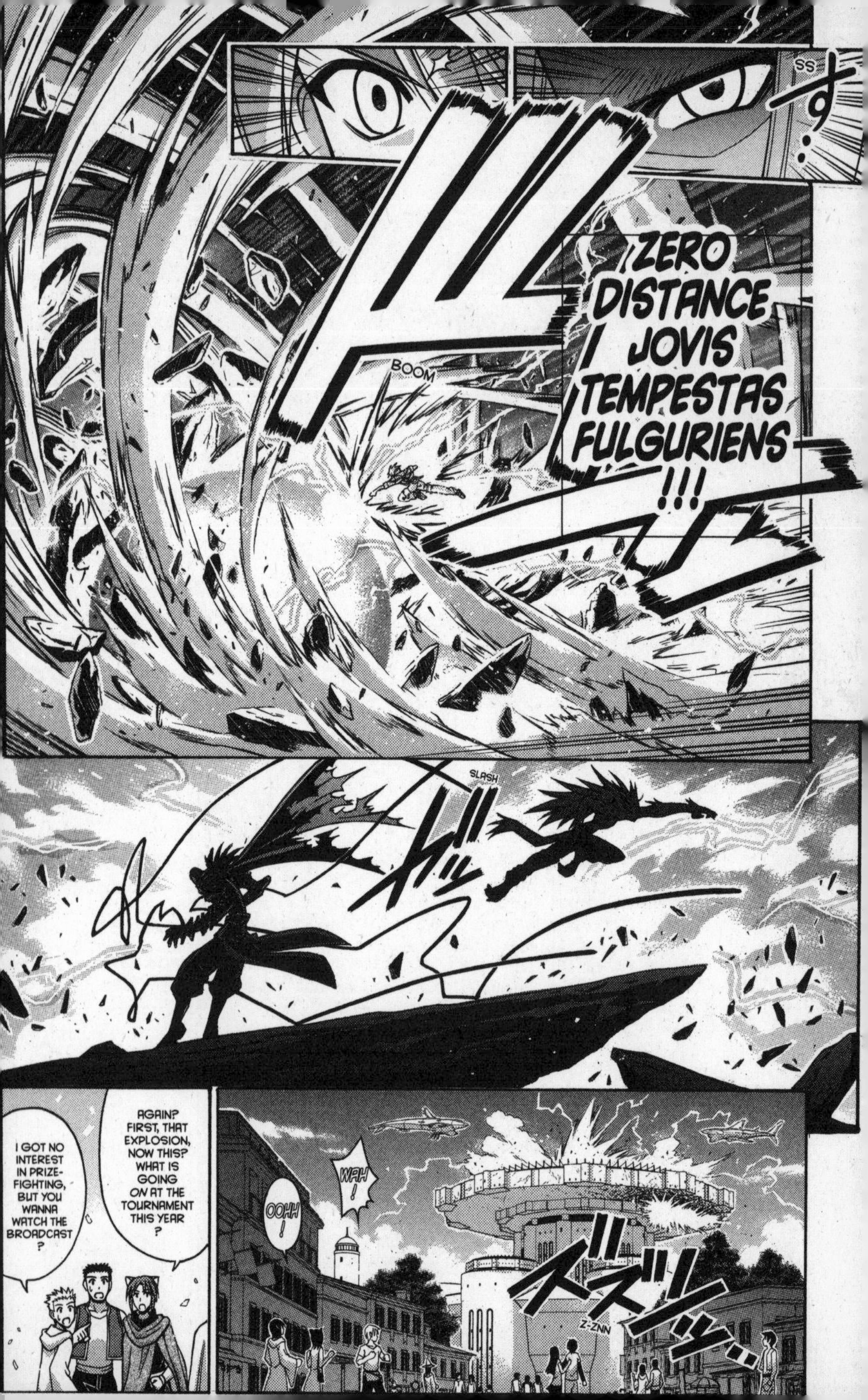
SS
ZERO DISTANCE JOVIS TEMPESTAS FULGURIENS !!!
BOOM
SLASH
WAH!
OOHH!
Z-ZNN
AGAIN? FIRST, THAT EXPLOSION, NOW THIS? WHAT IS GOING *ON* AT THE TOURNAMENT THIS YEAR?
I GOT NO INTEREST IN PRIZE-FIGHTING, BUT YOU WANNA WATCH THE BROADCAST?

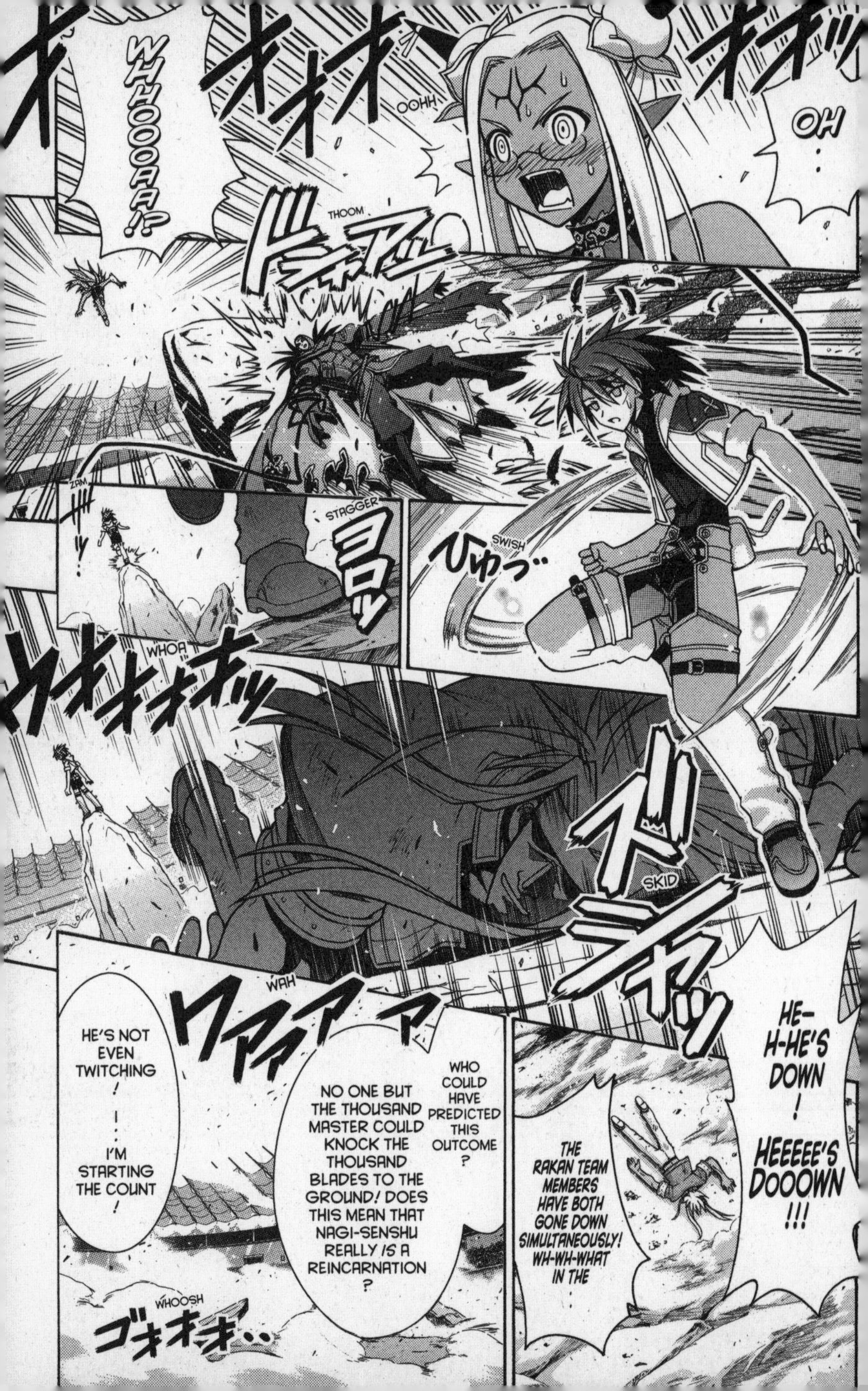
OH...
OOHH
WHHOOOAA!!?
THOOM
SWISH
STAGGER
ZAM
WHOA
SKID
HE-H-HE'S DOWN! HEEEEE'S DOOOWN!!!
THE RAKAN TEAM MEMBERS HAVE BOTH GONE DOWN SIMULTANEOUSLY! WH-WH-WHAT IN THE
WAH
WHO COULD HAVE PREDICTED THIS OUTCOME?
NO ONE BUT THE THOUSAND MASTER COULD KNOCK THE THOUSAND BLADES TO THE GROUND! DOES THIS MEAN THAT NAGI-SENSHU REALLY IS A REINCARNATION?
HE'S NOT EVEN TWITCHING! ...I'M STARTING THE COUNT!
WHOOSH

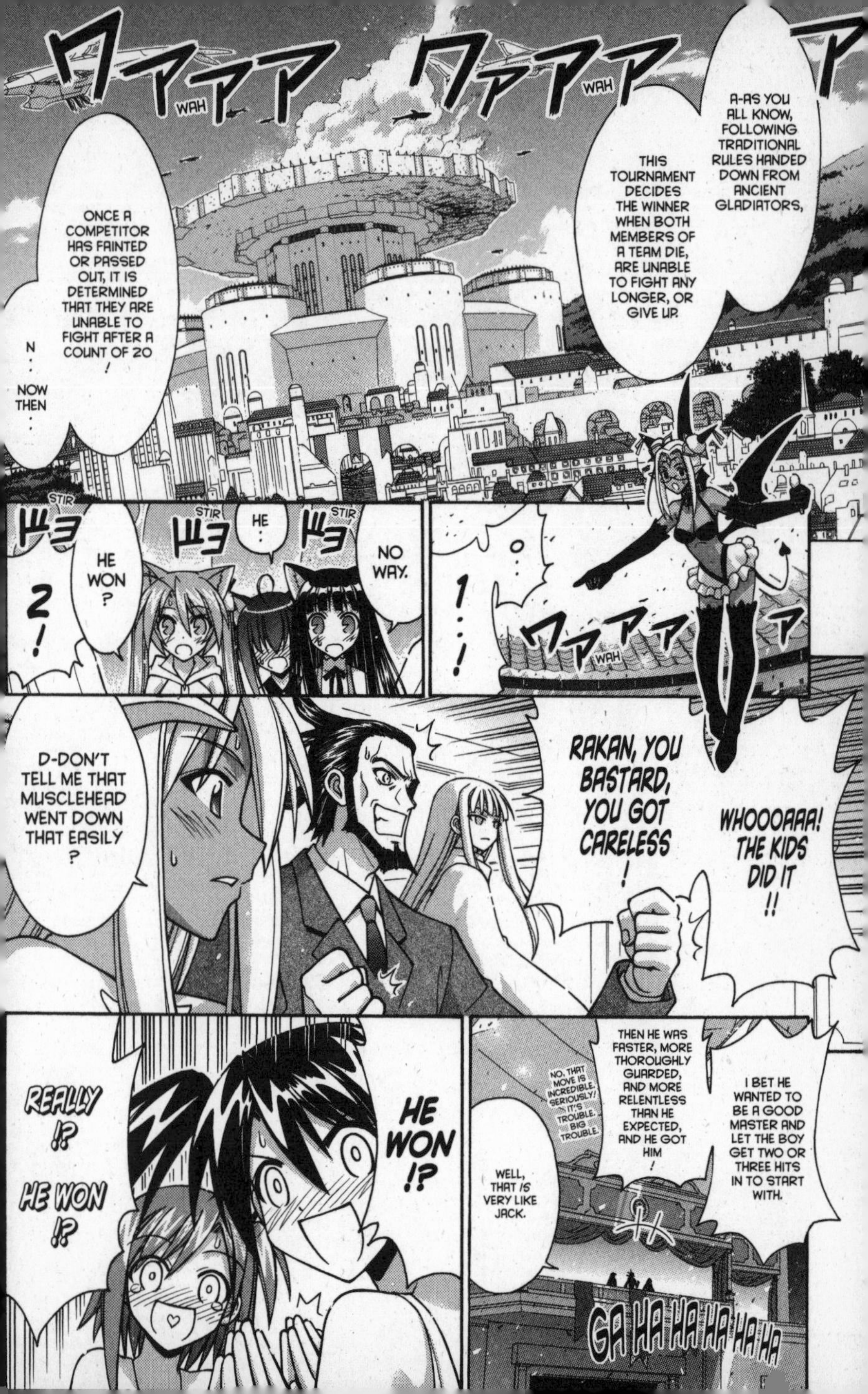
ワァァァ WAH ワァァァ WAH
A-AS YOU ALL KNOW, FOLLOWING TRADITIONAL RULES HANDED DOWN FROM ANCIENT GLADIATORS,
THIS TOURNAMENT DECIDES THE WINNER WHEN BOTH MEMBERS OF A TEAM DIE, ARE UNABLE TO FIGHT ANY LONGER, OR GIVE UP.
ONCE A COMPETITOR HAS FAINTED OR PASSED OUT, IT IS DETERMINED THAT THEY ARE UNABLE TO FIGHT AFTER A COUNT OF 20!
N... NOW THEN...
0...
1...!
ワァァァ WAH
NO WAY.
ドヨ STIR
HE...
ドヨ STIR
HE WON?
ドヨ STIR
2!
WHOOOAAA! THE KIDS DID IT!!
RAKAN, YOU BASTARD, YOU GOT CARELESS!
D-DON'T TELL ME THAT MUSCLEHEAD WENT DOWN THAT EASILY?
I BET HE WANTED TO BE A GOOD MASTER AND LET THE BOY GET TWO OR THREE HITS IN TO START WITH.
THEN HE WAS FASTER, MORE THOROUGHLY GUARDED, AND MORE RELENTLESS THAN HE EXPECTED, AND HE GOT HIM!
NO, THAT MOVE IS INCREDIBLE. SERIOUSLY! IT'S TROUBLE. BIG TROUBLE.
WELL, THAT IS VERY LIKE JACK.
GA HA HA HA HA HA HA
HE WON!?
REALLY!?
HE WON!?

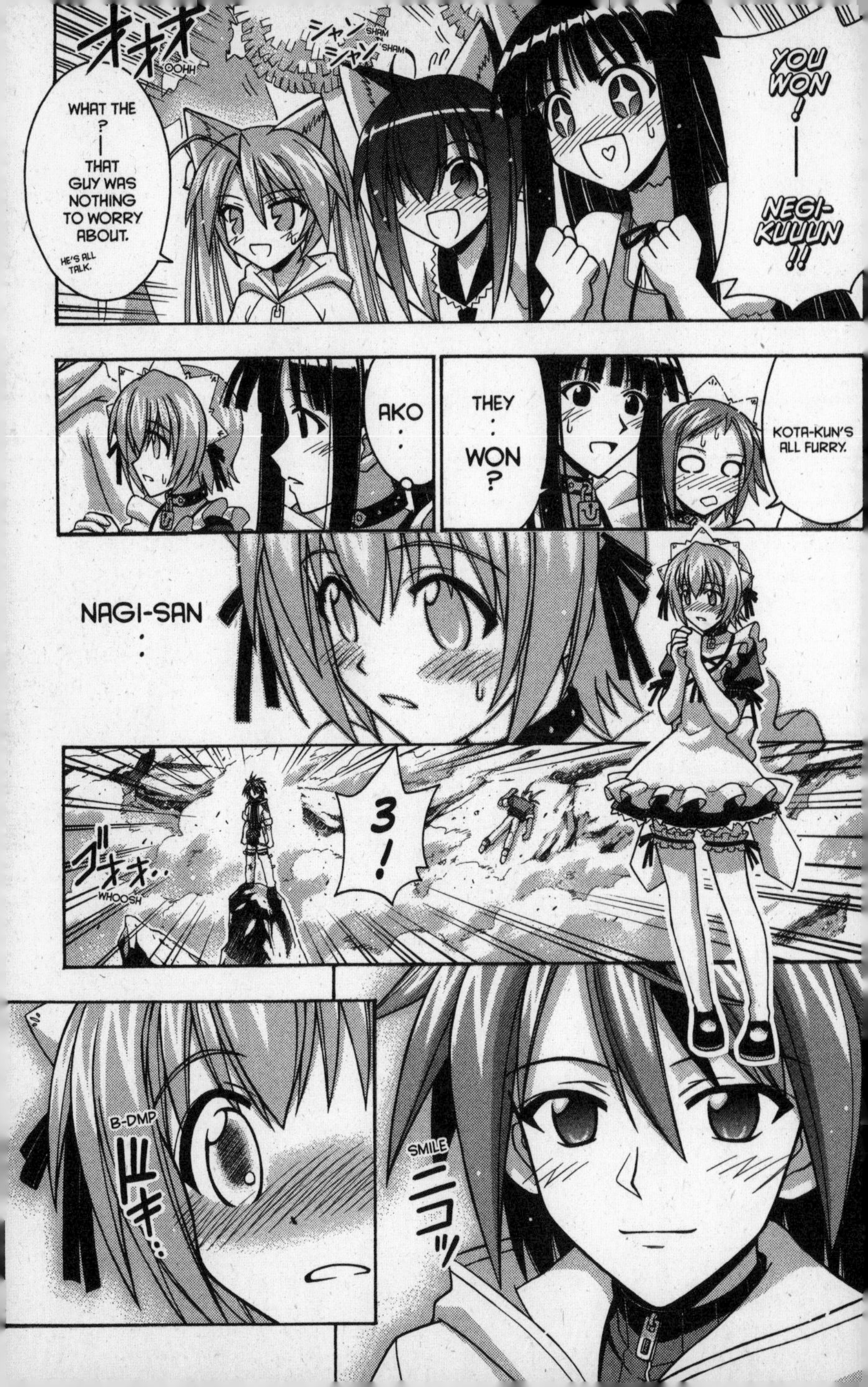
YOU WON! — NEGI-KUUUN!!
シャン SHAM
シャン SHAM
オォォ OOHH
WHAT THE? — THAT GUY WAS NOTHING TO WORRY ABOUT.
HE'S ALL TALK.
KOTA-KUN'S ALL FURRY.
THEY... WON?
AKO...
NAGI-SAN...
3!
ゴォォ... WHOOSH
ニコッ SMILE
ドキ... B-DMP

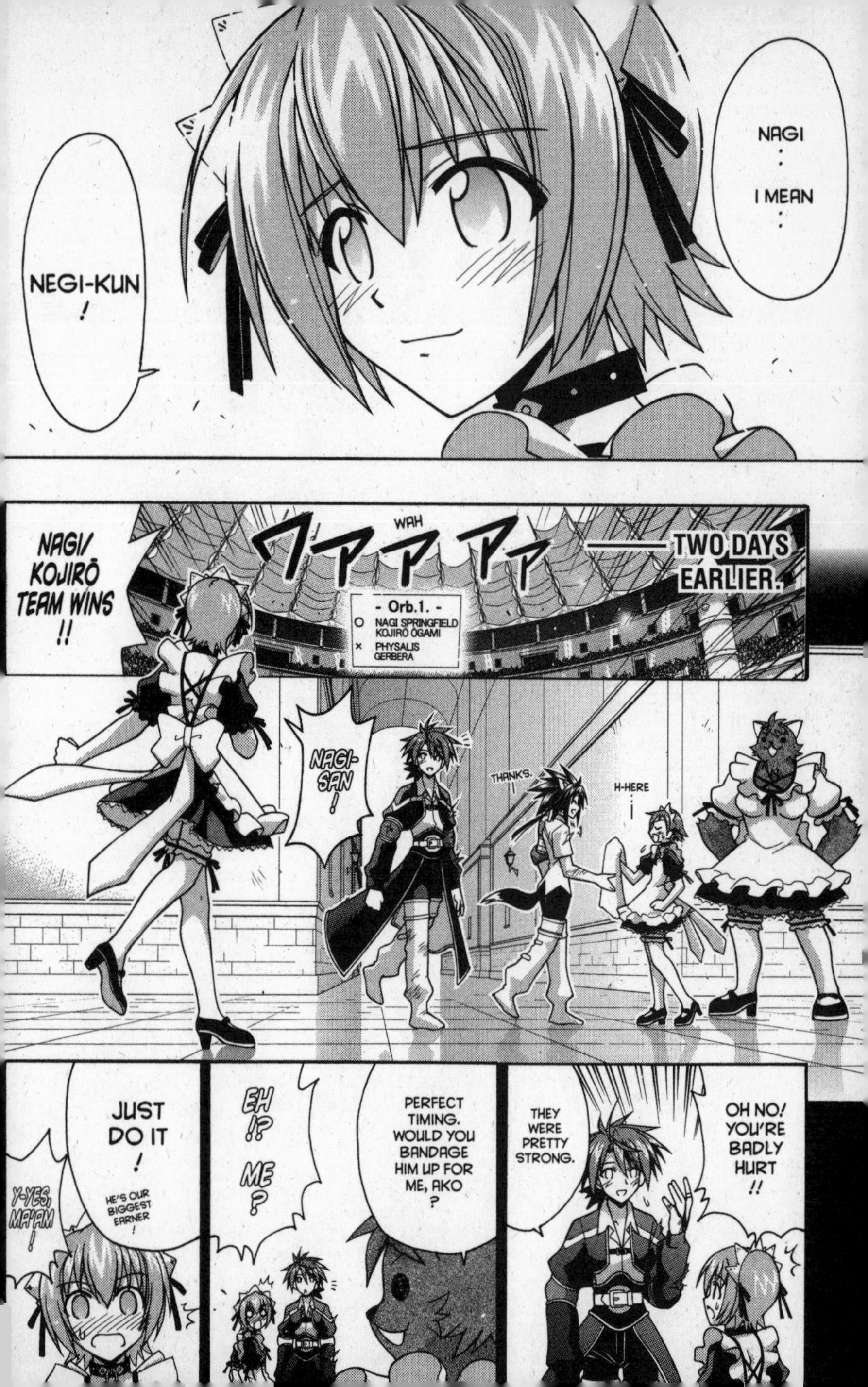
NAGI... I MEAN...
NEGI-KUN!
TWO DAYS EARLIER.
WAH
- Orb.1. -
○ NAGI SPRINGFIELD KOJIRŌ ŌGAMI
× PHYSALIS GERBERA
NAGI/ KOJIRŌ TEAM WINS!!
H-HERE...
THANKS.
NAGI-SAN!
OH NO! YOU'RE BADLY HURT!!
THEY WERE PRETTY STRONG.
PERFECT TIMING. WOULD YOU BANDAGE HIM UP FOR ME, AKO?
EH!? ME?
JUST DO IT!
HE'S OUR BIGGEST EARNER!
Y-YES, MA'AM!

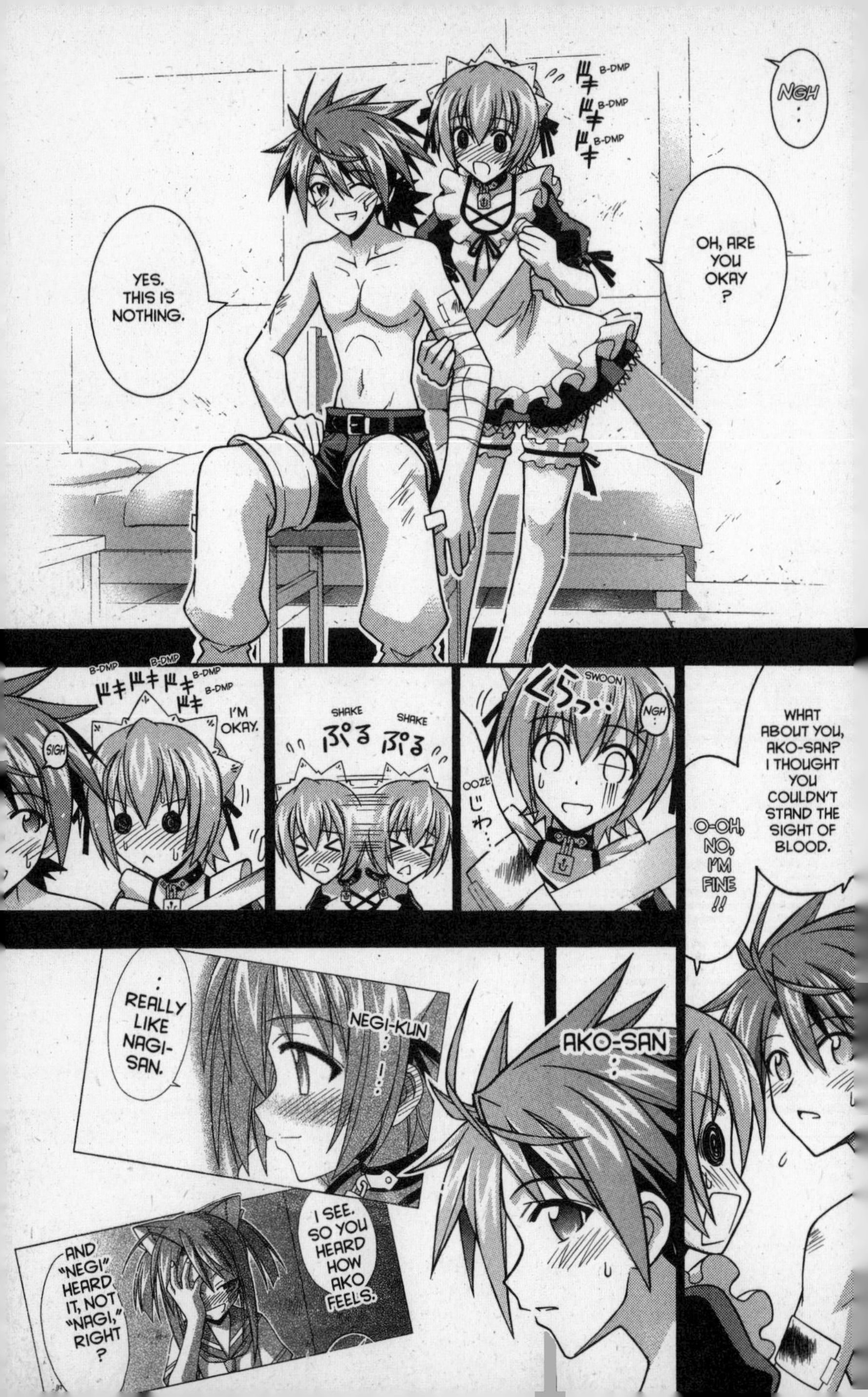
NGH
OH, ARE YOU OKAY?
B-DMP B-DMP B-DMP
YES. THIS IS NOTHING.
WHAT ABOUT YOU, AKO-SAN? I THOUGHT YOU COULDN'T STAND THE SIGHT OF BLOOD.
O-OH, NO, I'M FINE!!
くらっ SWOON
NGH
じわ… OOZE
ぷる SHAKE ぷる SHAKE
ドキ ドキ ドキ ドキ B-DMP B-DMP B-DMP B-DMP
I'M OKAY.
SIGH
AKO-SAN…
…REALLY LIKE NAGI-SAN.
NEGI-KUN…!
I SEE. SO YOU HEARD HOW AKO FEELS.
AND "NEGI" HEARD IT, NOT "NAGI," RIGHT?

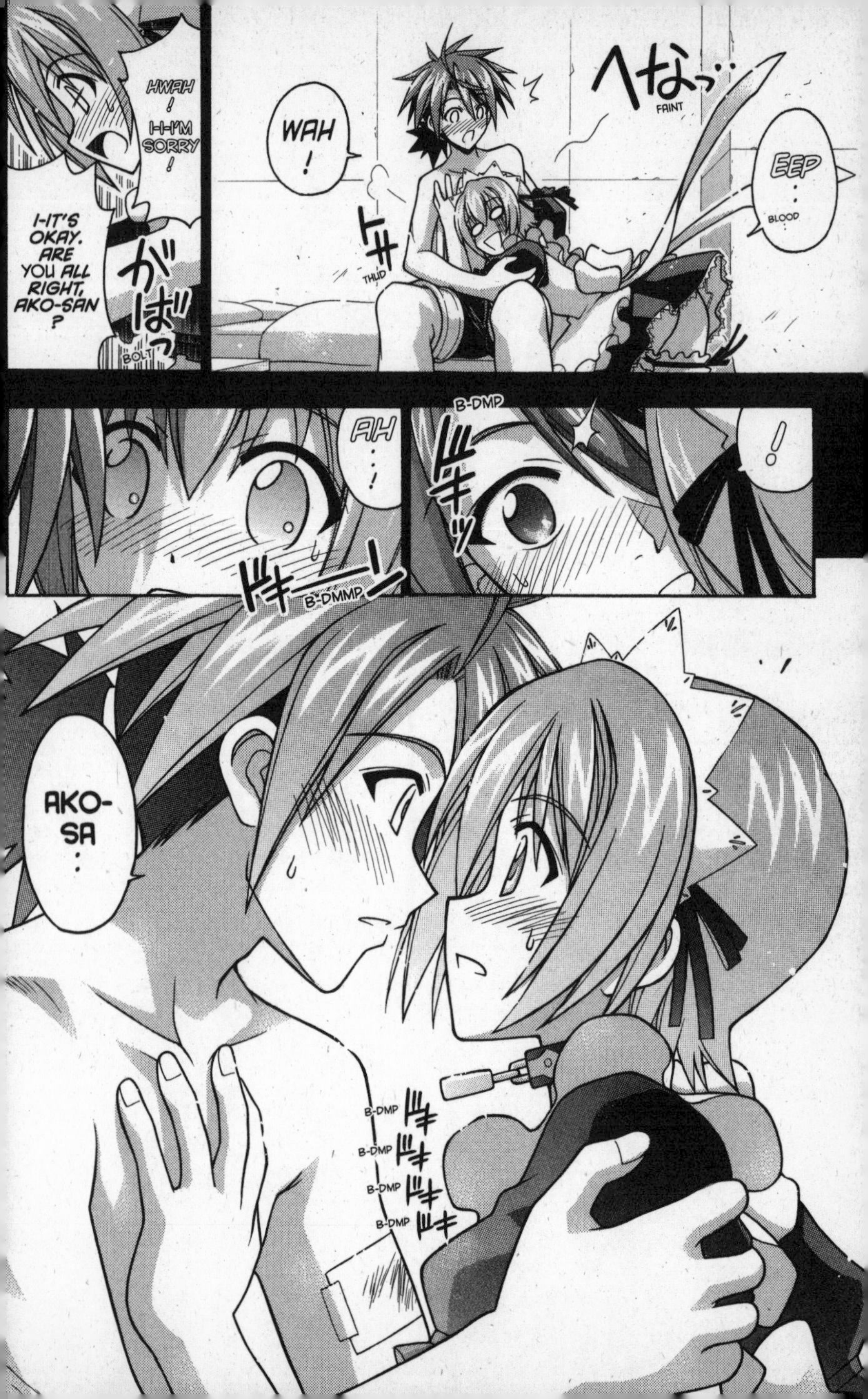

へなっ
FAINT
EEP... BLOOD...
WAH!
ドサ
THUD
HWAH! I-I-I'M SORRY!
I-IT'S OKAY. ARE YOU ALL RIGHT, AKO-SAN?
がばっ
BOLT
B-DMP
ドキッ
!
AH...!
ドキーーン
B-DMMP
...!
AKO-SA...
B-DMP ドキ
B-DMP ドキ
B-DMP ドキ
B-DMP ドキ

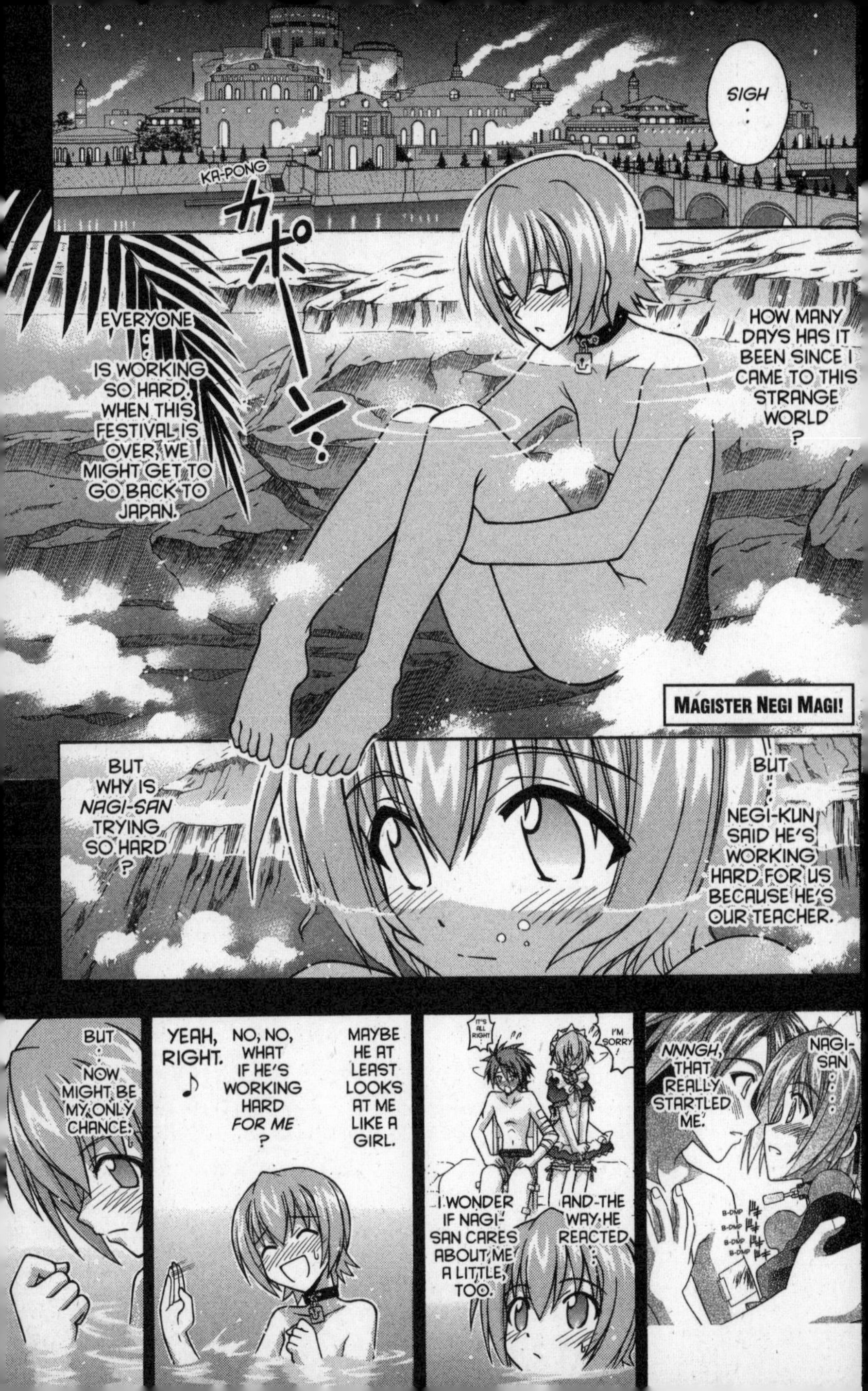
SIGH . .
KA-PONG
カポーン.
HOW MANY DAYS HAS IT BEEN SINCE I CAME TO THIS STRANGE WORLD ?
EVERYONE . . IS WORKING SO HARD. WHEN THIS FESTIVAL IS OVER, WE MIGHT GET TO GO BACK TO JAPAN.
MAGISTER NEGI MAGI!
BUT . . NEGI-KUN SAID HE'S WORKING HARD FOR US BECAUSE HE'S OUR TEACHER.
BUT WHY IS *NAGI-SAN* TRYING SO HARD ?
NAGI-SAN . . .
NNNGH, THAT REALLY STARTLED ME.
B-DMP
B-DMP
B-DMP
B-DMP
I'M SORRY !
IT'S ALL RIGHT . .
AND THE WAY HE REACTED . .
I WONDER IF NAGI-SAN CARES ABOUT ME A LITTLE, TOO.
MAYBE HE AT LEAST LOOKS AT ME LIKE A GIRL.
NO, NO, WHAT IF HE'S WORKING HARD *FOR ME* ?
YEAH, RIGHT. ♪
BUT . . NOW MIGHT BE MY ONLY CHANCE.

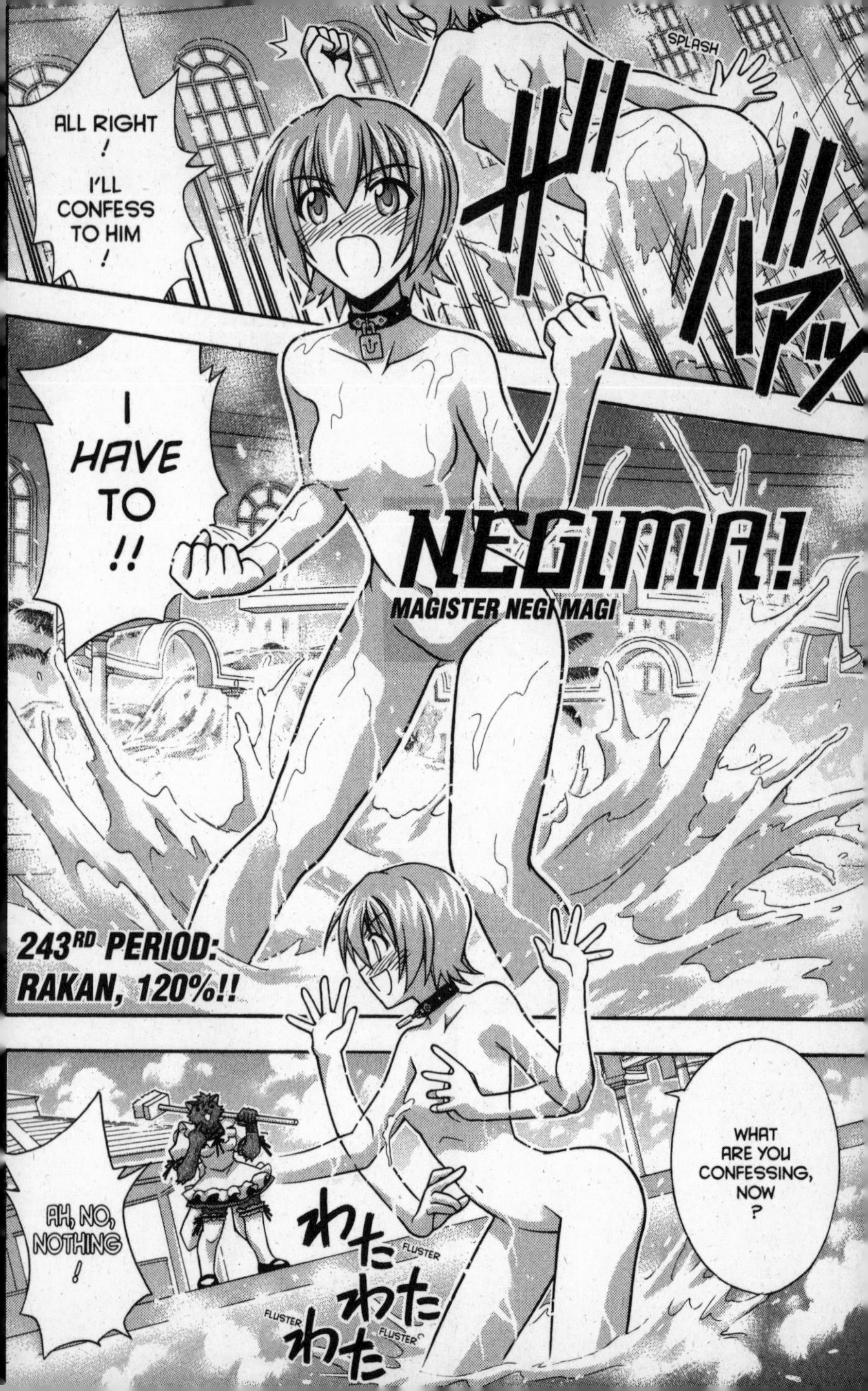

ザバァッ
SPLASH
ALL RIGHT! I'LL CONFESS TO HIM!
I HAVE TO!!
NEGIMA!
MAGISTER NEGI MAGI
243RD PERIOD: RAKAN, 120%!!
WHAT ARE YOU CONFESSING, NOW?
AH, NO, NOTHING!
わたわたわた
FLUSTER FLUSTER FLUSTER

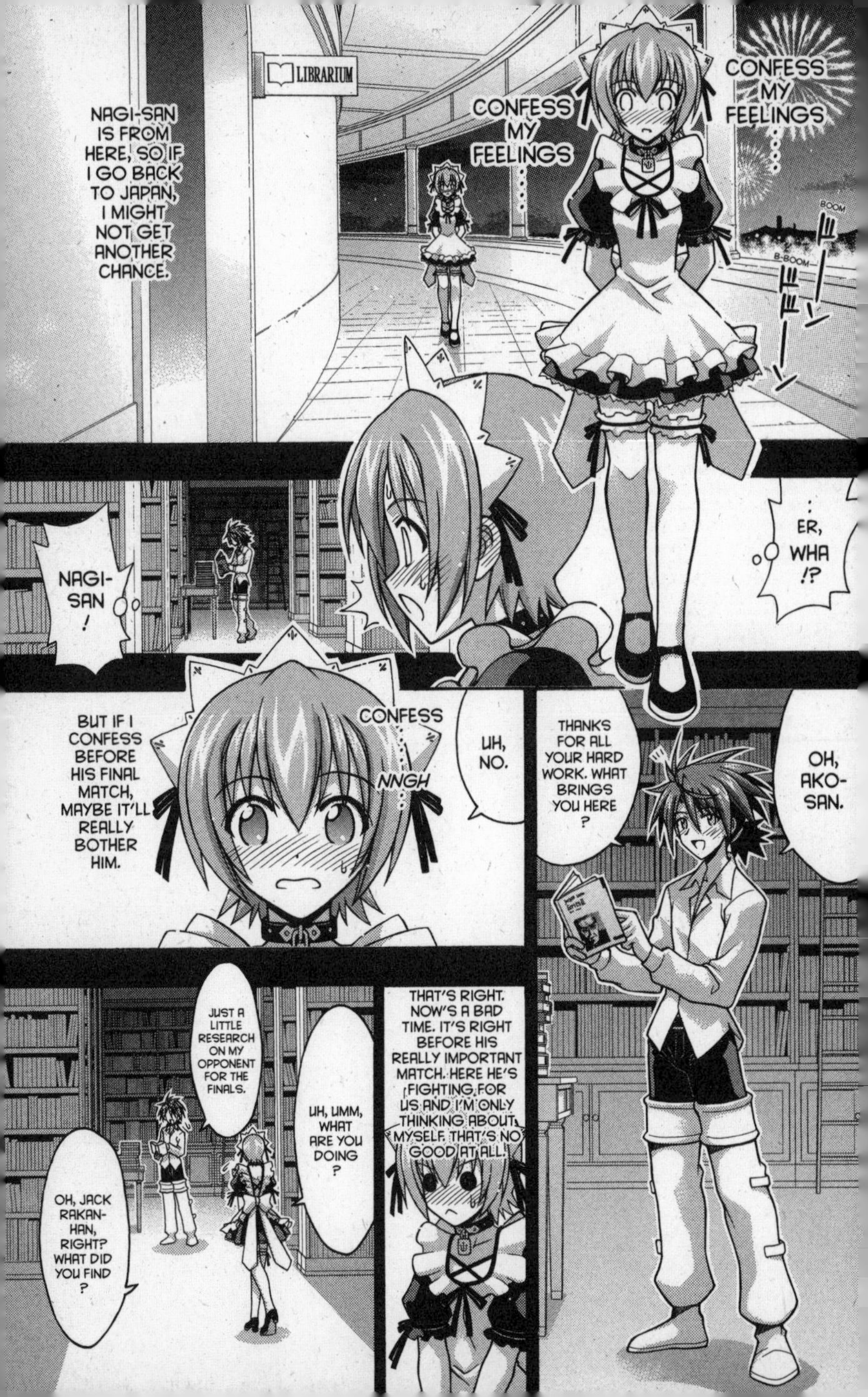

CONFESS MY FEELINGS
CONFESS MY FEELINGS
BOOM
B-BOOM
LIBRARIUM
NAGI-SAN IS FROM HERE, SO IF I GO BACK TO JAPAN, I MIGHT NOT GET ANOTHER CHANCE.
ER, WHA!?
NAGI-SAN!
OH, AKO-SAN.
THANKS FOR ALL YOUR HARD WORK. WHAT BRINGS YOU HERE?
UH, NO.
CONFESS
NNGH
BUT IF I CONFESS BEFORE HIS FINAL MATCH, MAYBE IT'LL REALLY BOTHER HIM.
THAT'S RIGHT. NOW'S A BAD TIME. IT'S RIGHT BEFORE HIS REALLY IMPORTANT MATCH. HERE HE'S FIGHTING FOR US AND I'M ONLY THINKING ABOUT MYSELF. THAT'S NO GOOD AT ALL.
UH, UMM, WHAT ARE YOU DOING?
JUST A LITTLE RESEARCH ON MY OPPONENT FOR THE FINALS.
OH, JACK RAKAN-HAN, RIGHT? WHAT DID YOU FIND?

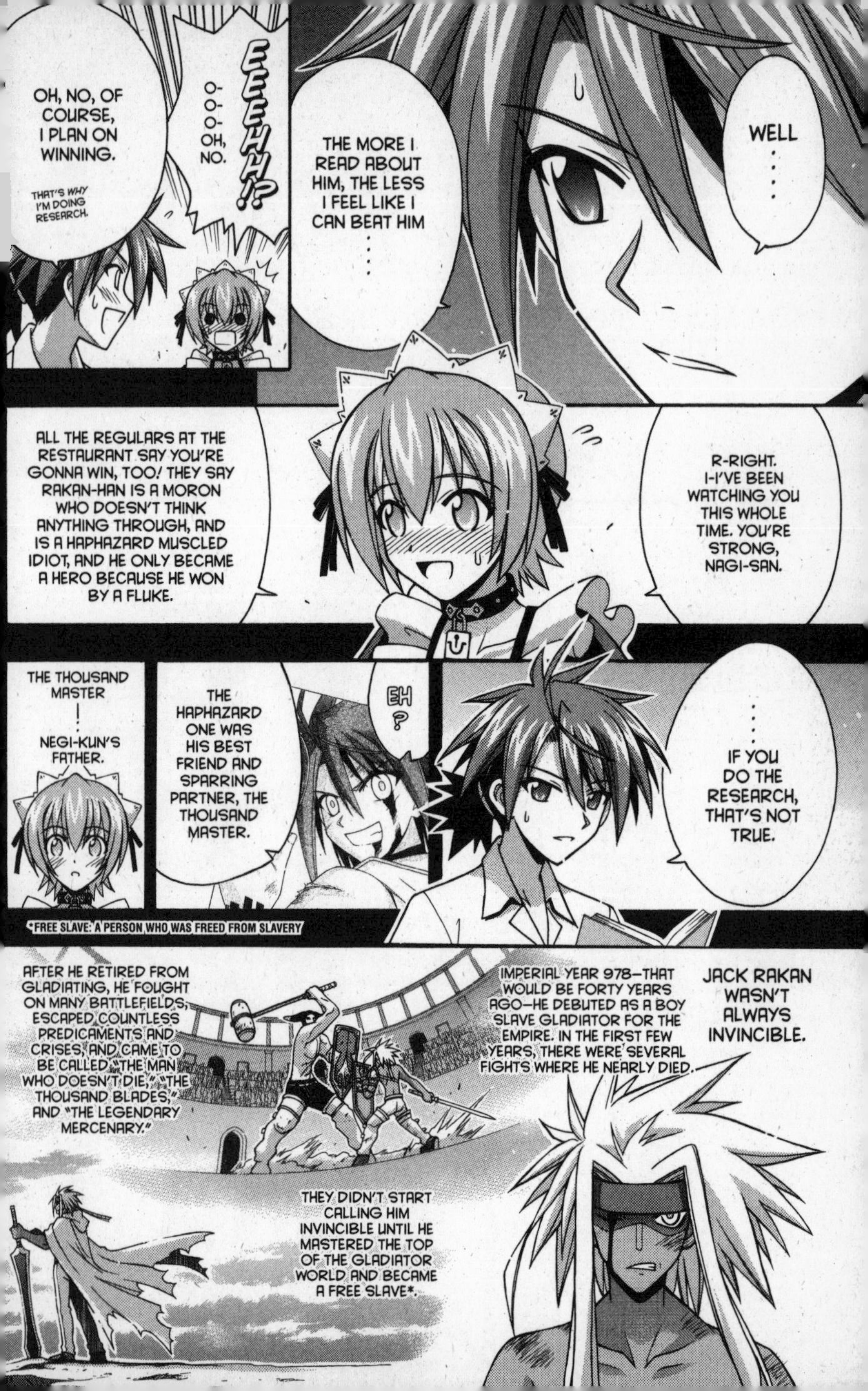
WELL......
THE MORE I READ ABOUT HIM, THE LESS I FEEL LIKE I CAN BEAT HIM......
EEEHH!?
O-O-O-OH, NO.
OH, NO, OF COURSE, I PLAN ON WINNING.
THAT'S WHY I'M DOING RESEARCH.
R-RIGHT. I-I'VE BEEN WATCHING YOU THIS WHOLE TIME. YOU'RE STRONG, NAGI-SAN.
ALL THE REGULARS AT THE RESTAURANT SAY YOU'RE GONNA WIN, TOO! THEY SAY RAKAN-HAN IS A MORON WHO DOESN'T THINK ANYTHING THROUGH, AND IS A HAPHAZARD MUSCLED IDIOT, AND HE ONLY BECAME A HERO BECAUSE HE WON BY A FLUKE.
... IF YOU DO THE RESEARCH, THAT'S NOT TRUE.
EH?
THE HAPHAZARD ONE WAS HIS BEST FRIEND AND SPARRING PARTNER, THE THOUSAND MASTER.
THE THOUSAND MASTER! NEGI-KUN'S FATHER.
*FREE SLAVE: A PERSON WHO WAS FREED FROM SLAVERY
JACK RAKAN WASN'T ALWAYS INVINCIBLE.
IMPERIAL YEAR 978—THAT WOULD BE FORTY YEARS AGO—HE DEBUTED AS A BOY SLAVE GLADIATOR FOR THE EMPIRE. IN THE FIRST FEW YEARS, THERE WERE SEVERAL FIGHTS WHERE HE NEARLY DIED.
AFTER HE RETIRED FROM GLADIATING, HE FOUGHT ON MANY BATTLEFIELDS, ESCAPED COUNTLESS PREDICAMENTS AND CRISES, AND CAME TO BE CALLED "THE MAN WHO DOESN'T DIE," "THE THOUSAND BLADES," AND "THE LEGENDARY MERCENARY."
THEY DIDN'T START CALLING HIM INVINCIBLE UNTIL HE MASTERED THE TOP OF THE GLADIATOR WORLD AND BECAME A FREE SLAVE*.

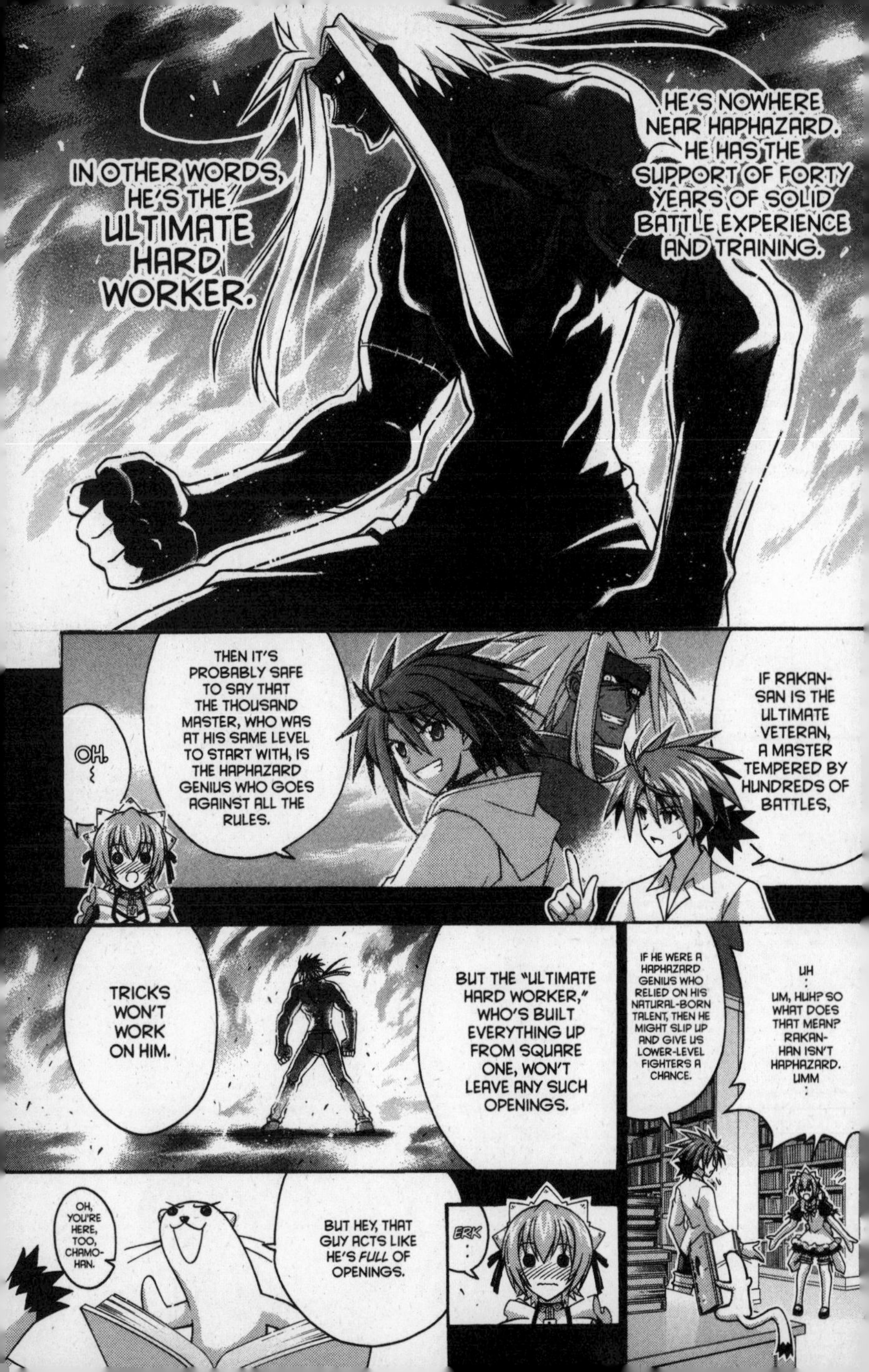
HE'S NOWHERE NEAR HAPHAZARD. HE HAS THE SUPPORT OF FORTY YEARS OF SOLID BATTLE EXPERIENCE AND TRAINING.
IN OTHER WORDS, HE'S THE ULTIMATE HARD WORKER.
IF RAKAN-SAN IS THE ULTIMATE VETERAN, A MASTER TEMPERED BY HUNDREDS OF BATTLES,
THEN IT'S PROBABLY SAFE TO SAY THAT THE THOUSAND MASTER, WHO WAS AT HIS SAME LEVEL TO START WITH, IS THE HAPHAZARD GENIUS WHO GOES AGAINST ALL THE RULES.
OH.
UH... UM, HUH? SO WHAT DOES THAT MEAN? RAKAN-HAN ISN'T HAPHAZARD. UMM...
IF HE WERE A HAPHAZARD GENIUS WHO RELIED ON HIS NATURAL-BORN TALENT, THEN HE MIGHT SLIP UP AND GIVE US LOWER-LEVEL FIGHTERS A CHANCE.
BUT THE "ULTIMATE HARD WORKER," WHO'S BUILT EVERYTHING UP FROM SQUARE ONE, WON'T LEAVE ANY SUCH OPENINGS.
TRICKS WON'T WORK ON HIM.
ERK
BUT HEY, THAT GUY ACTS LIKE HE'S *FULL* OF OPENINGS.
OH, YOU'RE HERE, TOO, CHAMO-HAN.

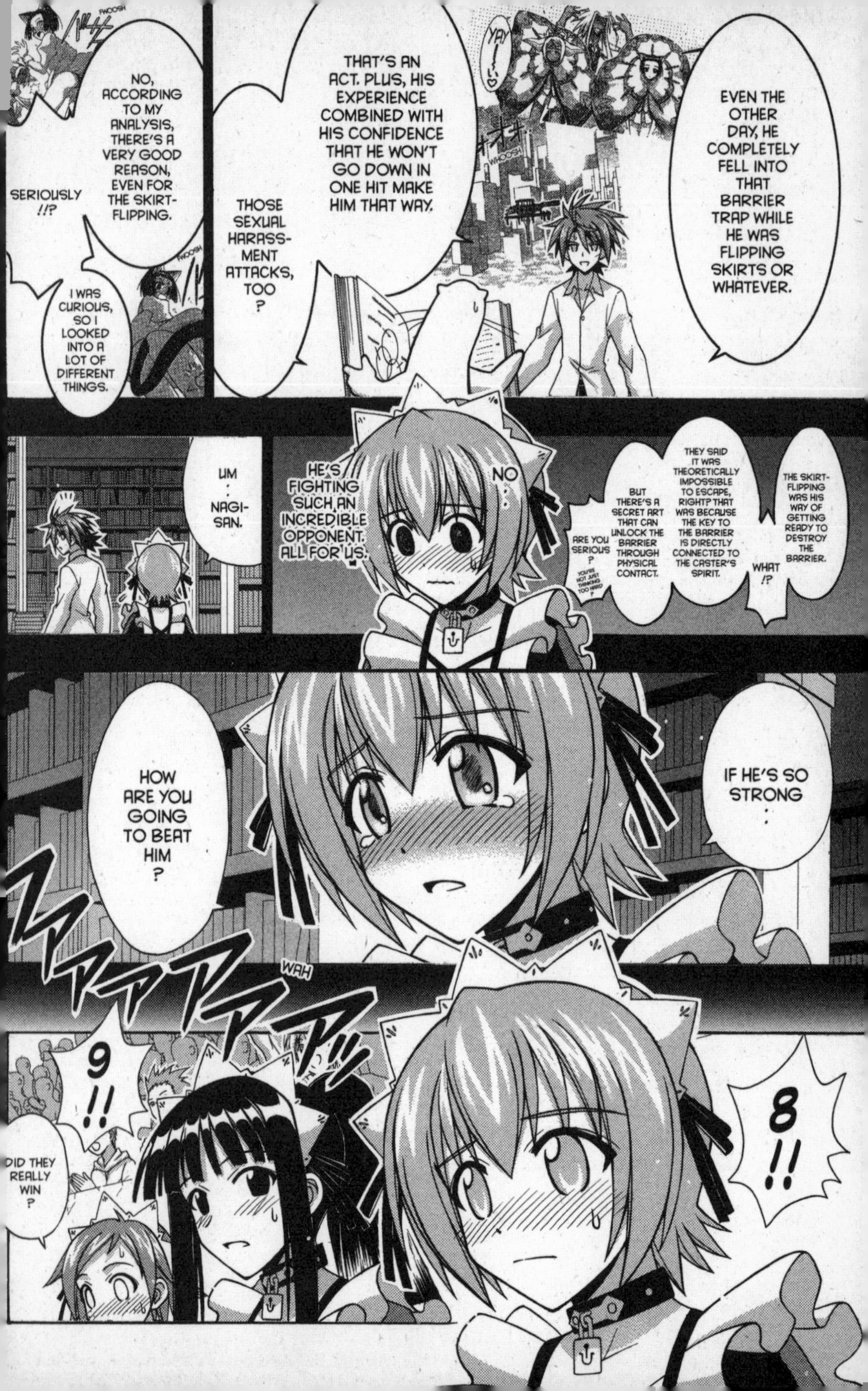
YAY!
WHOOSH
EVEN THE OTHER DAY, HE COMPLETELY FELL INTO THAT BARRIER TRAP WHILE HE WAS FLIPPING SKIRTS OR WHATEVER.
THAT'S AN ACT. PLUS, HIS EXPERIENCE COMBINED WITH HIS CONFIDENCE THAT HE WON'T GO DOWN IN ONE HIT MAKE HIM THAT WAY.
THOSE SEXUAL HARASS-MENT ATTACKS, TOO?
PWOOSH
NO, ACCORDING TO MY ANALYSIS, THERE'S A VERY GOOD REASON, EVEN FOR THE SKIRT-FLIPPING.
SERIOUSLY!!?
PWOOSH
I WAS CURIOUS, SO I LOOKED INTO A LOT OF DIFFERENT THINGS.
THE SKIRT-FLIPPING WAS HIS WAY OF GETTING READY TO DESTROY THE BARRIER.
WHAT!?
THEY SAID IT WAS THEORETICALLY IMPOSSIBLE TO ESCAPE, RIGHT? THAT WAS BECAUSE THE KEY TO THE BARRIER IS DIRECTLY CONNECTED TO THE CASTER'S SPIRIT.
BUT THERE'S A SECRET ART THAT CAN UNLOCK THE BARRIER THROUGH PHYSICAL CONTACT.
ARE YOU SERIOUS?
YOU'RE NOT JUST THINKING TOO HARD?
NO
HE'S FIGHTING SUCH AN INCREDIBLE OPPONENT. ALL FOR US.
UM : NAGI-SAN.
IF HE'S SO STRONG :
HOW ARE YOU GOING TO BEAT HIM?
8!!
WAH
9!!
DID THEY REALLY WIN?

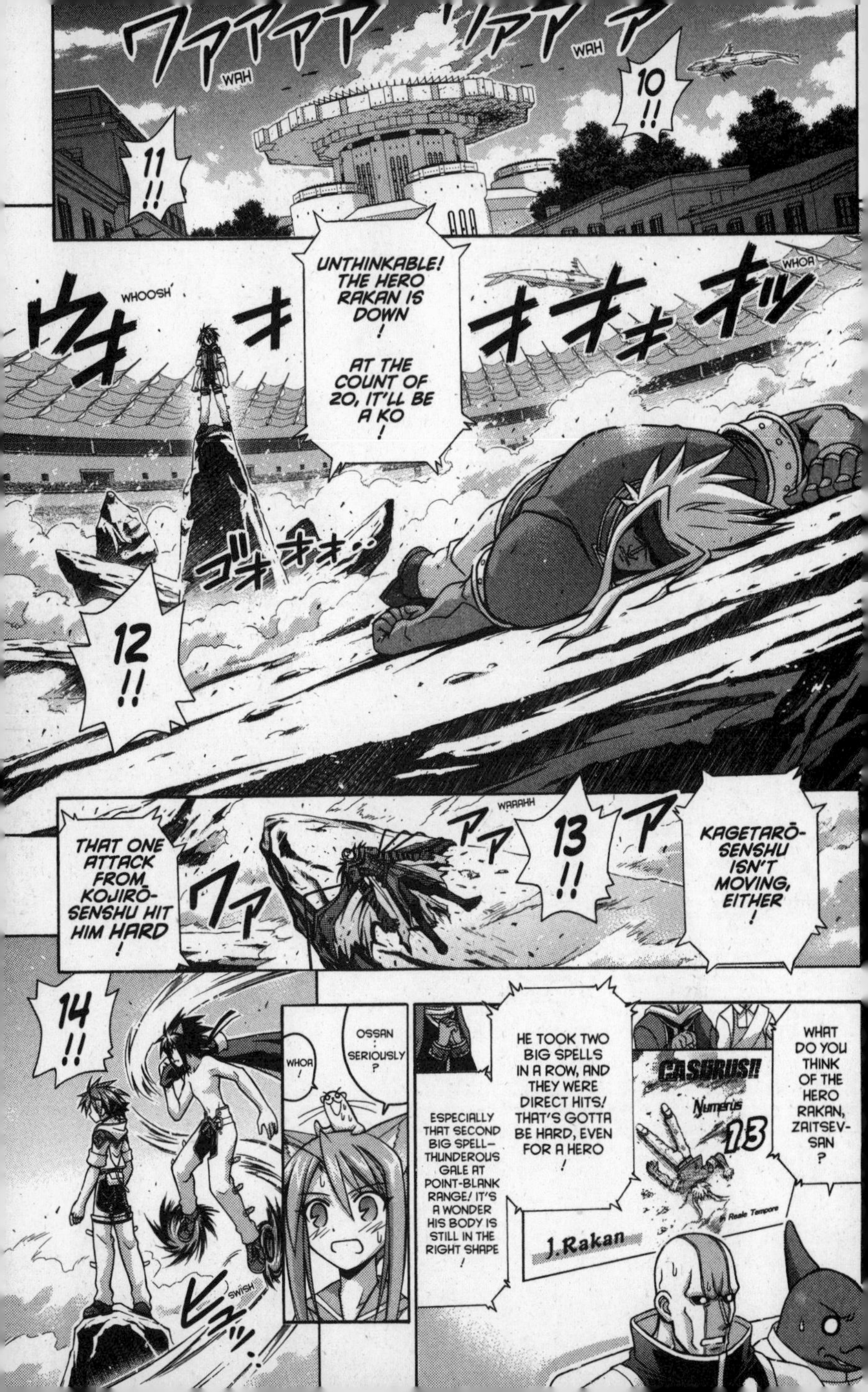
10 !!
WAH
WAH
11 !!
WHOA
UNTHINKABLE! THE HERO RAKAN IS DOWN!
AT THE COUNT OF 20, IT'LL BE A KO!
WHOOSH
12 !!
KAGETARŌ-SENSHU ISN'T MOVING, EITHER!
13 !!
WAAAHH
THAT ONE ATTACK FROM KOJIRŌ-SENSHU HIT HIM HARD!
WHAT DO YOU THINK OF THE HERO RAKAN, ZAITSEV-SAN?
CASURUS!!
Numerus 13
J.Rakan
HE TOOK TWO BIG SPELLS IN A ROW, AND THEY WERE DIRECT HITS! THAT'S GOTTA BE HARD, EVEN FOR A HERO!
ESPECIALLY THAT SECOND BIG SPELL—THUNDEROUS GALE AT POINT-BLANK RANGE! IT'S A WONDER HIS BODY IS STILL IN THE RIGHT SHAPE!
OSSAN... SERIOUSLY?
WHOA!
14 !!
SWISH

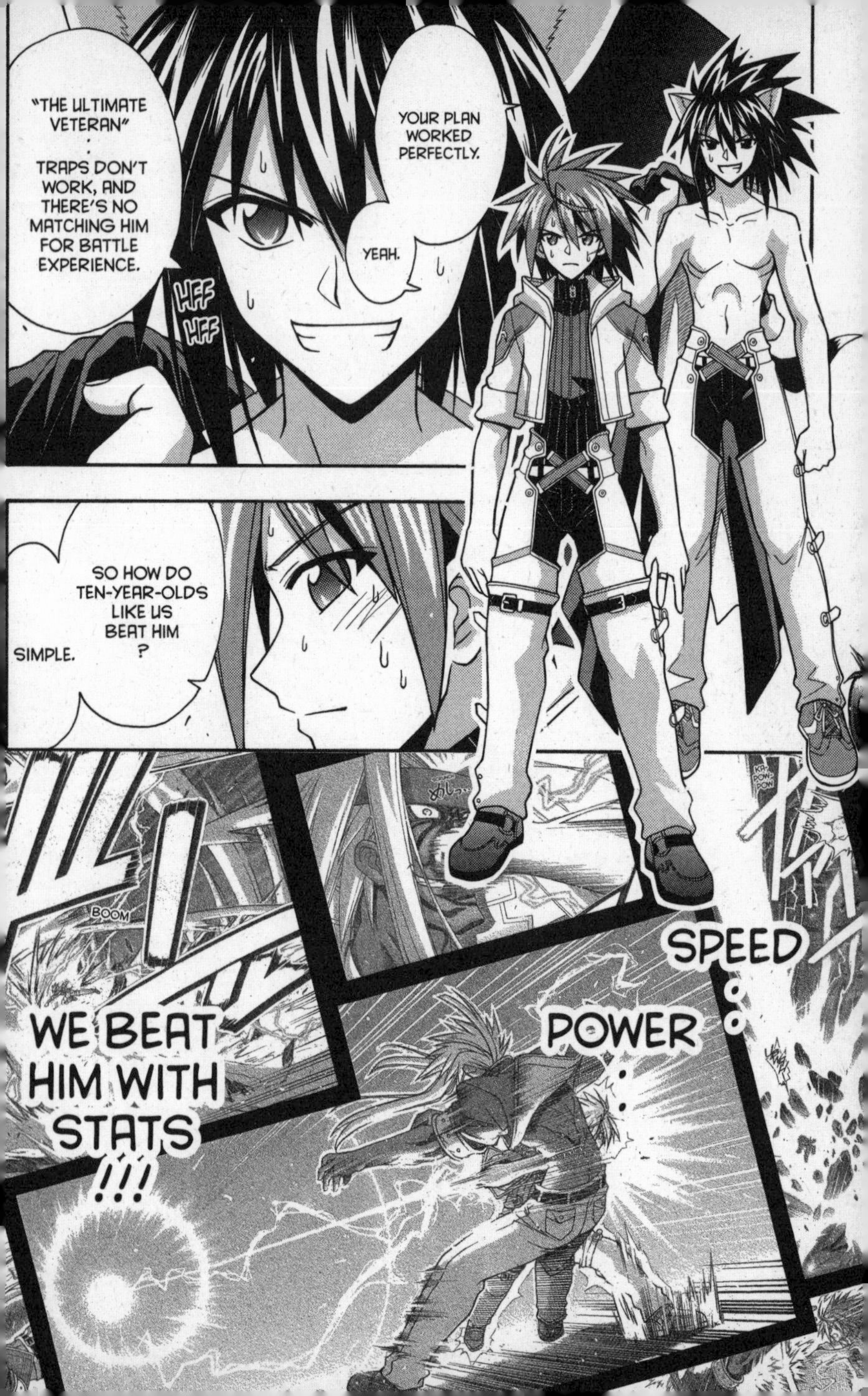
YOUR PLAN WORKED PERFECTLY.
YEAH.
"THE ULTIMATE VETERAN" : TRAPS DON'T WORK, AND THERE'S NO MATCHING HIM FOR BATTLE EXPERIENCE.
HFF HFF
SO HOW DO TEN-YEAR-OLDS LIKE US BEAT HIM ?
SIMPLE.
KA-POW-POW
BOOM
SPEED :
POWER . . .
WE BEAT HIM WITH STATS !!!

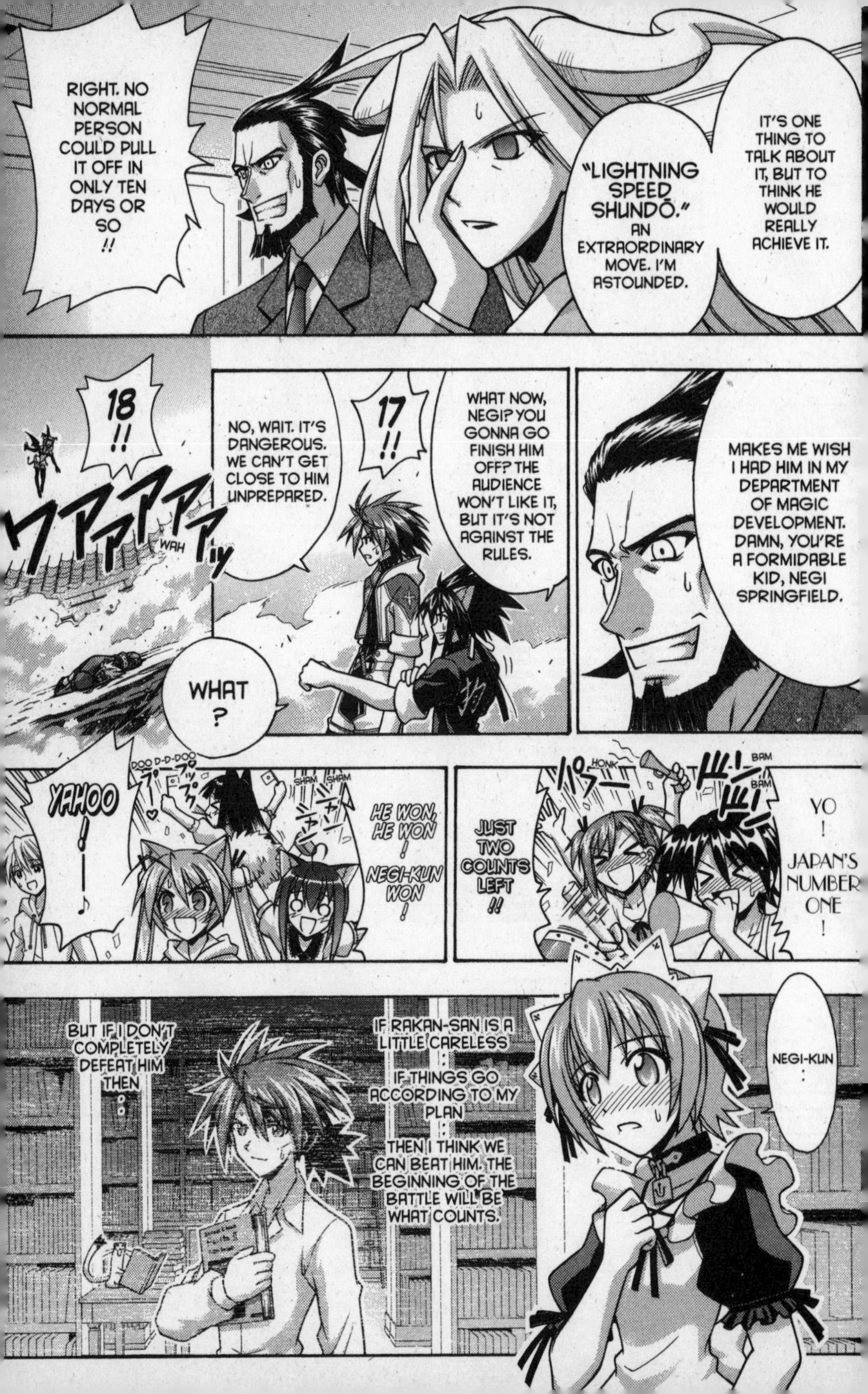
IT'S ONE THING TO TALK ABOUT IT, BUT TO THINK HE WOULD REALLY ACHIEVE IT.
"LIGHTNING SPEED SHUNDŌ." AN EXTRAORDINARY MOVE. I'M ASTOUNDED.
RIGHT. NO NORMAL PERSON COULD PULL IT OFF IN ONLY TEN DAYS OR SO !!
MAKES ME WISH I HAD HIM IN MY DEPARTMENT OF MAGIC DEVELOPMENT. DAMN, YOU'RE A FORMIDABLE KID, NEGI SPRINGFIELD.
WHAT NOW, NEGI? YOU GONNA GO FINISH HIM OFF? THE AUDIENCE WON'T LIKE IT, BUT IT'S NOT AGAINST THE RULES.
17 !!
NO, WAIT. IT'S DANGEROUS. WE CAN'T GET CLOSE TO HIM UNPREPARED.
WHAT ?
18 !!
WAH
YO ! JAPAN'S NUMBER ONE !
BAM
BAM
HONK
JUST TWO COUNTS LEFT !!
HE WON, HE WON ! NEGI-KUN WON !
SHAM
SHAM
DOO D-D-DOO
YAHOO ! ♪
NEGI-KUN :
IF RAKAN-SAN IS A LITTLE CARELESS : IF THINGS GO ACCORDING TO MY PLAN : THEN I THINK WE CAN BEAT HIM. THE BEGINNING OF THE BATTLE WILL BE WHAT COUNTS.
BUT IF I DON'T COMPLETELY DEFEAT HIM THEN :

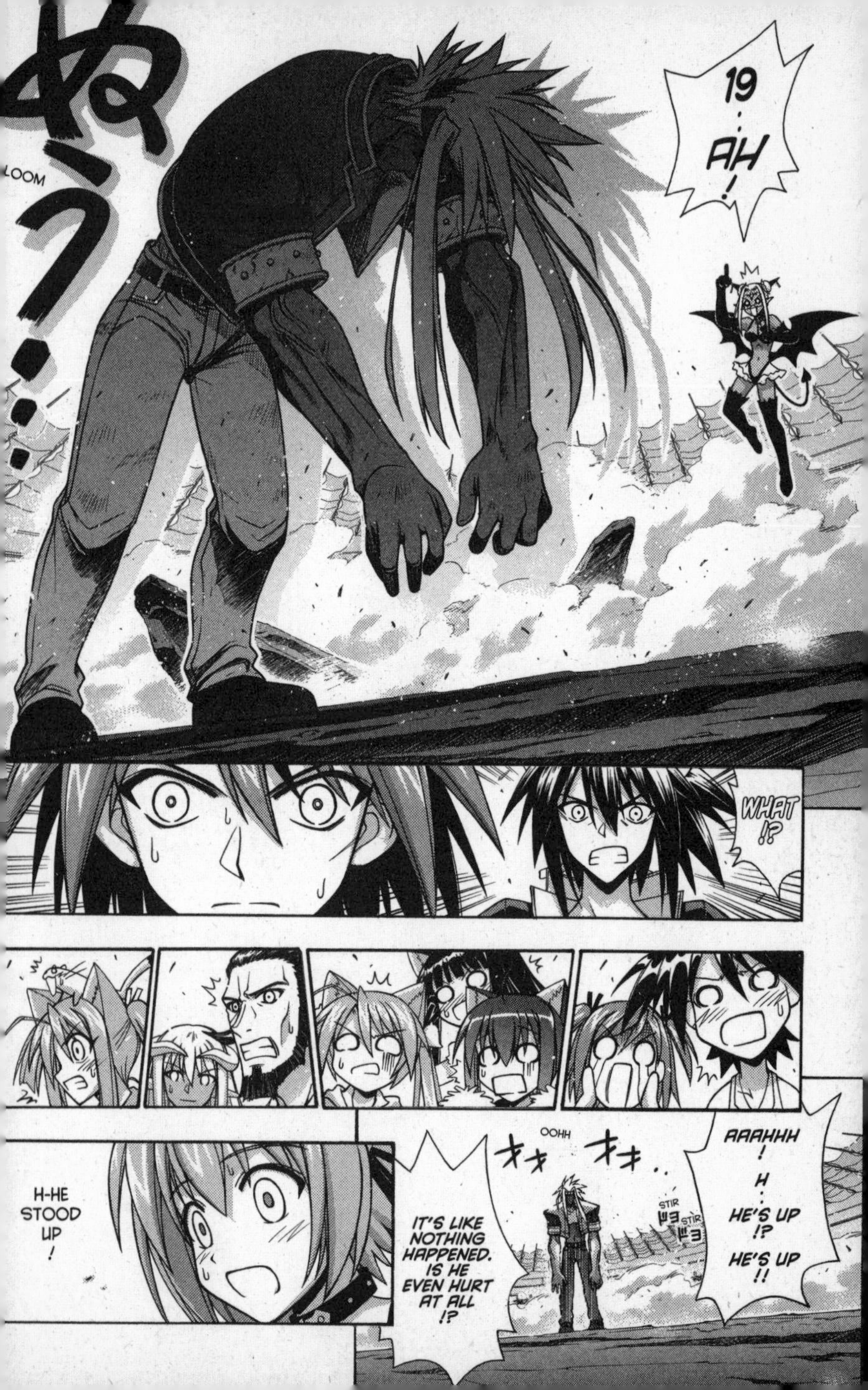
19... AH!
ぬう…
LOOM
WHAT!?
AAAHHH! H... HE'S UP!? HE'S UP!!
オォ オォ
OOHH
ドヨ ドヨ
STIR STIR
IT'S LIKE NOTHING HAPPENED. IS HE EVEN HURT AT ALL!?
H-HE STOOD UP!

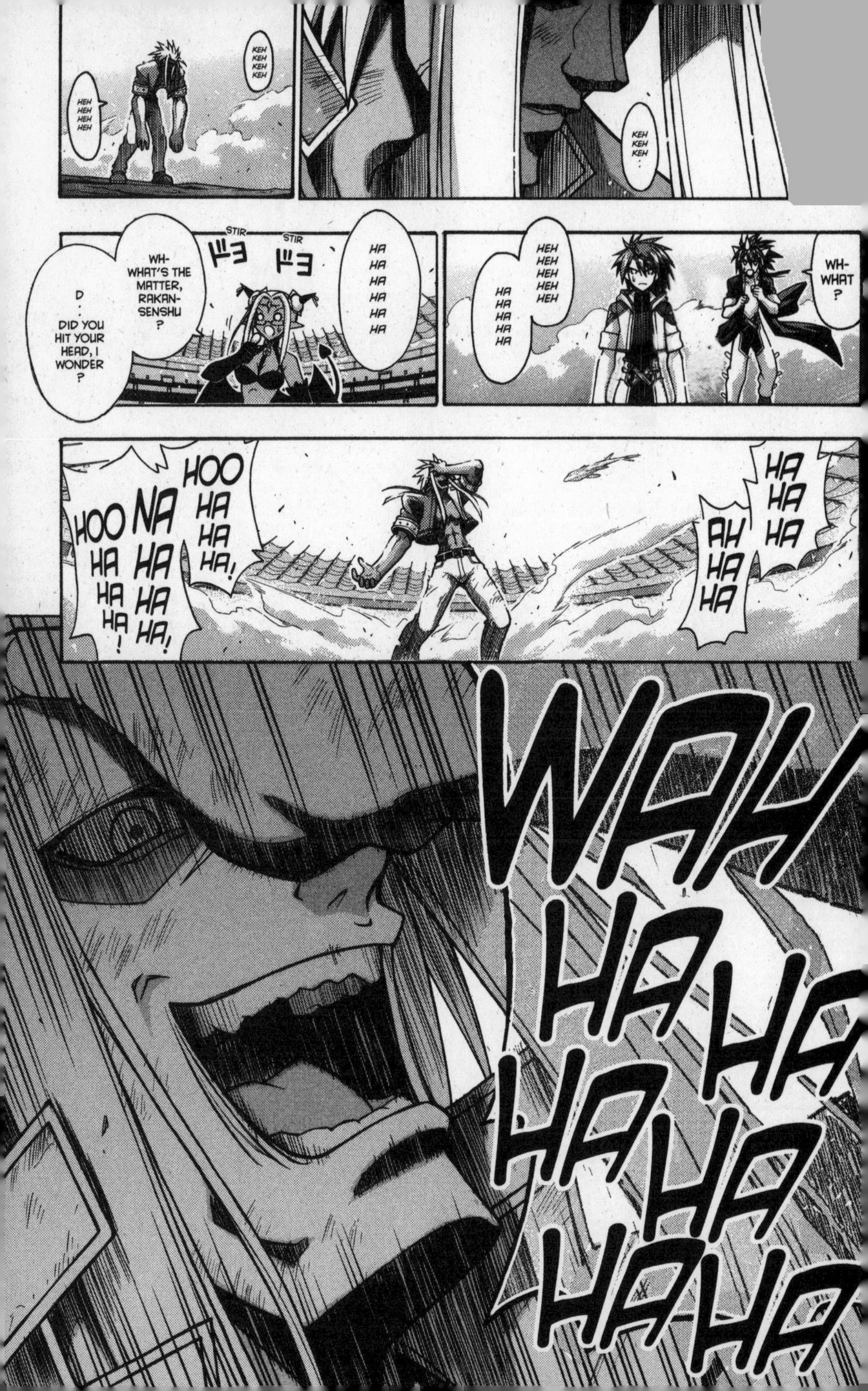
KEH KEH KEH ...
KEH KEH KEH KEH
HEH HEH HEH HEH HEH
WH- WHAT?
HEH HEH HEH HEH HEH
HA HA HA HA HA
HA HA HA HA HA HA HA
STIR ドヨ
STIR ドヨ
WH- WHAT'S THE MATTER, RAKAN-SENSHU?
D... DID YOU HIT YOUR HEAD, I WONDER?
HA HA HA
AH HA HA HA
HOO HA HA HA!
NA HA HA HA!
HOO HA HA HA!
WAH HA HA HA HA HA HA HA HA HA HA

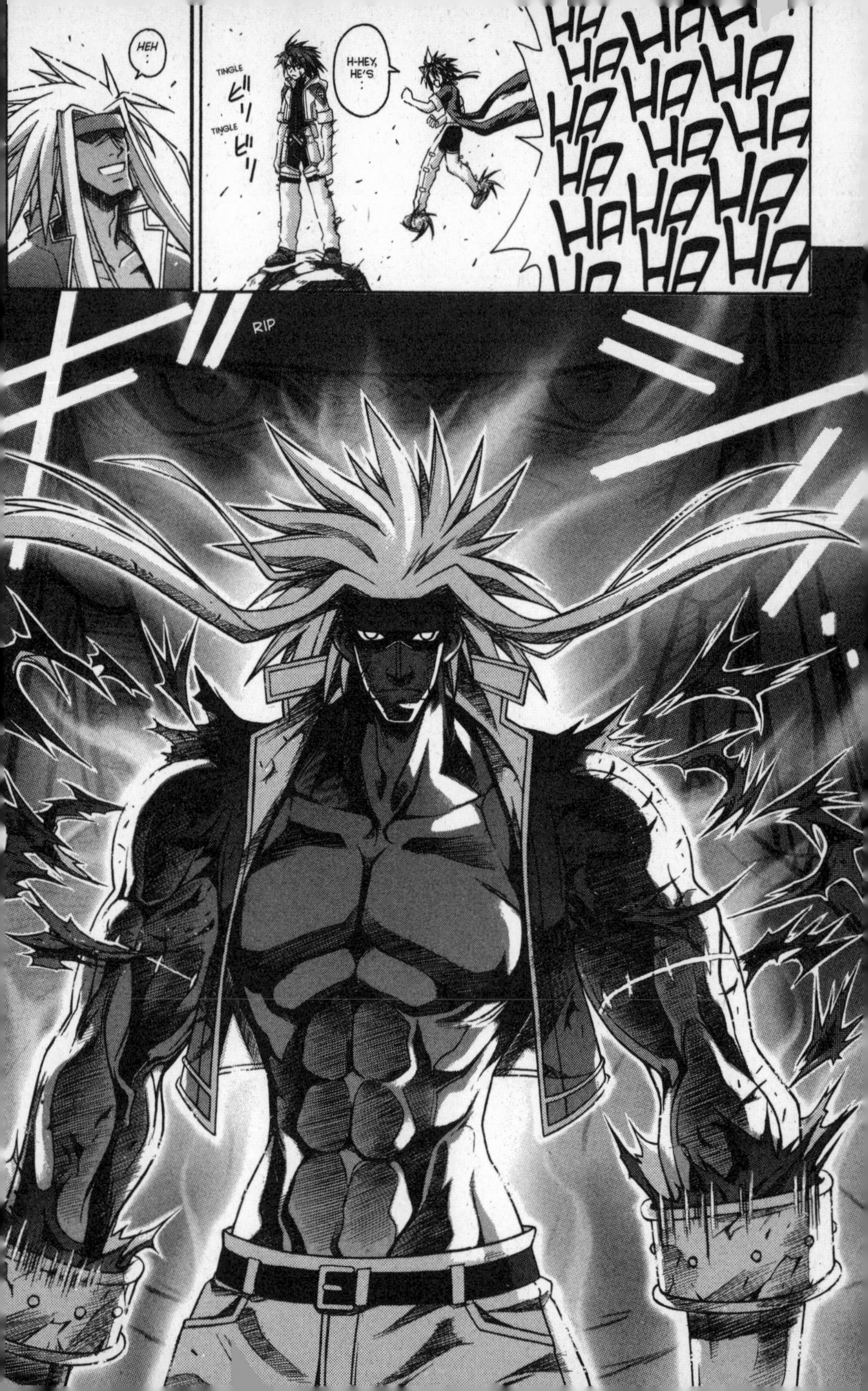
HA HA HA HA HA HA HA HA HA HA HA HA HA HA HA HA HA HA HA HA HA
H-HEY, HE'S...
TINGLE ビリ
TINGLE ビリ
HEH...
RIP

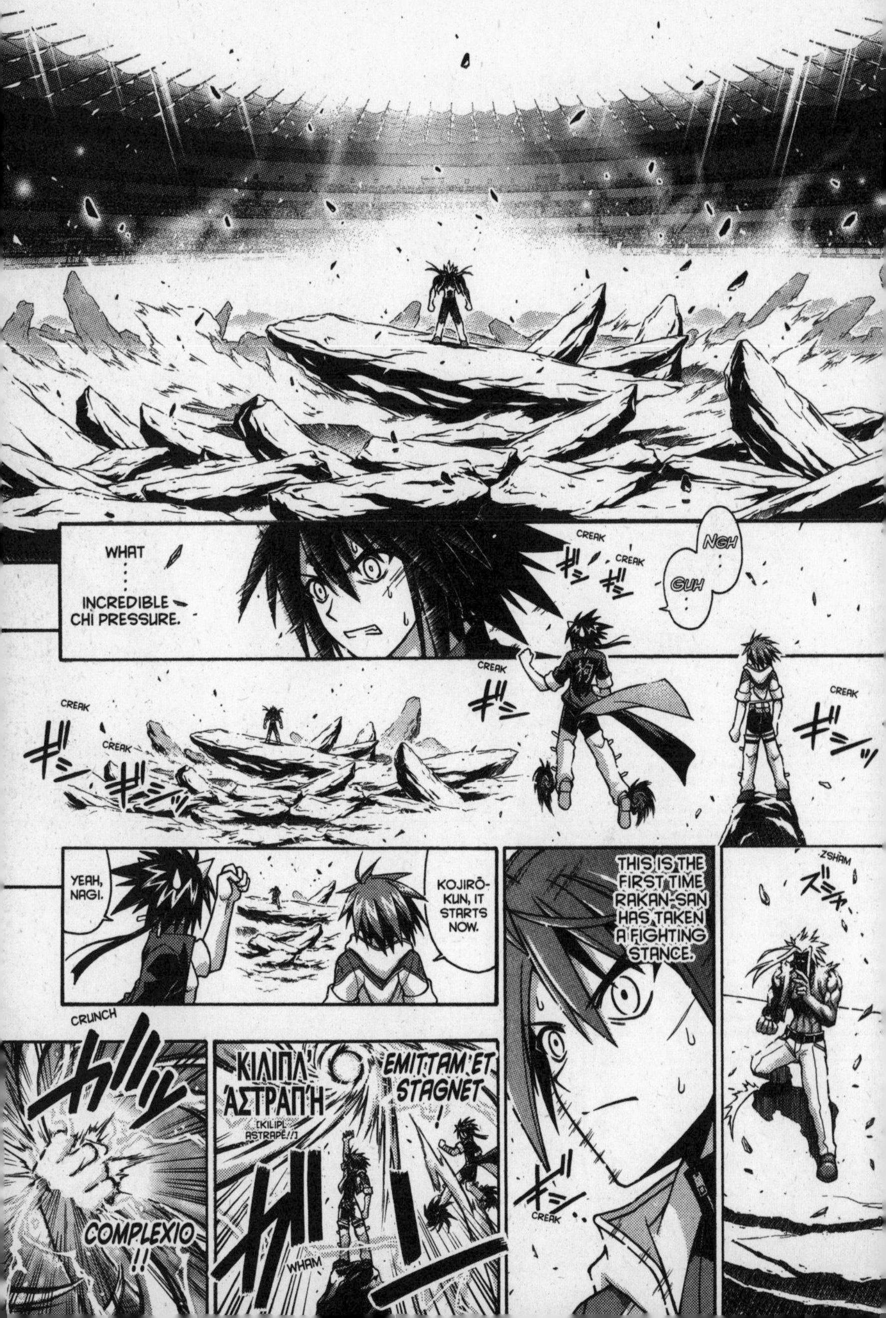
NGH
GUH
CREAK
CREAK
WHAT ... INCREDIBLE CHI PRESSURE.
CREAK
CREAK
CREAK
CREAK
ZSHAM
THIS IS THE FIRST TIME RAKAN-SAN HAS TAKEN A FIGHTING STANCE.
CREAK
KOJIRŌ-KUN, IT STARTS NOW.
YEAH, NAGI.
EMITTAM ET STAGNET!
ΚΙΛΙΠΛ' ΆΣΤΡΑΠΉ
[KILIPL ASTRAPÉ!!]
WHAM
CRUNCH
COMPLEXIO!!

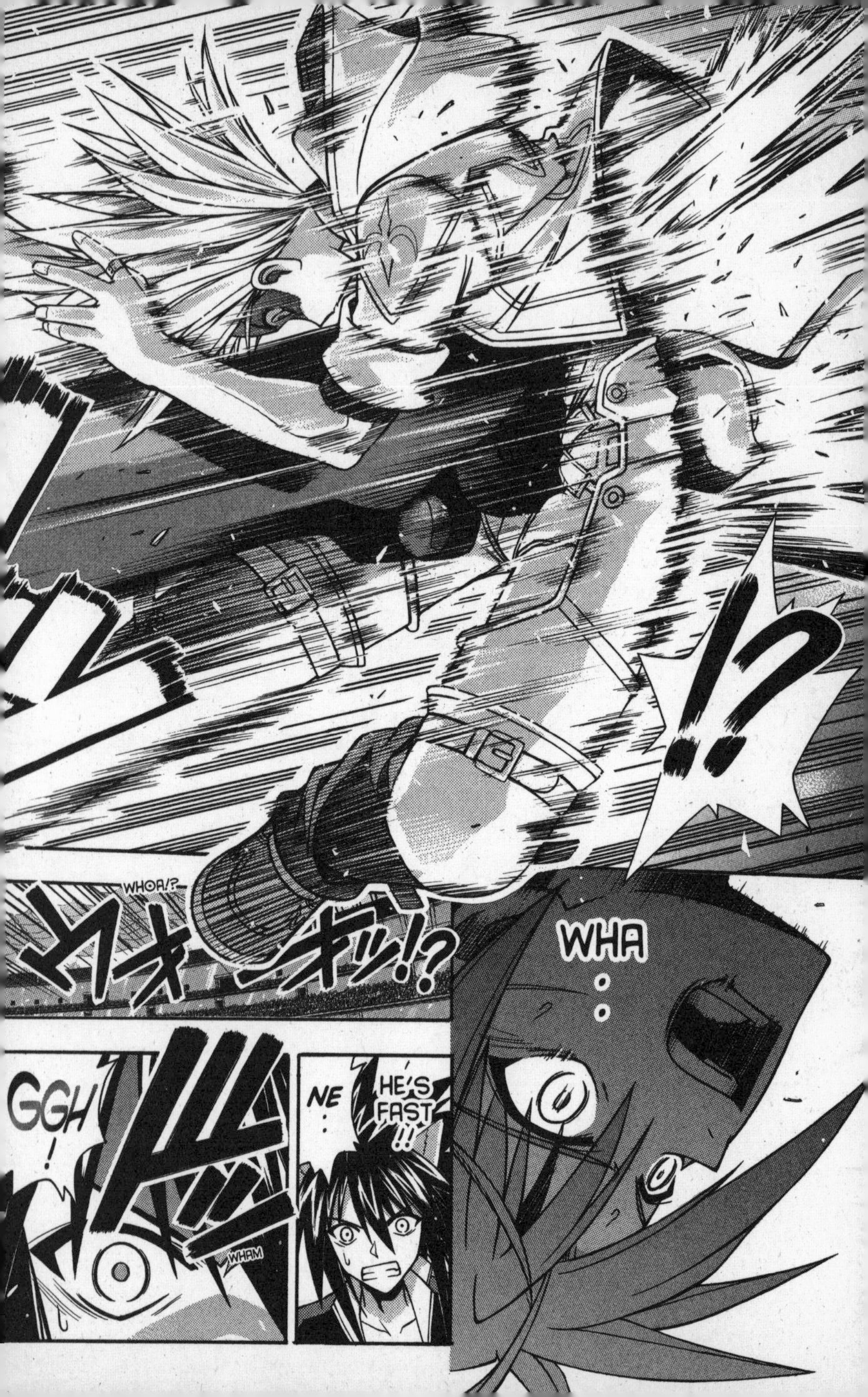
!?
WHA . . .
WHOA!?
NE . . .
HE'S FAST!!
GGH!
WHAM

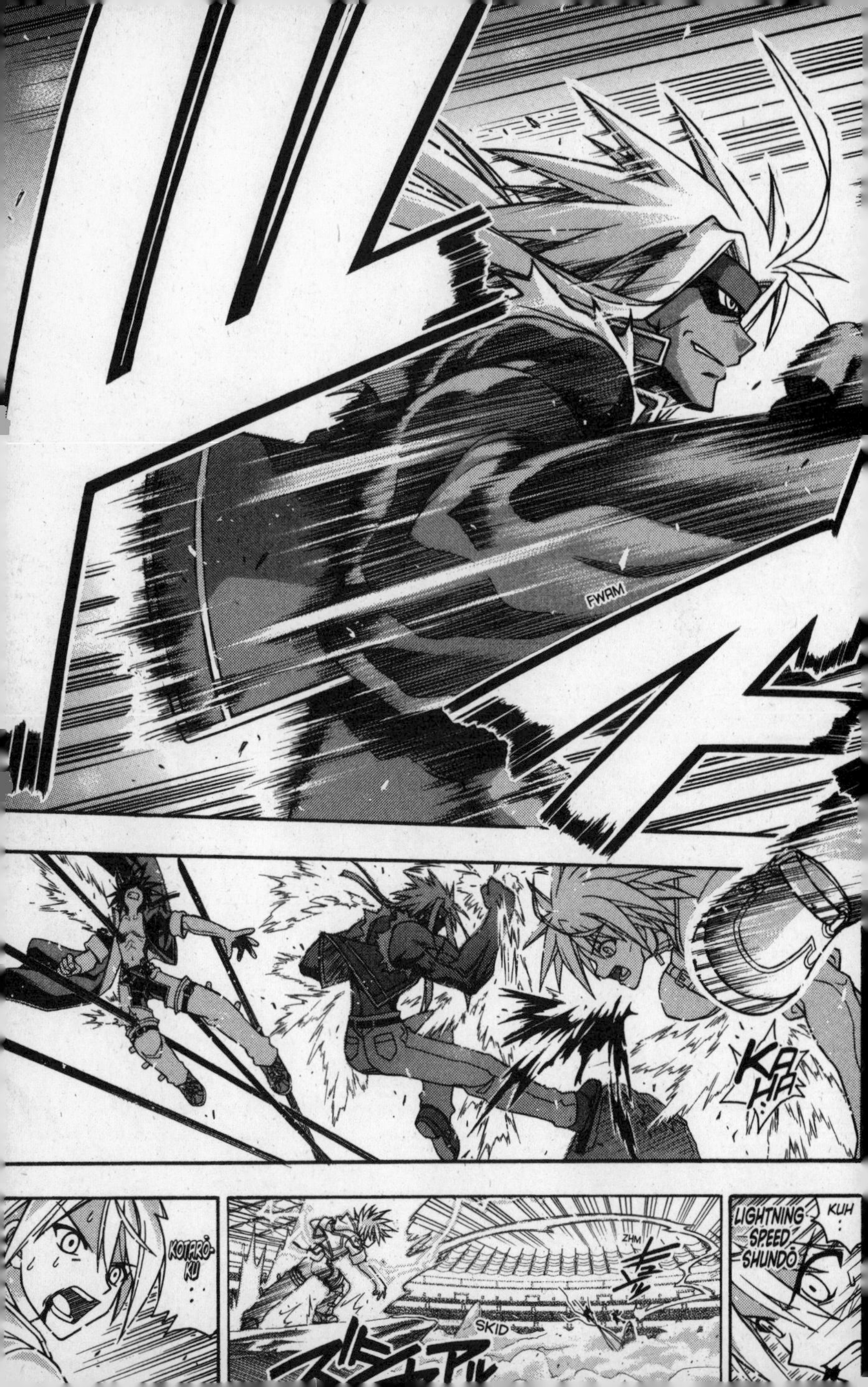
FWAM
KA-HA
LIGHTNING SPEED SHUNDŌ
KUH
ZHM
SKID
KOTARŌ-KU

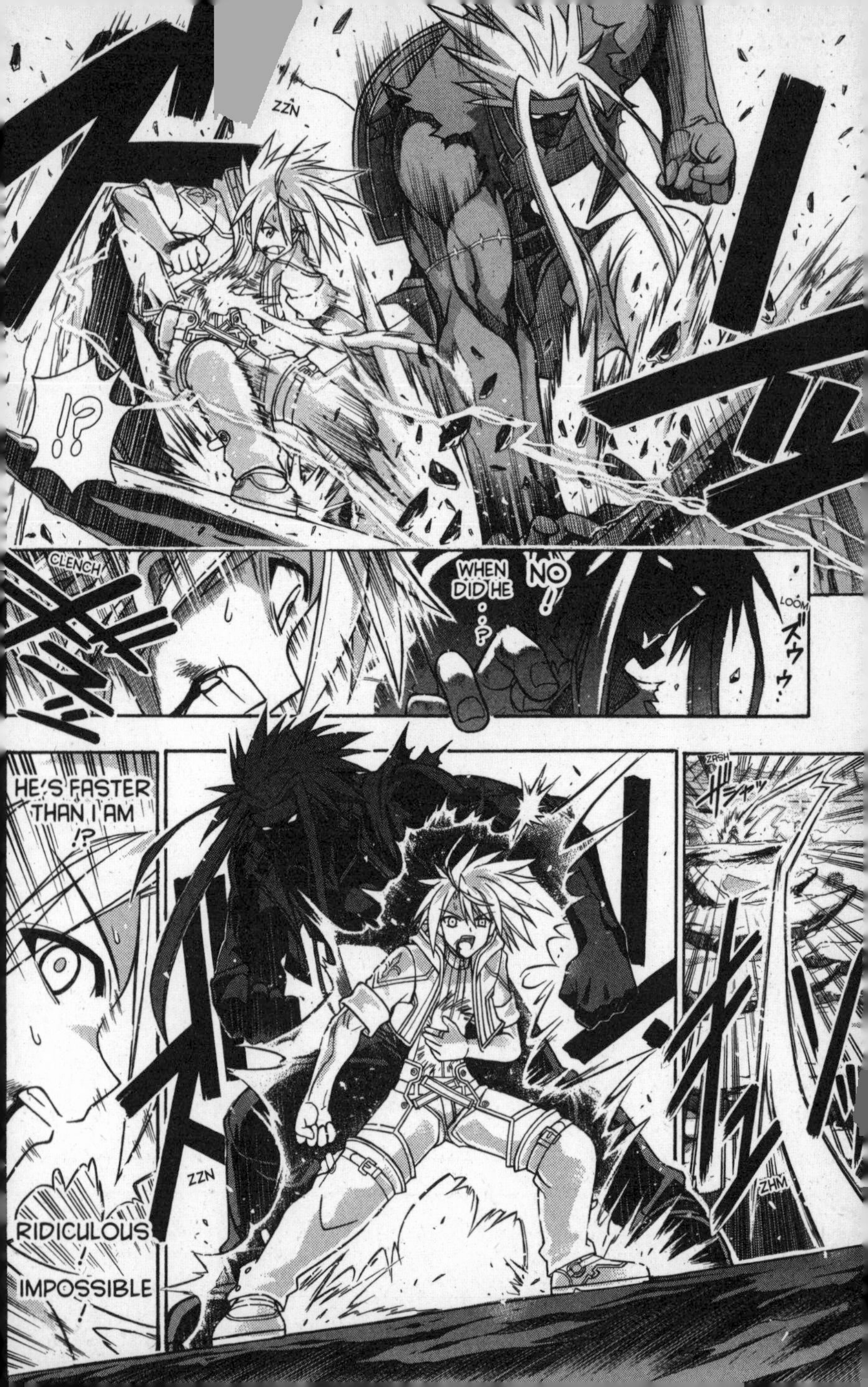
ZZN
!?
!!
CLENCH
NO!
WHEN DID HE...?
LOOM
ズウゥ...
ZASH
ザシャッ
ZHM
HE'S FASTER THAN I AM!?
ZZN
RIDICULOUS!
IMPOSSIBLE!

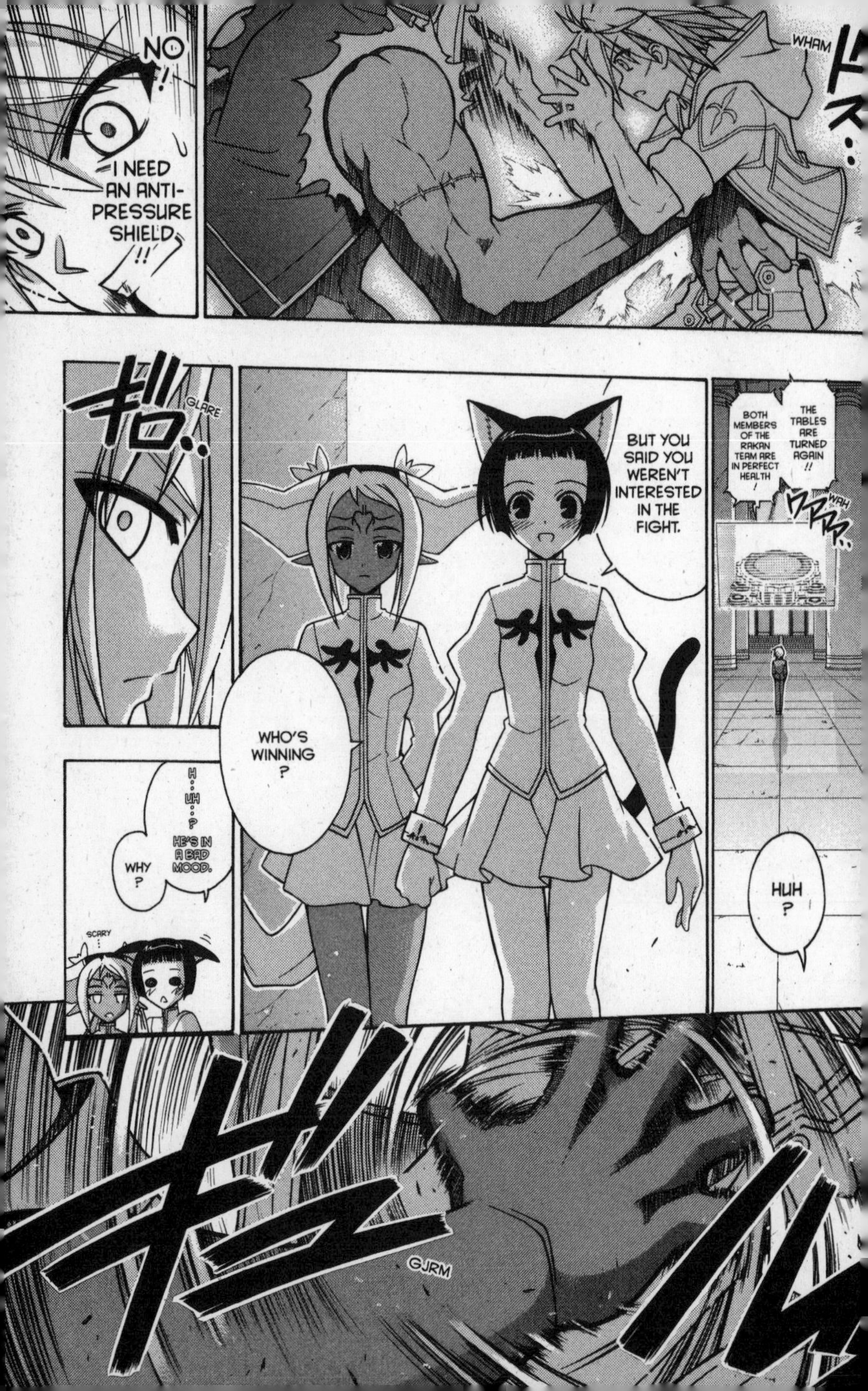

WHAM
ドス...
NO !?
I NEED AN ANTI-PRESSURE SHIELD !!
THE TABLES ARE TURNED AGAIN !!
BOTH MEMBERS OF THE RAKAN TEAM ARE IN PERFECT HEALTH !
WAH
HUH ?
BUT YOU SAID YOU WEREN'T INTERESTED IN THE FIGHT.
WHO'S WINNING ?
GLARE
H... UH...?
HE'S IN A BAD MOOD.
WHY ?
SCARY...
GJRM

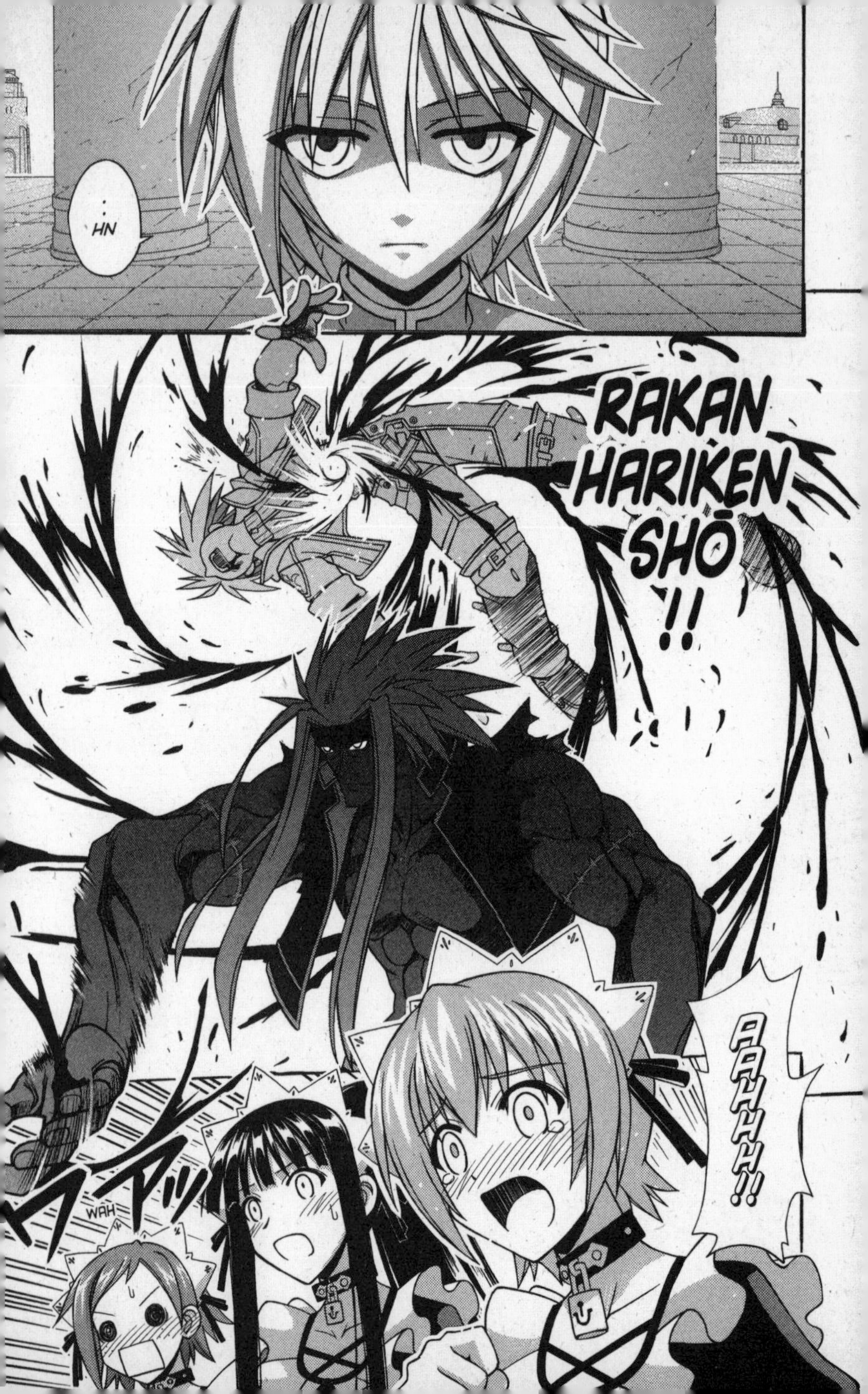

...HN
RAKAN HARIKEN SHŌ!!
AAHHHH!!
WAH

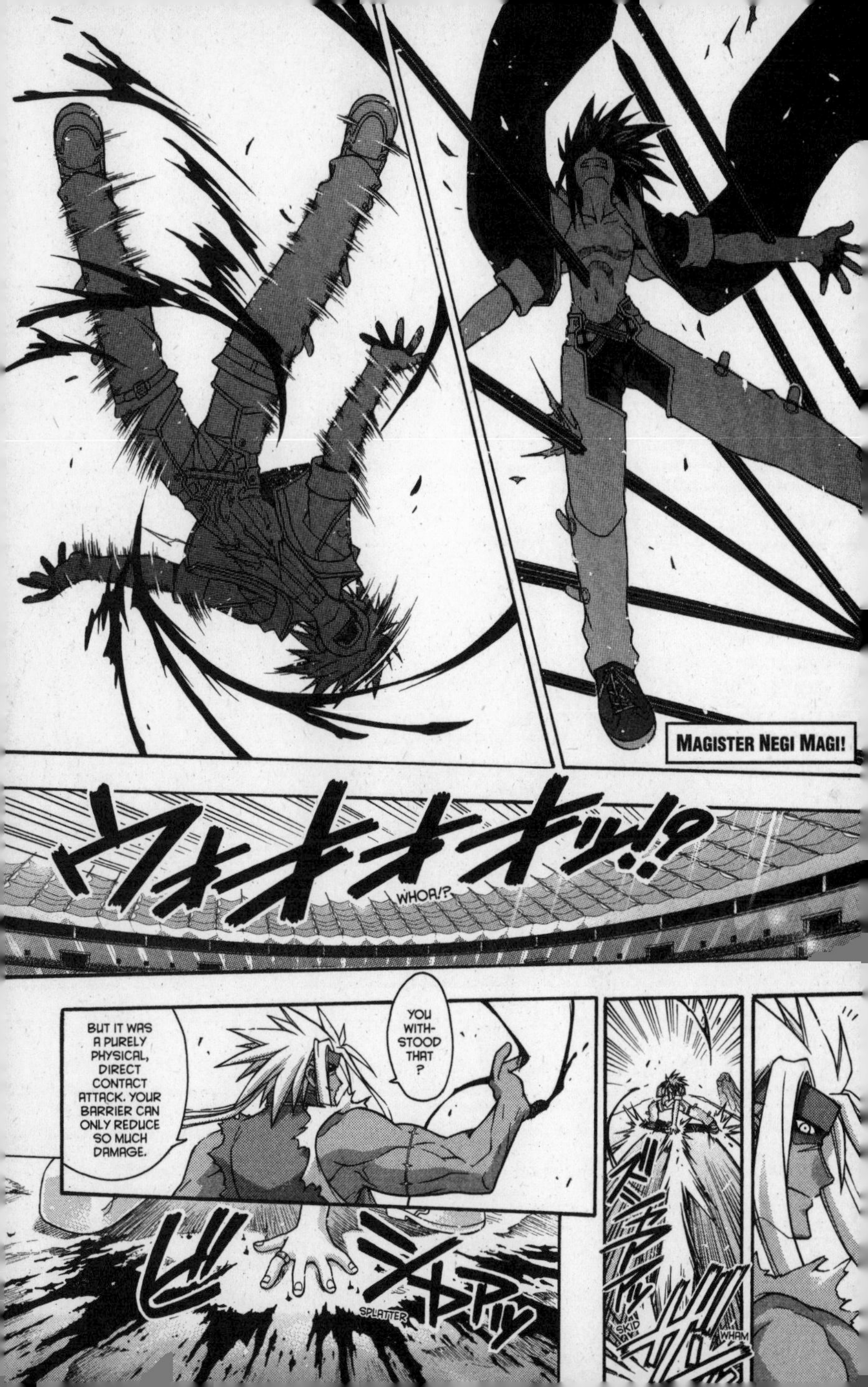
MAGISTER NEGI MAGI!
ウォオオオッ!?
WHOA!?
SKID
WHAM
YOU WITH-STOOD THAT?
BUT IT WAS A PURELY PHYSICAL, DIRECT CONTACT ATTACK. YOUR BARRIER CAN ONLY REDUCE SO MUCH DAMAGE.
SPLATTER

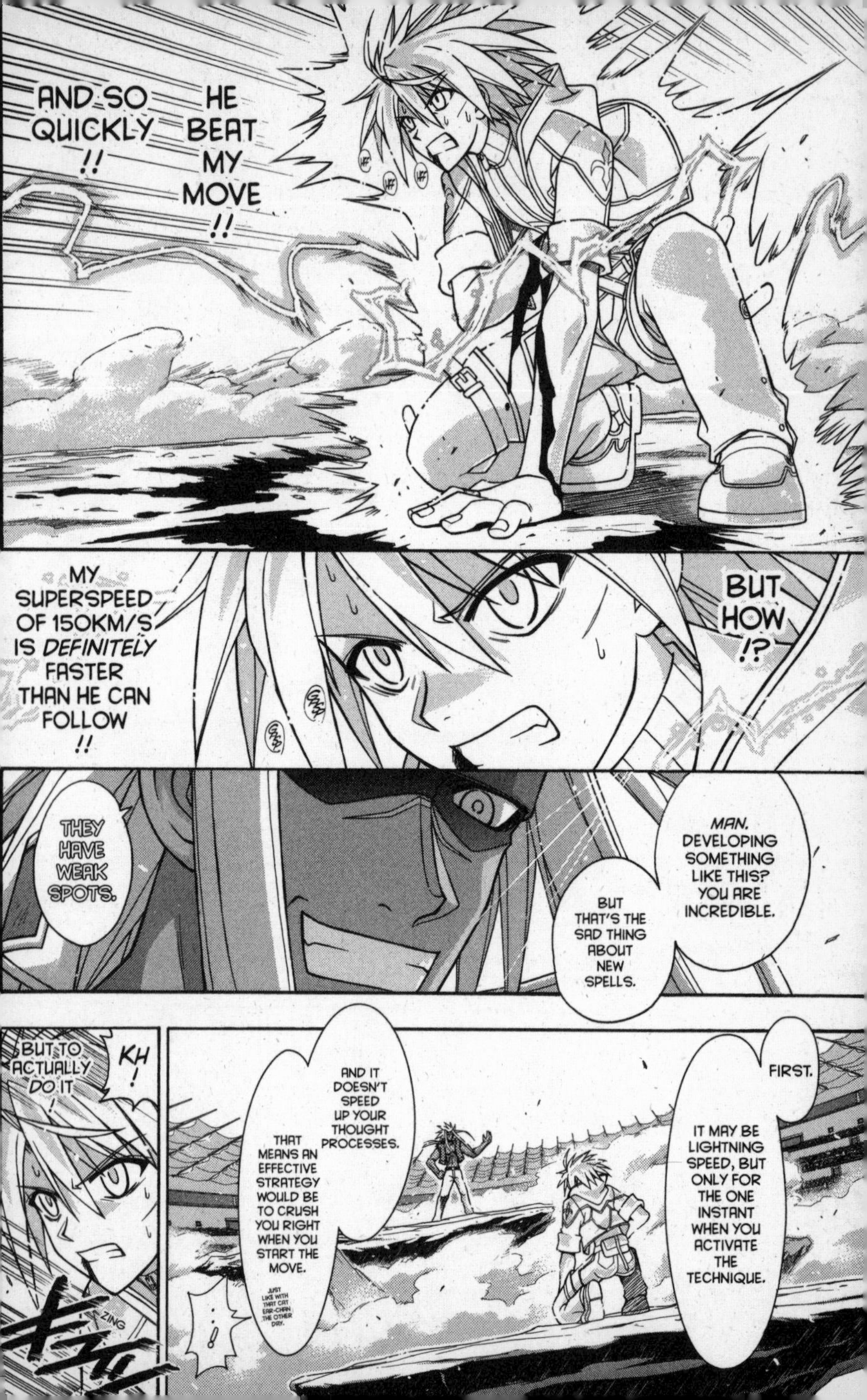
HE BEAT MY MOVE!!
AND SO QUICKLY!!
BUT HOW!?
MY SUPERSPEED OF 150KM/S IS *DEFINITELY* FASTER THAN HE CAN FOLLOW!!
MAN. DEVELOPING SOMETHING LIKE THIS? YOU ARE INCREDIBLE.
BUT THAT'S THE SAD THING ABOUT NEW SPELLS.
THEY HAVE WEAK SPOTS.
FIRST.
IT MAY BE LIGHTNING SPEED, BUT ONLY FOR THE ONE INSTANT WHEN YOU ACTIVATE THE TECHNIQUE.
AND IT DOESN'T SPEED UP YOUR THOUGHT PROCESSES.
THAT MEANS AN EFFECTIVE STRATEGY WOULD BE TO CRUSH YOU RIGHT WHEN YOU START THE MOVE.
JUST LIKE WITH THAT CAT EAR-CHAN THE OTHER DAY.
...!
KH!
BUT TO ACTUALLY *DO* IT!
ZING

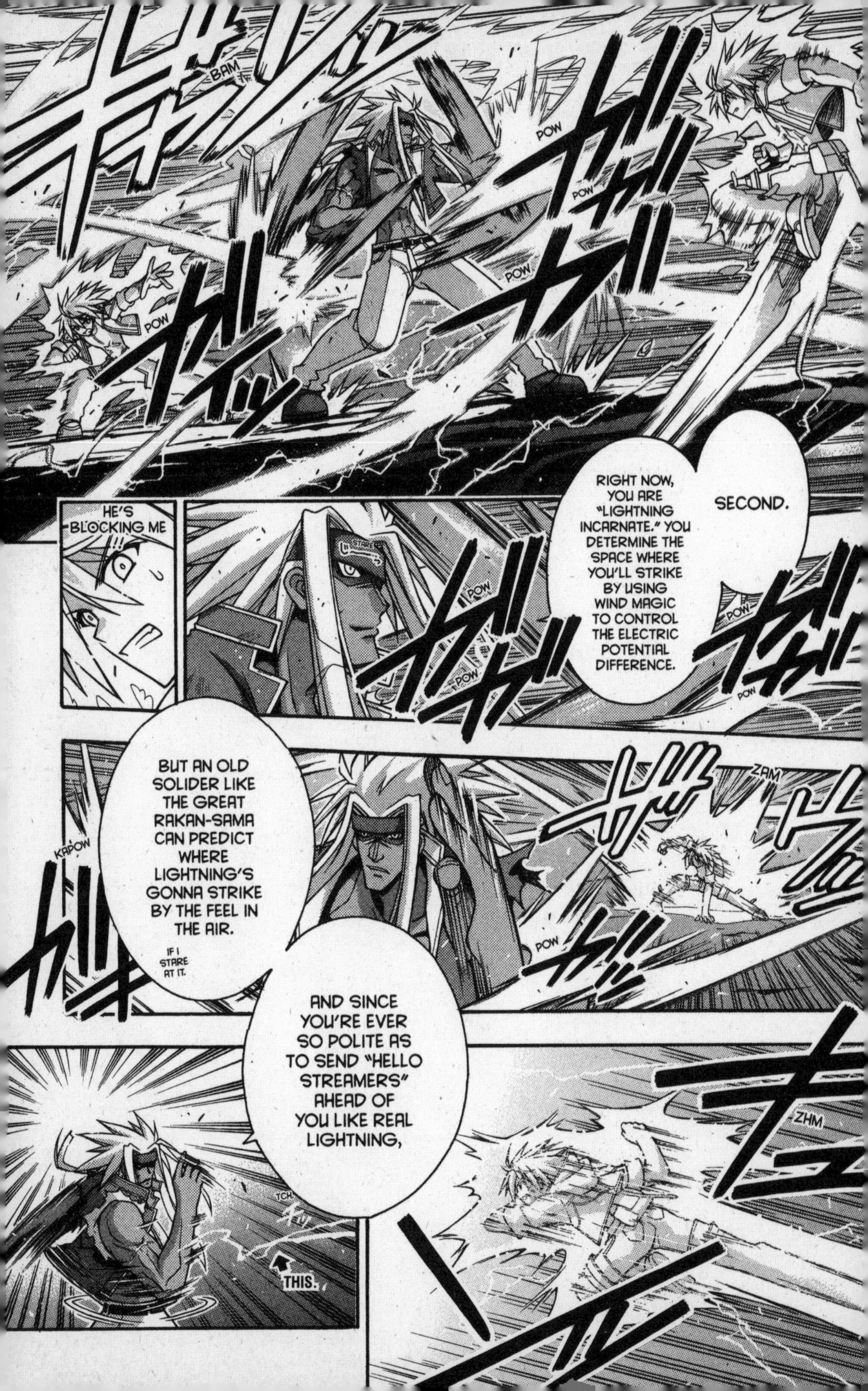
POW
POW
BAM
POW
POW
SECOND.
RIGHT NOW, YOU ARE "LIGHTNING INCARNATE." YOU DETERMINE THE SPACE WHERE YOU'LL STRIKE BY USING WIND MAGIC TO CONTROL THE ELECTRIC POTENTIAL DIFFERENCE.
POW
POW
POW
POW
STARE
HE'S BLOCKING ME!!!
ZAM
POW
BUT AN OLD SOLIDER LIKE THE GREAT RAKAN-SAMA CAN PREDICT WHERE LIGHTNING'S GONNA STRIKE BY THE FEEL IN THE AIR.
IF I STARE AT IT.
KAPOW
ZHM
AND SINCE YOU'RE EVER SO POLITE AS TO SEND "HELLO STREAMERS" AHEAD OF YOU LIKE REAL LIGHTNING,
TCH
THIS.

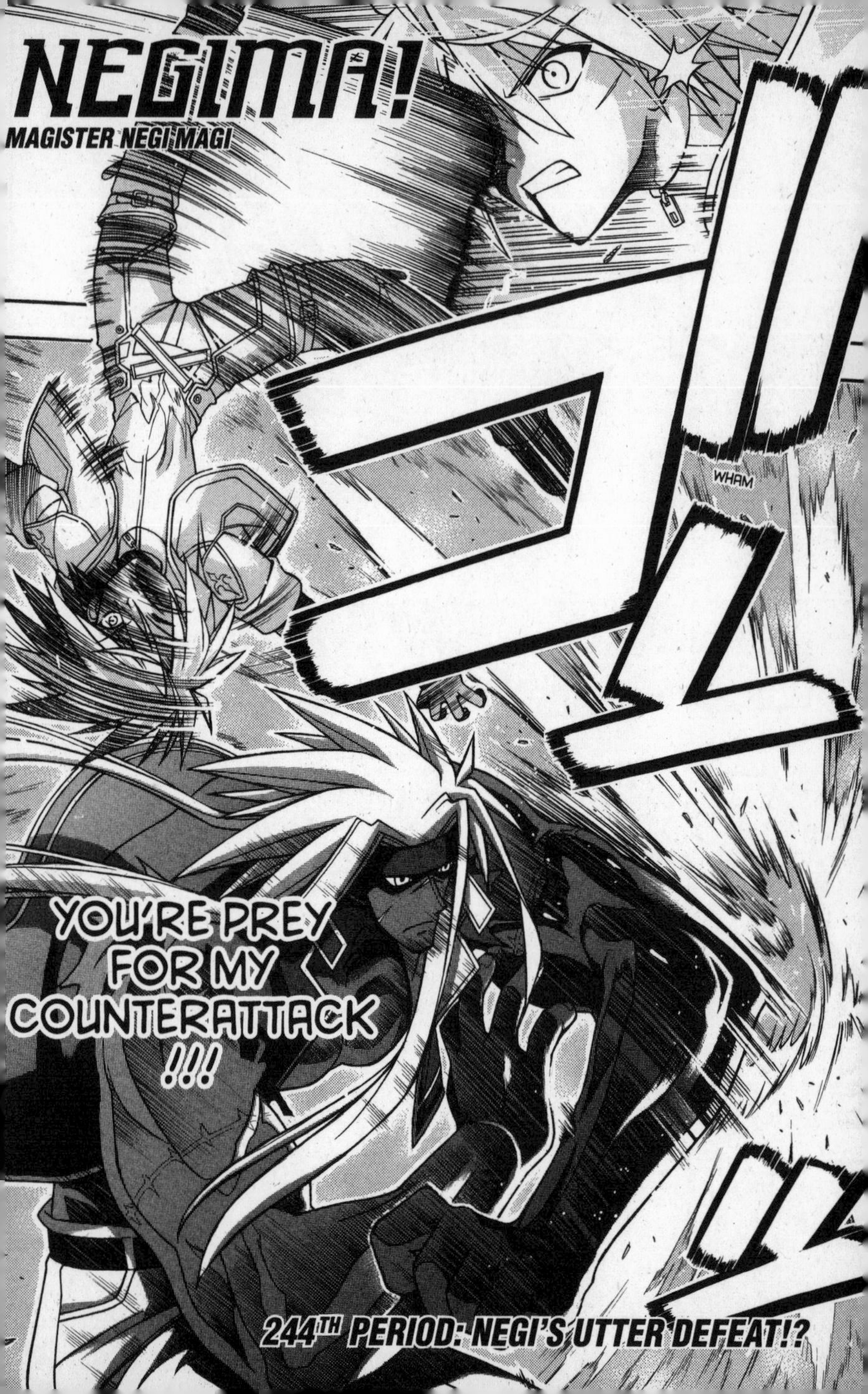
NEGIMA!
MAGISTER NEGI MAGI
WHAM
YOU'RE PREY FOR MY COUNTERATTACK !!!
244TH PERIOD: NEGI'S UTTER DEFEAT!?

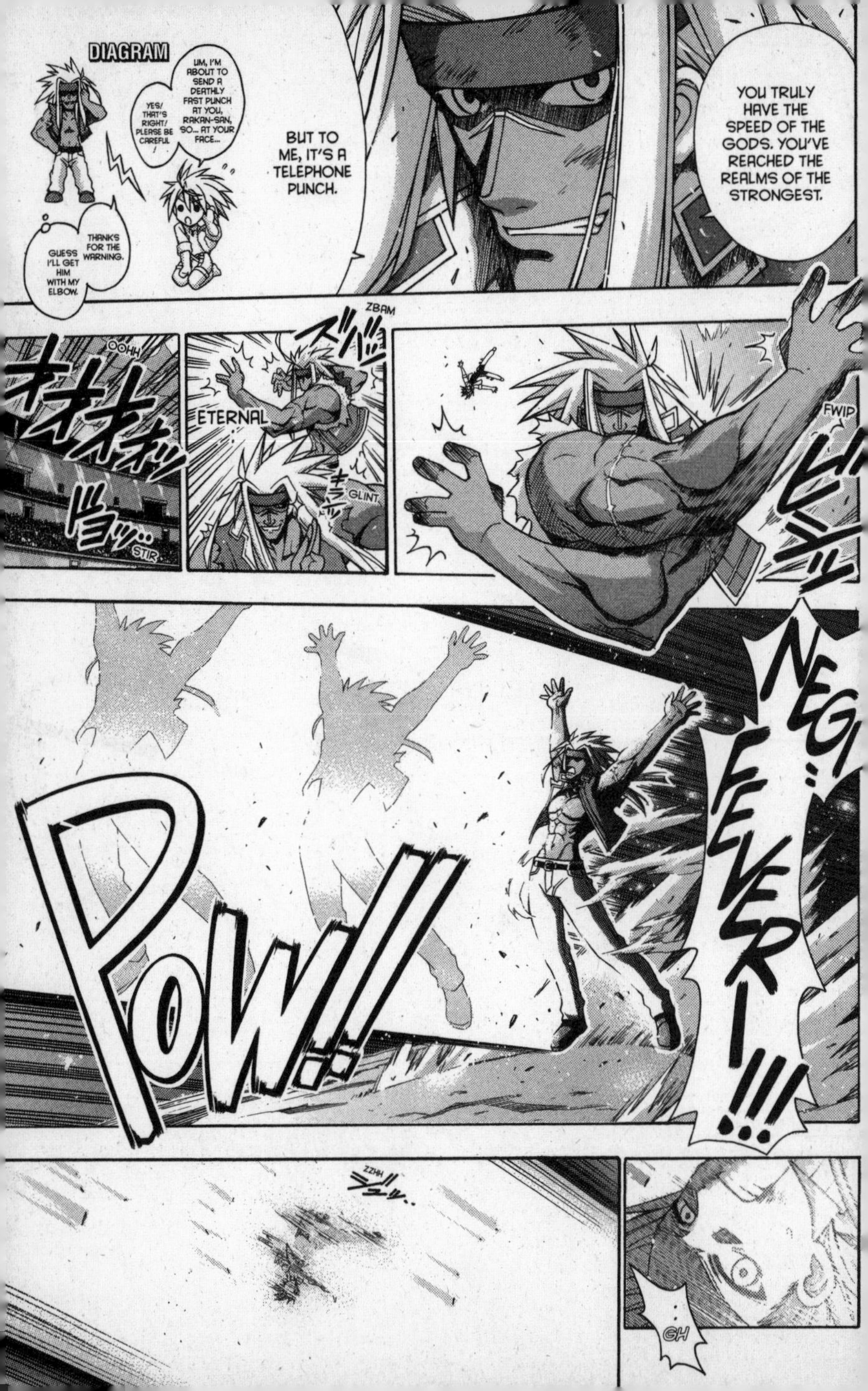
YOU TRULY HAVE THE SPEED OF THE GODS. YOU'VE REACHED THE REALMS OF THE STRONGEST.
BUT TO ME, IT'S A TELEPHONE PUNCH.
DIAGRAM
UM, I'M ABOUT TO SEND A DEATHLY FAST PUNCH AT YOU, RAKAN-SAN, SO... AT YOUR FACE...
YES/ THAT'S RIGHT/ PLEASE BE CAREFUL/
THANKS FOR THE WARNING.
GUESS I'LL GET HIM WITH MY ELBOW.
FWIP
ZBAM
ETERNAL
GLINT
OOHH
STIR
NEGI FEEVER!!!
POW!!
GH
ZZHH

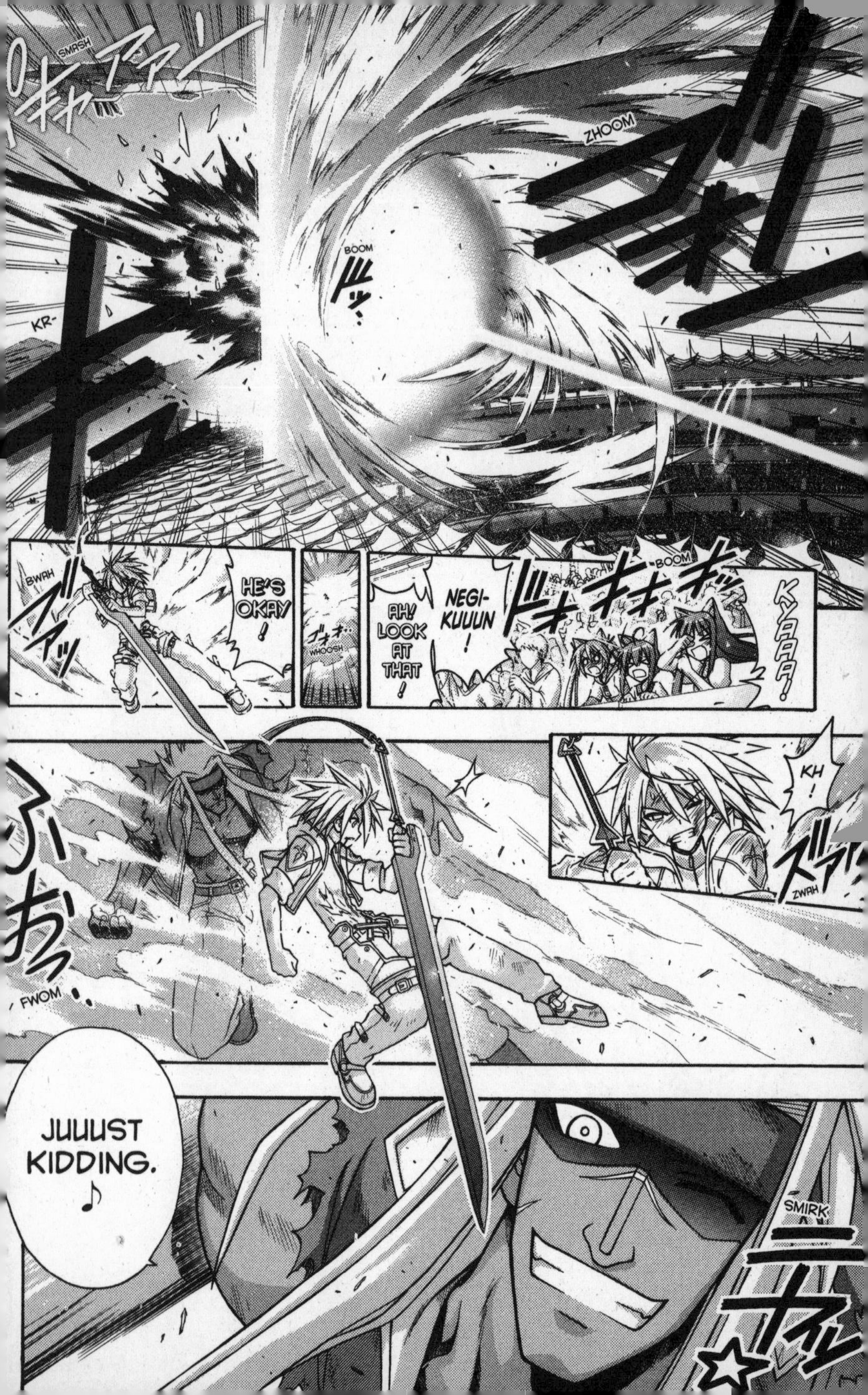
ZHOOM
BOOM
SMASH
KR-
BOOM
KYAAAA!
NEGI-KUUUN!
AH! LOOK AT THAT!
WHOOSH
HE'S OKAY!
BWAH
KH!
ZWAH
FWOM
SMIRK
JUUUST KIDDING. ♪

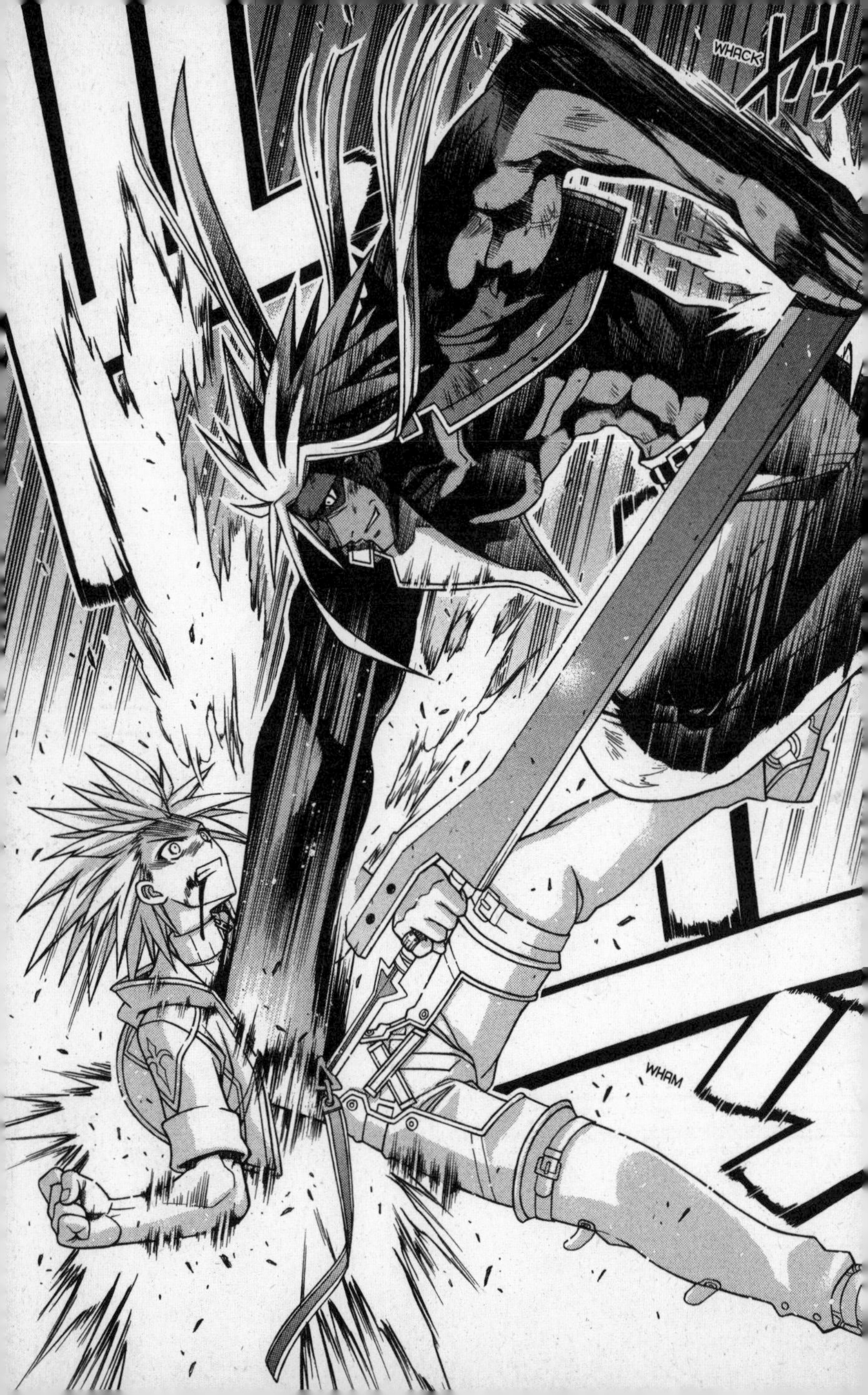
WHACK
WHAM

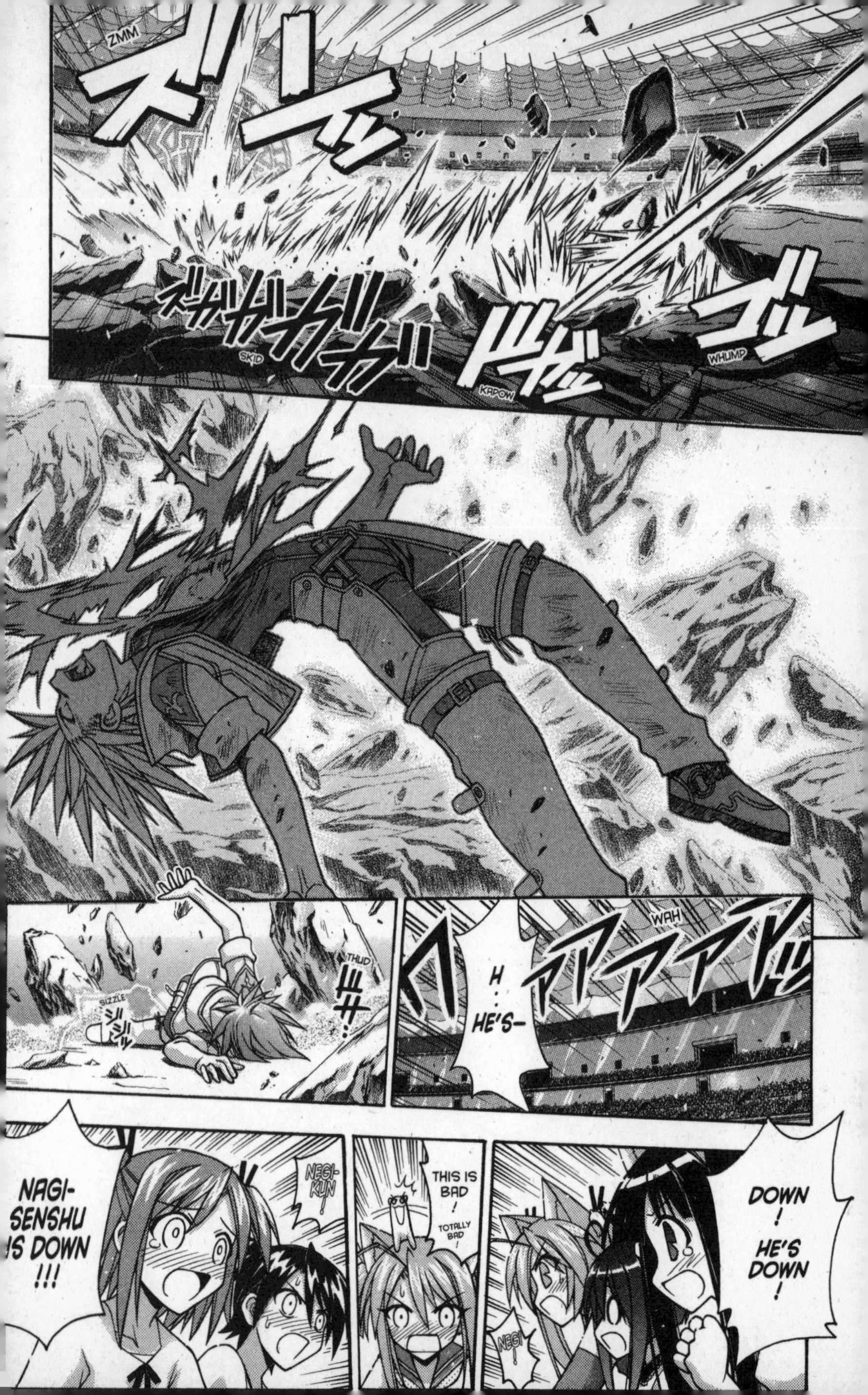
ZMM
WHUMP
KAPOW
SKID
WAH
H... HE'S—
THUD
SIZZLE
DOWN! HE'S DOWN!
NEGI!
THIS IS BAD!
TOTALLY BAD!
NEGI-KUN!
NAGI-SENSHU IS DOWN!!!

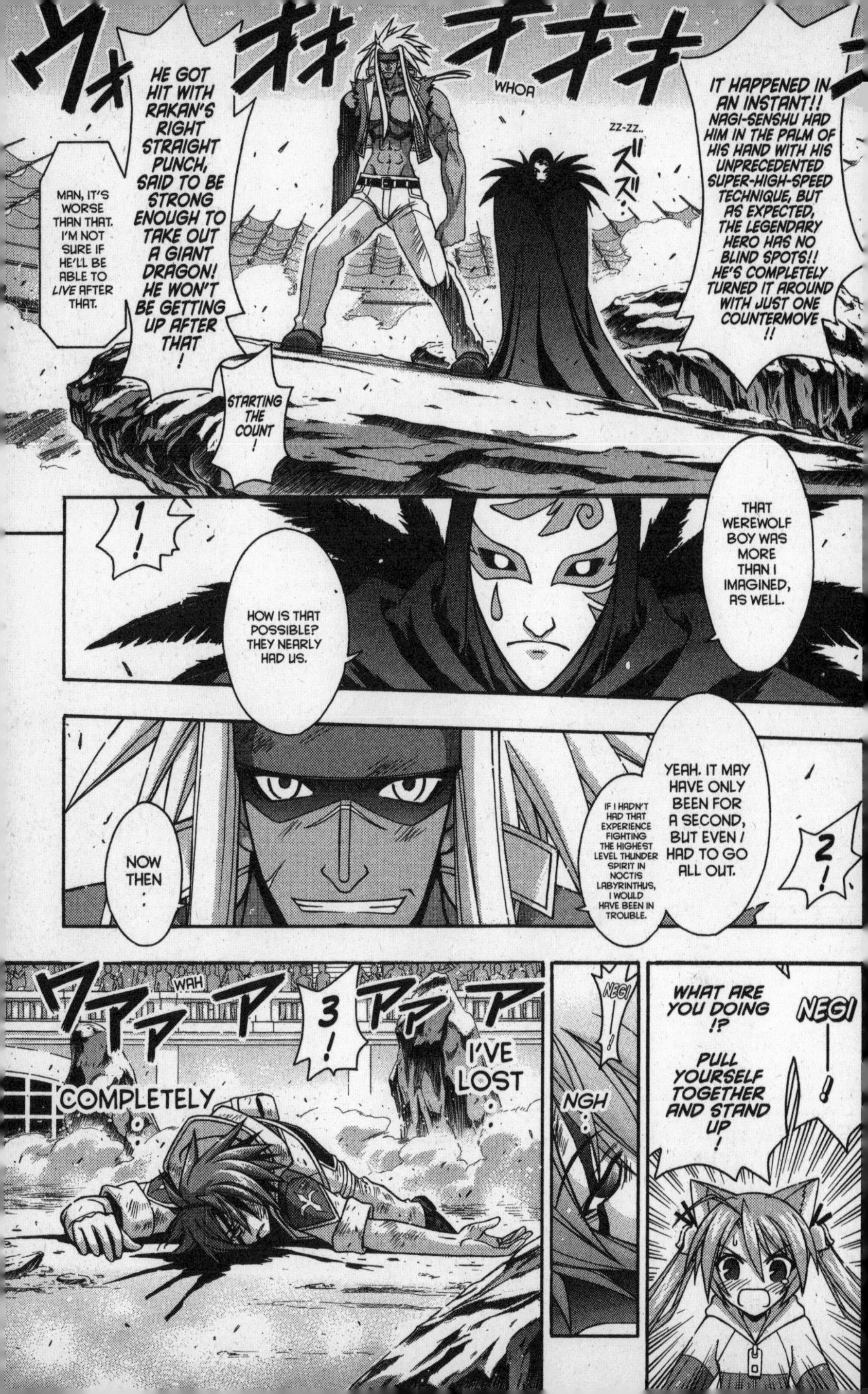
IT HAPPENED IN AN INSTANT!! NAGI-SENSHU HAD HIM IN THE PALM OF HIS HAND WITH HIS UNPRECEDENTED SUPER-HIGH-SPEED TECHNIQUE, BUT AS EXPECTED, THE LEGENDARY HERO HAS NO BLIND SPOTS!! HE'S COMPLETELY TURNED IT AROUND WITH JUST ONE COUNTERMOVE!!
ZZ-ZZ..
WHOA
HE GOT HIT WITH RAKAN'S RIGHT STRAIGHT PUNCH, SAID TO BE STRONG ENOUGH TO TAKE OUT A GIANT DRAGON! HE WON'T BE GETTING UP AFTER THAT!
MAN, IT'S WORSE THAN THAT. I'M NOT SURE IF HE'LL BE ABLE TO *LIVE* AFTER THAT.
STARTING THE COUNT!
THAT WEREWOLF BOY WAS MORE THAN I IMAGINED, AS WELL.
1!
HOW IS THAT POSSIBLE? THEY NEARLY HAD US.
2!
YEAH. IT MAY HAVE ONLY BEEN FOR A SECOND, BUT EVEN *I* HAD TO GO ALL OUT.
IF I HADN'T HAD THAT EXPERIENCE FIGHTING THE HIGHEST LEVEL THUNDER SPIRIT IN NOCTIS LABYRINTHUS, I WOULD HAVE BEEN IN TROUBLE.
NOW THEN..
NEGI!
WHAT ARE YOU DOING!? PULL YOURSELF TOGETHER AND STAND UP!
NEGI!
NGH..
WAH
3!
I'VE LOST..
COMPLETELY..

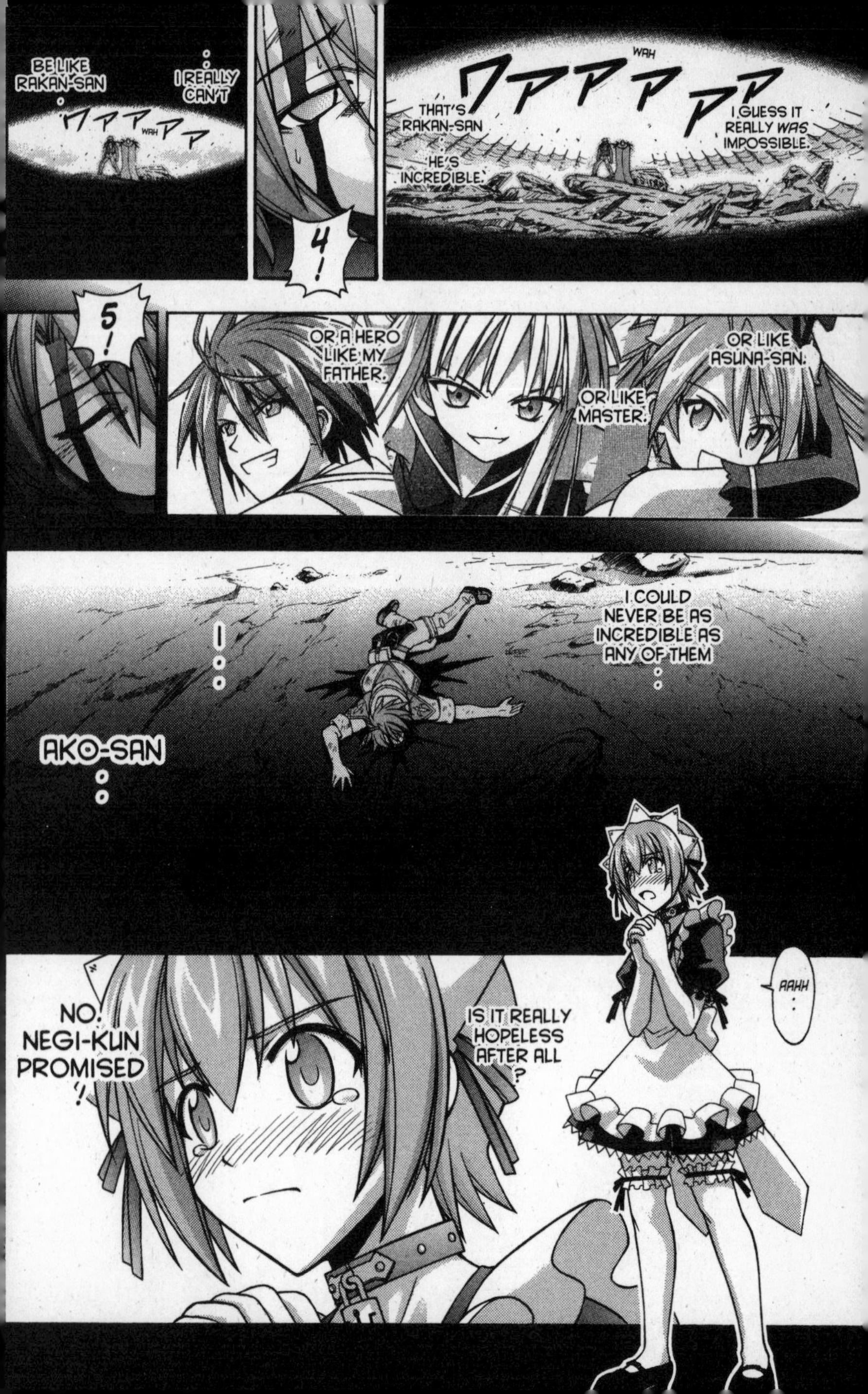
WAH
ワアアアアア
I GUESS IT REALLY WAS IMPOSSIBLE.
THAT'S RAKAN-SAN
HE'S INCREDIBLE.
I REALLY CAN'T...
4!
BE LIKE RAKAN-SAN.
ワアア WAH アア
OR LIKE ASUNA-SAN.
OR LIKE MASTER.
OR A HERO LIKE MY FATHER.
5!
I COULD NEVER BE AS INCREDIBLE AS ANY OF THEM...
I...
AKO-SAN...
AAHH...
IS IT REALLY HOPELESS AFTER ALL?
NO. NEGI-KUN PROMISED!

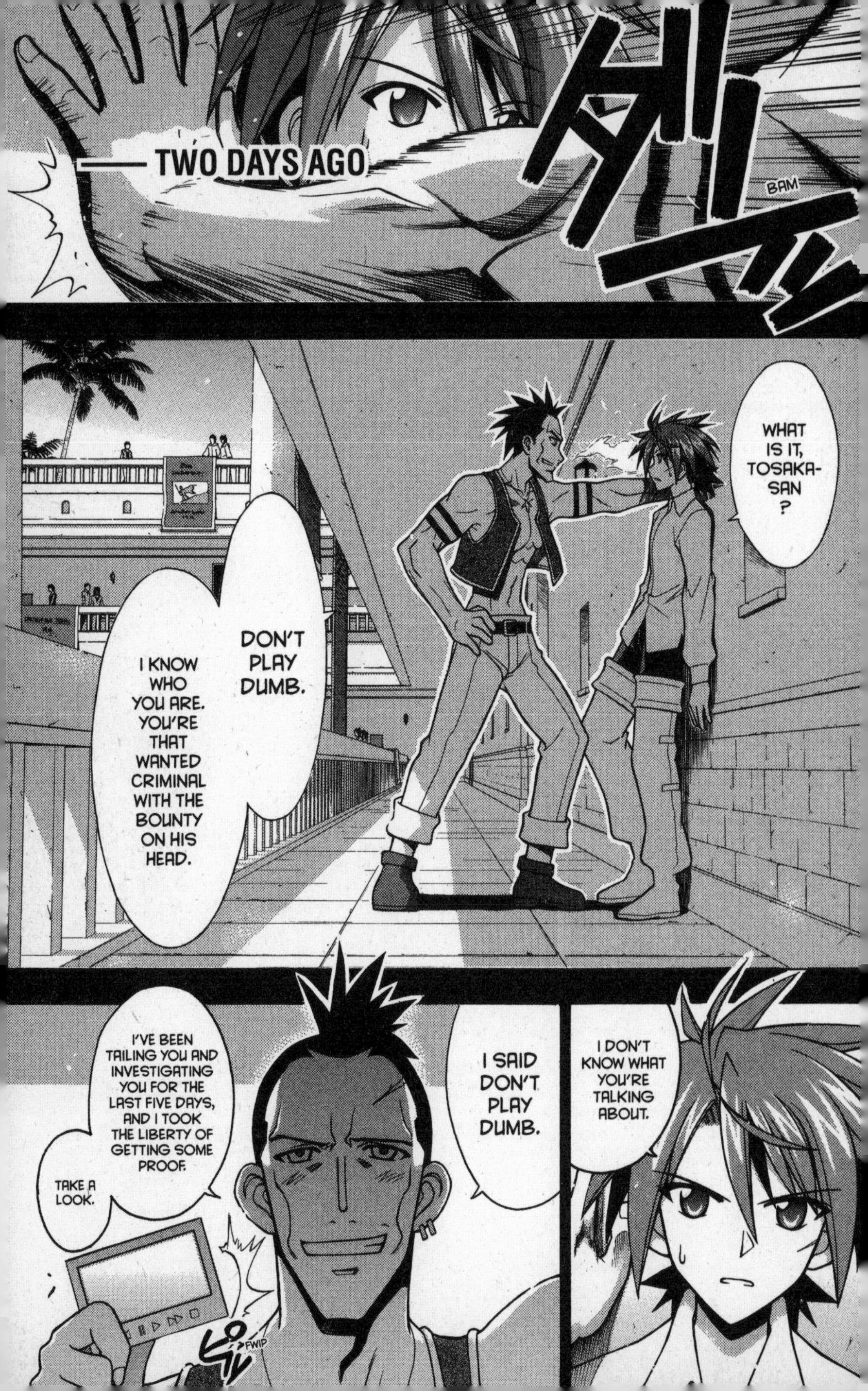
—TWO DAYS AGO
BAM
WHAT IS IT, TOSAKA-SAN?
DON'T PLAY DUMB.
I KNOW WHO YOU ARE. YOU'RE THAT WANTED CRIMINAL WITH THE BOUNTY ON HIS HEAD.
I DON'T KNOW WHAT YOU'RE TALKING ABOUT.
I SAID DON'T PLAY DUMB.
I'VE BEEN TAILING YOU AND INVESTIGATING YOU FOR THE LAST FIVE DAYS, AND I TOOK THE LIBERTY OF GETTING SOME PROOF.
TAKE A LOOK.
FWIP

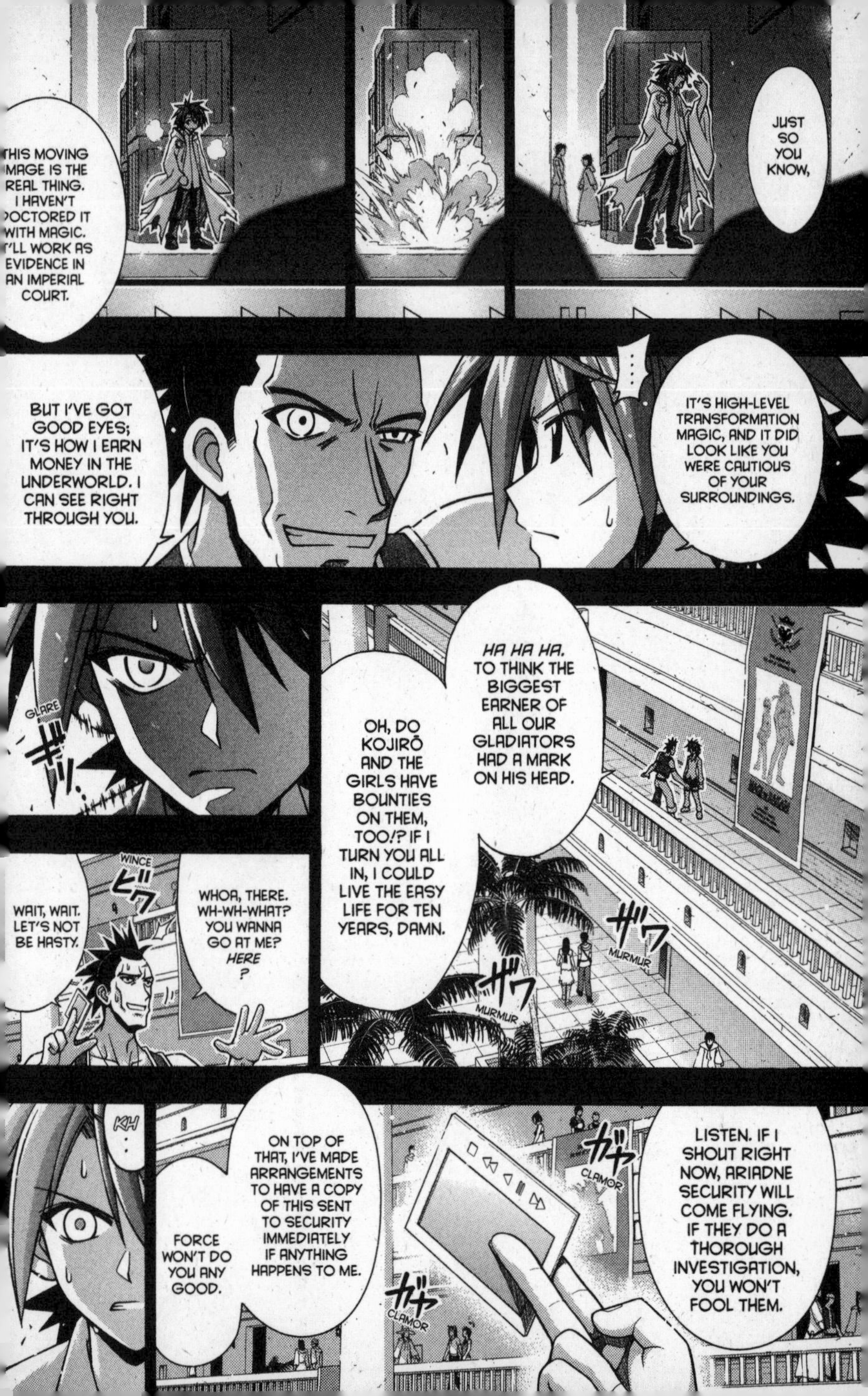

JUST SO YOU KNOW,
THIS MOVING IMAGE IS THE REAL THING. I HAVEN'T DOCTORED IT WITH MAGIC. IT'LL WORK AS EVIDENCE IN AN IMPERIAL COURT.
IT'S HIGH-LEVEL TRANSFORMATION MAGIC, AND IT DID LOOK LIKE YOU WERE CAUTIOUS OF YOUR SURROUNDINGS.
...!
BUT I'VE GOT GOOD EYES; IT'S HOW I EARN MONEY IN THE UNDERWORLD. I CAN SEE RIGHT THROUGH YOU.
HA HA HA. TO THINK THE BIGGEST EARNER OF ALL OUR GLADIATORS HAD A MARK ON HIS HEAD.
OH, DO KOJIRŌ AND THE GIRLS HAVE BOUNTIES ON THEM, TOO!? IF I TURN YOU ALL IN, I COULD LIVE THE EASY LIFE FOR TEN YEARS, DAMN.
MURMUR
MURMUR
GLARE
...
WINCE
WHOA, THERE. WH-WH-WHAT? YOU WANNA GO AT ME? *HERE*?
WAIT, WAIT. LET'S NOT BE HASTY.
LISTEN. IF I SHOUT RIGHT NOW, ARIADNE SECURITY WILL COME FLYING. IF THEY DO A THOROUGH INVESTIGATION, YOU WON'T FOOL THEM.
CLAMOR
CLAMOR
ON TOP OF THAT, I'VE MADE ARRANGEMENTS TO HAVE A COPY OF THIS SENT TO SECURITY IMMEDIATELY IF ANYTHING HAPPENS TO ME.
FORCE WON'T DO YOU ANY GOOD.
KH
...

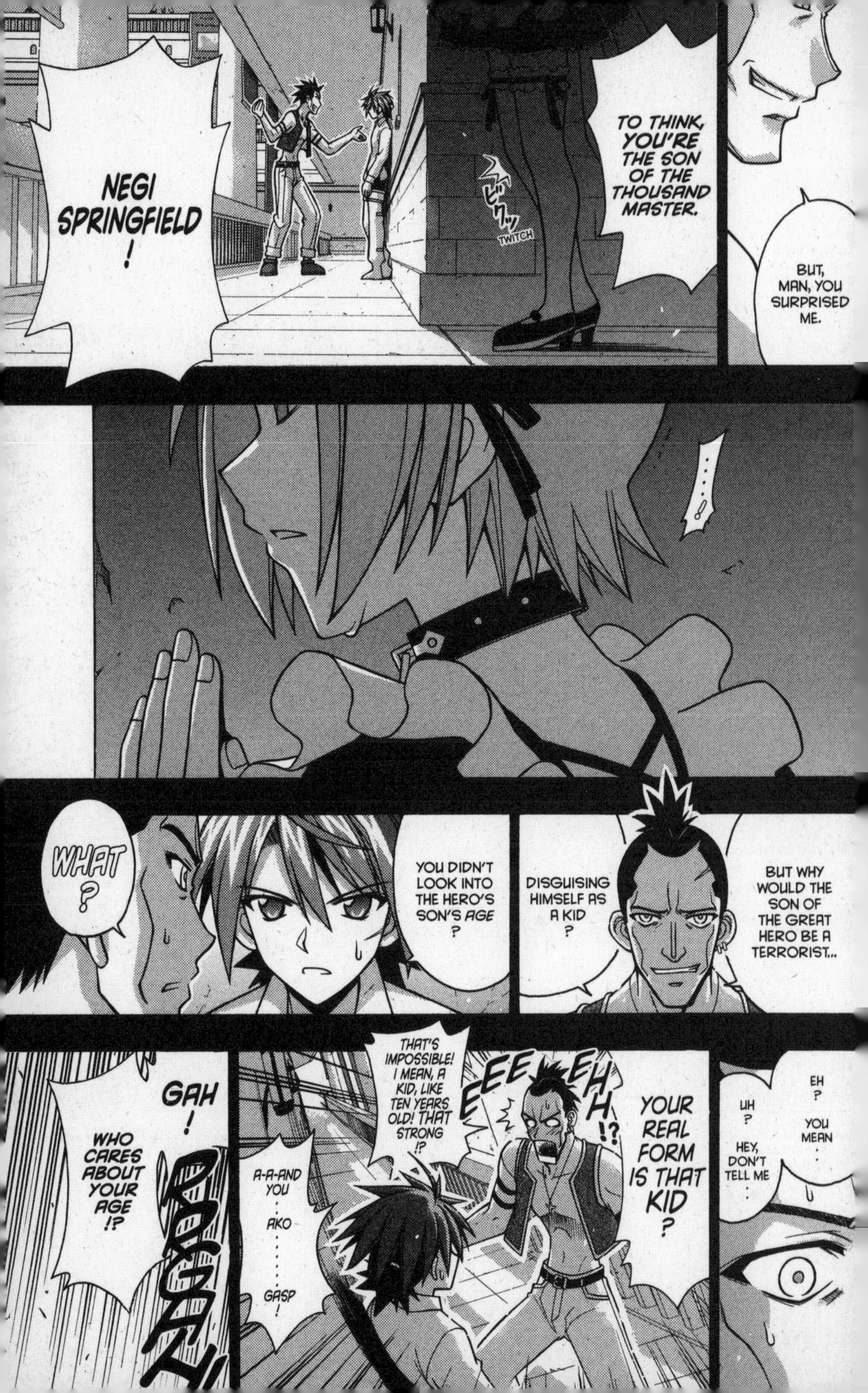
BUT, MAN, YOU SURPRISED ME.
TO THINK, YOU'RE THE SON OF THE THOUSAND MASTER.
ビクッ
TWITCH
NEGI SPRINGFIELD !
...!
BUT WHY WOULD THE SON OF THE GREAT HERO BE A TERRORIST...
DISGUISING HIMSELF AS A KID ?
YOU DIDN'T LOOK INTO THE HERO'S SON'S AGE ?
WHAT ?
EH ? YOU MEAN...
UH ? HEY, DON'T TELL ME...
YOUR REAL FORM IS THAT KID ?
EEEEHH !?
THAT'S IMPOSSIBLE! I MEAN, A KID, LIKE TEN YEARS OLD! THAT STRONG !?
A-A-AND YOU... AKO......
GASP !
GAH !
WHO CARES ABOUT YOUR AGE !?

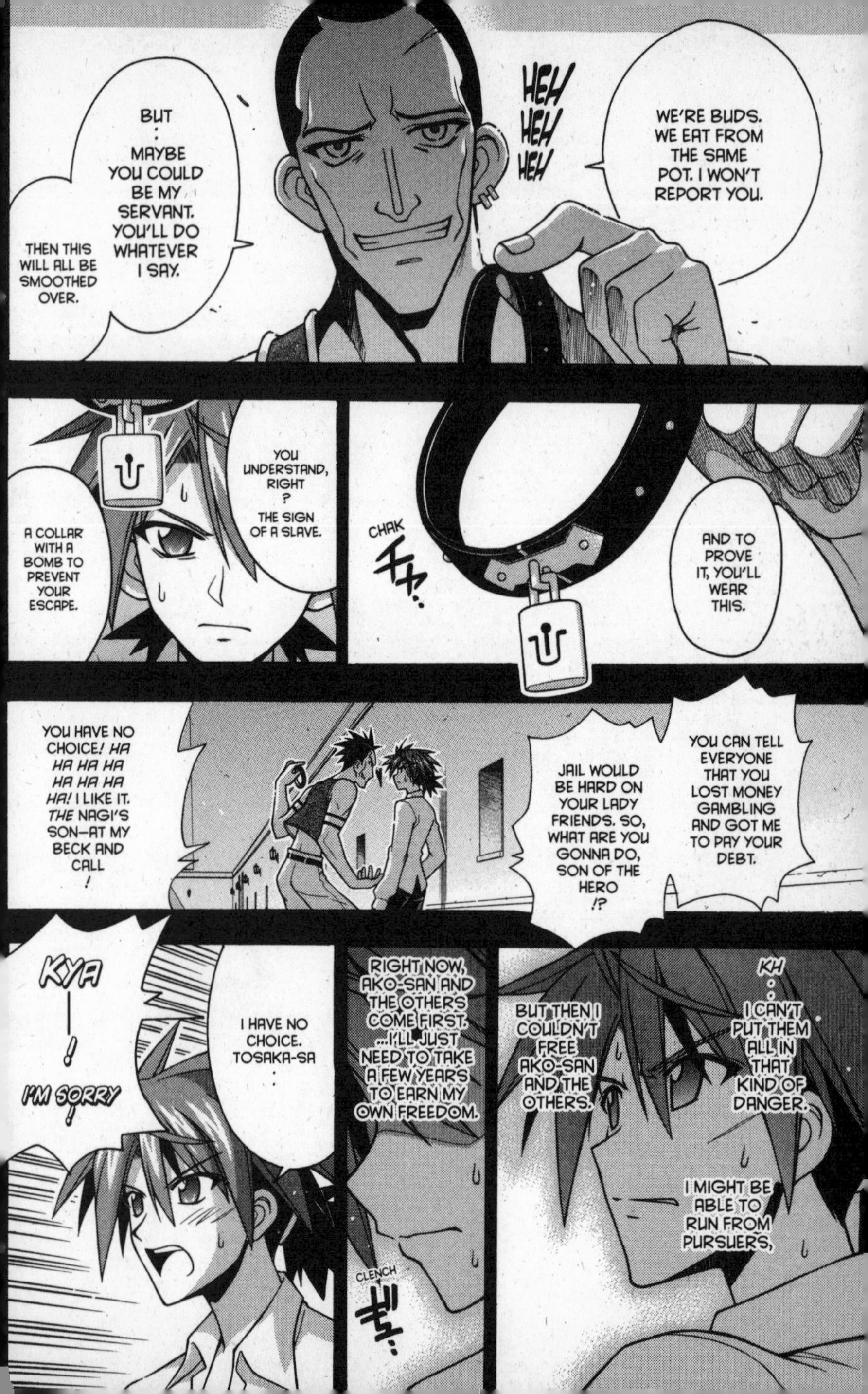

WE'RE BUDS. WE EAT FROM THE SAME POT. I WON'T REPORT YOU.
HEH HEH HEH
BUT : MAYBE YOU COULD BE MY SERVANT. YOU'LL DO WHATEVER I SAY.
THEN THIS WILL ALL BE SMOOTHED OVER.
AND TO PROVE IT, YOU'LL WEAR THIS.
CHAK
YOU UNDERSTAND, RIGHT? THE SIGN OF A SLAVE.
A COLLAR WITH A BOMB TO PREVENT YOUR ESCAPE.
YOU CAN TELL EVERYONE THAT YOU LOST MONEY GAMBLING AND GOT ME TO PAY YOUR DEBT.
JAIL WOULD BE HARD ON YOUR LADY FRIENDS. SO, WHAT ARE YOU GONNA DO, SON OF THE HERO!?
YOU HAVE NO CHOICE! *HA HA HA HA HA HA HA HA!* I LIKE IT. *THE* NAGI'S SON—AT MY BECK AND CALL!
KH : : I CAN'T PUT THEM ALL IN THAT KIND OF DANGER.
BUT THEN I COULDN'T FREE AKO-SAN AND THE OTHERS.
I MIGHT BE ABLE TO RUN FROM PURSUERS,
RIGHT NOW, AKO-SAN AND THE OTHERS COME FIRST. ...I'LL JUST NEED TO TAKE A FEW YEARS TO EARN MY OWN FREEDOM.
CLENCH
I HAVE NO CHOICE. TOSAKA-SA :
KYA—!
I'M SORRY!

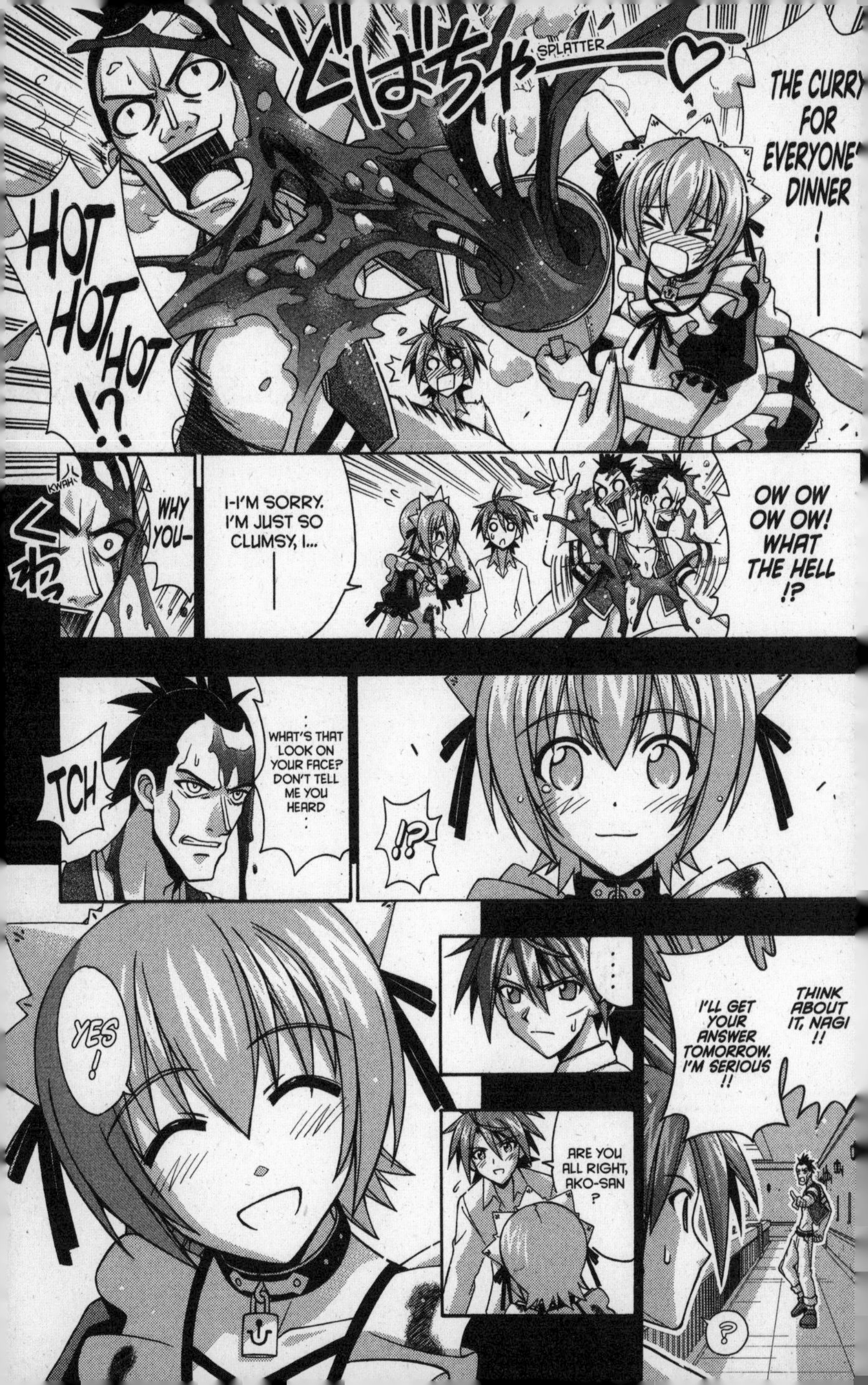
THE CURRY FOR EVERYONE'S DINNER!
どばちゃー
SPLATTER
HOT HOT HOT HOT!?
OW OW OW OW! WHAT THE HELL!?
I-I'M SORRY. I'M JUST SO CLUMSY, I...
くわっ
KWAH
WHY YOU-
!?
...WHAT'S THAT LOOK ON YOUR FACE? DON'T TELL ME YOU HEARD...
TCH
THINK ABOUT IT, NAGI!!
I'LL GET YOUR ANSWER TOMORROW. I'M SERIOUS!!
?
....
ARE YOU ALL RIGHT, AKO-SAN?
YES!

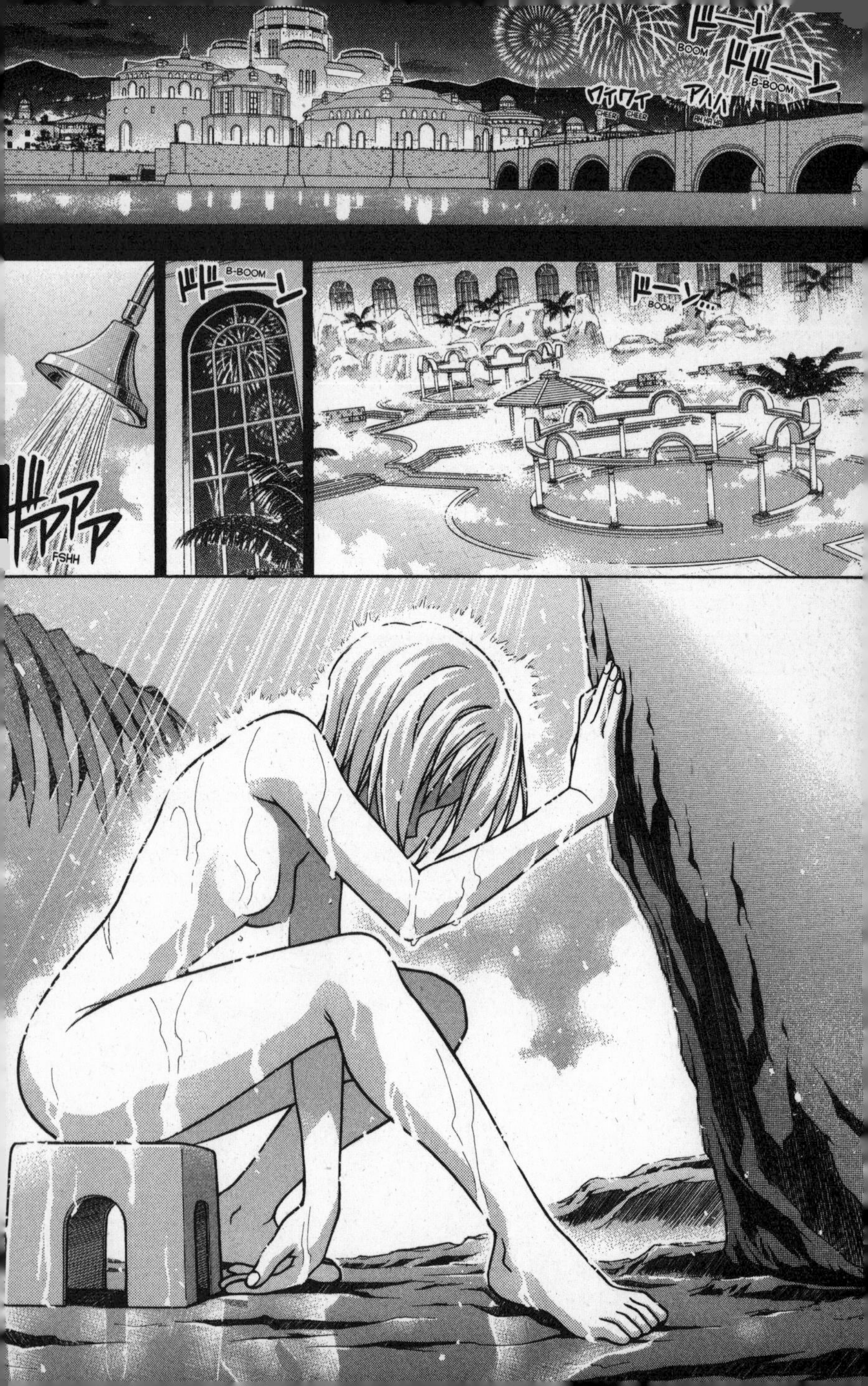
ドーン
BOOM
ドドーン
B-BOOM
アハハ
AH HA HA
ワイワイ
CHEER CHEER
ドーン…
BOOM
ドドーン
B-BOOM
ザァァァ
FSHH

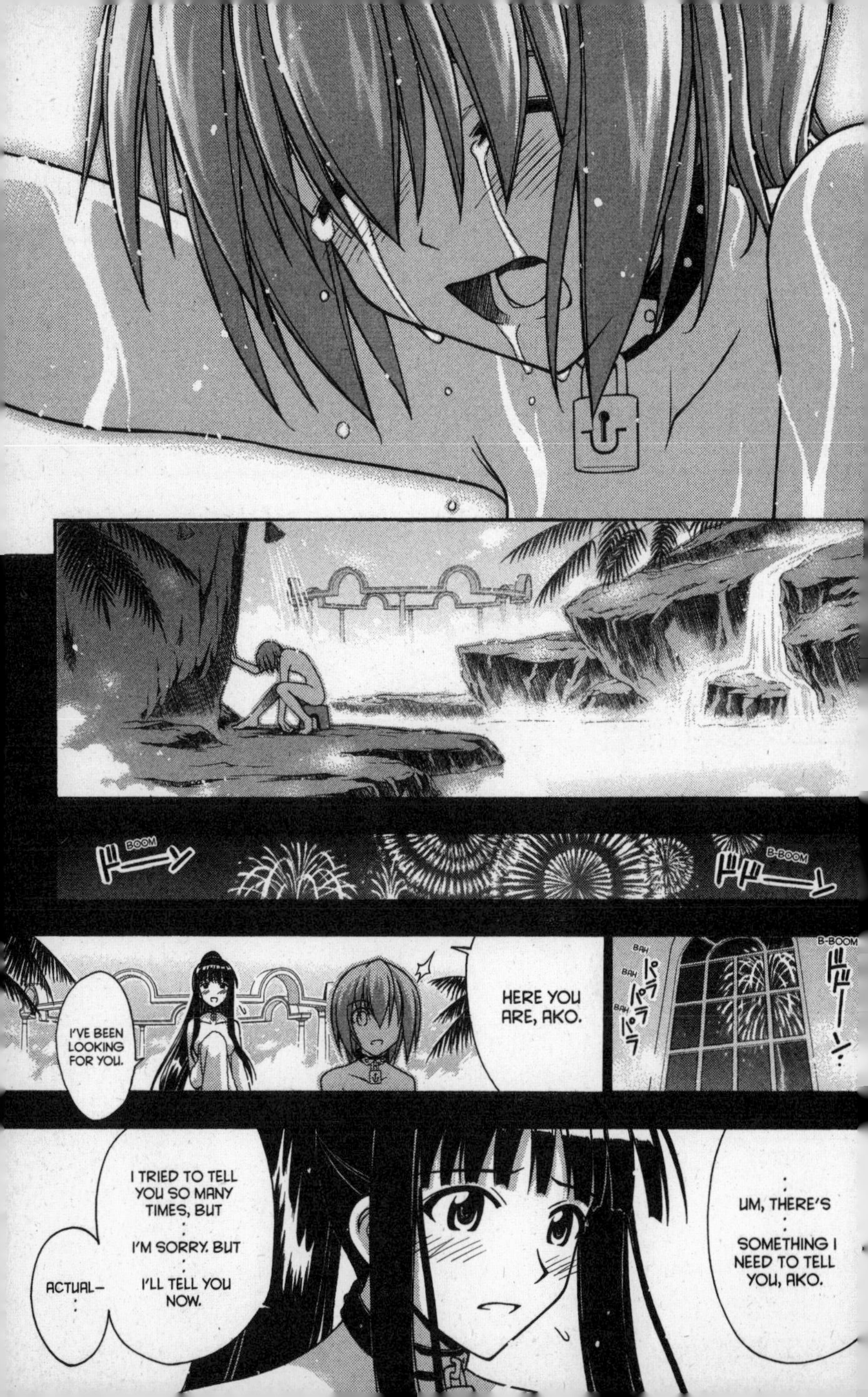
B-BOOM
BOOM
B-BOOM
BAH
BAH
BAH
HERE YOU ARE, AKO.
I'VE BEEN LOOKING FOR YOU.
...UM, THERE'S... SOMETHING I NEED TO TELL YOU, AKO.
I TRIED TO TELL YOU SO MANY TIMES, BUT... I'M SORRY. BUT... I'LL TELL YOU NOW.
ACTUAL—...

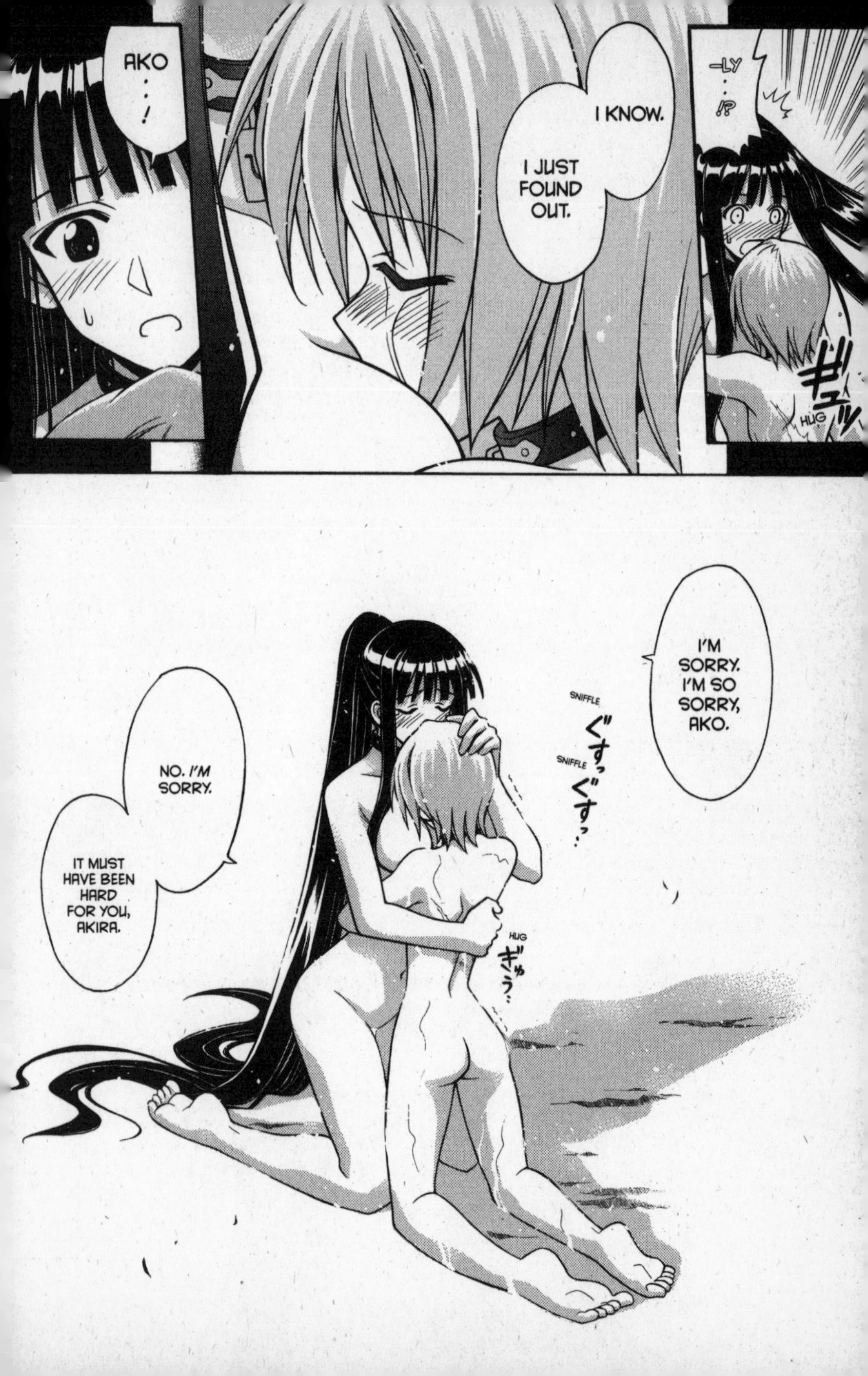
—LY
. . !?
ギュッ
HUG
I KNOW.
I JUST FOUND OUT.
AKO . . . !
I'M SORRY. I'M SO SORRY, AKO.
SNIFFLE
ぐすっ
SNIFFLE
ぐすっ. .
HUG
ぎゅう. .
NO. I'M SORRY.
IT MUST HAVE BEEN HARD FOR YOU, AKIRA.

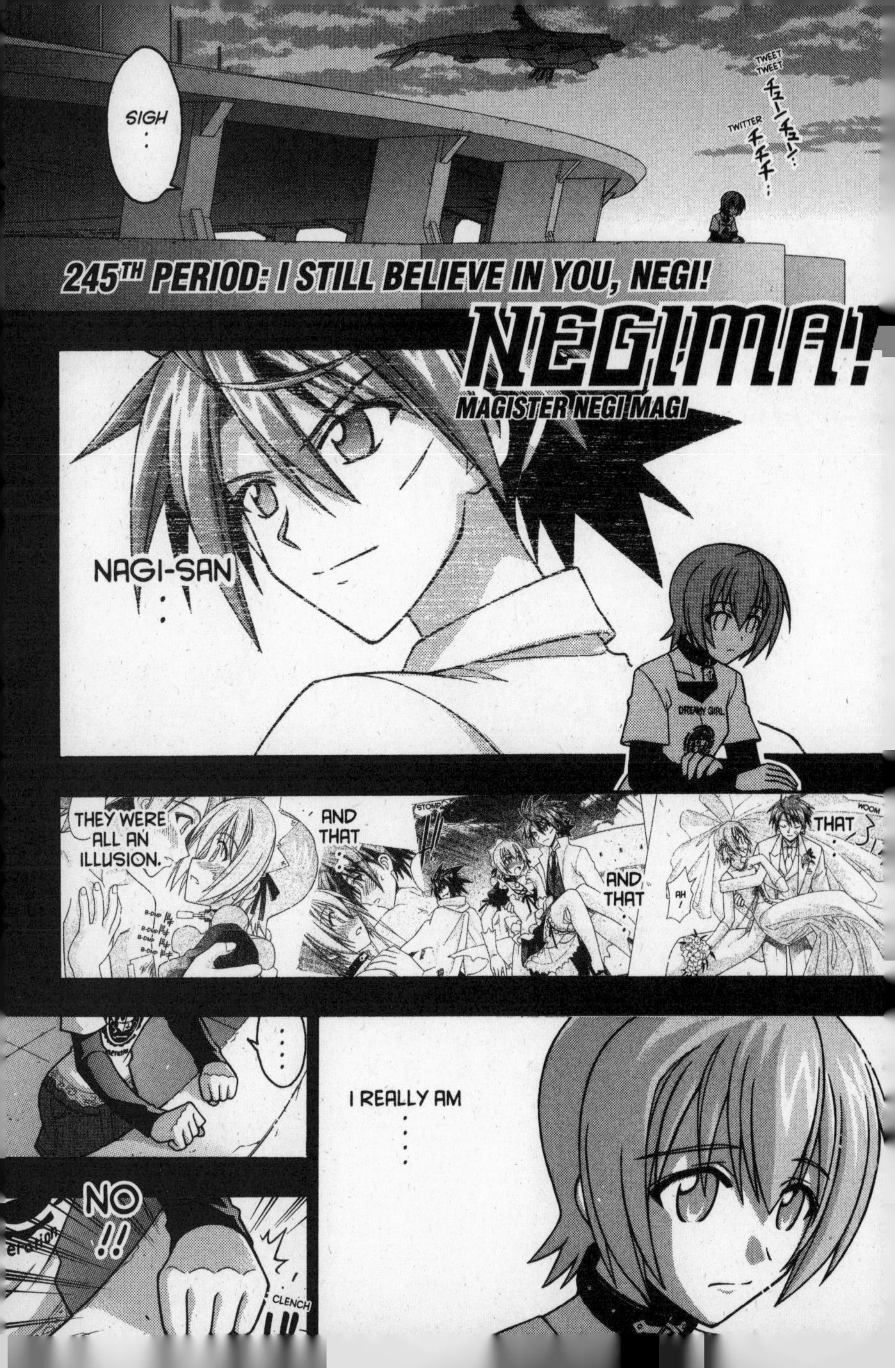
TWEET TWEET
チューンチューン..
TWITTER
チチチ..
SIGH
..
245TH PERIOD: I STILL BELIEVE IN YOU, NEGI!
NEGIMA!
MAGISTER NEGI MAGI
NAGI-SAN
..
WOOM
THAT
AH!
AND THAT
...
STOMP
AND THAT
THEY WERE ALL AN ILLUSION.
B-DMP
B-DMP
B-DMP
I REALLY AM
...
....
NO !!
CLENCH

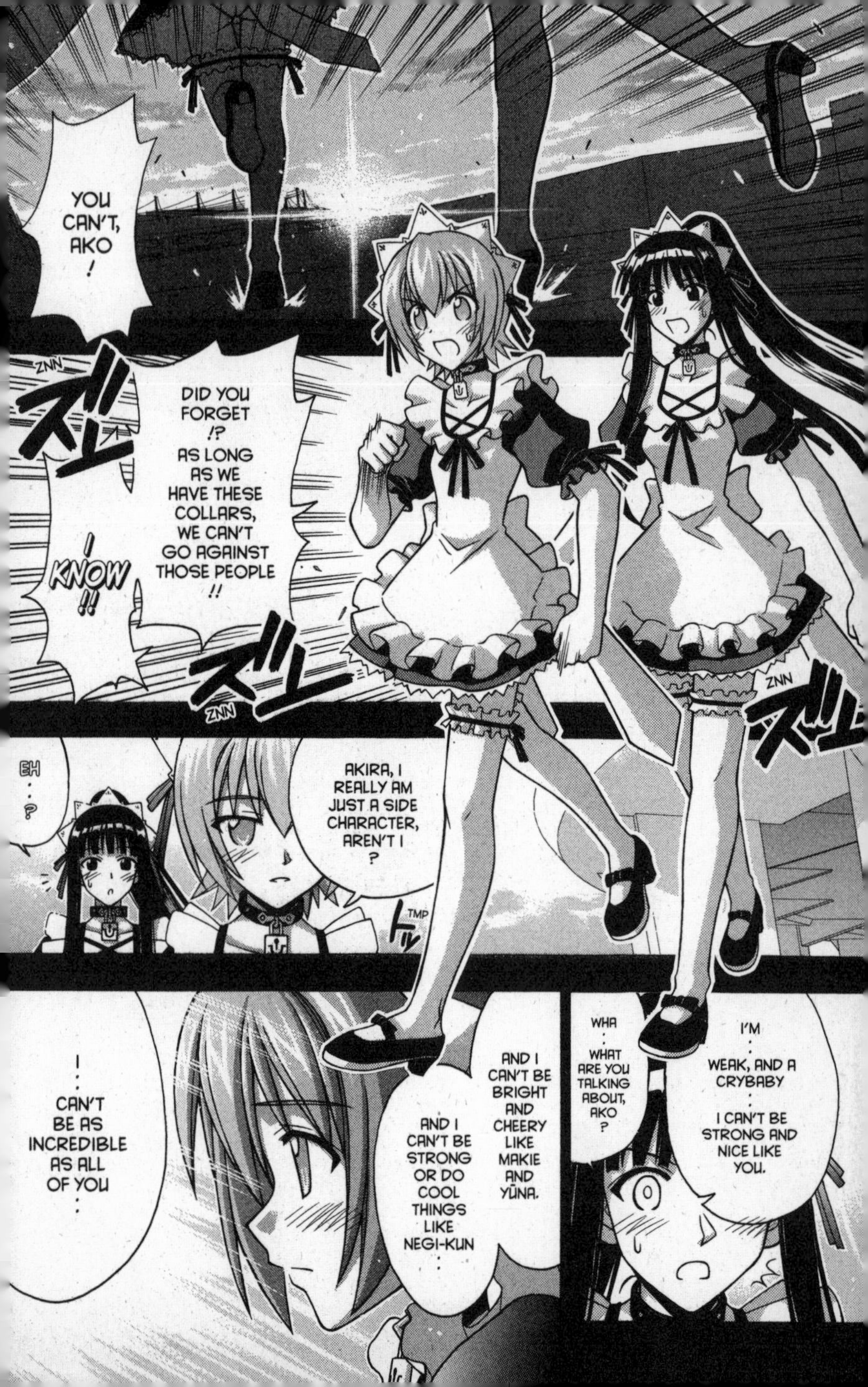
YOU CAN'T, AKO!
ZNN
DID YOU FORGET!? AS LONG AS WE HAVE THESE COLLARS, WE CAN'T GO AGAINST THOSE PEOPLE!!
I KNOW!!
ZNN
ZNN
AKIRA, I REALLY AM JUST A SIDE CHARACTER, AREN'T I?
EH...?
TMP
I'M... WEAK, AND A CRYBABY... I CAN'T BE STRONG AND NICE LIKE YOU.
WHA... WHAT ARE YOU TALKING ABOUT, AKO?
AND I CAN'T BE BRIGHT AND CHEERY LIKE MAKIE AND YŪNA.
AND I CAN'T BE STRONG OR DO COOL THINGS LIKE NEGI-KUN...
I... CAN'T BE AS INCREDIBLE AS ALL OF YOU...

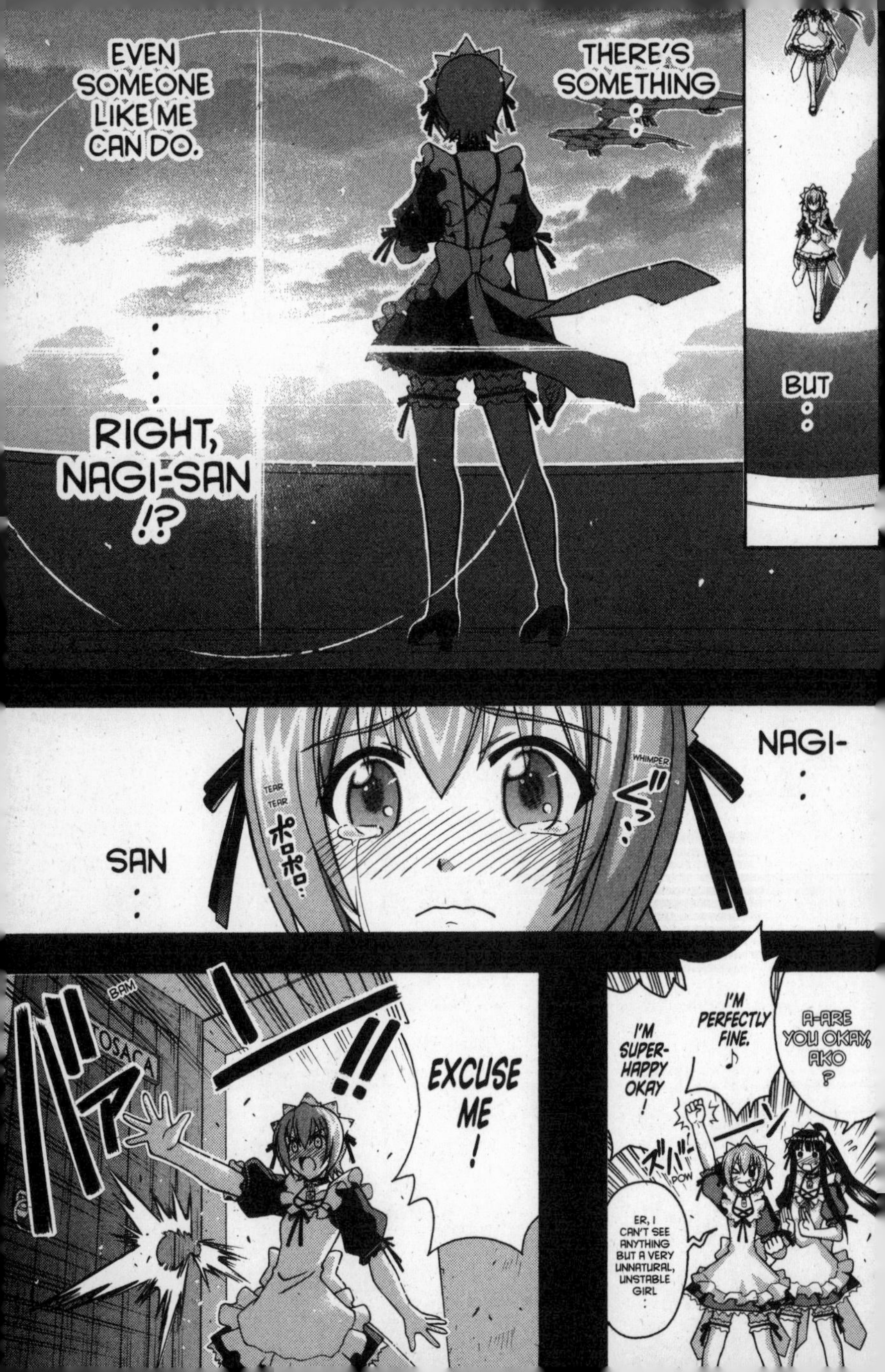
BUT..
THERE'S SOMETHING...
EVEN SOMEONE LIKE ME CAN DO.
....
RIGHT, NAGI-SAN!?
NAGI-..
WHIMPER
ぐっ..
TEAR TEAR
ポロポロ..
SAN..
A-ARE YOU OKAY, AKO?
I'M PERFECTLY FINE. ♪
I'M SUPER-HAPPY OKAY!
ズバー
POW
ER, I CAN'T SEE ANYTHING BUT A VERY UNNATURAL, UNSTABLE GIRL..
EXCUSE ME!
BAM

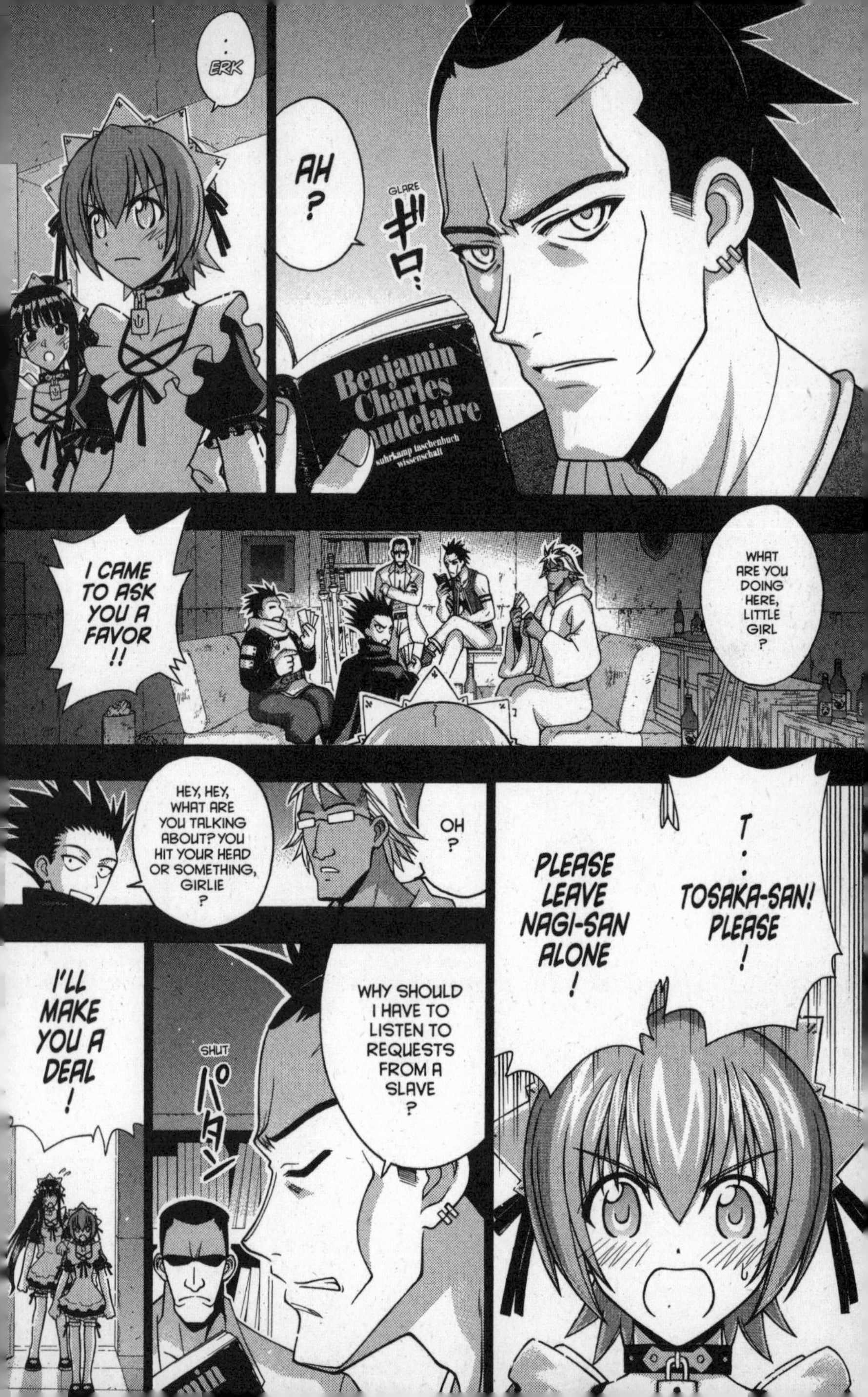
AH?
GLARE
ギロ
Benjamin
Charles
udelaire
suhrkamp taschenbuch wissenschaft
... ERK
WHAT ARE YOU DOING HERE, LITTLE GIRL?
I CAME TO ASK YOU A FAVOR!!
T.. TOSAKA-SAN! PLEASE!
PLEASE LEAVE NAGI-SAN ALONE!
OH?
HEY, HEY, WHAT ARE YOU TALKING ABOUT? YOU HIT YOUR HEAD OR SOMETHING, GIRLIE?
WHY SHOULD I HAVE TO LISTEN TO REQUESTS FROM A SLAVE?
SHUT
パタン
I'LL MAKE YOU A DEAL!

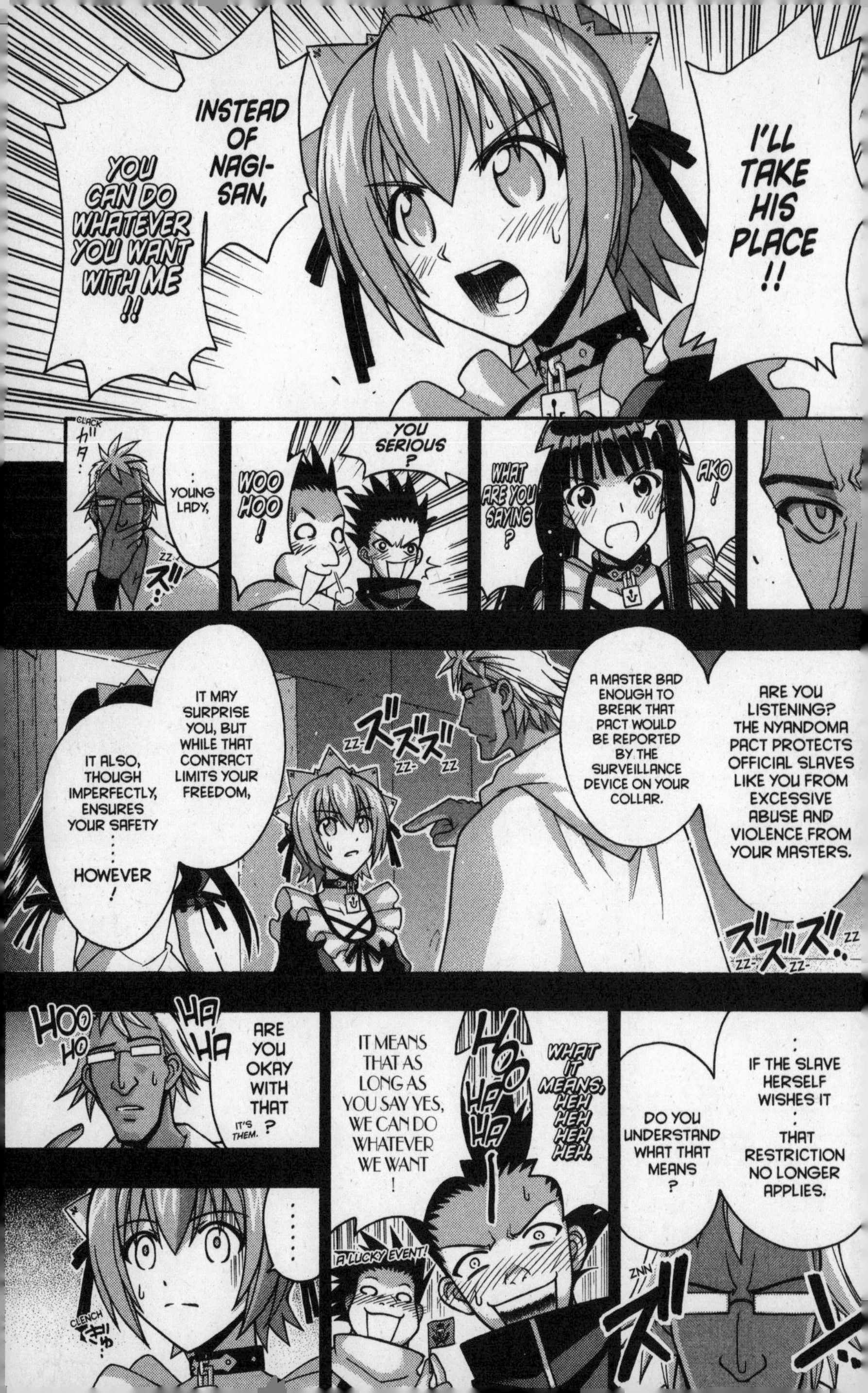
I'LL TAKE HIS PLACE!!
INSTEAD OF NAGI-SAN,
YOU CAN DO WHATEVER YOU WANT WITH ME!!
AKO!
WHAT ARE YOU SAYING?
YOU SERIOUS?
WOO HOO!
CLACK
...YOUNG LADY,
ZZ
ARE YOU LISTENING? THE NYANDOMA PACT PROTECTS OFFICIAL SLAVES LIKE YOU FROM EXCESSIVE ABUSE AND VIOLENCE FROM YOUR MASTERS.
A MASTER BAD ENOUGH TO BREAK THAT PACT WOULD BE REPORTED BY THE SURVEILLANCE DEVICE ON YOUR COLLAR.
ZZ ZZ- ZZ- ZZ
ZZ- ZZ- ZZ
IT MAY SURPRISE YOU, BUT WHILE THAT CONTRACT LIMITS YOUR FREEDOM,
IT ALSO, THOUGH IMPERFECTLY, ENSURES YOUR SAFETY ...... HOWEVER!
...IF THE SLAVE HERSELF WISHES IT... THAT RESTRICTION NO LONGER APPLIES.
DO YOU UNDERSTAND WHAT THAT MEANS?
ZNN
WHAT IT MEANS, HEH HEH HEH HEH.
HOO HA HA
IT MEANS THAT AS LONG AS YOU SAY YES, WE CAN DO WHATEVER WE WANT!
A LUCKY EVENT!
HOO HO
HA HA
ARE YOU OKAY WITH THAT?
IT'S THEM.
......
CLENCH

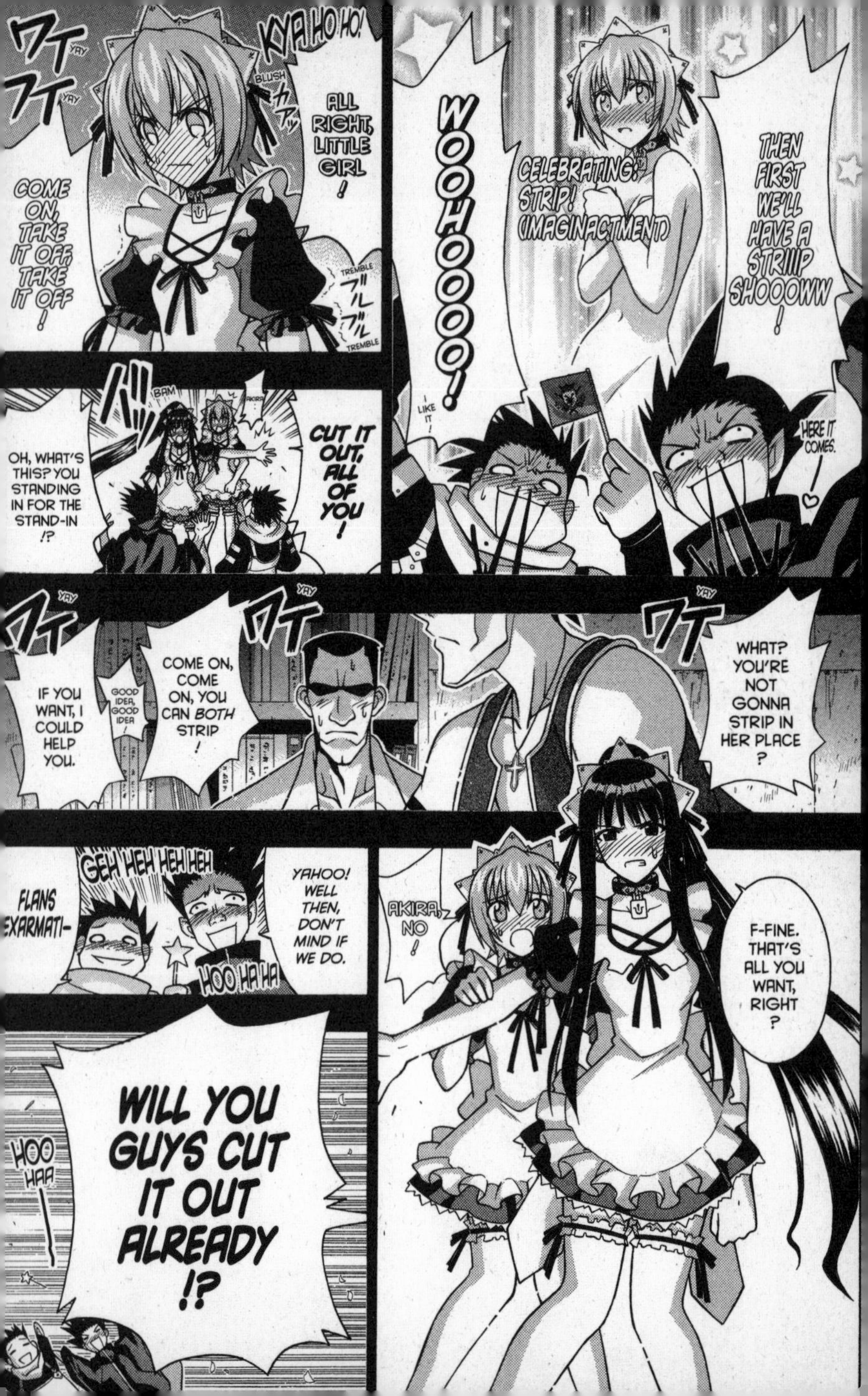
THEN FIRST WE'LL HAVE A STRIIIP SHOOOWW!
CELEBRATING: STRIP! (IMAGINACTMENT)
WOOHOOOOOO!
I LIKE IT!
HERE IT COMES. ♡
KYA HO HO!
ALL RIGHT, LITTLE GIRL!
BLUSH
YAY
YAY
COME ON, TAKE IT OFF, TAKE IT OFF!
TREMBLE
TREMBLE
BAM
AKIRA
CUT IT OUT, ALL OF YOU!
OH, WHAT'S THIS? YOU STANDING IN FOR THE STAND-IN!?
YAY
WHAT? YOU'RE NOT GONNA STRIP IN HER PLACE?
YAY
COME ON, COME ON, YOU CAN BOTH STRIP!
GOOD IDEA, GOOD IDEA!
IF YOU WANT, I COULD HELP YOU.
YAY
F-FINE. THAT'S ALL YOU WANT, RIGHT?
AKIRA, NO!
YAHOO! WELL THEN, DON'T MIND IF WE DO.
GEH HEH HEH HEH
HOO HA HA
FLANS EXARMATI-
WILL YOU GUYS CUT IT OUT ALREADY!?
HOO HAA—

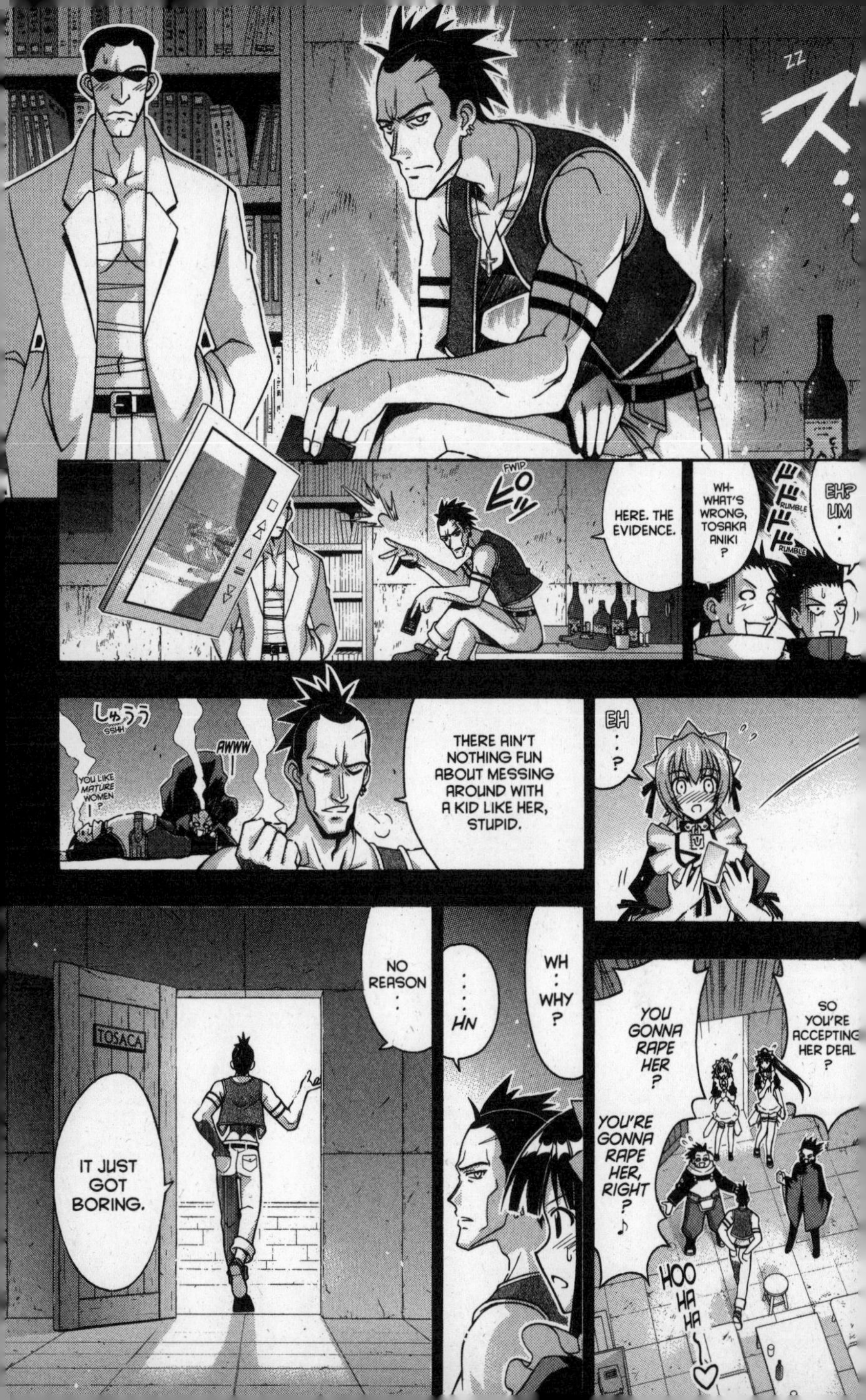

ZZ
EH? UM . . .
WH- WHAT'S WRONG, TOSAKA ANIKI ?
RUMBLE
RUMBLE
HERE. THE EVIDENCE.
FWIP
EH . . . ?
THERE AIN'T NOTHING FUN ABOUT MESSING AROUND WITH A KID LIKE HER, STUPID.
SSHH
AWWW!
YOU LIKE MATURE WOMEN!?
SO YOU'RE ACCEPTING HER DEAL?
YOU GONNA RAPE HER?
YOU'RE GONNA RAPE HER, RIGHT?♪
HOO HA HA~♥
WH . . WHY?
. . . .HN
NO REASON . . .
TOSACA
IT JUST GOT BORING.

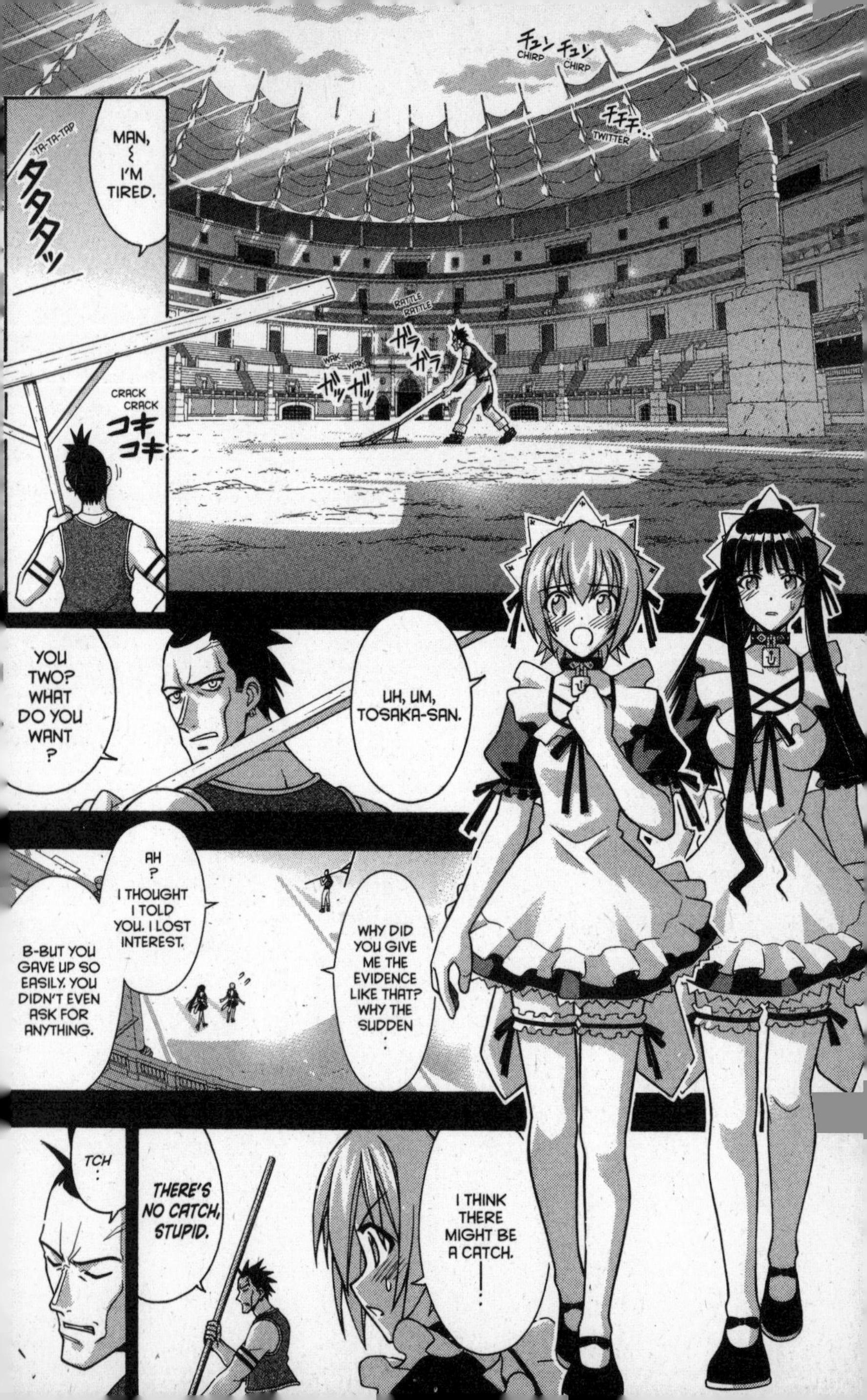
チュン チュン
CHIRP CHIRP
チチチ…
TWITTER
ガラ ガラ
RATTLE RATTLE
ガッ ガッ
WAK WAK
タタタッ
TA-TA-TAP
MAN, ~ I'M TIRED.
コキ コキ
CRACK CRACK
UH, UM, TOSAKA-SAN.
YOU TWO? WHAT DO YOU WANT ?
WHY DID YOU GIVE ME THE EVIDENCE LIKE THAT? WHY THE SUDDEN . . .
AH ? I THOUGHT I TOLD YOU. I LOST INTEREST.
B-BUT YOU GAVE UP SO EASILY. YOU DIDN'T EVEN ASK FOR ANYTHING.
I THINK THERE MIGHT BE A CATCH. . . !
TCH . . .
THERE'S NO CATCH, STUPID.

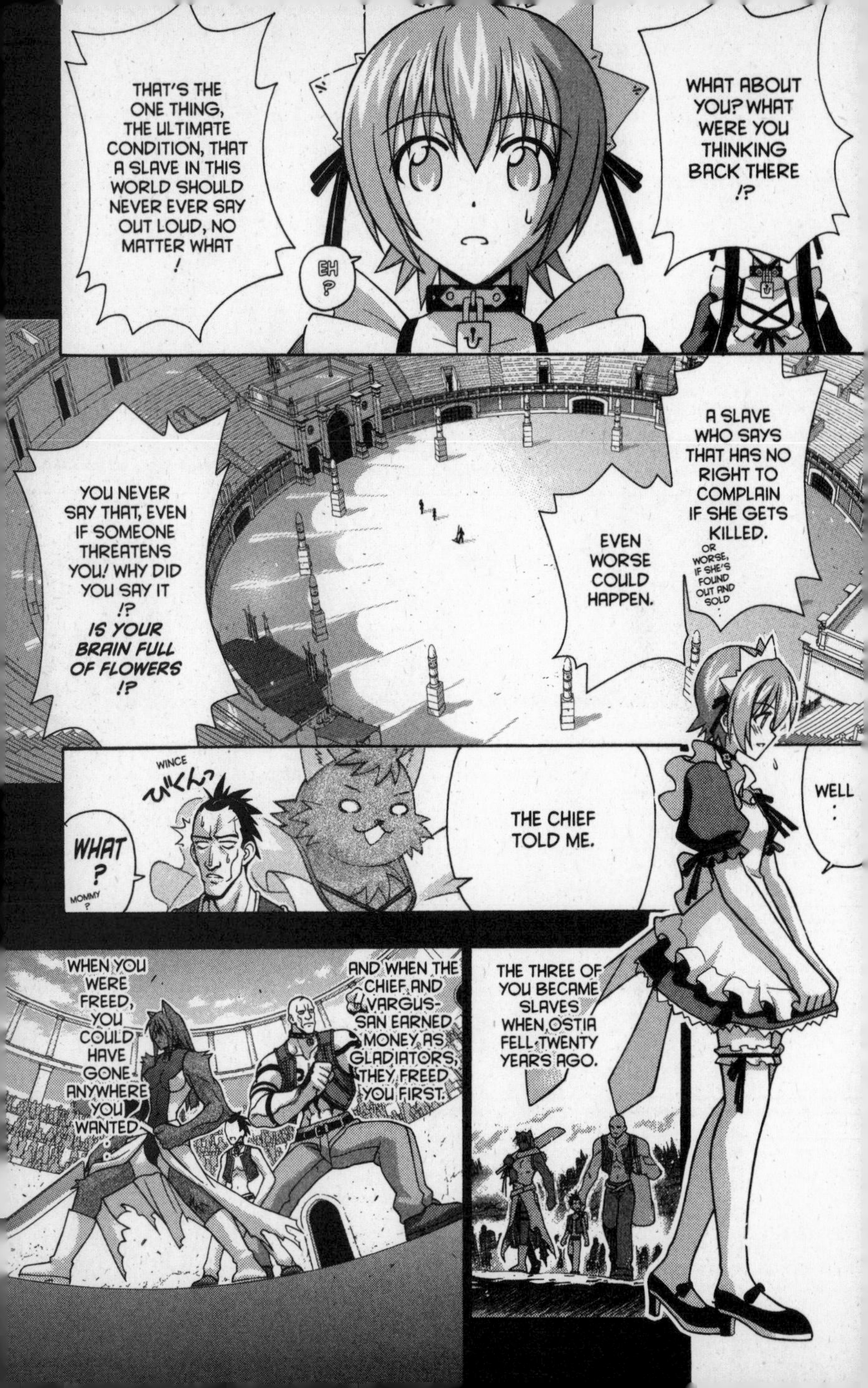
WHAT ABOUT YOU? WHAT WERE YOU THINKING BACK THERE !?
EH ?
THAT'S THE ONE THING, THE ULTIMATE CONDITION, THAT A SLAVE IN THIS WORLD SHOULD NEVER EVER SAY OUT LOUD, NO MATTER WHAT !
A SLAVE WHO SAYS THAT HAS NO RIGHT TO COMPLAIN IF SHE GETS KILLED.
OR WORSE, IF SHE'S FOUND OUT AND SOLD
EVEN WORSE COULD HAPPEN.
YOU NEVER SAY THAT, EVEN IF SOMEONE THREATENS YOU! WHY DID YOU SAY IT !? IS YOUR BRAIN FULL OF FLOWERS !?
WELL :
THE CHIEF TOLD ME.
WINCE
WHAT ?
MOMMY ?
THE THREE OF YOU BECAME SLAVES WHEN OSTIA FELL TWENTY YEARS AGO.
AND WHEN THE CHIEF AND VARGUS-SAN EARNED MONEY AS GLADIATORS, THEY FREED YOU FIRST.
WHEN YOU WERE FREED, YOU COULD HAVE GONE ANYWHERE YOU WANTED

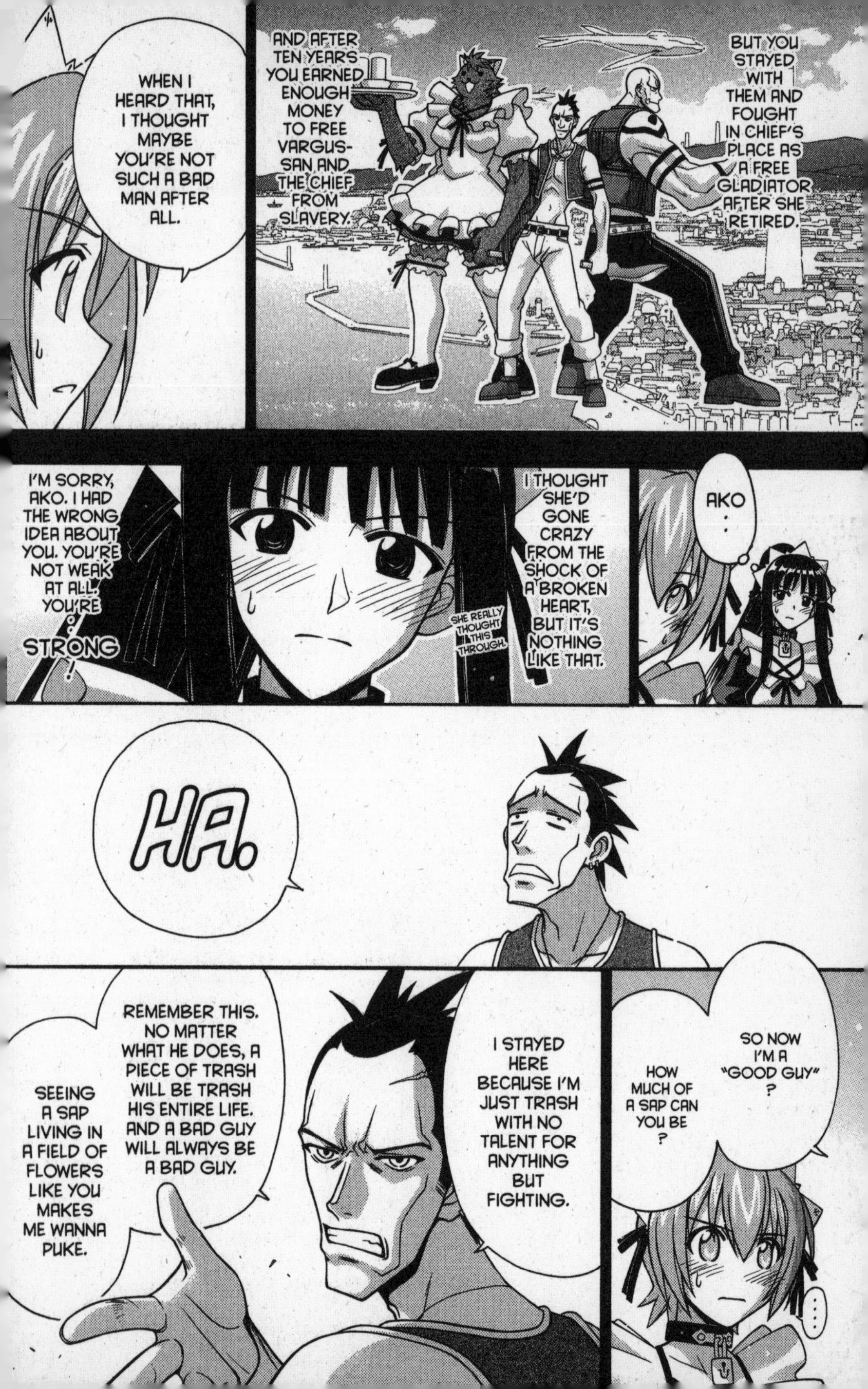
AND AFTER TEN YEARS YOU EARNED ENOUGH MONEY TO FREE VARGUS-SAN AND THE CHIEF FROM SLAVERY.
BUT YOU STAYED WITH THEM AND FOUGHT IN CHIEF'S PLACE AS A FREE GLADIATOR AFTER SHE RETIRED.
WHEN I HEARD THAT, I THOUGHT MAYBE YOU'RE NOT SUCH A BAD MAN AFTER ALL.
AKO...
I THOUGHT SHE'D GONE CRAZY FROM THE SHOCK OF A BROKEN HEART, BUT IT'S NOTHING LIKE THAT.
SHE REALLY THOUGHT THIS THROUGH.
I'M SORRY, AKO. I HAD THE WRONG IDEA ABOUT YOU. YOU'RE NOT WEAK AT ALL. YOU'RE... STRONG!
HA.
SO NOW I'M A "GOOD GUY"?
HOW MUCH OF A SAP CAN YOU BE?
...
I STAYED HERE BECAUSE I'M JUST TRASH WITH NO TALENT FOR ANYTHING BUT FIGHTING.
REMEMBER THIS. NO MATTER WHAT HE DOES, A PIECE OF TRASH WILL BE TRASH HIS ENTIRE LIFE. AND A BAD GUY WILL ALWAYS BE A BAD GUY.
SEEING A SAP LIVING IN A FIELD OF FLOWERS LIKE YOU MAKES ME WANNA PUKE.

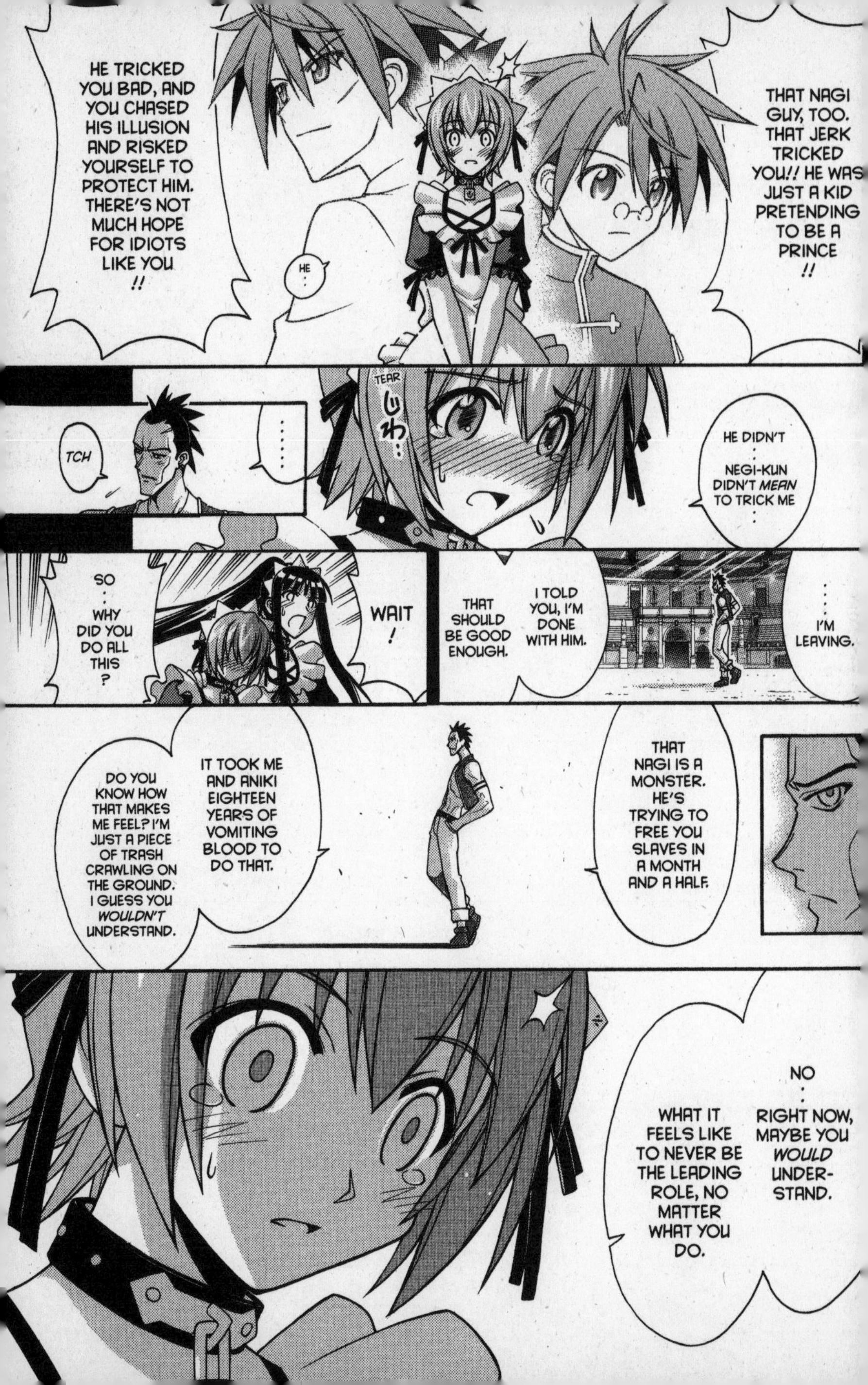
THAT NAGI GUY, TOO. THAT JERK TRICKED YOU!! HE WAS JUST A KID PRETENDING TO BE A PRINCE!!
HE TRICKED YOU BAD, AND YOU CHASED HIS ILLUSION AND RISKED YOURSELF TO PROTECT HIM. THERE'S NOT MUCH HOPE FOR IDIOTS LIKE YOU!!
HE...
HE DIDN'T... NEGI-KUN DIDN'T *MEAN* TO TRICK ME...
TEAR
じわ...
......
TCH
...... I'M LEAVING.
I TOLD YOU, I'M DONE WITH HIM.
THAT SHOULD BE GOOD ENOUGH.
WAIT!
SO... WHY DID YOU DO ALL THIS?
THAT NAGI IS A MONSTER. HE'S TRYING TO FREE YOU SLAVES IN A MONTH AND A HALF.
IT TOOK ME AND ANIKI EIGHTEEN YEARS OF VOMITING BLOOD TO DO THAT.
DO YOU KNOW HOW THAT MAKES ME FEEL? I'M JUST A PIECE OF TRASH CRAWLING ON THE GROUND. I GUESS YOU *WOULDN'T* UNDERSTAND.
NO... RIGHT NOW, MAYBE YOU *WOULD* UNDER-STAND.
WHAT IT FEELS LIKE TO NEVER BE THE LEADING ROLE, NO MATTER WHAT YOU DO.

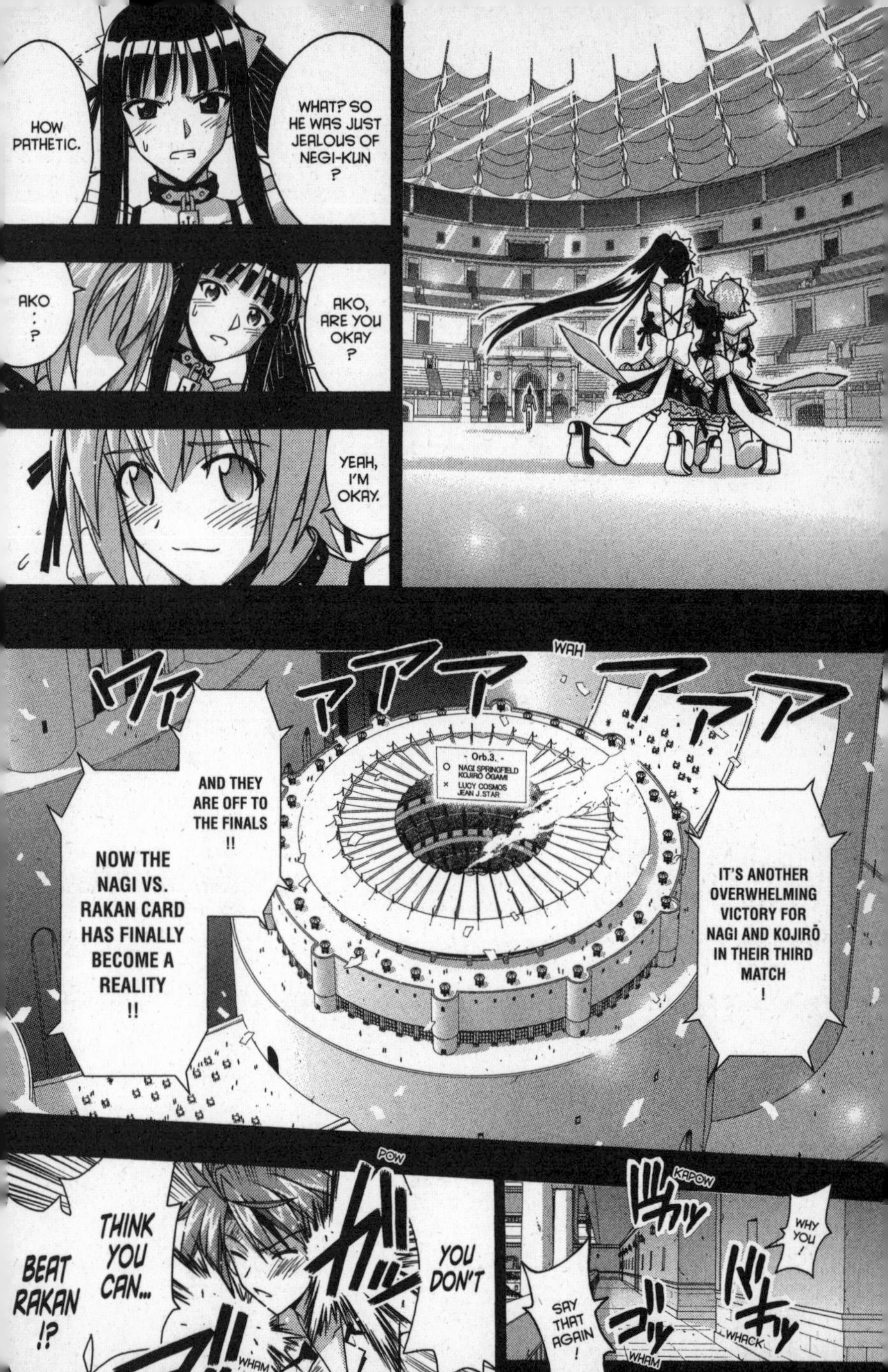
WHAT? SO HE WAS JUST JEALOUS OF NEGI-KUN ?
HOW PATHETIC.
AKO, ARE YOU OKAY ?
AKO . . . ?
YEAH, I'M OKAY.
ワァァアア アァアア
WAH
- Orb.3. -
○ NAGI SPRINGFIELD KOJIRŌ ŌGAMI
× LUCY COSMOS JEAN J.STAR
IT'S ANOTHER OVERWHELMING VICTORY FOR NAGI AND KOJIRŌ IN THEIR THIRD MATCH !
AND THEY ARE OFF TO THE FINALS !!
NOW THE NAGI VS. RAKAN CARD HAS FINALLY BECOME A REALITY !!
ドカッ
KAPOW
WHY YOU !
SAY THAT AGAIN !
ドカッ
WHACK
ゴッ
WHAM
ガッ
POW
YOU DON'T
THINK YOU CAN...
BEAT RAKAN !?
ゴッ
WHAM

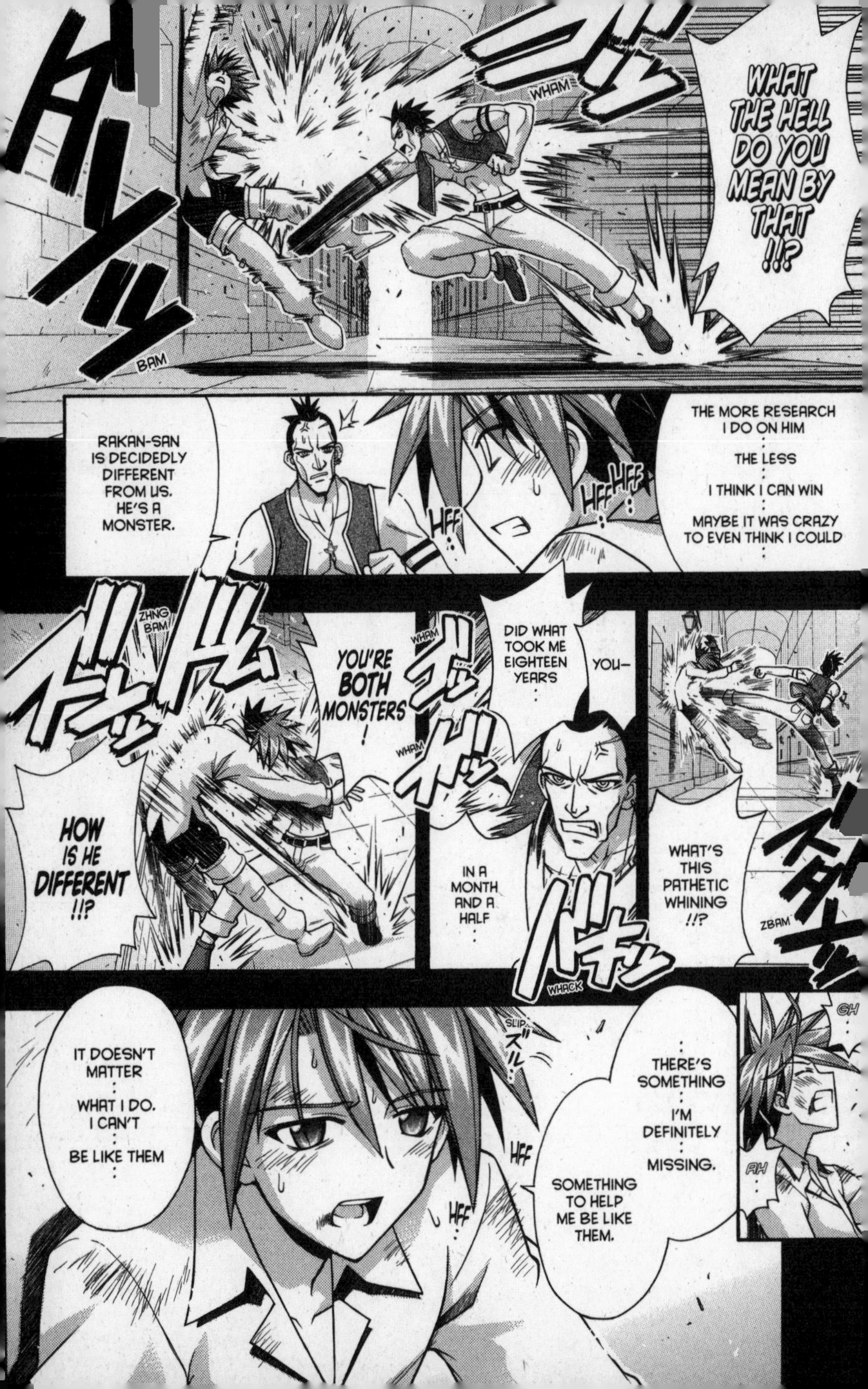
WHAT THE HELL DO YOU MEAN BY THAT!!?
WHAM
BAM
THE MORE RESEARCH I DO ON HIM... THE LESS... I THINK I CAN WIN... MAYBE IT WAS CRAZY TO EVEN THINK I COULD...
HFF HFF
HFF
RAKAN-SAN IS DECIDEDLY DIFFERENT FROM US. HE'S A MONSTER.
WHAT'S THIS PATHETIC WHINING!!?
ZBAM
YOU—
DID WHAT TOOK ME EIGHTEEN YEARS...
IN A MONTH AND A HALF...
WHACK
WHAM
WHAM
YOU'RE BOTH MONSTERS!
ZHNG BAM
HOW IS HE DIFFERENT!!?
GH...
AH
...THERE'S SOMETHING... I'M DEFINITELY... MISSING.
SOMETHING TO HELP ME BE LIKE THEM.
SLIP
HFF
HFF
IT DOESN'T MATTER... WHAT I DO. I CAN'T... BE LIKE THEM...

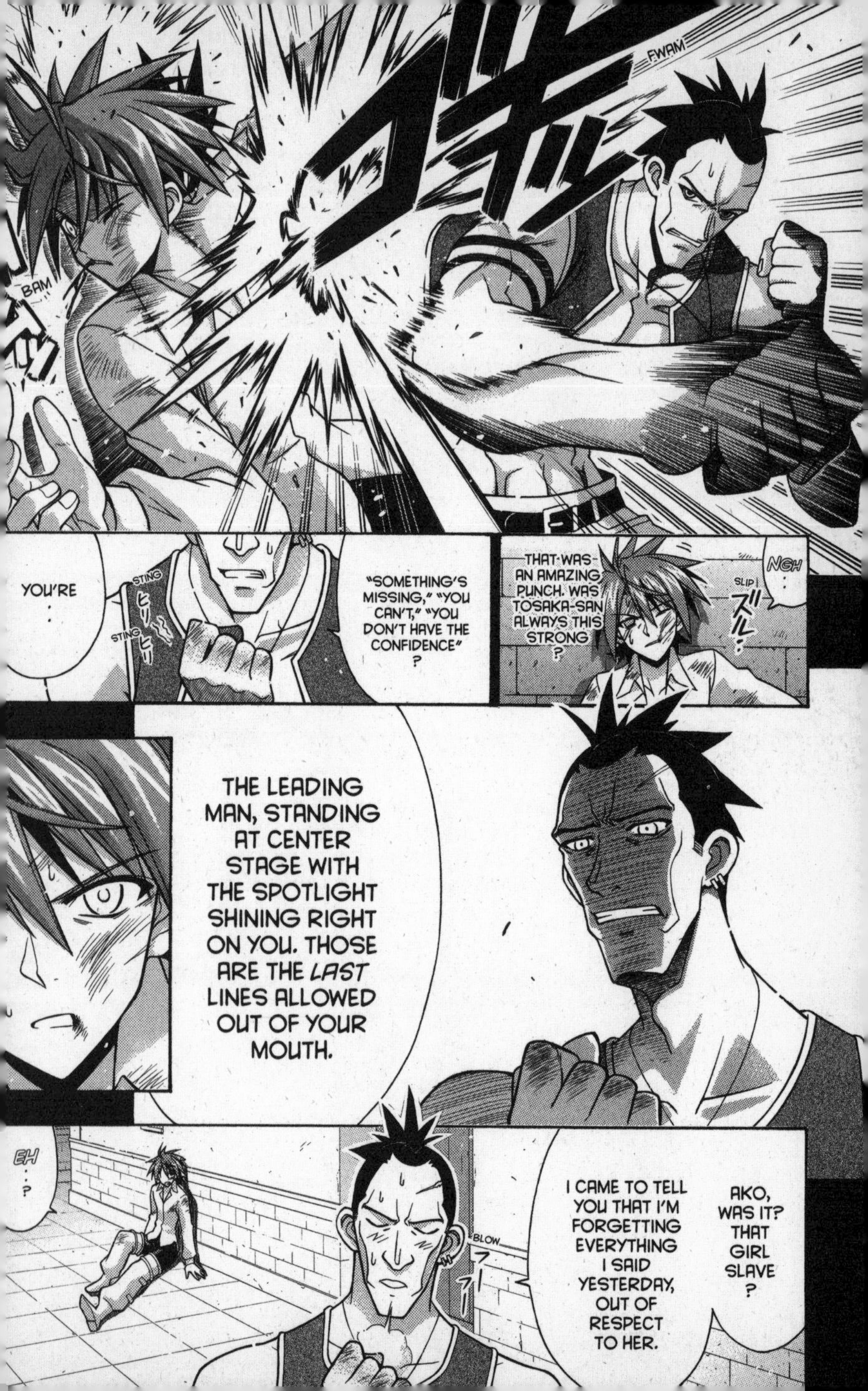
FWAM
BAM
NGH
SLIP
THAT WAS AN AMAZING PUNCH. WAS TOSAKA-SAN ALWAYS THIS STRONG?
"SOMETHING'S MISSING," "YOU CAN'T," "YOU DON'T HAVE THE CONFIDENCE"?
STING
STING
YOU'RE
THE LEADING MAN, STANDING AT CENTER STAGE WITH THE SPOTLIGHT SHINING RIGHT ON YOU. THOSE ARE THE *LAST* LINES ALLOWED OUT OF YOUR MOUTH.
AKO, WAS IT? THAT GIRL SLAVE?
I CAME TO TELL YOU THAT I'M FORGETTING EVERYTHING I SAID YESTERDAY, OUT OF RESPECT TO HER.
BLOW
EH...?

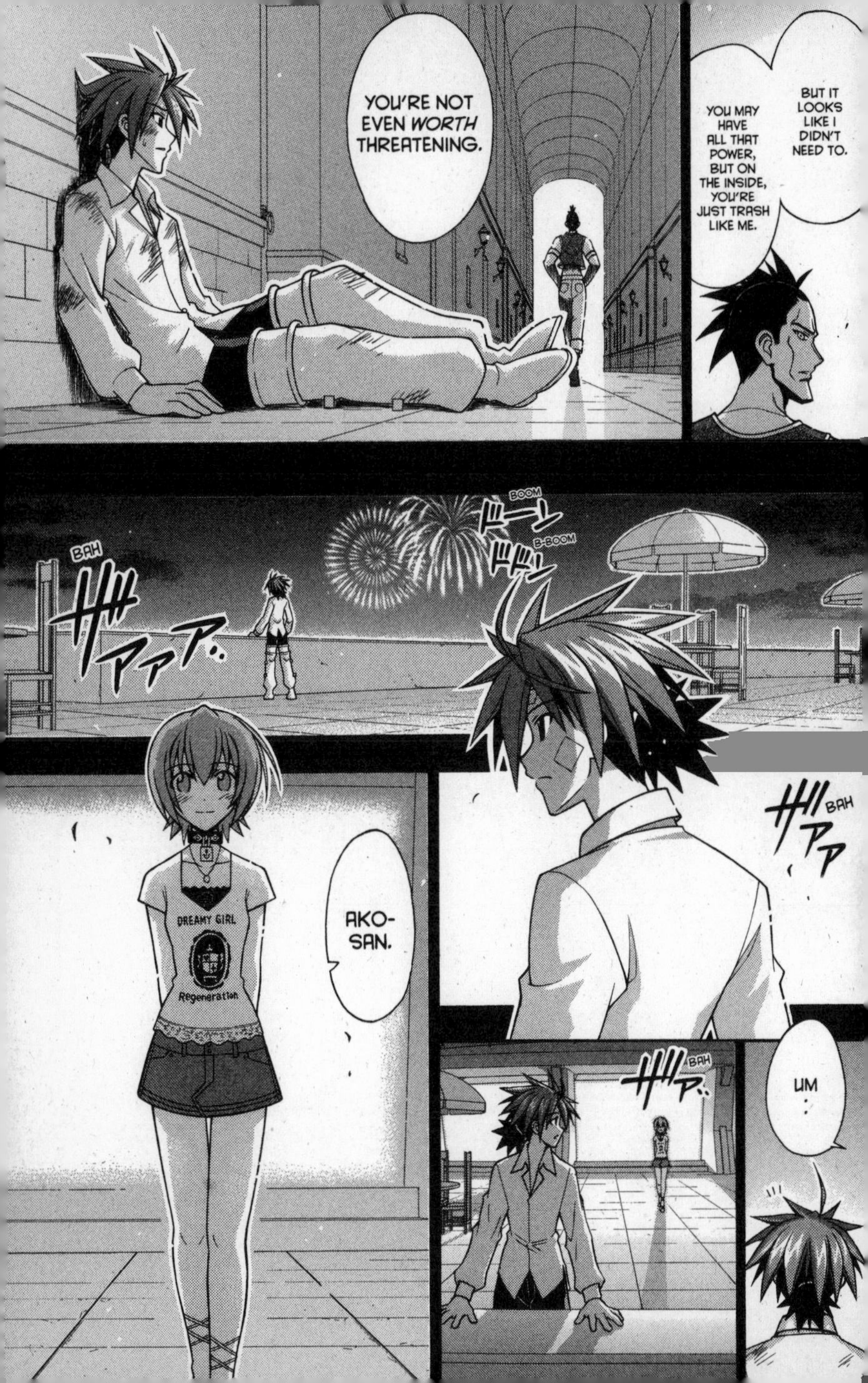
BUT IT LOOKS LIKE I DIDN'T NEED TO.
YOU MAY HAVE ALL THAT POWER, BUT ON THE INSIDE, YOU'RE JUST TRASH LIKE ME.
YOU'RE NOT EVEN *WORTH* THREATENING.
BOOM
ドーン
B-BOOM
ドドン
BAH
ザァァァ
BAH
ザァァ
UM...
BAH
ザァァ
AKO-SAN.
DREAMY GIRL
Regeneration

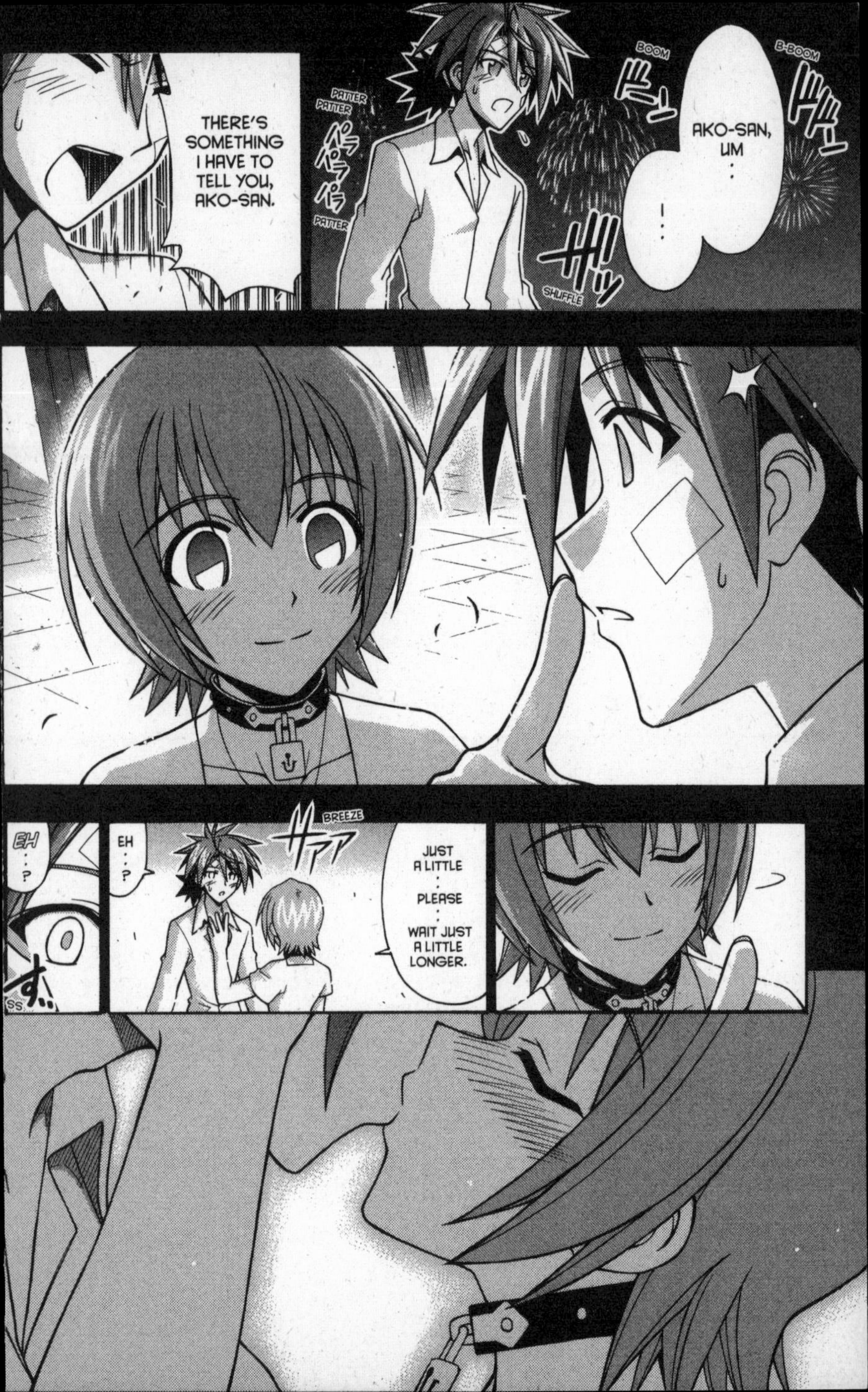
B-BOOM
BOOM
AKO-SAN, UM . . .
! . . .
SHUFFLE
PATTER PATTER
PATTER
THERE'S SOMETHING I HAVE TO TELL YOU, AKO-SAN.
JUST A LITTLE . . . PLEASE . . . WAIT JUST A LITTLE LONGER.
BREEZE
EH . . . ?
EH . . . ?
SS...

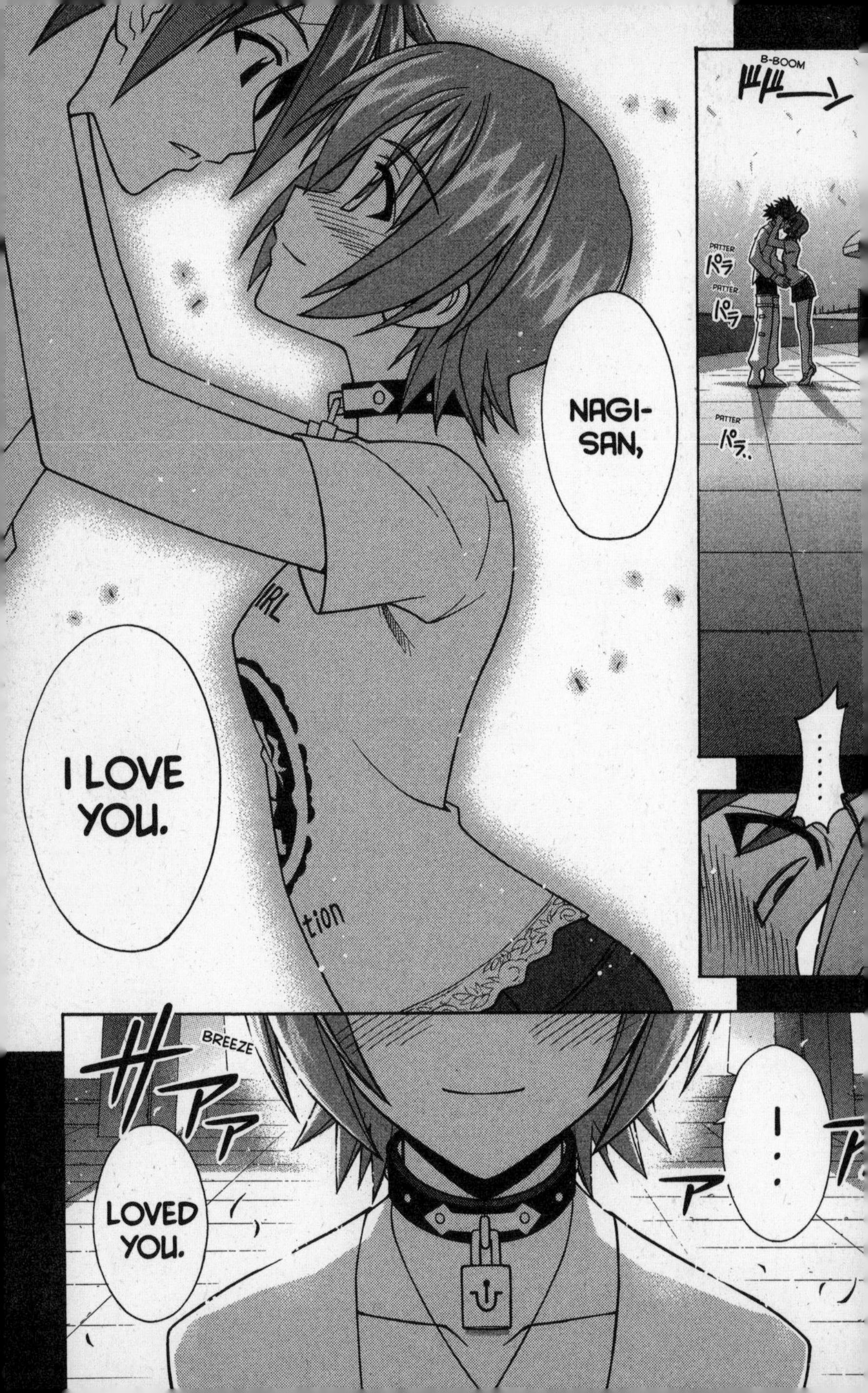
B-BOOM
ドドーン
PATTER
パラ
PATTER
パラ
PATTER
パラ..
......
NAGI-SAN,
I LOVE YOU.
!..
BREEZE
サァァ
LOVED YOU.

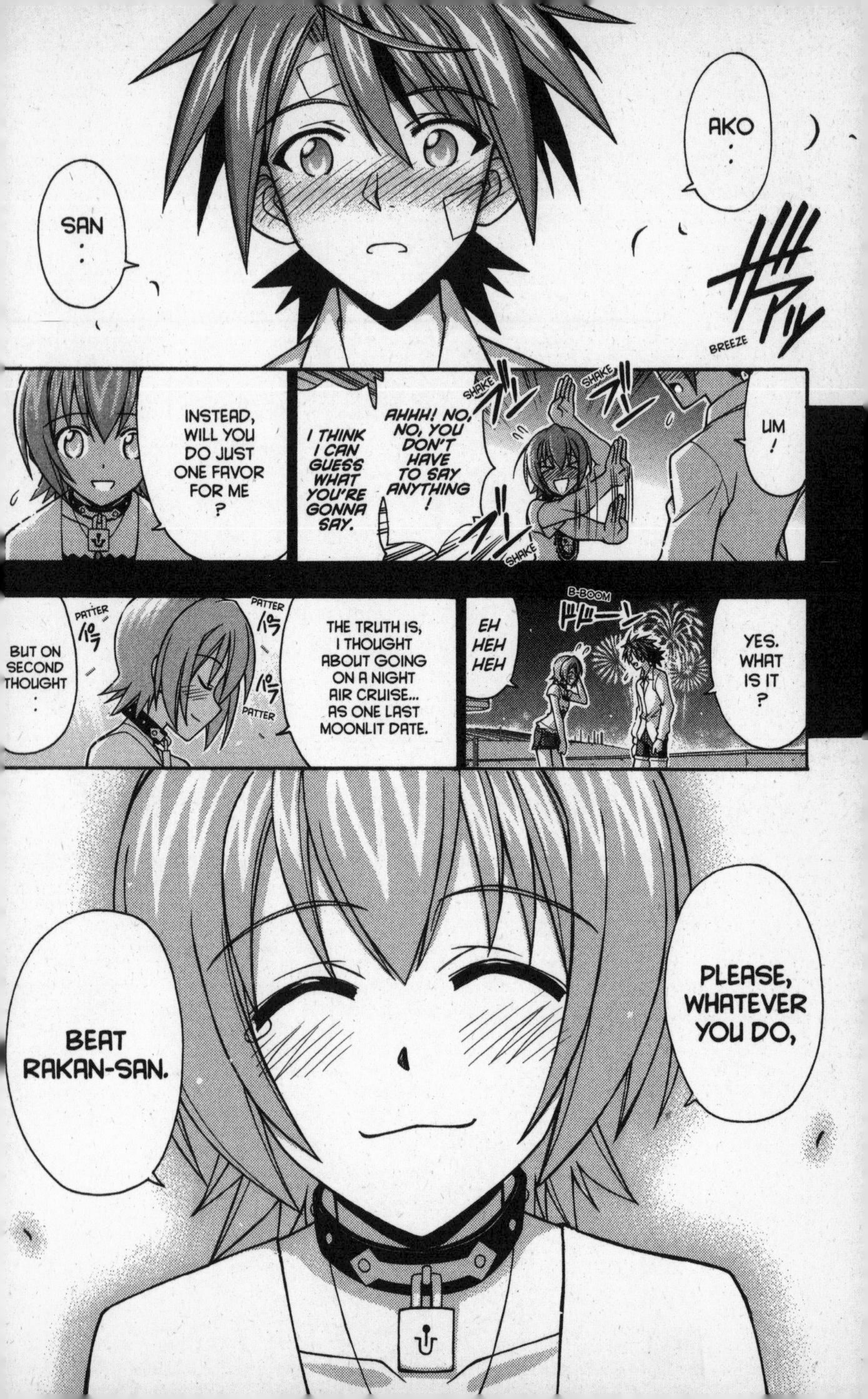
AKO...
SAN...
BREEZE
UM!
SHAKE
SHAKE
AHHH! NO, NO, YOU DON'T HAVE TO SAY ANYTHING!
I THINK I CAN GUESS WHAT YOU'RE GONNA SAY.
SHAKE
INSTEAD, WILL YOU DO JUST ONE FAVOR FOR ME?
YES. WHAT IS IT?
B-BOOM
EH HEH HEH
THE TRUTH IS, I THOUGHT ABOUT GOING ON A NIGHT AIR CRUISE... AS ONE LAST MOONLIT DATE.
PATTER
PATTER
PATTER
BUT ON SECOND THOUGHT...
PLEASE, WHATEVER YOU DO,
BEAT RAKAN-SAN.

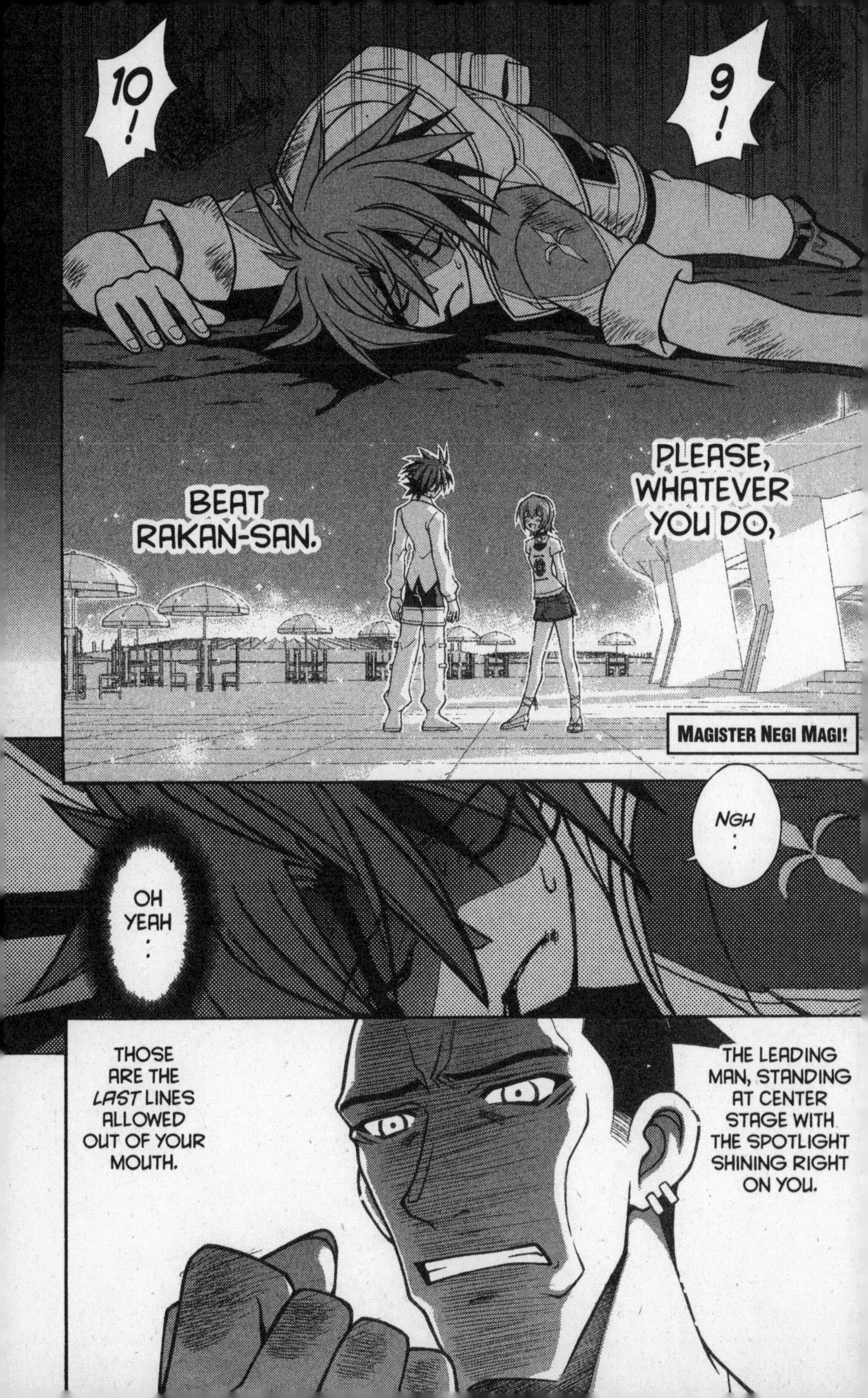
9!
10!
PLEASE, WHATEVER YOU DO,
BEAT RAKAN-SAN.
MAGISTER NEGI MAGI!
NGH :
OH YEAH :
THE LEADING MAN, STANDING AT CENTER STAGE WITH THE SPOTLIGHT SHINING RIGHT ON YOU.
THOSE ARE THE *LAST* LINES ALLOWED OUT OF YOUR MOUTH.

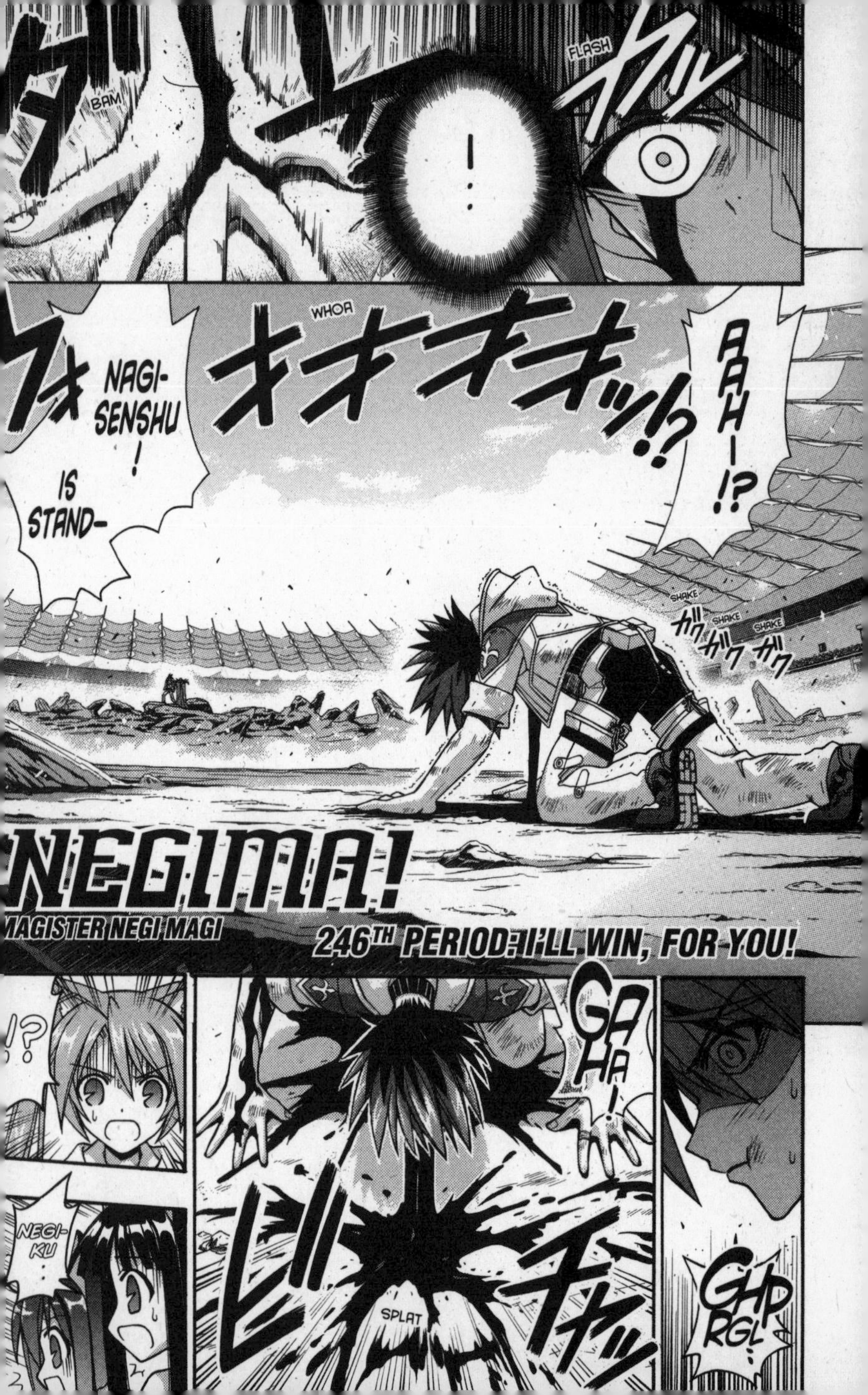
FLASH
!
BAM
AAH-!?
WHOA
NAGI-SENSHU!
IS STAND-
SHAKE
SHAKE
SHAKE
NEGIMA!
MAGISTER NEGI MAGI
246TH PERIOD: I'LL WIN, FOR YOU!
GHPRGL!
GAHA!
SPLAT
!?
NEGI-KU

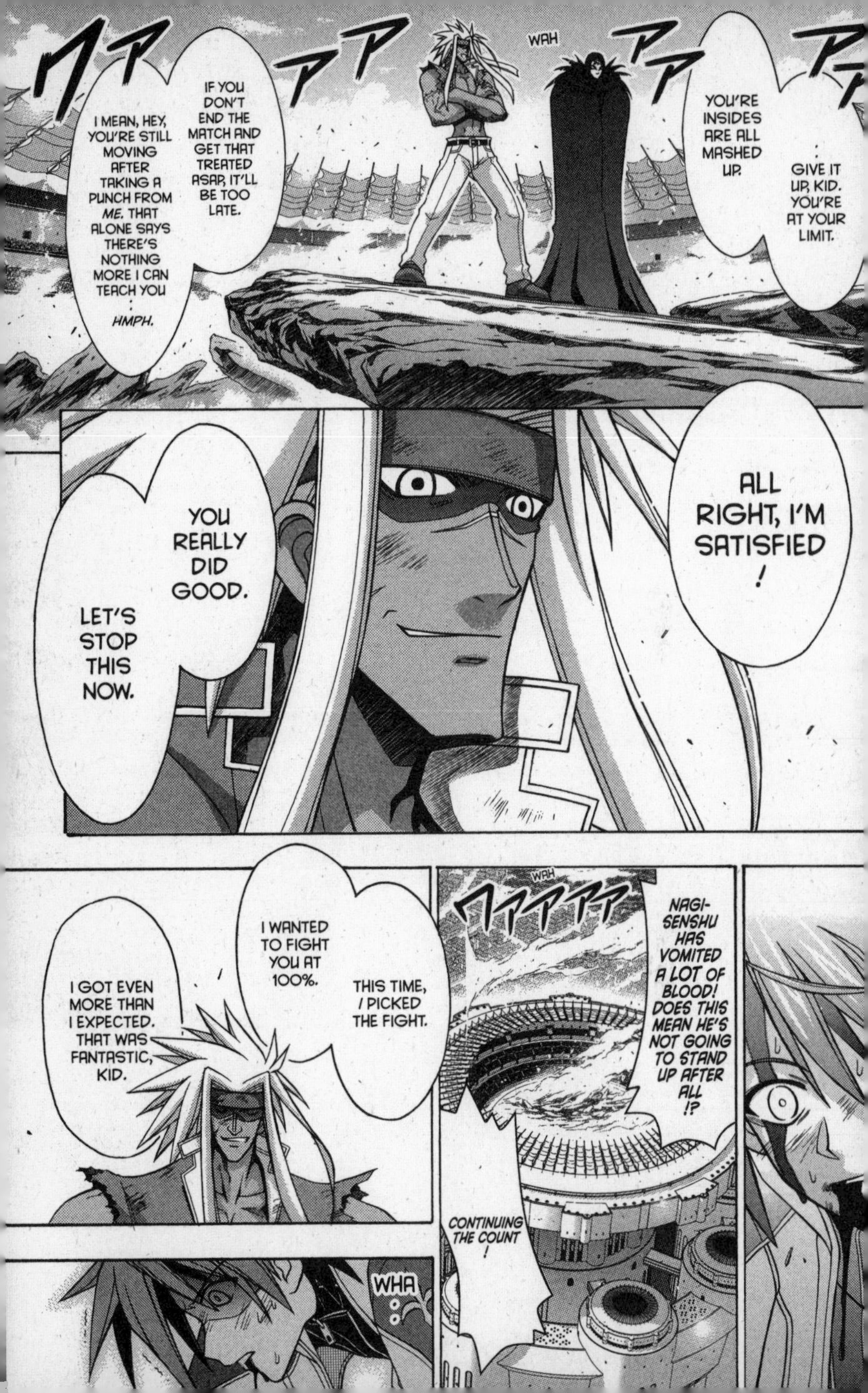
WAH
GIVE IT UP, KID. YOU'RE AT YOUR LIMIT.
YOU'RE INSIDES ARE ALL MASHED UP.
IF YOU DON'T END THE MATCH AND GET THAT TREATED ASAP, IT'LL BE TOO LATE.
I MEAN, HEY, YOU'RE STILL MOVING AFTER TAKING A PUNCH FROM *ME*. THAT ALONE SAYS THERE'S NOTHING MORE I CAN TEACH YOU :
HMPH.
ALL RIGHT, I'M SATISFIED !
YOU REALLY DID GOOD.
LET'S STOP THIS NOW.
WAH
NAGI-SENSHU HAS VOMITED A LOT OF BLOOD! DOES THIS MEAN HE'S NOT GOING TO STAND UP AFTER ALL !?
CONTINUING THE COUNT !
THIS TIME, *I* PICKED THE FIGHT.
I WANTED TO FIGHT YOU AT 100%.
I GOT EVEN MORE THAN I EXPECTED. THAT WAS FANTASTIC, KID.
WHA ..

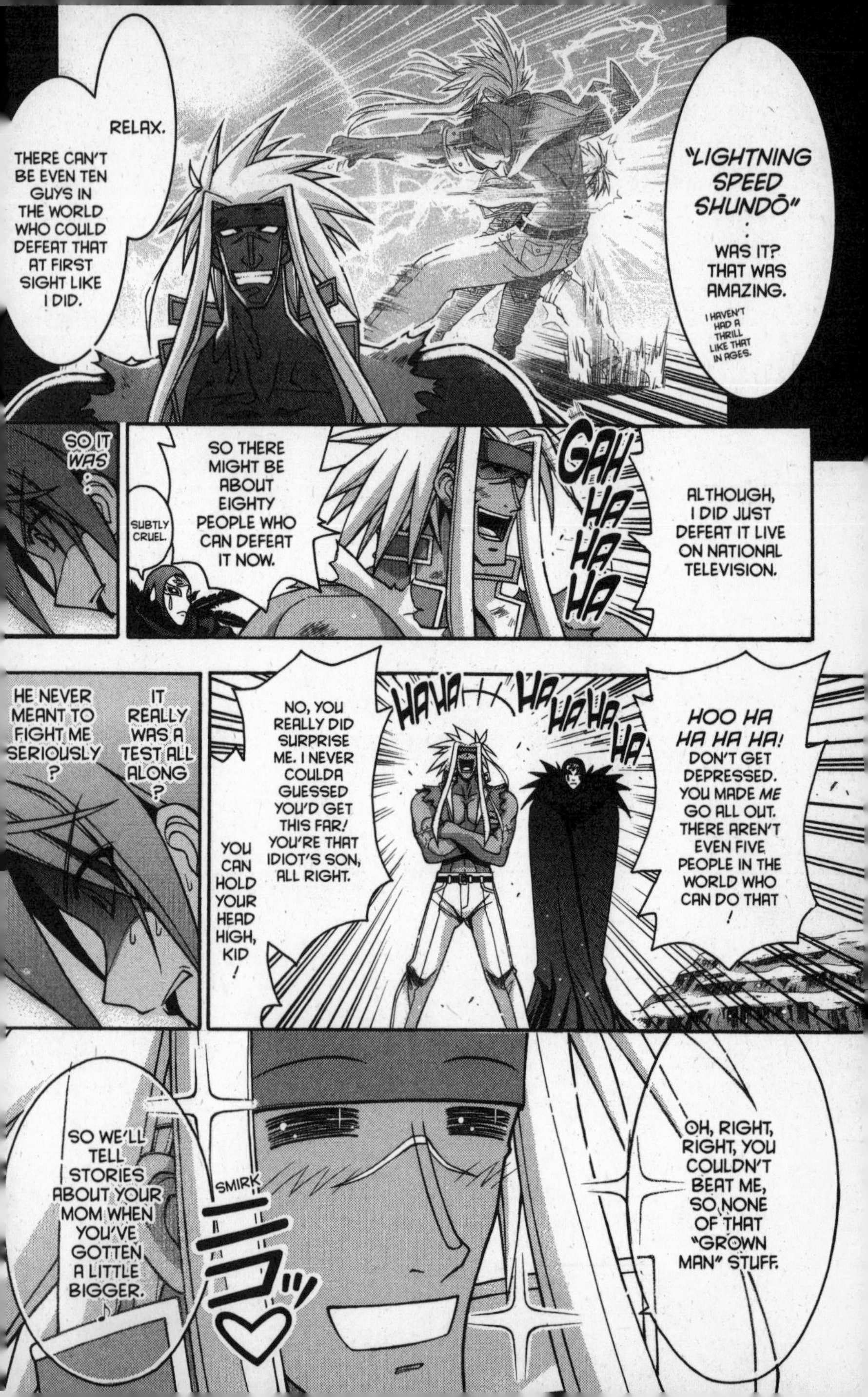
"LIGHTNING SPEED SHUNDŌ"
...WAS IT? THAT WAS AMAZING.
I HAVEN'T HAD A THRILL LIKE THAT IN AGES.
RELAX.
THERE CAN'T BE EVEN TEN GUYS IN THE WORLD WHO COULD DEFEAT THAT AT FIRST SIGHT LIKE I DID.
GAH HA HA HA HA
ALTHOUGH, I DID JUST DEFEAT IT LIVE ON NATIONAL TELEVISION.
SO THERE MIGHT BE ABOUT EIGHTY PEOPLE WHO CAN DEFEAT IT NOW.
SUBTLY CRUEL.
SO IT WAS...
HOO HA HA HA HA! DON'T GET DEPRESSED. YOU MADE *ME* GO ALL OUT. THERE AREN'T EVEN FIVE PEOPLE IN THE WORLD WHO CAN DO THAT!
HA HA HA HA HA HA
NO, YOU REALLY DID SURPRISE ME. I NEVER COULDA GUESSED YOU'D GET THIS FAR! YOU'RE THAT IDIOT'S SON, ALL RIGHT.
YOU CAN HOLD YOUR HEAD HIGH, KID!
IT REALLY WAS A TEST ALL ALONG?
HE NEVER MEANT TO FIGHT ME SERIOUSLY?
OH, RIGHT, RIGHT, YOU COULDN'T BEAT ME, SO NONE OF THAT "GROWN MAN" STUFF.
SO WE'LL TELL STORIES ABOUT YOUR MOM WHEN YOU'VE GOTTEN A LITTLE BIGGER.
SMIRK

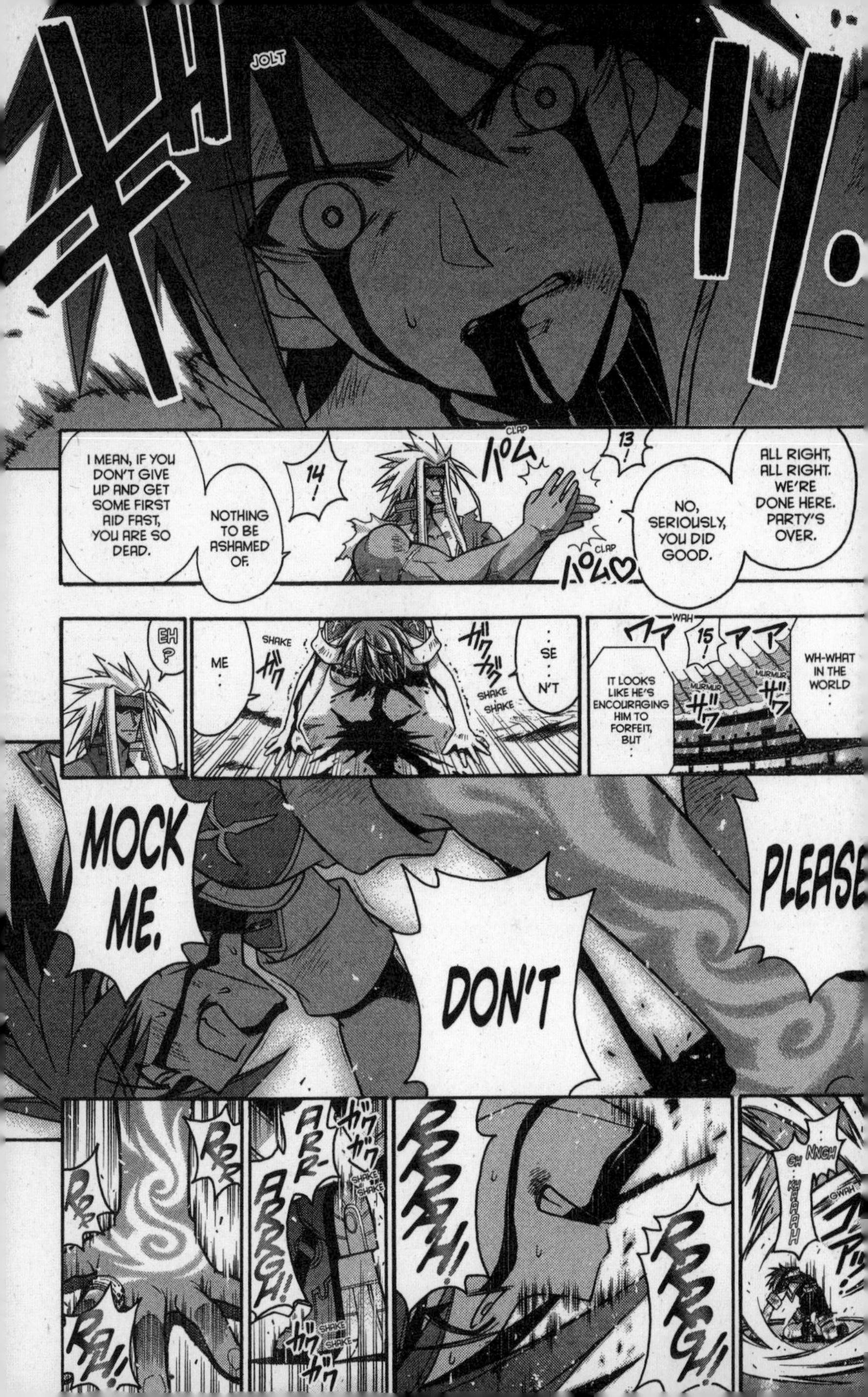
JOLT
ALL RIGHT, ALL RIGHT. WE'RE DONE HERE. PARTY'S OVER.
13!
NO, SERIOUSLY, YOU DID GOOD.
CLAP
CLAP
14!
NOTHING TO BE ASHAMED OF.
I MEAN, IF YOU DON'T GIVE UP AND GET SOME FIRST AID FAST, YOU ARE SO DEAD.
WH-WHAT IN THE WORLD...
WAH
15!
MURMUR
MURMUR
IT LOOKS LIKE HE'S ENCOURAGING HIM TO FORFEIT, BUT...
...SE... N'T
SHAKE
SHAKE
SHAKE
ME...
EH?
PLEASE
DON'T
MOCK ME.
NNGH
GH
GWAH
SHAKE SHAKE
ARR- ARRRGH!!
SHAKE SHAKE

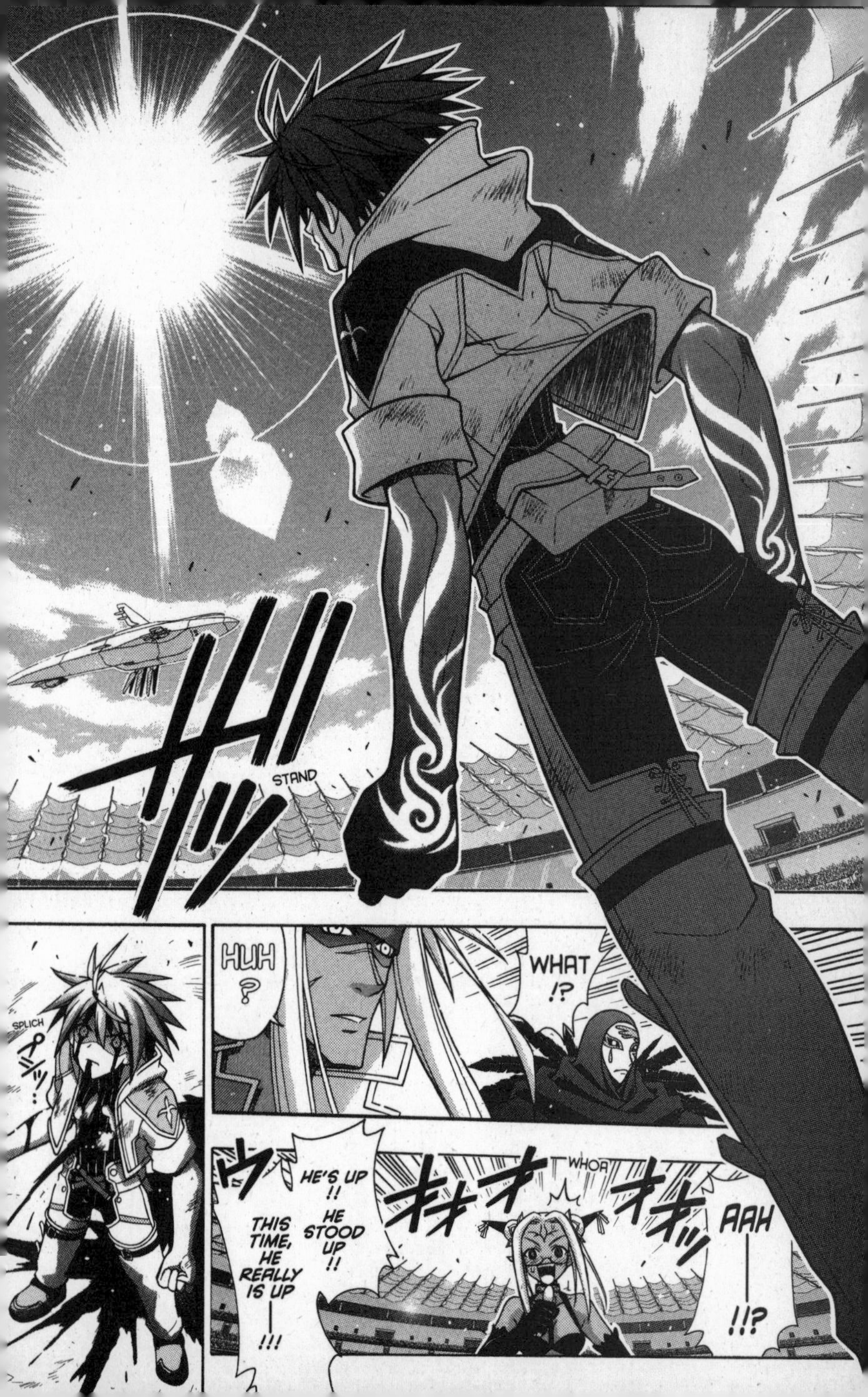
STAND
WHAT !?
HUH ?
AAH —— !!?
WHOA
HE'S UP !!
HE STOOD UP !!
THIS TIME, HE REALLY IS UP —— !!!
SPLICH

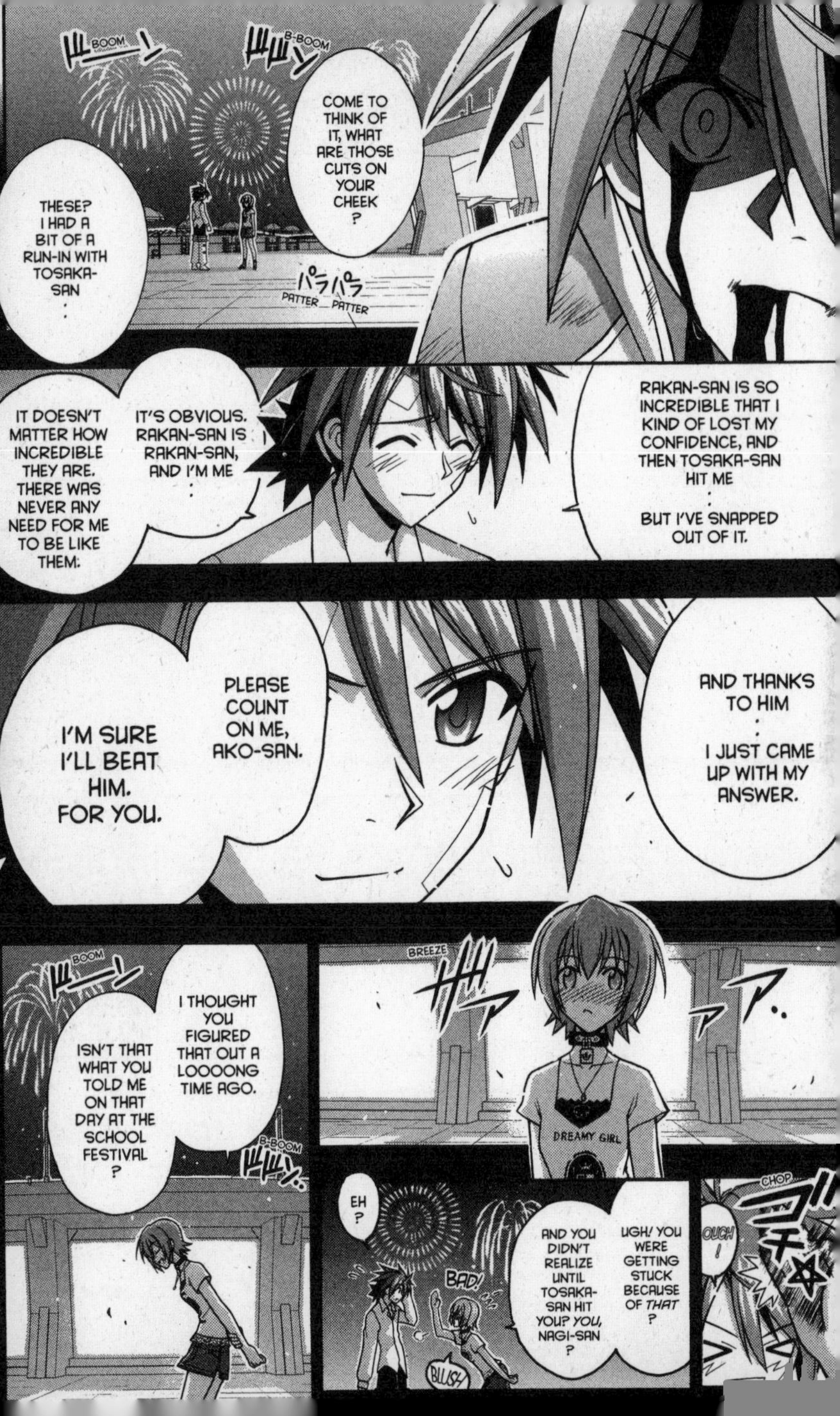
B-BOOM
BOOM
COME TO THINK OF IT, WHAT ARE THOSE CUTS ON YOUR CHEEK?
THESE? I HAD A BIT OF A RUN-IN WITH TOSAKA-SAN...
PATTER PATTER
RAKAN-SAN IS SO INCREDIBLE THAT I KIND OF LOST MY CONFIDENCE, AND THEN TOSAKA-SAN HIT ME... BUT I'VE SNAPPED OUT OF IT.
IT'S OBVIOUS. RAKAN-SAN IS RAKAN-SAN, AND I'M ME...
IT DOESN'T MATTER HOW INCREDIBLE THEY ARE. THERE WAS NEVER ANY NEED FOR ME TO BE LIKE THEM.
AND THANKS TO HIM... I JUST CAME UP WITH MY ANSWER.
PLEASE COUNT ON ME, AKO-SAN.
I'M SURE I'LL BEAT HIM. FOR YOU.
BREEZE
CHOP
OUCH!
UGH! YOU WERE GETTING STUCK BECAUSE OF *THAT*?
AND YOU DIDN'T REALIZE UNTIL TOSAKA-SAN HIT YOU? *YOU*, NAGI-SAN?
EH?
BAD!
BLUSH
BOOM
I THOUGHT YOU FIGURED THAT OUT A LOOOONG TIME AGO.
ISN'T THAT WHAT YOU TOLD ME ON THAT DAY AT THE SCHOOL FESTIVAL?
B-BOOM

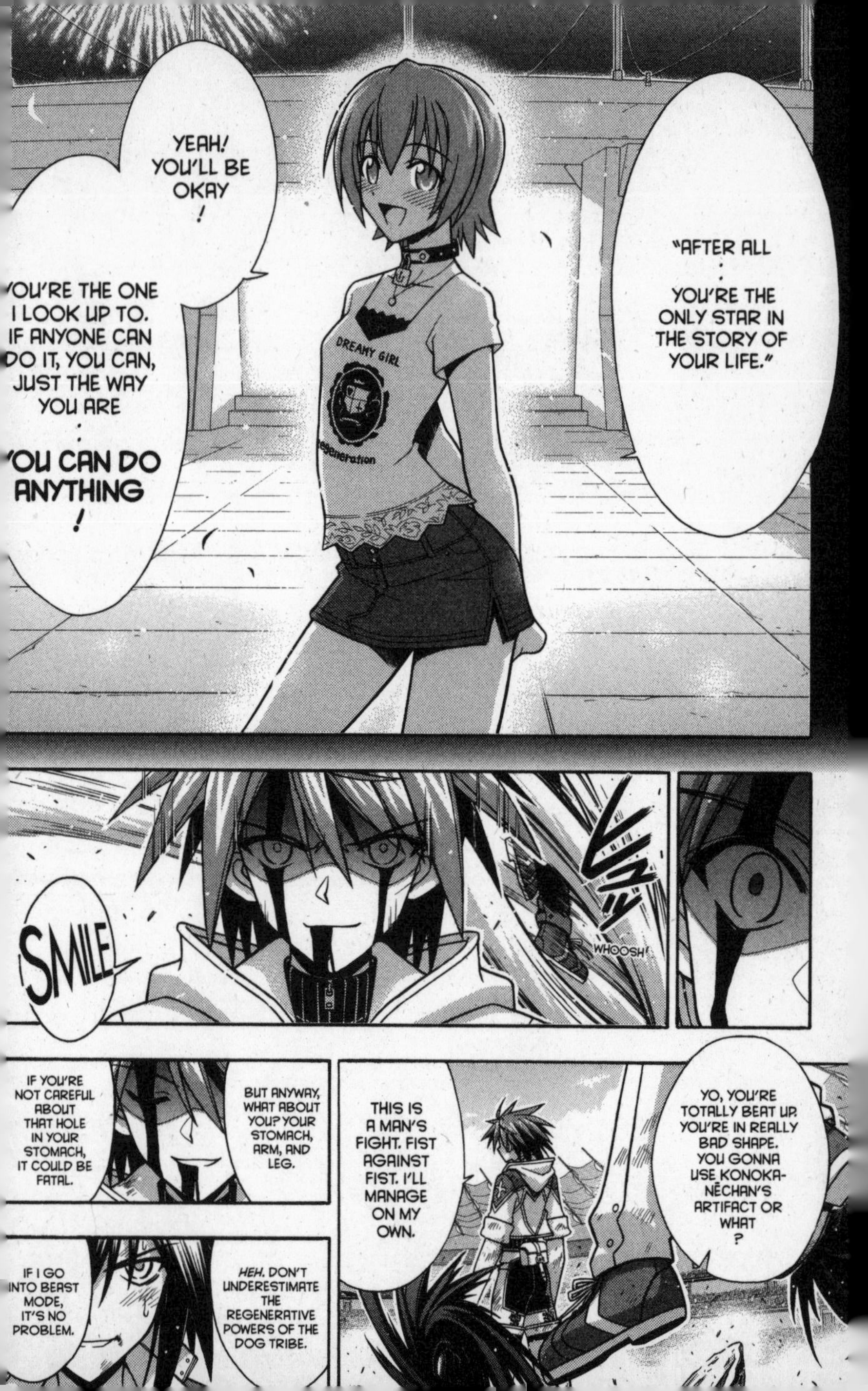
YEAH! YOU'LL BE OKAY!
YOU'RE THE ONE I LOOK UP TO. IF ANYONE CAN DO IT, YOU CAN, JUST THE WAY YOU ARE... YOU CAN DO ANYTHING!
"AFTER ALL... YOU'RE THE ONLY STAR IN THE STORY OF YOUR LIFE."
WHOOSH
SMILE
YO, YOU'RE TOTALLY BEAT UP. YOU'RE IN REALLY BAD SHAPE. YOU GONNA USE KONOKA-NÉCHAN'S ARTIFACT OR WHAT?
THIS IS A MAN'S FIGHT. FIST AGAINST FIST. I'LL MANAGE ON MY OWN.
BUT ANYWAY, WHAT ABOUT YOU? YOUR STOMACH, ARM, AND LEG.
IF YOU'RE NOT CAREFUL ABOUT THAT HOLE IN YOUR STOMACH, IT COULD BE FATAL.
HEH. DON'T UNDERESTIMATE THE REGENERATIVE POWERS OF THE DOG TRIBE.
IF I GO INTO BEAST MODE, IT'S NO PROBLEM.

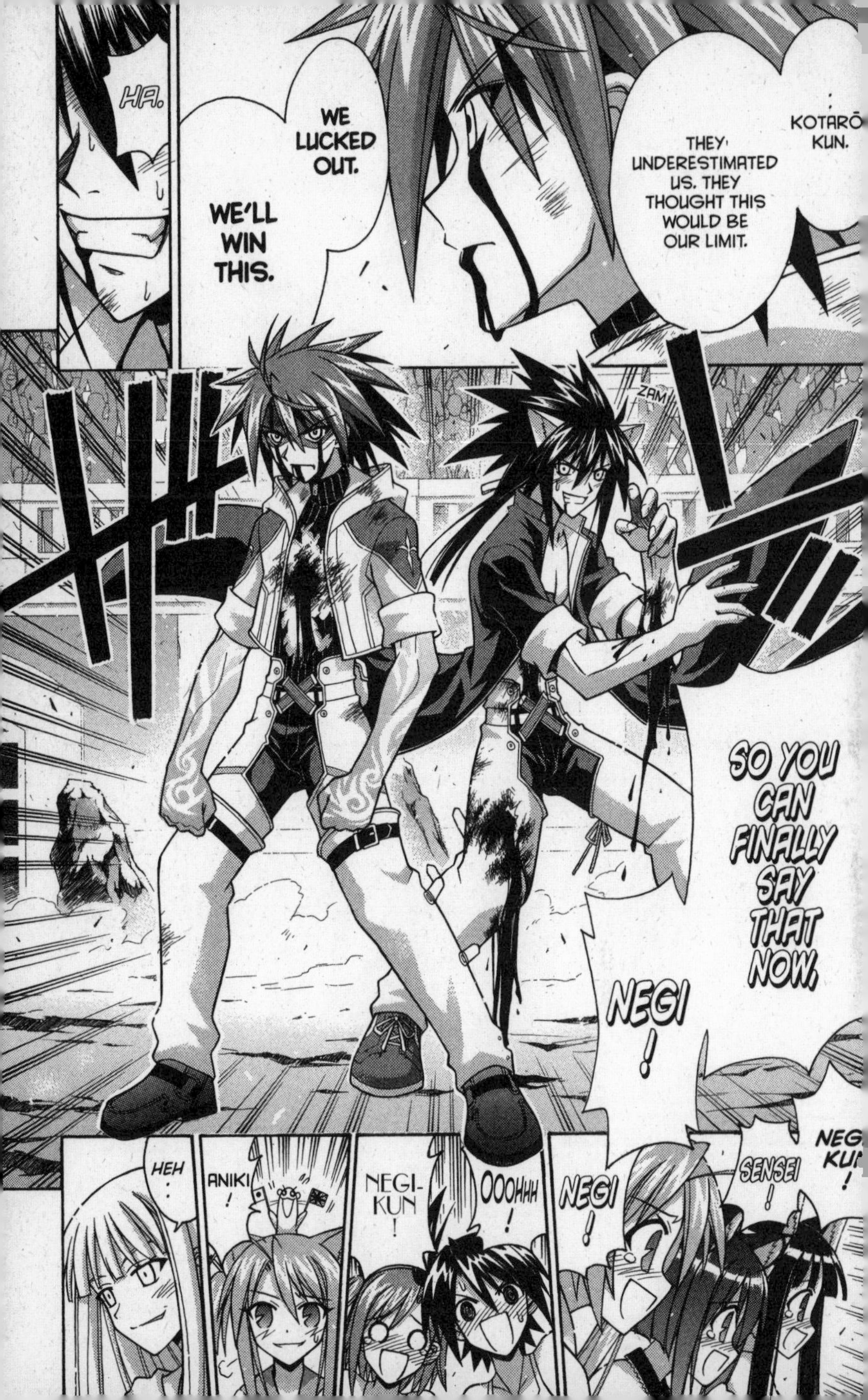
KOTARŌ KUN.
THEY UNDERESTIMATED US. THEY THOUGHT THIS WOULD BE OUR LIMIT.
WE LUCKED OUT.
WE'LL WIN THIS.
HA.
ZAM
SO YOU CAN FINALLY SAY THAT NOW.
NEGI!
NEGI KUN!
SENSEI!
NEGI!
OOOHHH!
NEGI-KUN!
ANIKI!
HEH…

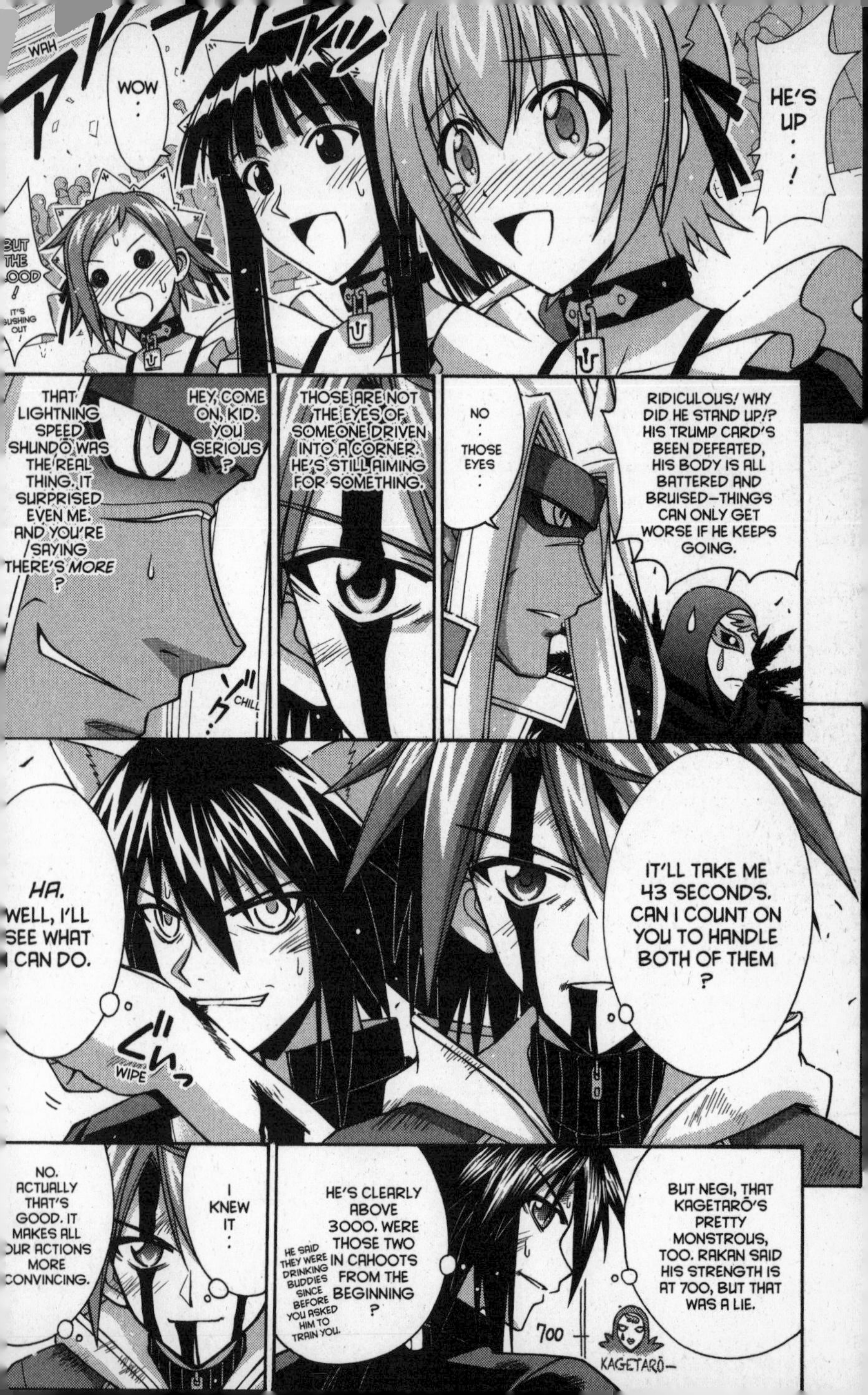
HE'S UP . . . !
WAH
WOW . . .
BUT THE OOD! IT'S GUSHING OUT!
RIDICULOUS! WHY DID HE STAND UP!? HIS TRUMP CARD'S BEEN DEFEATED, HIS BODY IS ALL BATTERED AND BRUISED—THINGS CAN ONLY GET WORSE IF HE KEEPS GOING.
NO . . . THOSE EYES . . .
THOSE ARE NOT THE EYES OF SOMEONE DRIVEN INTO A CORNER. HE'S STILL AIMING FOR SOMETHING.
HEY, COME ON, KID. YOU SERIOUS?
THAT LIGHTNING SPEED SHUNDŌ WAS THE REAL THING. IT SURPRISED EVEN ME. AND YOU'RE SAYING THERE'S *MORE*?
CHILL
IT'LL TAKE ME 43 SECONDS. CAN I COUNT ON YOU TO HANDLE BOTH OF THEM?
HA. WELL, I'LL SEE WHAT CAN DO.
WIPE
BUT NEGI, THAT KAGETARŌ'S PRETTY MONSTROUS, TOO. RAKAN SAID HIS STRENGTH IS AT 700, BUT THAT WAS A LIE.
700 — KAGETARŌ—
HE'S CLEARLY ABOVE 3000. WERE THOSE TWO IN CAHOOTS FROM THE BEGINNING?
HE SAID THEY WERE DRINKING BUDDIES SINCE BEFORE YOU ASKED HIM TO TRAIN YOU.
I KNEW IT . . .
NO. ACTUALLY THAT'S GOOD. IT MAKES ALL UR ACTIONS MORE CONVINCING.

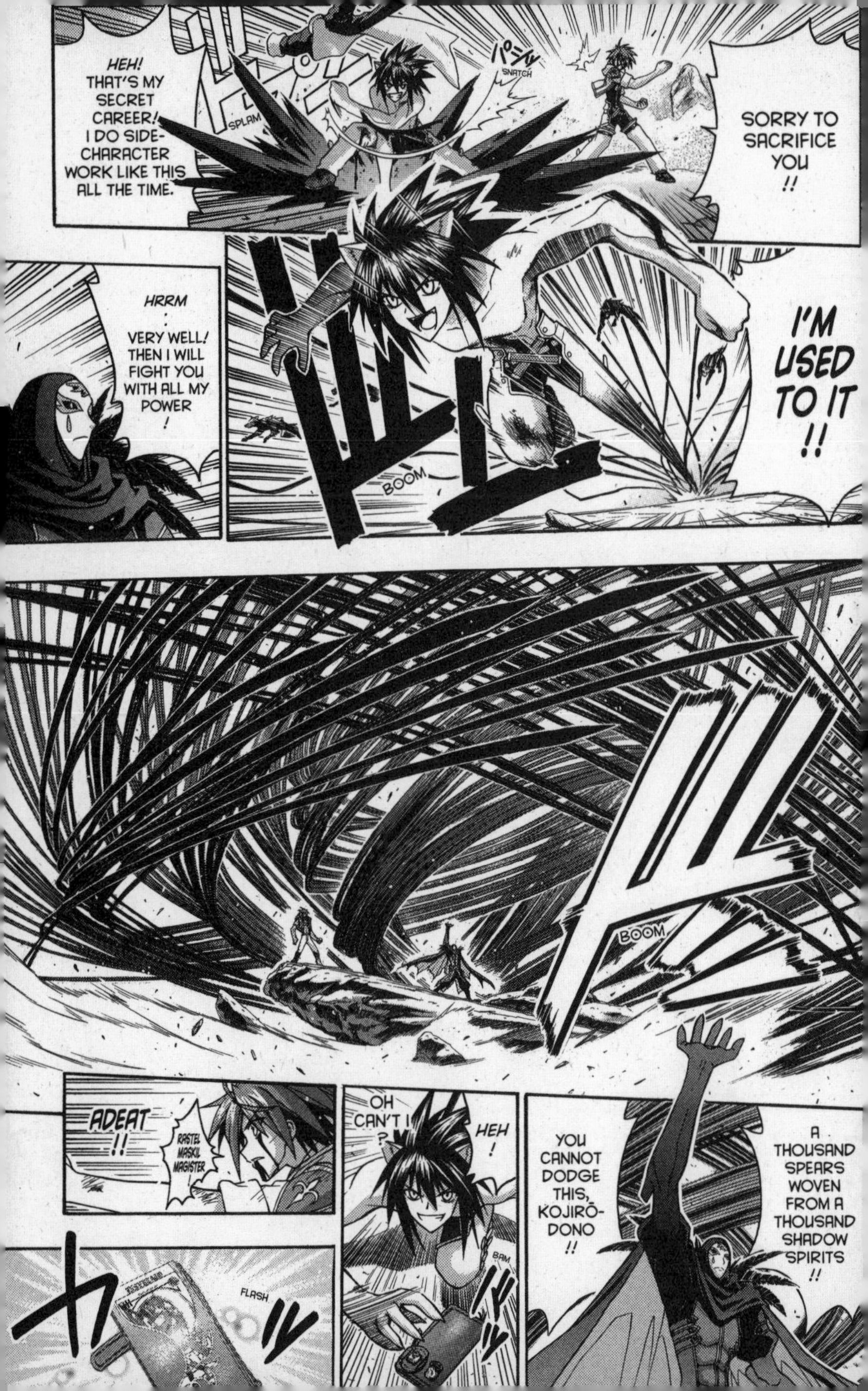
SORRY TO SACRIFICE YOU!!
SNATCH
HEH! THAT'S MY SECRET CAREER! I DO SIDE-CHARACTER WORK LIKE THIS ALL THE TIME.
SPLAM
I'M USED TO IT!!
BOOM
HRRM
:
VERY WELL! THEN I WILL FIGHT YOU WITH ALL MY POWER!
BOOM
A THOUSAND SPEARS WOVEN FROM A THOUSAND SHADOW SPIRITS!!
YOU CANNOT DODGE THIS, KOJIRŌ-DONO!!
HEH!
OH CAN'T I?
BAM
ADEAT!!
RASTEL MASKIL MAGISTER!
FLASH

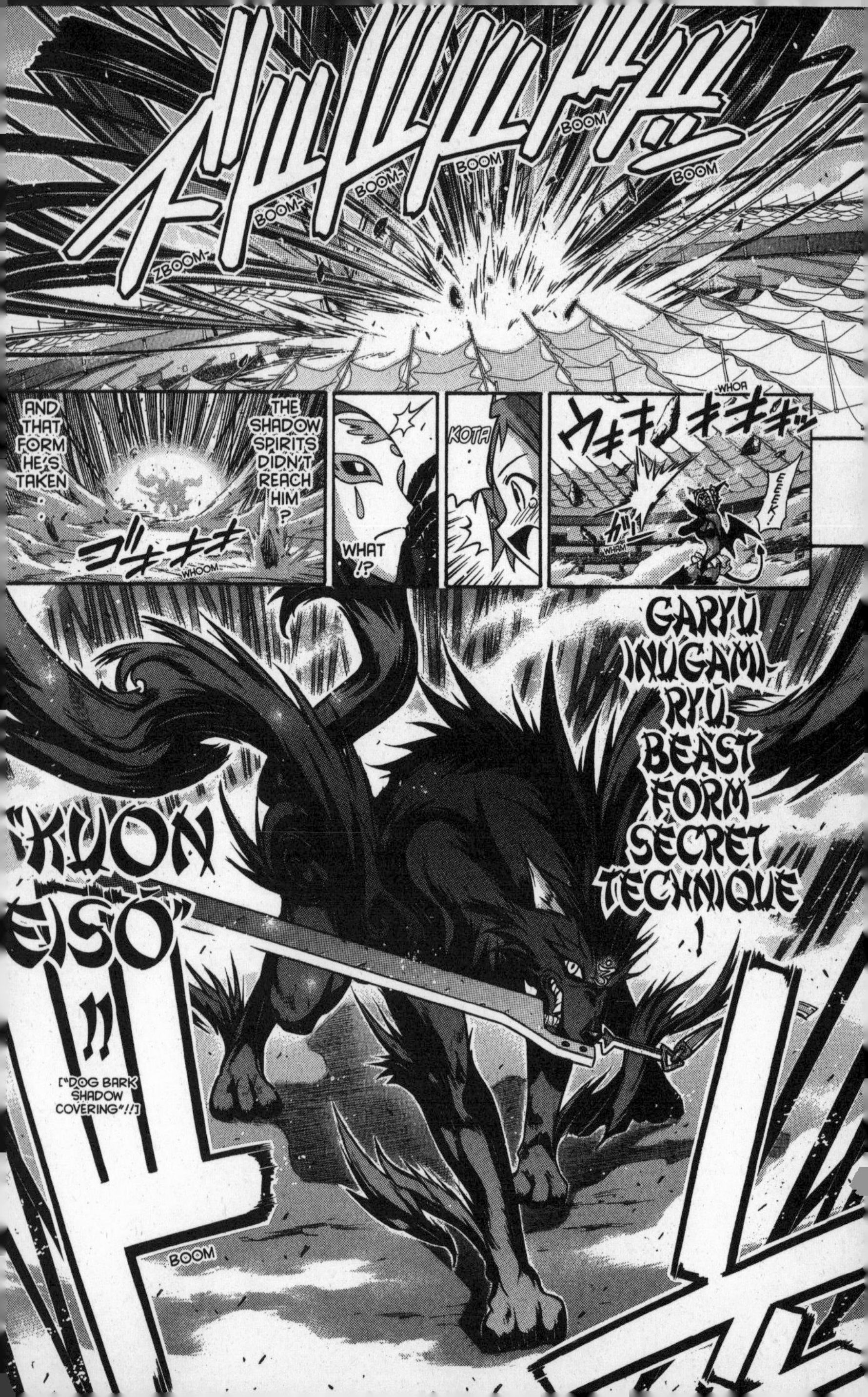

ZBOOM-
BOOM-
BOOM-
BOOM
BOOM
BOOM
WHOA
ウォオノオオオッ
EEEK!
ガッ
WHAM
KOTA
...
WHAT!?
THE SHADOW SPIRITS DIDN'T REACH HIM?
AND THAT FORM HE'S TAKEN
ゴオオオ
WHOOM
GARYŪ INUGAMI RYŪ BEAST FORM SECRET TECHNIQUE
"KUON EISŌ"!!
["DOG BARK SHADOW COVERING"!!]
BOOM

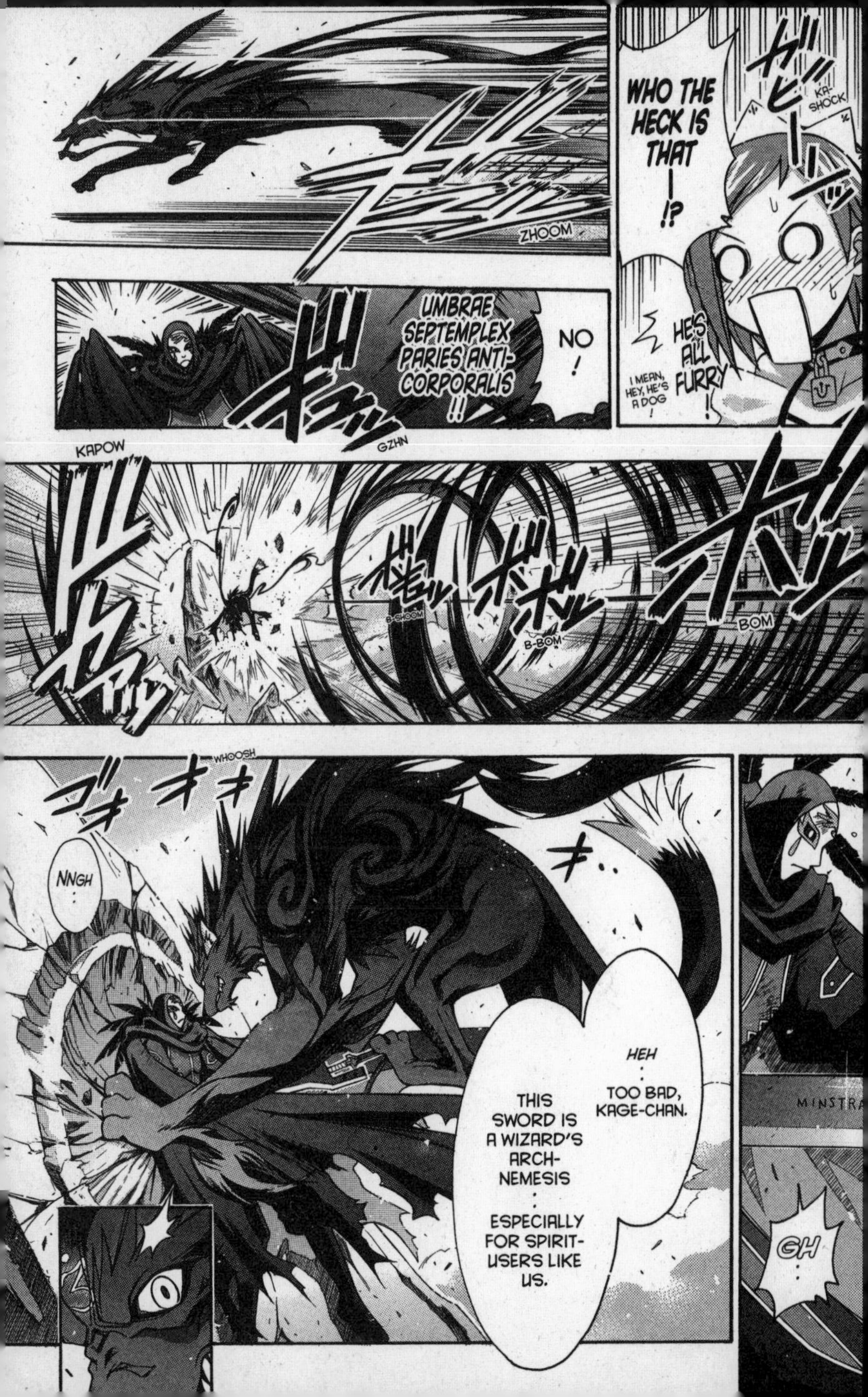
KA-SHOCK
WHO THE HECK IS THAT—!?
HE'S ALL FURRY!
I MEAN, HEY, HE'S A DOG
ZHOOM
NO!
UMBRAE SEPTEMPLEX PARIES ANTI-CORPORALIS!!
GZHN
BOM
B-BOM
B-SHOOM
KAPOW
GH...
WHOOSH
NNGH...
HEH... TOO BAD, KAGE-CHAN.
THIS SWORD IS A WIZARD'S ARCH-NEMESIS... ESPECIALLY FOR SPIRIT-USERS LIKE US.

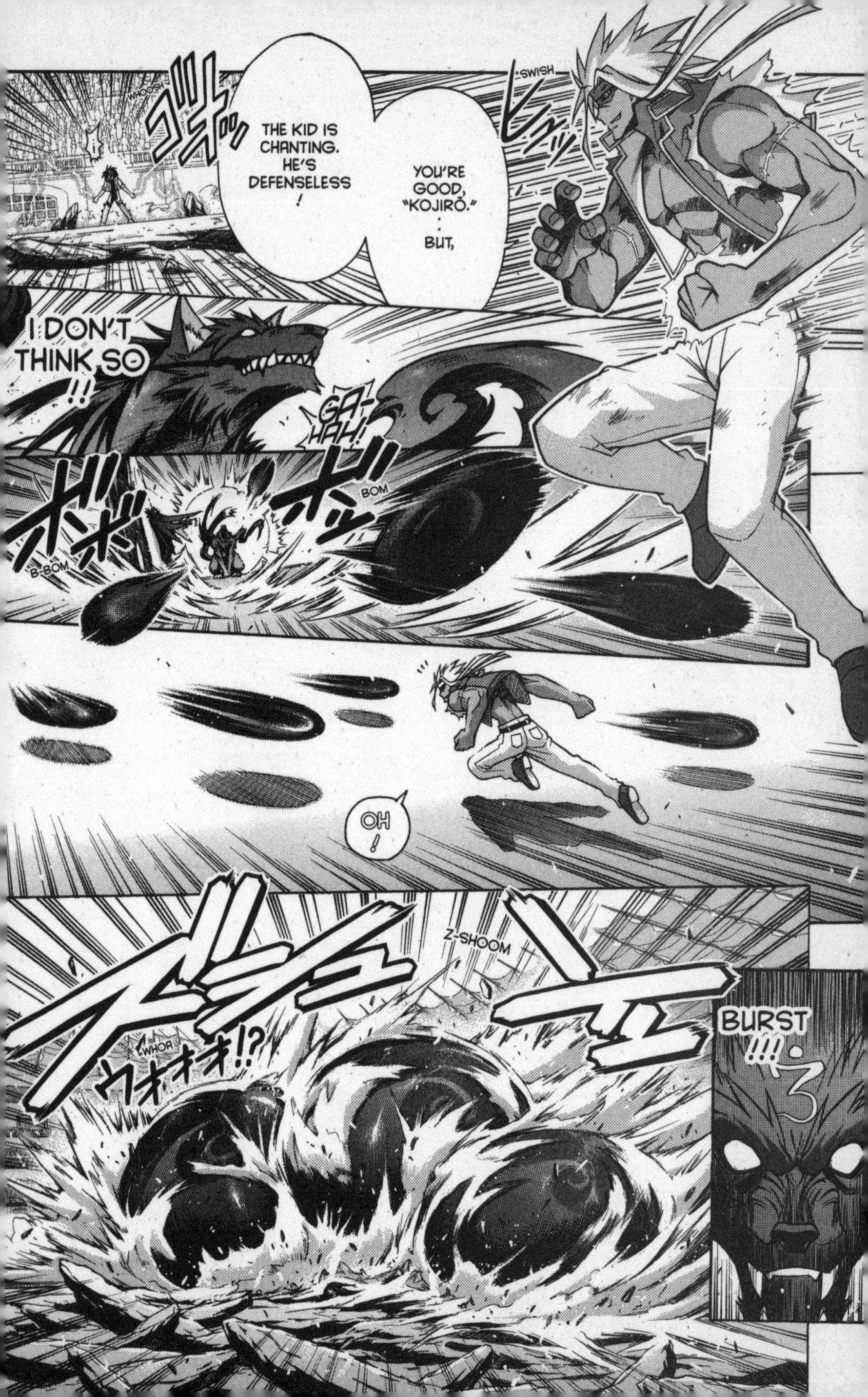
SWISH
YOU'RE GOOD, "KOJIRŌ." BUT,
THE KID IS CHANTING. HE'S DEFENSELESS!
WHOOSH
I DON'T THINK SO!!
GA-HAH!
BOM
B-BOM
OH!
BURST!!!
Z-SHOOM
WHOA

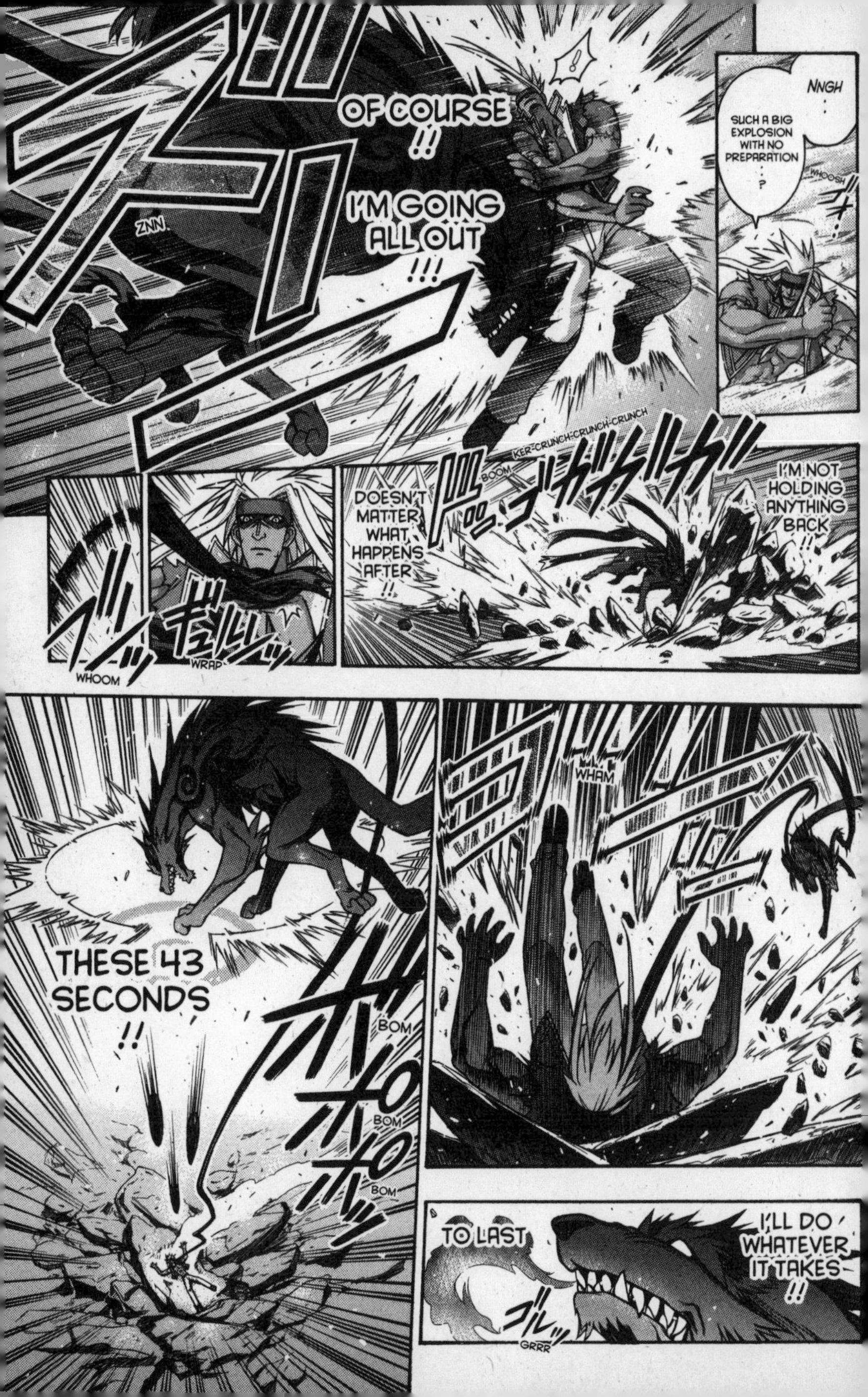
NNGH
SUCH A BIG EXPLOSION WITH NO PREPARATION . . . ?
WHOOSH
!
OF COURSE!!
I'M GOING ALL OUT!!!
ZNN
KER-CRUNCH-CRUNCH-CRUNCH
BOOM
I'M NOT HOLDING ANYTHING BACK!!
DOESN'T MATTER WHAT HAPPENS AFTER!!
WRAP
WHOOM
WHAM
I'LL DO WHATEVER IT TAKES!!
TO LAST
GRRR
THESE 43 SECONDS!!
BOM
BOM
BOM

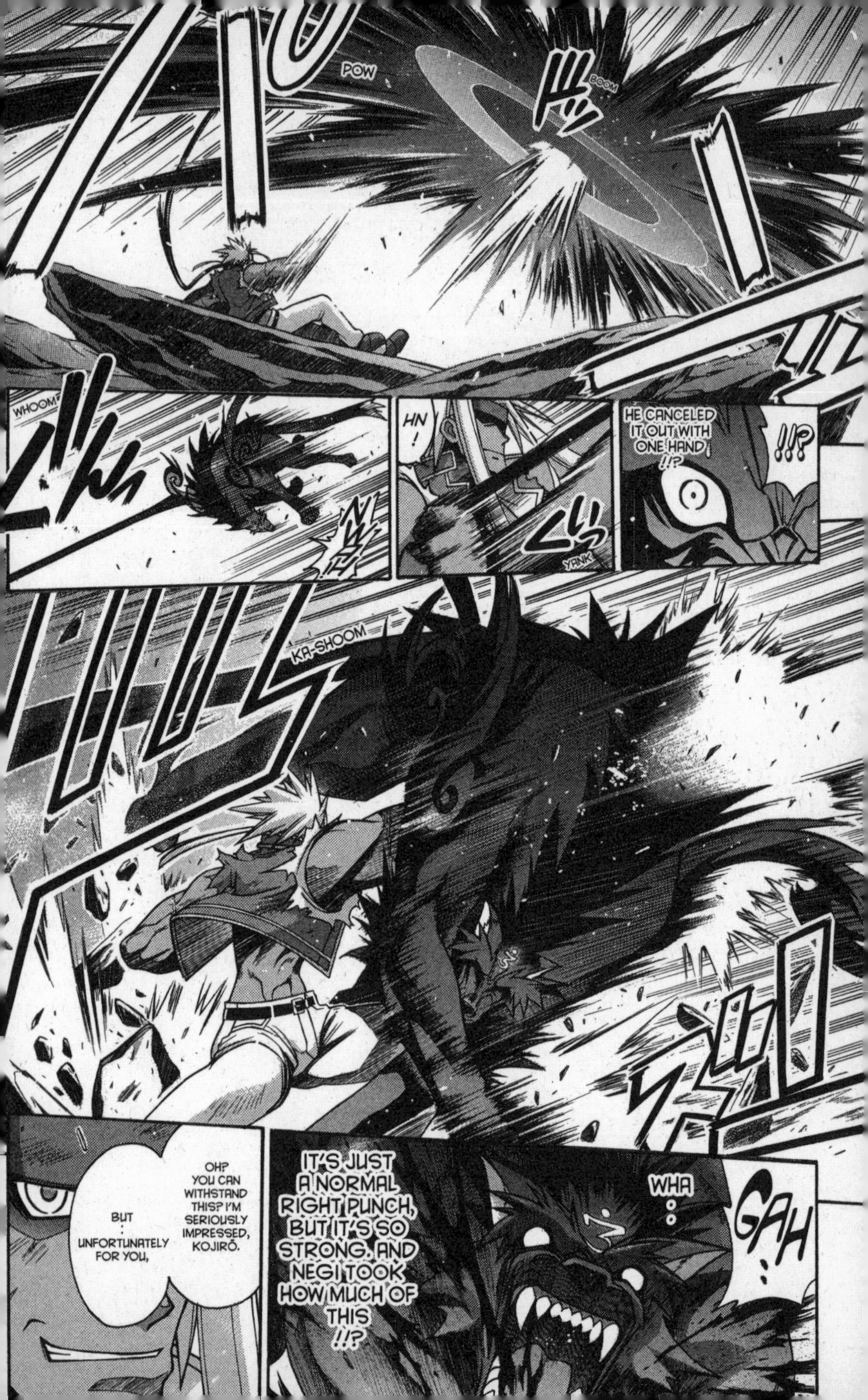
BOOM
POW
HE CANCELED IT OUT WITH ONE HAND !!?
!!?
HN !
YANK
WHOOM
KA-SHOOM
WHA...
GAH
IT'S JUST A NORMAL RIGHT PUNCH, BUT IT'S SO STRONG. AND NEGI TOOK HOW MUCH OF THIS !!?
OH? YOU CAN WITHSTAND THIS? I'M SERIOUSLY IMPRESSED, KOJIRŌ.
BUT... UNFORTUNATELY FOR YOU,

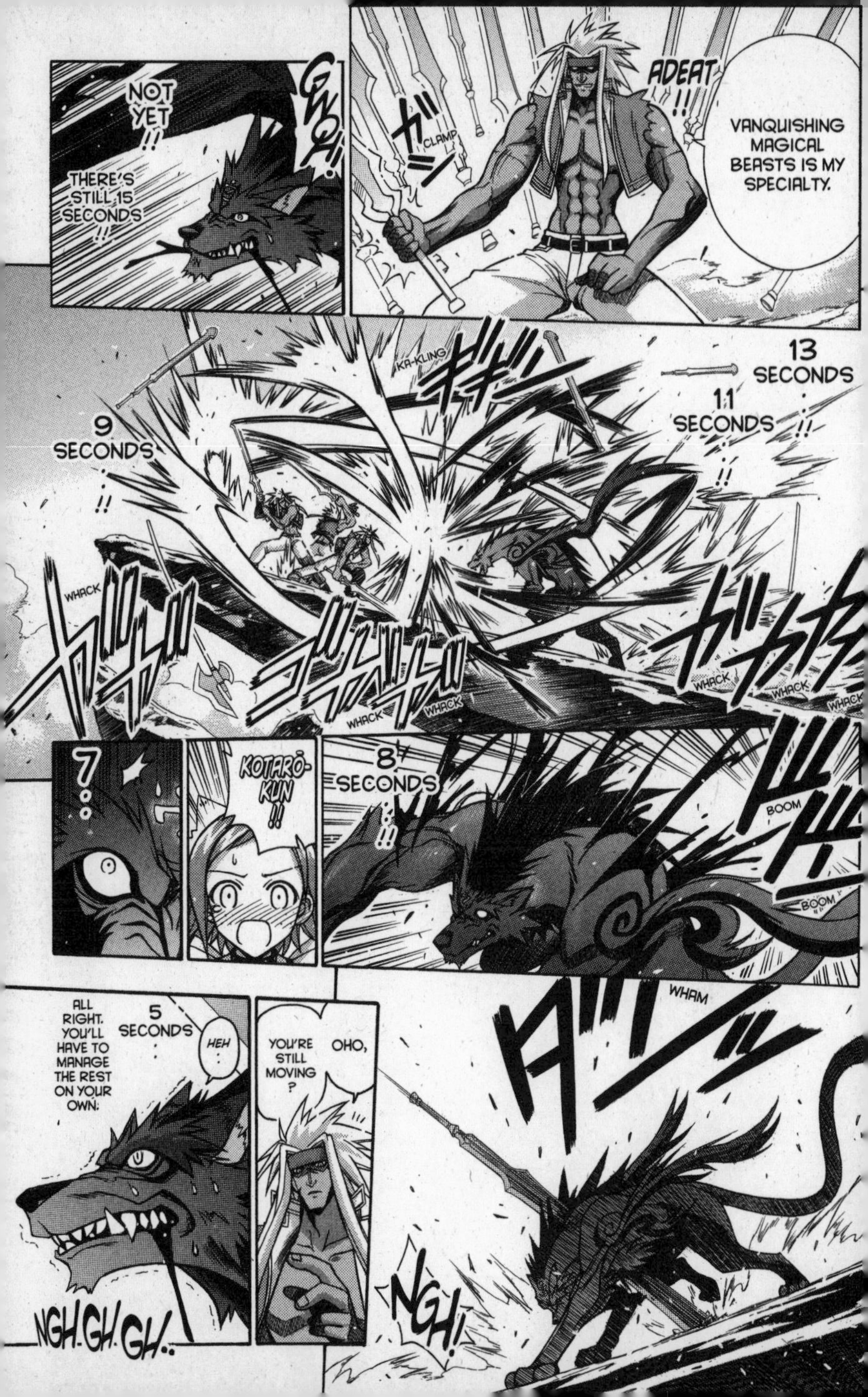
ADEAT!!
CLAMP
VANQUISHING MAGICAL BEASTS IS MY SPECIALTY.
GWOH!
NOT YET!!
THERE'S STILL 15 SECONDS!!
KA-KLING
13 SECONDS
11 SECONDS!!
9 SECONDS!!
WHACK
WHACK
WHACK
WHACK
WHACK
WHACK
BOOM
BOOM
8 SECONDS!!
KOTARÔ-KUN!!
7...
WHAM
NGH!
OHO,
YOU'RE STILL MOVING?
HEH
5 SECONDS
ALL RIGHT. YOU'LL HAVE TO MANAGE THE REST ON YOUR OWN.
NGH..GH..GH..

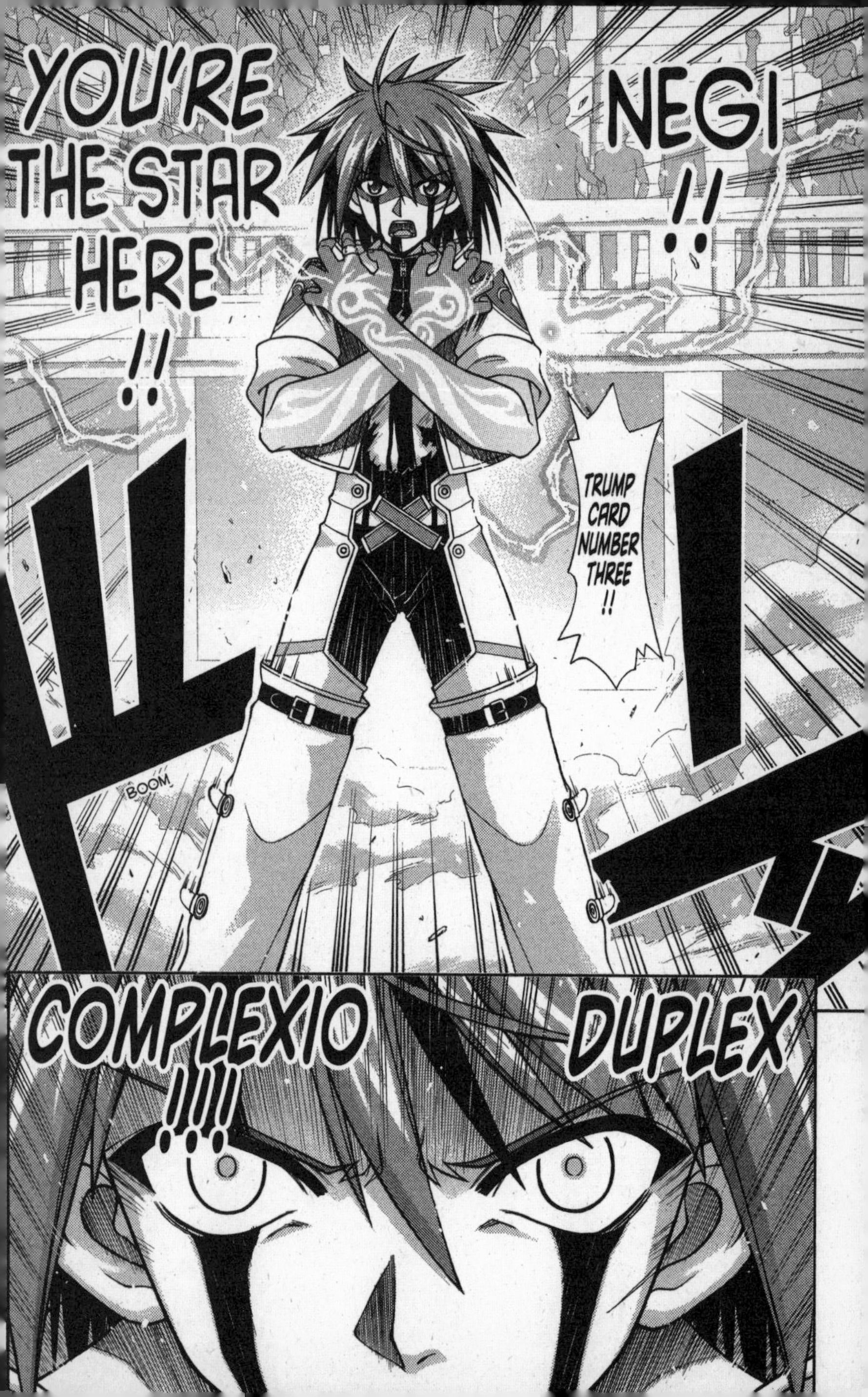
NEGI!!
YOU'RE THE STAR HERE!!
TRUMP CARD NUMBER THREE!!
BOOM
COMPLEXIO DUPLEX!!!!

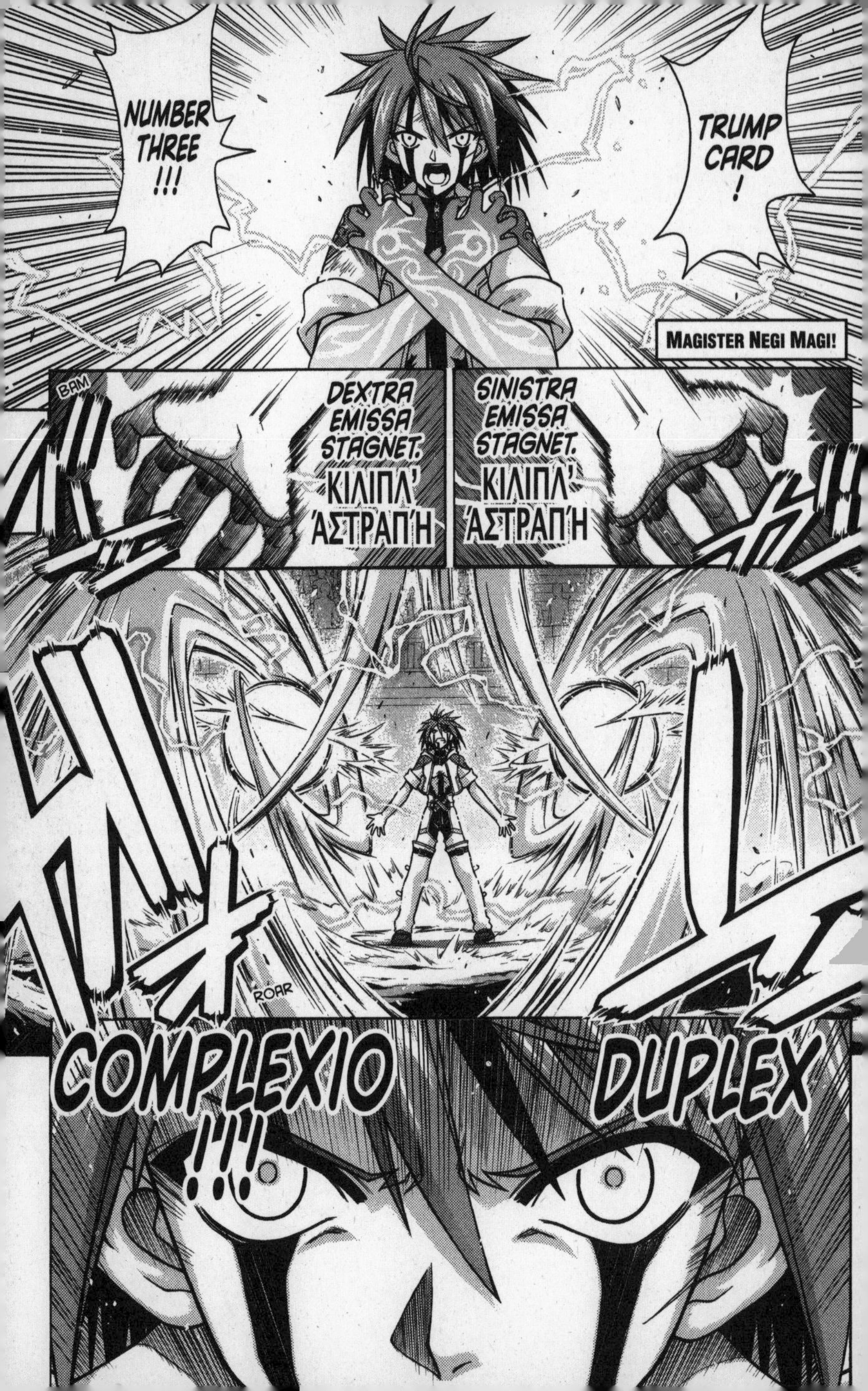
TRUMP CARD !
NUMBER THREE !!!
MAGISTER NEGI MAGI!
SINISTRA EMISSA STAGNET. ΚΙΛΙΠΛ' ΆΣΤΡΑΠ'Η
DEXTRA EMISSA STAGNET. ΚΙΛΙΠΛ' ΆΣΤΡΑΠ'Η
BAM
ROAR
COMPLEXIO DUPLEX !!!!

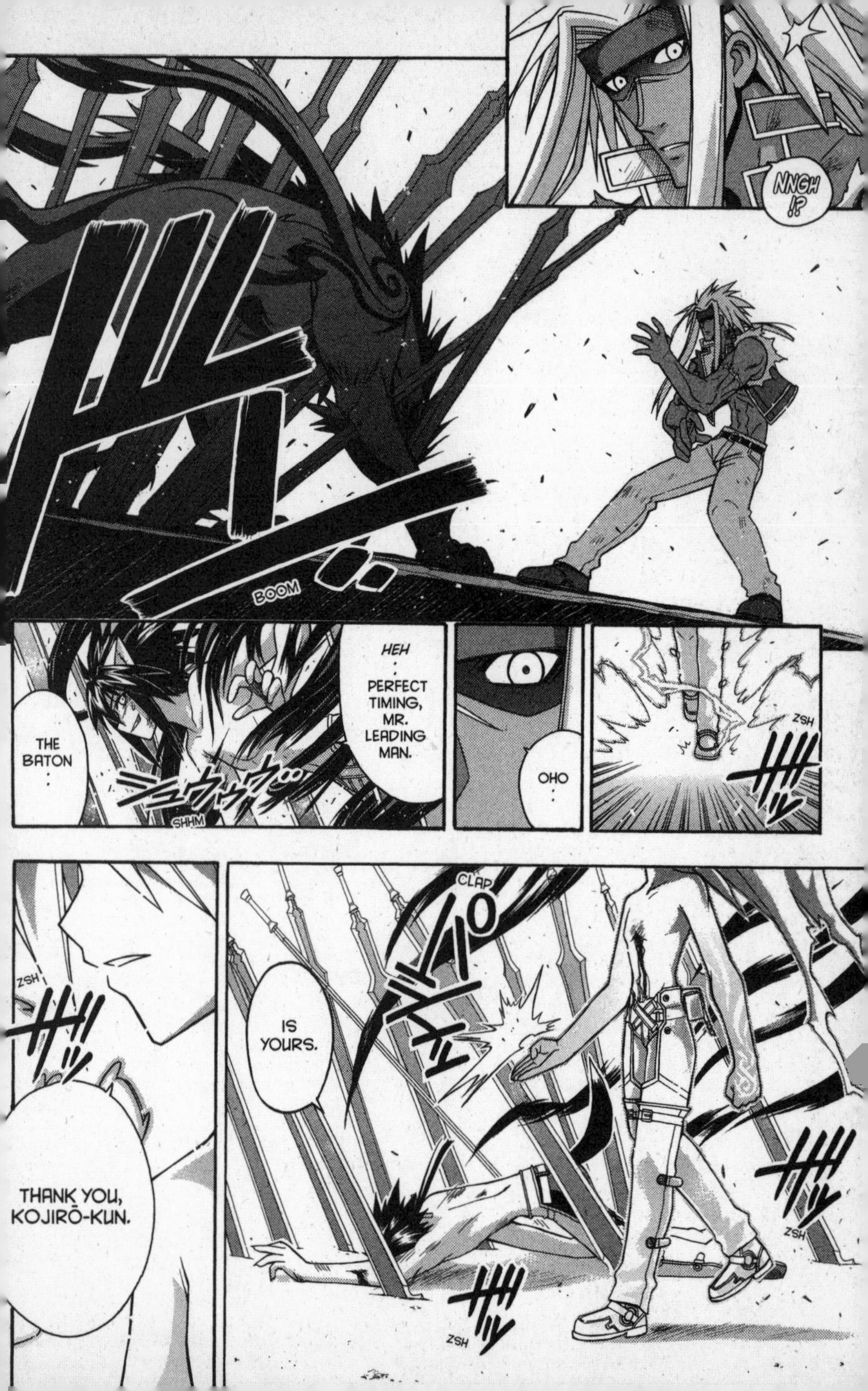
NNGH !?
BOOM
ZSH
OHO . . .
HEH . . . PERFECT TIMING, MR. LEADING MAN.
THE BATON . . .
SHHM
CLAP
IS YOURS.
ZSH
ZSH
ZSH
THANK YOU, KOJIRŌ-KUN.

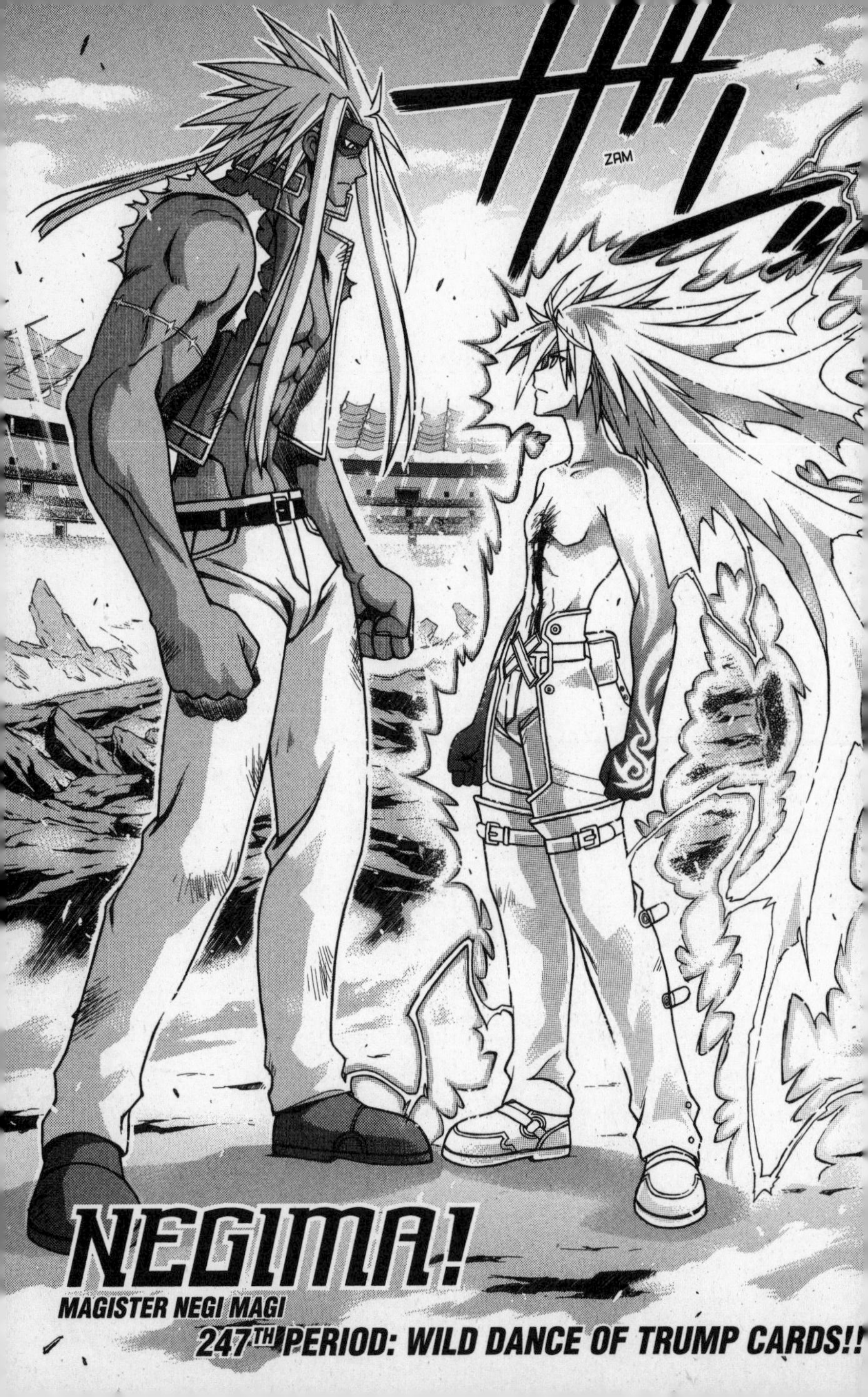
ZAM
NEGIMA!
MAGISTER NEGI MAGI
247TH PERIOD: WILD DANCE OF TRUMP CARDS!!

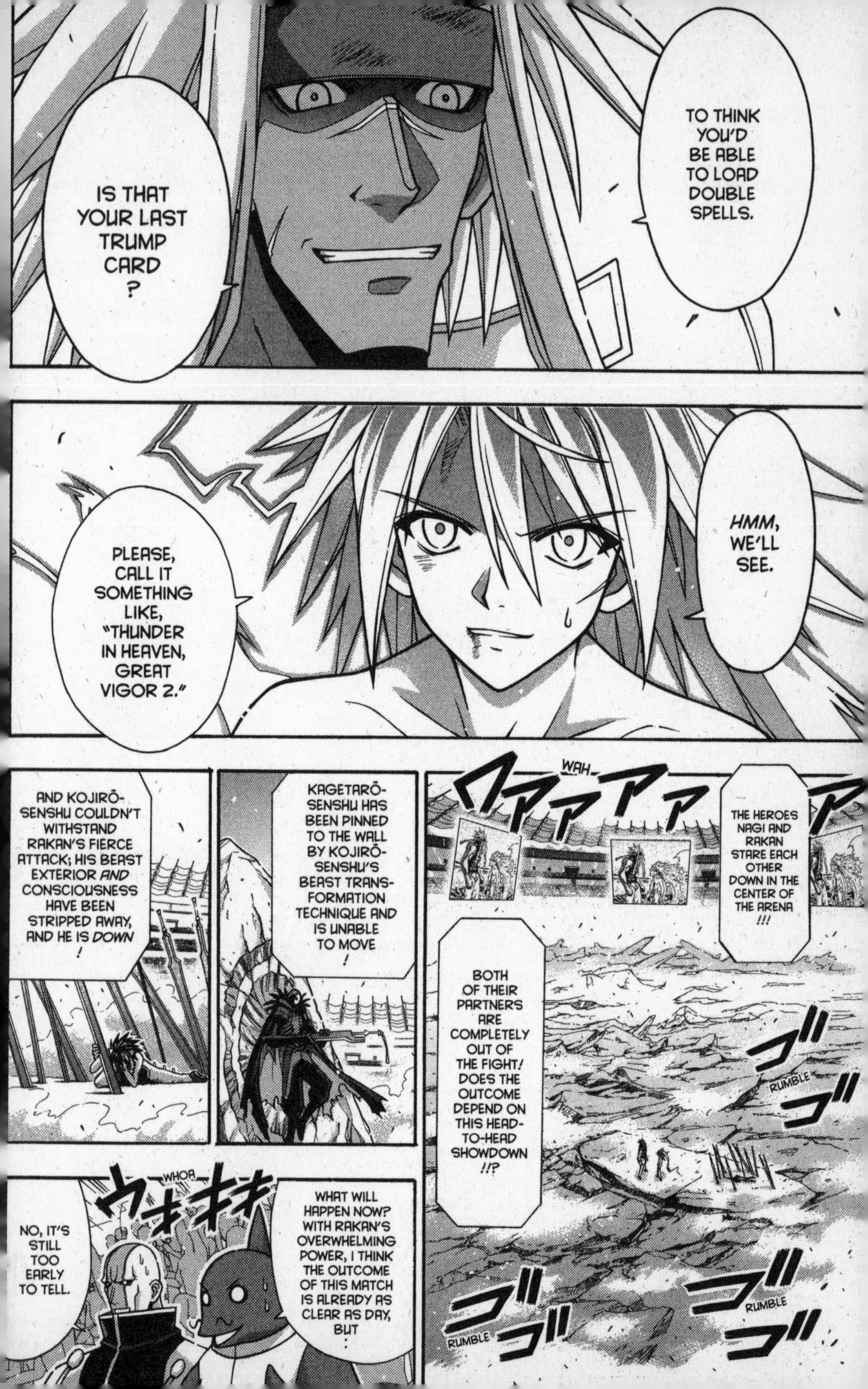

TO THINK YOU'D BE ABLE TO LOAD DOUBLE SPELLS.
IS THAT YOUR LAST TRUMP CARD?
HMM, WE'LL SEE.
PLEASE, CALL IT SOMETHING LIKE, "THUNDER IN HEAVEN, GREAT VIGOR 2."
WAH
THE HEROES NAGI AND RAKAN STARE EACH OTHER DOWN IN THE CENTER OF THE ARENA!!!
BOTH OF THEIR PARTNERS ARE COMPLETELY OUT OF THE FIGHT! DOES THE OUTCOME DEPEND ON THIS HEAD-TO-HEAD SHOWDOWN!!?
RUMBLE
RUMBLE
RUMBLE
KAGETARŌ-SENSHU HAS BEEN PINNED TO THE WALL BY KOJIRŌ-SENSHU'S BEAST TRANSFORMATION TECHNIQUE AND IS UNABLE TO MOVE!
AND KOJIRŌ-SENSHU COULDN'T WITHSTAND RAKAN'S FIERCE ATTACK; HIS BEAST EXTERIOR *AND* CONSCIOUSNESS HAVE BEEN STRIPPED AWAY, AND HE IS *DOWN*!
WHOA
WHAT WILL HAPPEN NOW? WITH RAKAN'S OVERWHELMING POWER, I THINK THE OUTCOME OF THIS MATCH IS ALREADY AS CLEAR AS DAY, BUT!
NO, IT'S STILL TOO EARLY TO TELL.

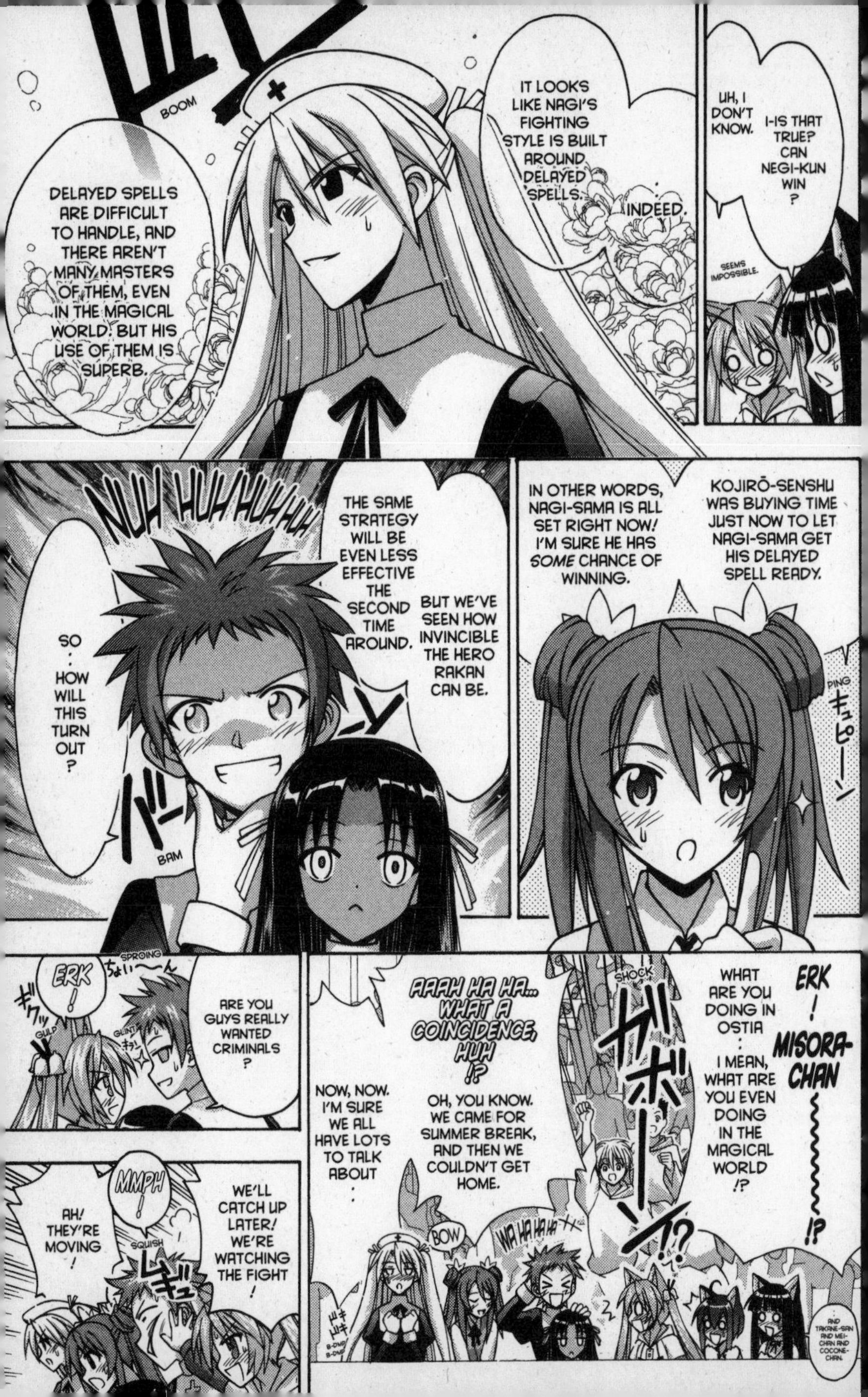
I-IS THAT TRUE? CAN NEGI-KUN WIN?
UH, I DON'T KNOW.
SEEMS IMPOSSIBLE.
BOOM
IT LOOKS LIKE NAGI'S FIGHTING STYLE IS BUILT AROUND DELAYED SPELLS.
INDEED.
DELAYED SPELLS ARE DIFFICULT TO HANDLE, AND THERE AREN'T MANY MASTERS OF THEM, EVEN IN THE MAGICAL WORLD. BUT HIS USE OF THEM IS SUPERB.
KOJIRŌ-SENSHU WAS BUYING TIME JUST NOW TO LET NAGI-SAMA GET HIS DELAYED SPELL READY.
IN OTHER WORDS, NAGI-SAMA IS ALL SET RIGHT NOW! I'M SURE HE HAS *SOME* CHANCE OF WINNING.
PING
THE SAME STRATEGY WILL BE EVEN LESS EFFECTIVE THE SECOND TIME AROUND.
BUT WE'VE SEEN HOW INVINCIBLE THE HERO RAKAN CAN BE.
NUH HUHHUHHUH
SO... HOW WILL THIS TURN OUT?
BAM
ERK! MISORA-CHAN~!?
WHAT ARE YOU DOING IN OSTIA... I MEAN, WHAT ARE YOU EVEN DOING IN THE MAGICAL WORLD!?
SHOCK
AAAH HA HA... WHAT A COINCIDENCE, HUH!?
OH, YOU KNOW. WE CAME FOR SUMMER BREAK, AND THEN WE COULDN'T GET HOME.
NOW, NOW. I'M SURE WE ALL HAVE LOTS TO TALK ABOUT...
BOW
WA HA HA HA
B-DMP B-DMP
AND TAKANE-SAN AND MEI-CHAN AND COCONE-CHAN.
ARE YOU GUYS REALLY WANTED CRIMINALS?
SPROING
GLINT
ERK!
GULP
WE'LL CATCH UP LATER! WE'RE WATCHING THE FIGHT!
MMPH!
SQUISH
AH! THEY'RE MOVING!

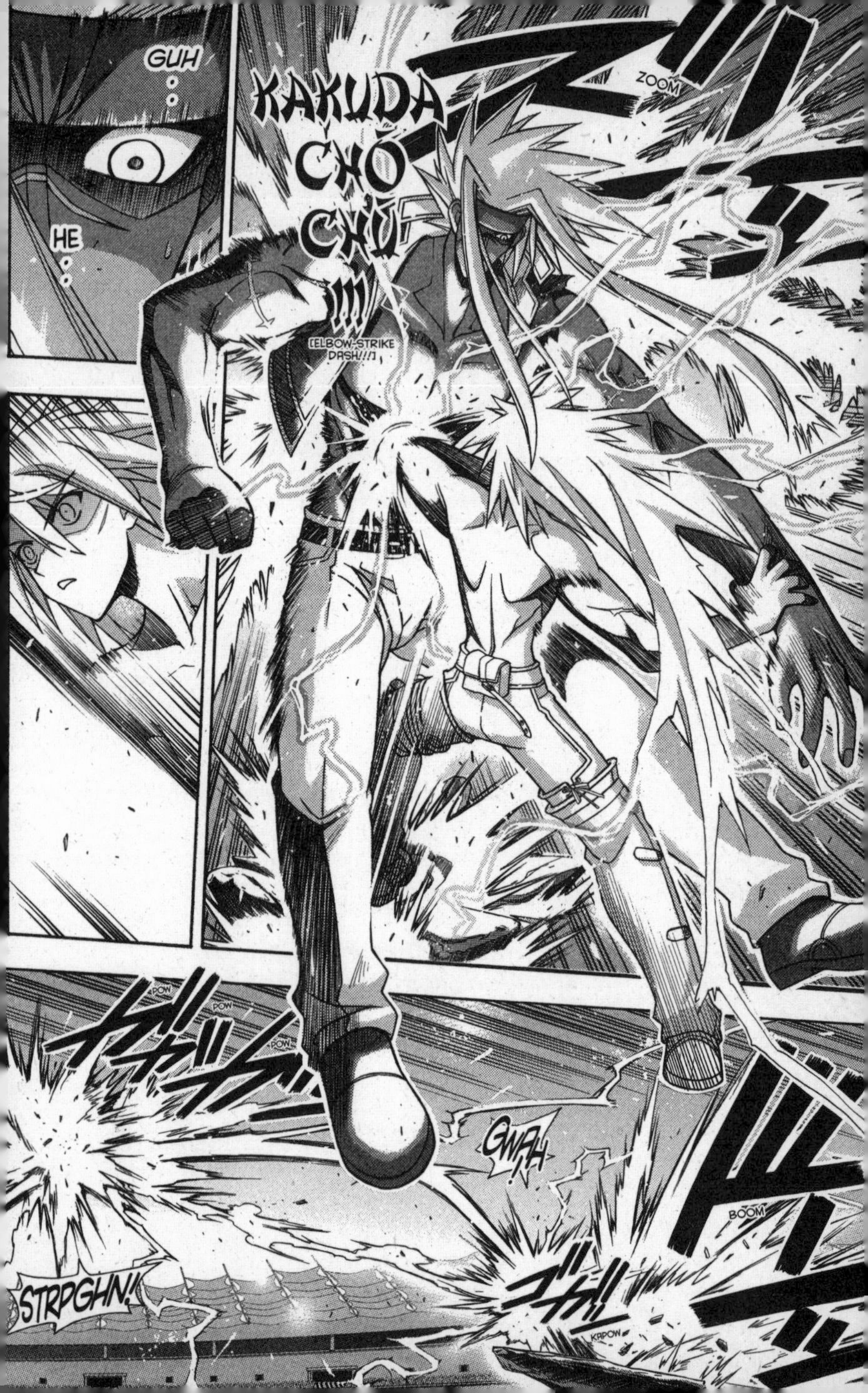
ZOOM
KAKUDA CHŌ CHŪ!!!
[ELBOW-STRIKE DASH!!!]
GUH...
HE...
BOOM
GWAH!
POW
POW
POW
KAPOW
STRPGHN!

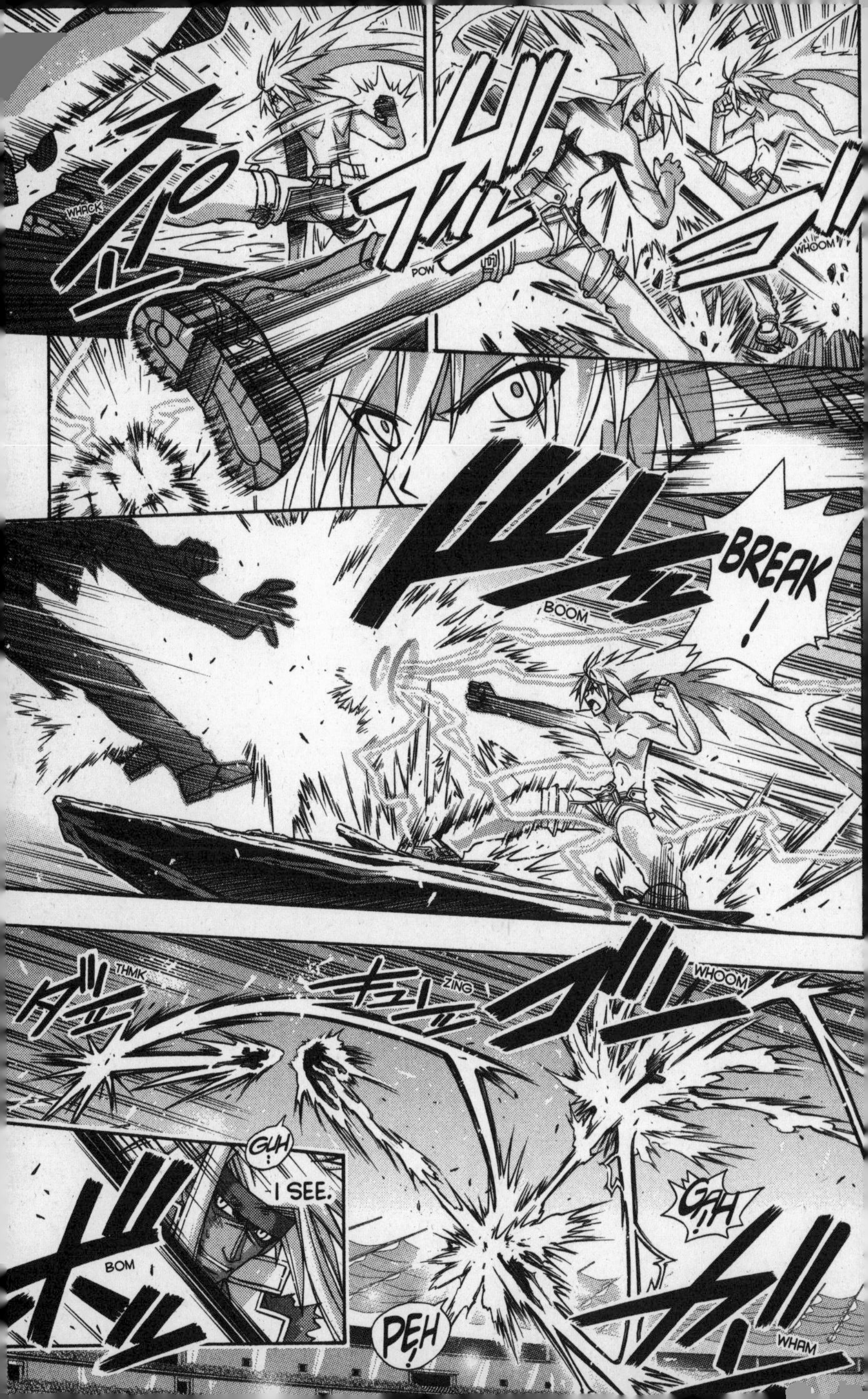
WHOOM
POW
WHACK
BREAK!
BOOM
WHOOM
ZING
THMK
GAH!
PEH!
WHAM
GUH!
I SEE.
BOM

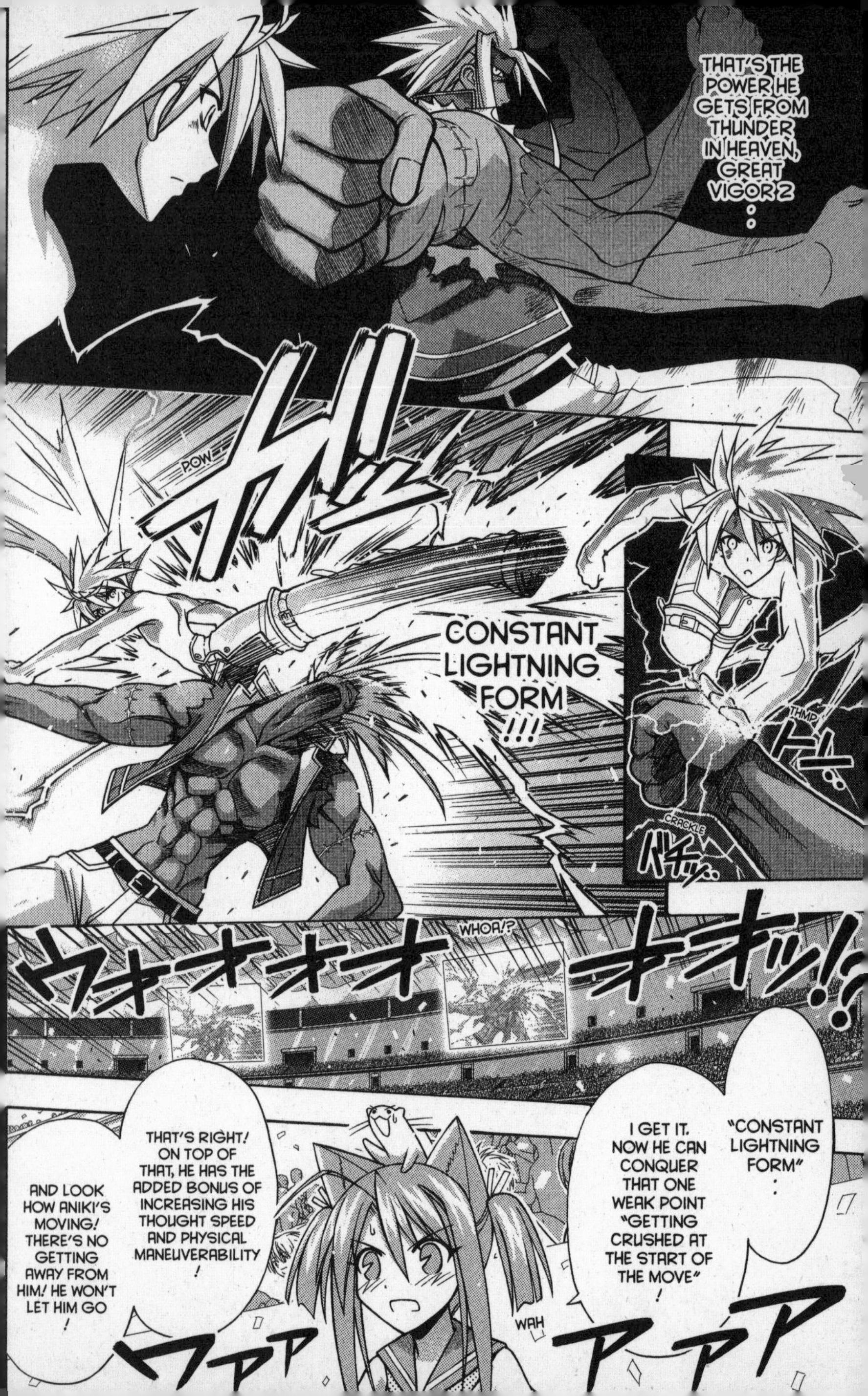

THAT'S THE POWER HE GETS FROM THUNDER IN HEAVEN, GREAT VIGOR 2 ..
THMP
CRACKLE
POW
CONSTANT LIGHTNING FORM !!!
WHOA!?
"CONSTANT LIGHTNING FORM" ..
I GET IT. NOW HE CAN CONQUER THAT ONE WEAK POINT "GETTING CRUSHED AT THE START OF THE MOVE" !
THAT'S RIGHT! ON TOP OF THAT, HE HAS THE ADDED BONUS OF INCREASING HIS THOUGHT SPEED AND PHYSICAL MANEUVERABILITY !
AND LOOK HOW ANIKI'S MOVING! THERE'S NO GETTING AWAY FROM HIM! HE WON'T LET HIM GO !
WAH

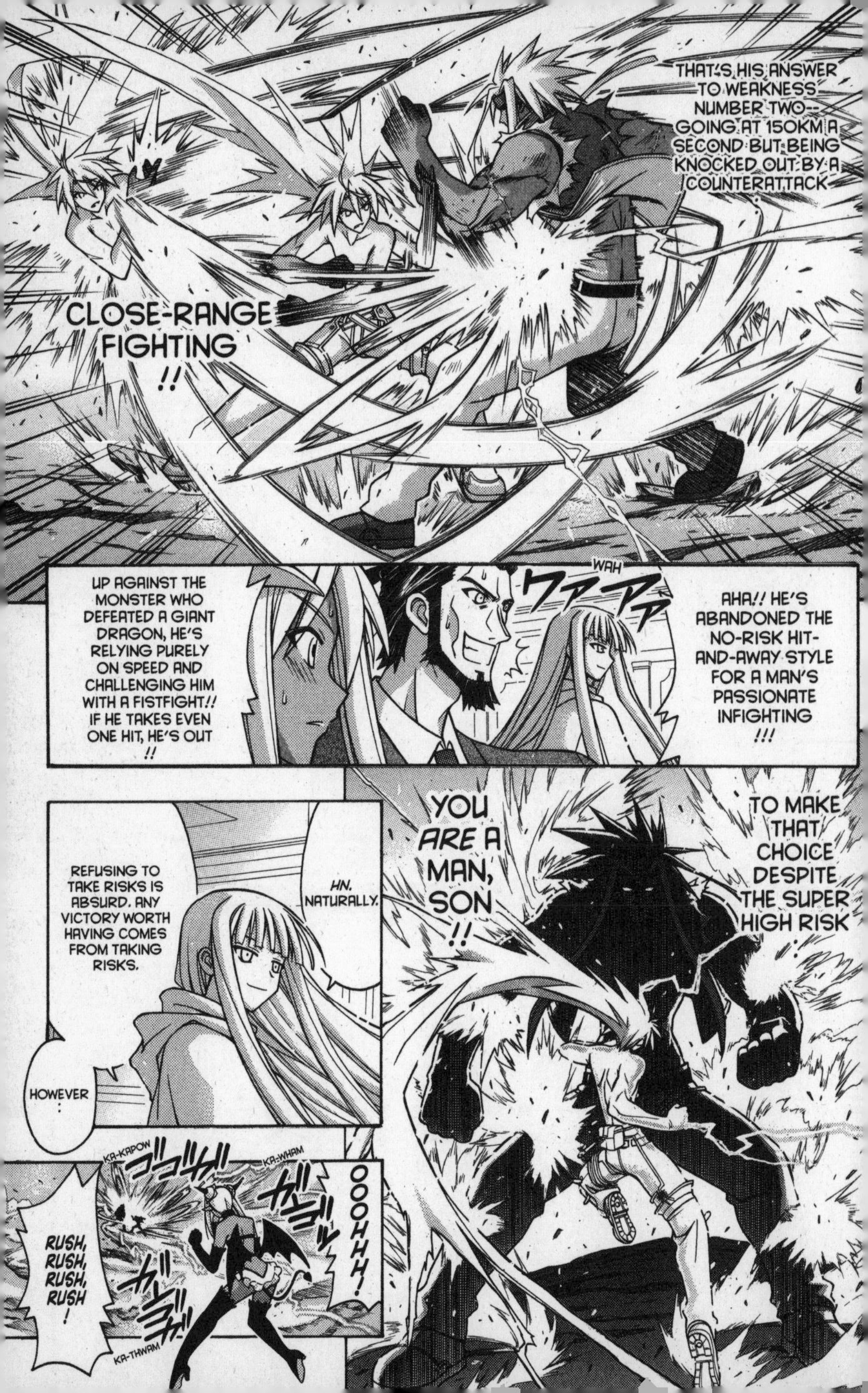
THAT'S HIS ANSWER TO WEAKNESS NUMBER TWO-- GOING AT 150KM A SECOND BUT BEING KNOCKED OUT BY A COUNTERATTACK
CLOSE-RANGE FIGHTING !!
WAH
AHA!! HE'S ABANDONED THE NO-RISK HIT-AND-AWAY STYLE FOR A MAN'S PASSIONATE INFIGHTING !!!
UP AGAINST THE MONSTER WHO DEFEATED A GIANT DRAGON, HE'S RELYING PURELY ON SPEED AND CHALLENGING HIM WITH A FISTFIGHT!! IF HE TAKES EVEN ONE HIT, HE'S OUT !!
TO MAKE THAT CHOICE DESPITE THE SUPER HIGH RISK
YOU *ARE* A MAN, SON !!
HN. NATURALLY.
REFUSING TO TAKE RISKS IS ABSURD. ANY VICTORY WORTH HAVING COMES FROM TAKING RISKS.
HOWEVER
OOOHHH!
KA-WHAM
KA-KAPOW
RUSH, RUSH, RUSH, RUSH !
KA-THWAM

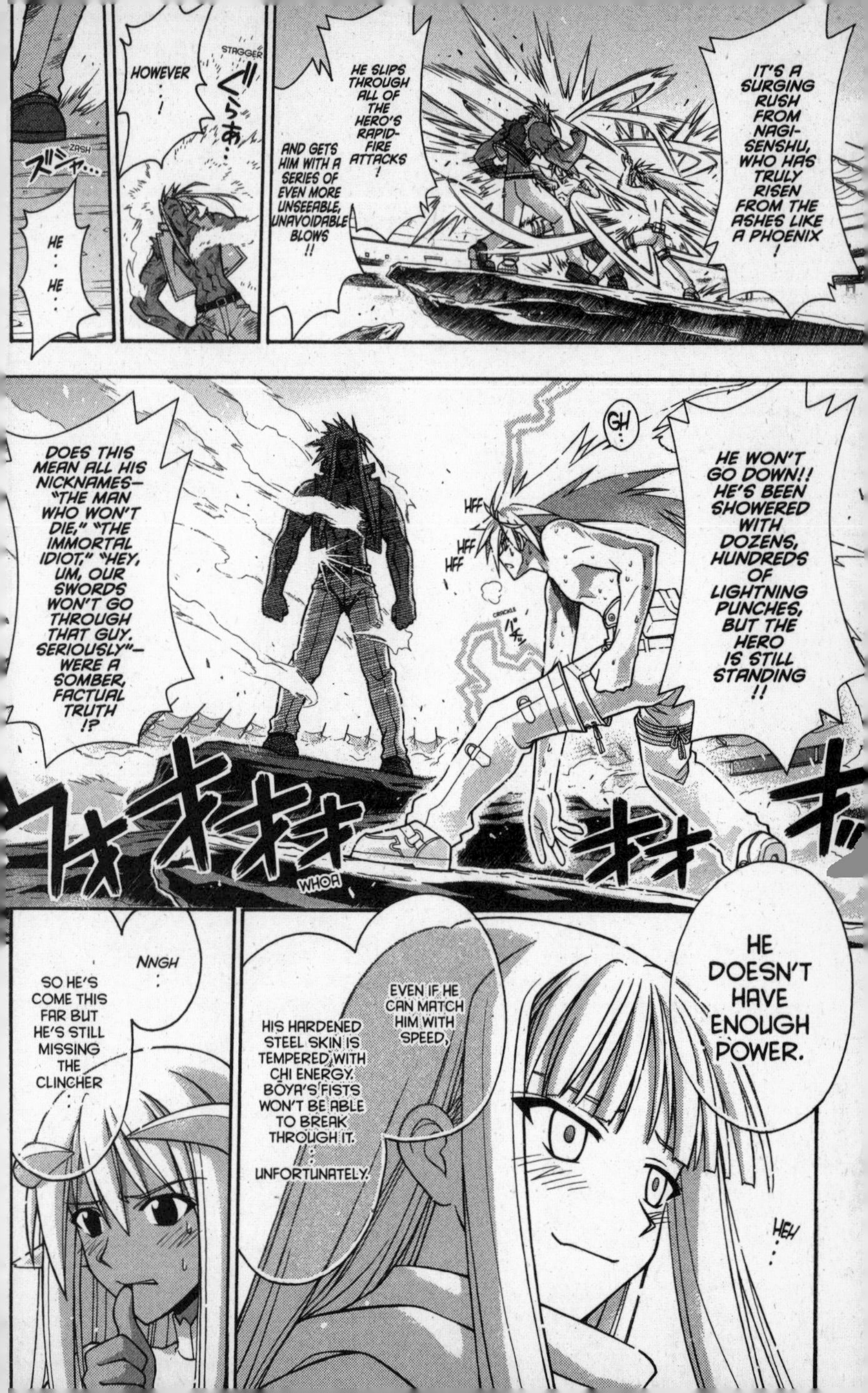
IT'S A SURGING RUSH FROM NAGI-SENSHU, WHO HAS TRULY RISEN FROM THE ASHES LIKE A PHOENIX!
HE SLIPS THROUGH ALL OF THE HERO'S RAPID-FIRE ATTACKS!
AND GETS HIM WITH A SERIES OF EVEN MORE UNSEEABLE, UNAVOIDABLE BLOWS!!
STAGGER
HOWEVER...!
ZASH
HE... HE...
HE WON'T GO DOWN!! HE'S BEEN SHOWERED WITH DOZENS, HUNDREDS OF LIGHTNING PUNCHES, BUT THE HERO IS STILL STANDING!!
GH...
HFF HFF HFF
CRACKLE
DOES THIS MEAN ALL HIS NICKNAMES—"THE MAN WHO WON'T DIE," "THE IMMORTAL IDIOT," "HEY, UM, OUR SWORDS WON'T GO THROUGH THAT GUY. SERIOUSLY"—WERE A SOMBER, FACTUAL TRUTH!?
WHOA
HE DOESN'T HAVE ENOUGH POWER.
HEH...
EVEN IF HE CAN MATCH HIM WITH SPEED,
HIS HARDENED STEEL SKIN IS TEMPERED WITH CHI ENERGY. BŌYA'S FISTS WON'T BE ABLE TO BREAK THROUGH IT...
UNFORTUNATELY.
NNGH...
SO HE'S COME THIS FAR BUT HE'S STILL MISSING THE CLINCHER...

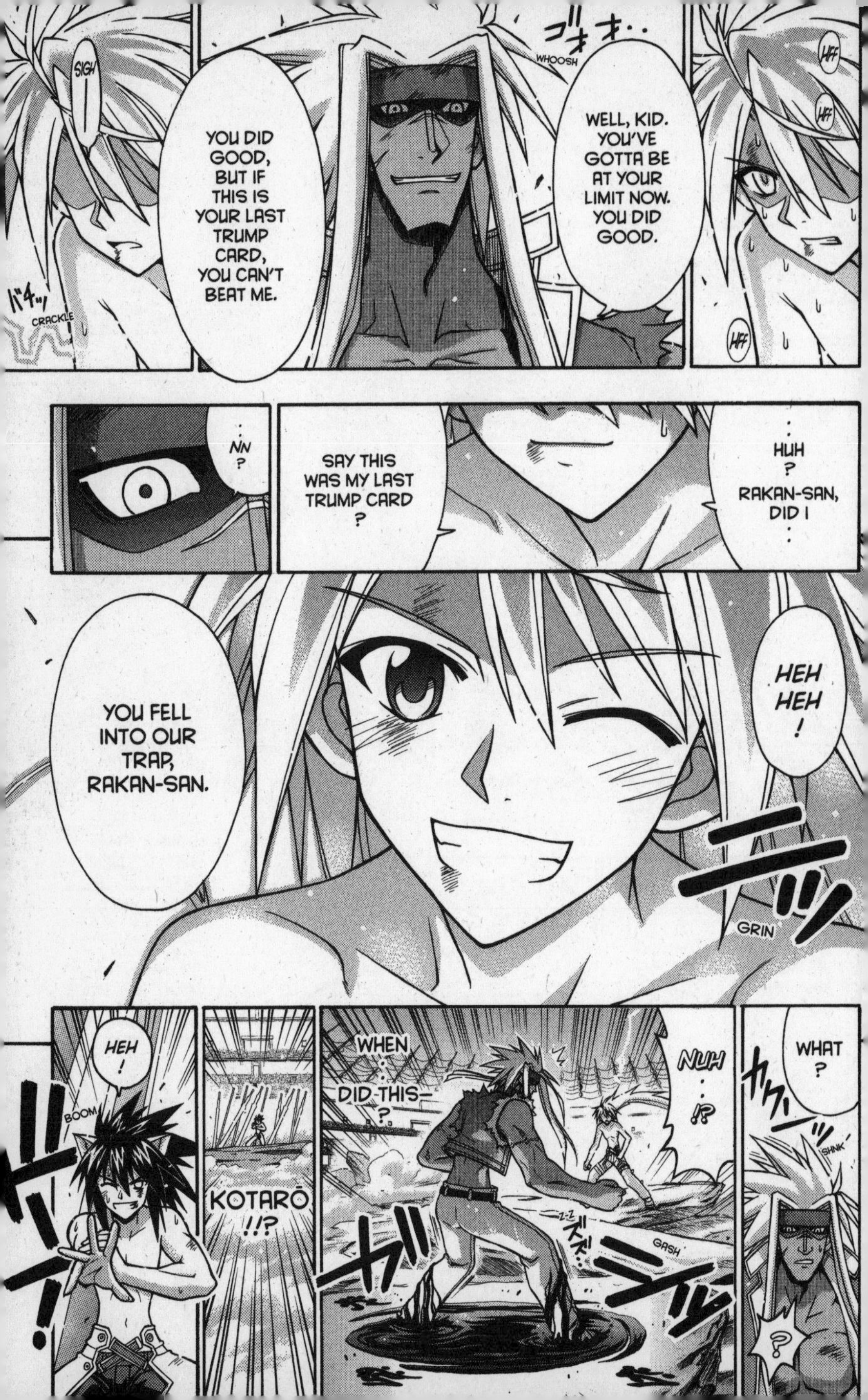
HFF
HFF
HFF
WHOOSH
WELL, KID. YOU'VE GOTTA BE AT YOUR LIMIT NOW. YOU DID GOOD.
YOU DID GOOD, BUT IF THIS IS YOUR LAST TRUMP CARD, YOU CAN'T BEAT ME.
SIGH
CRACKLE
...HUH? RAKAN-SAN, DID I...
SAY THIS WAS MY LAST TRUMP CARD?
...NN?
HEH HEH!
YOU FELL INTO OUR TRAP, RAKAN-SAN.
GRIN
WHAT?
SHNK
NUH...!?
WHEN... DID THIS—?
GASH
KOTARŌ!!?
HEH!
BOOM

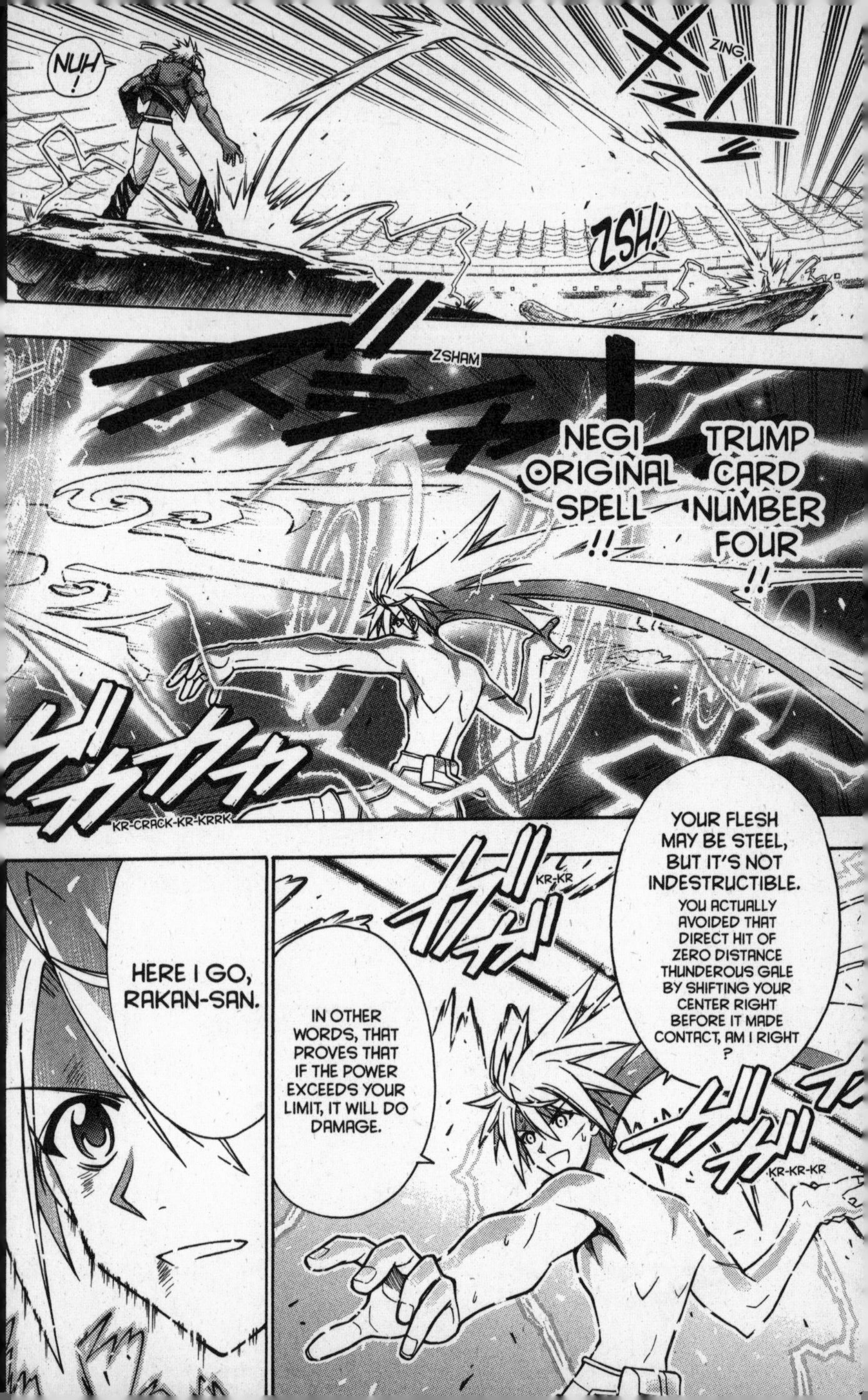
ZING
ZSH!!
NUH!
ZSHAM
TRUMP CARD NUMBER FOUR!!
NEGI ORIGINAL SPELL!!
KR-CRACK-KR-KRRK
YOUR FLESH MAY BE STEEL, BUT IT'S NOT INDESTRUCTIBLE. YOU ACTUALLY AVOIDED THAT DIRECT HIT OF ZERO DISTANCE THUNDEROUS GALE BY SHIFTING YOUR CENTER RIGHT BEFORE IT MADE CONTACT, AM I RIGHT?
KR-KR
KR-KR-KR
IN OTHER WORDS, THAT PROVES THAT IF THE POWER EXCEEDS YOUR LIMIT, IT WILL DO DAMAGE.
HERE I GO, RAKAN-SAN.

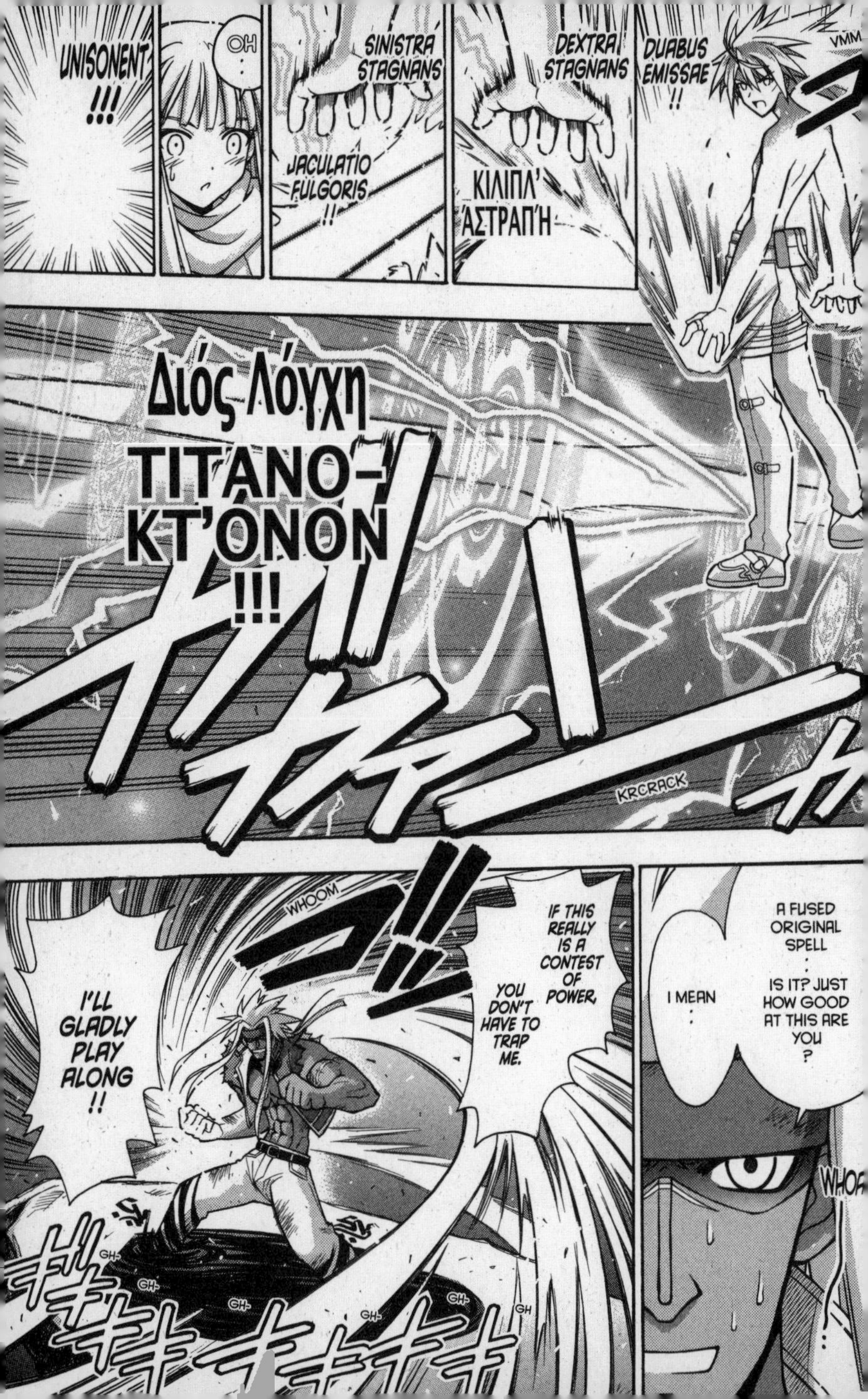
VMM
DUABUS EMISSAE !!
DEXTRA STAGNANS
ΚΙΛΙΠΛ’ ἈΣΤΡΑΠΉ
SINISTRA STAGNANS
JACULATIO FULGORIS !!
OH . .
UNISONENT !!!
Διός Λόγχη
TITANO-KT’ÓNON !!!
KRCRACK
A FUSED ORIGINAL SPELL . . IS IT? JUST HOW GOOD AT THIS ARE YOU ?
I MEAN . .
WHOOM
IF THIS REALLY IS A CONTEST OF POWER,
YOU DON’T HAVE TO TRAP ME.
I’LL GLADLY PLAY ALONG !!
GH- GH- GH- GH- GH

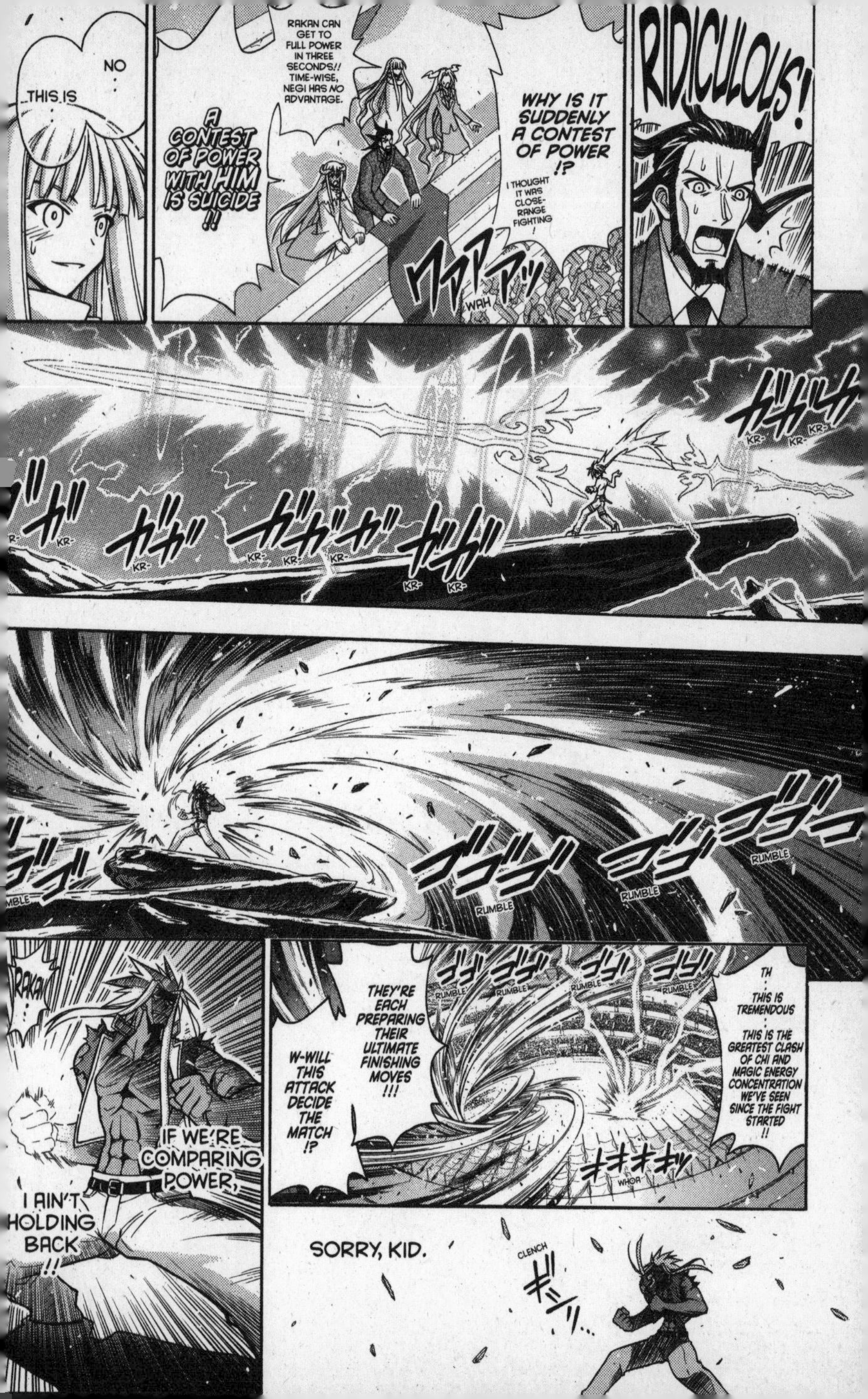
RIDICULOUS!
WHY IS IT SUDDENLY A CONTEST OF POWER !?
I THOUGHT IT WAS CLOSE-RANGE FIGHTING !
RAKAN CAN GET TO FULL POWER IN THREE SECONDS!! TIME-WISE, NEGI HAS NO ADVANTAGE.
A CONTEST OF POWER WITH HIM IS SUICIDE !!
WAH
NO
THIS IS
KR- KR- KR-
KR- KR- KR- KR- KR- KR- KR-
RUMBLE RUMBLE RUMBLE RUMBLE
TH... THIS IS TREMENDOUS... THIS IS THE GREATEST CLASH OF CHI AND MAGIC ENERGY CONCENTRATION WE'VE SEEN SINCE THE FIGHT STARTED !!
RUMBLE RUMBLE RUMBLE RUMBLE
THEY'RE EACH PREPARING THEIR ULTIMATE FINISHING MOVES !!!
W-WILL THIS ATTACK DECIDE THE MATCH !?
WHOA
CLENCH
SORRY, KID.
RAKAN...!
IF WE'RE COMPARING POWER,
I AIN'T HOLDING BACK !!

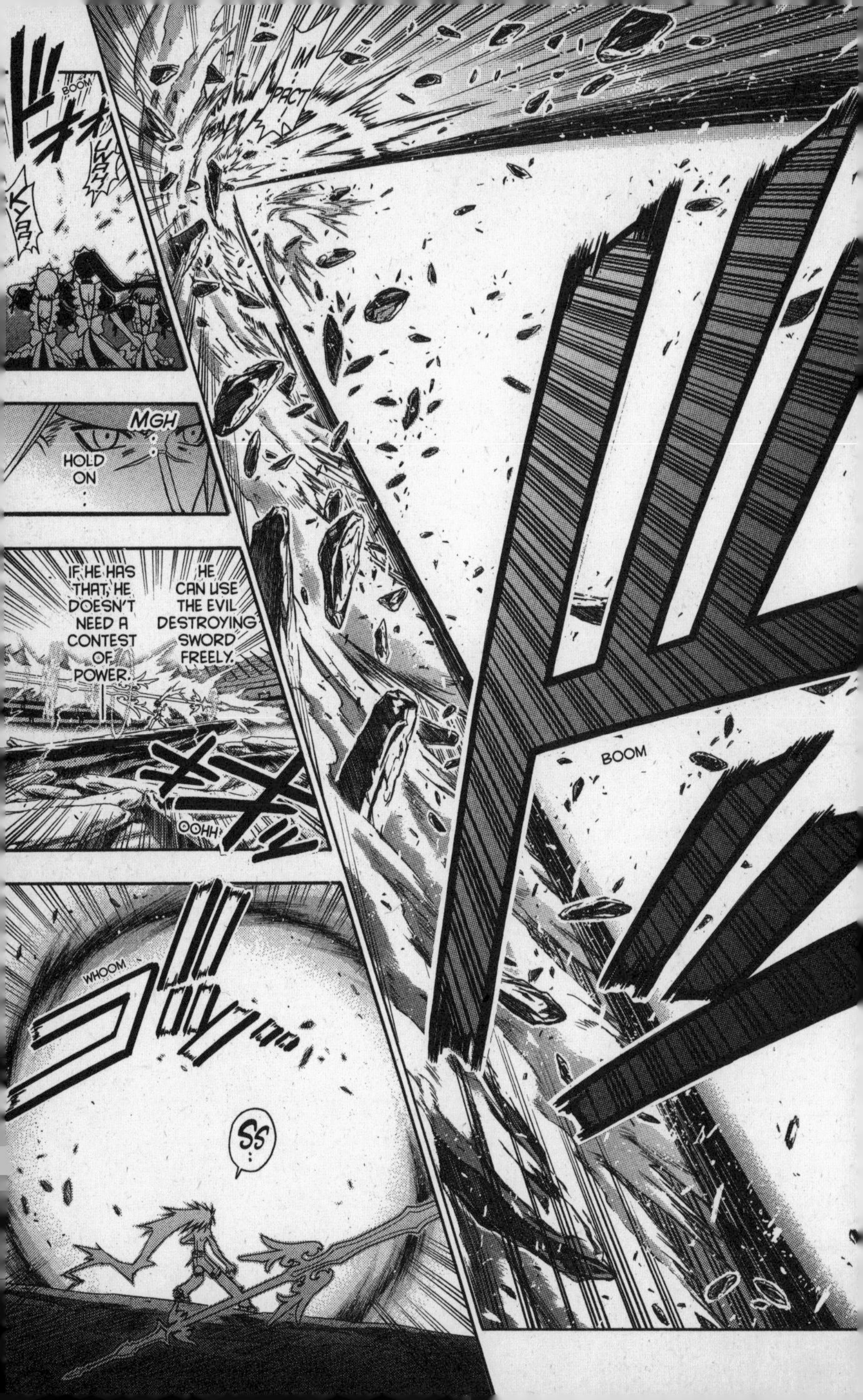
IMPACT
BOOM
BOOM
UWAH
KYAA
MGH
HOLD ON
HE CAN USE THE EVIL DESTROYING SWORD FREELY.
IF HE HAS THAT, HE DOESN'T NEED A CONTEST OF POWER.
OOHH
WHOOM
SS

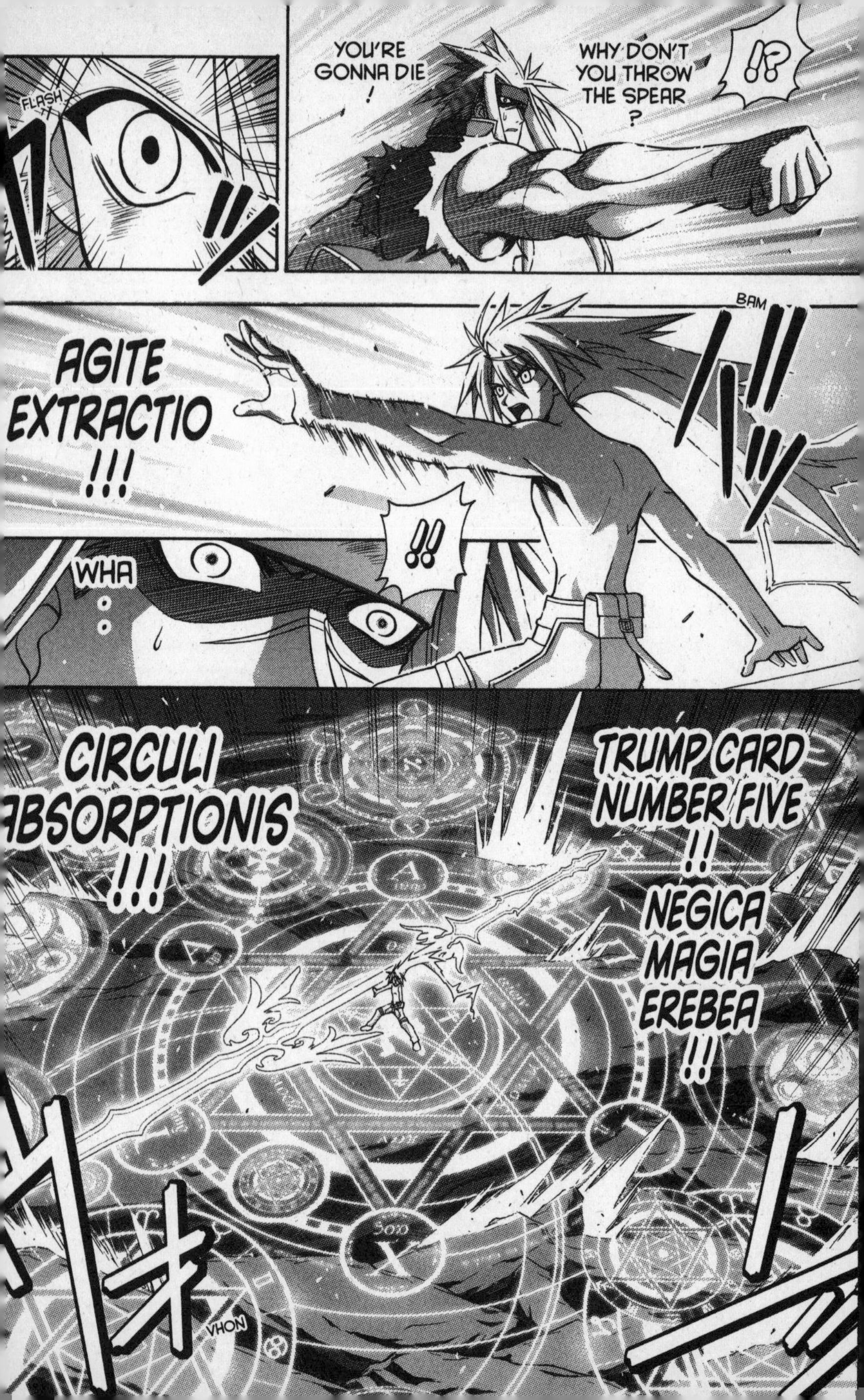
!?
WHY DON'T YOU THROW THE SPEAR?
YOU'RE GONNA DIE!
FLASH
BAM
AGITE EXTRACTIO!!!
!!
WHA..
TRUMP CARD NUMBER FIVE!!
NEGICA MAGIA EREBEA!!
CIRCULI ABSORPTIONIS!!!
VHON

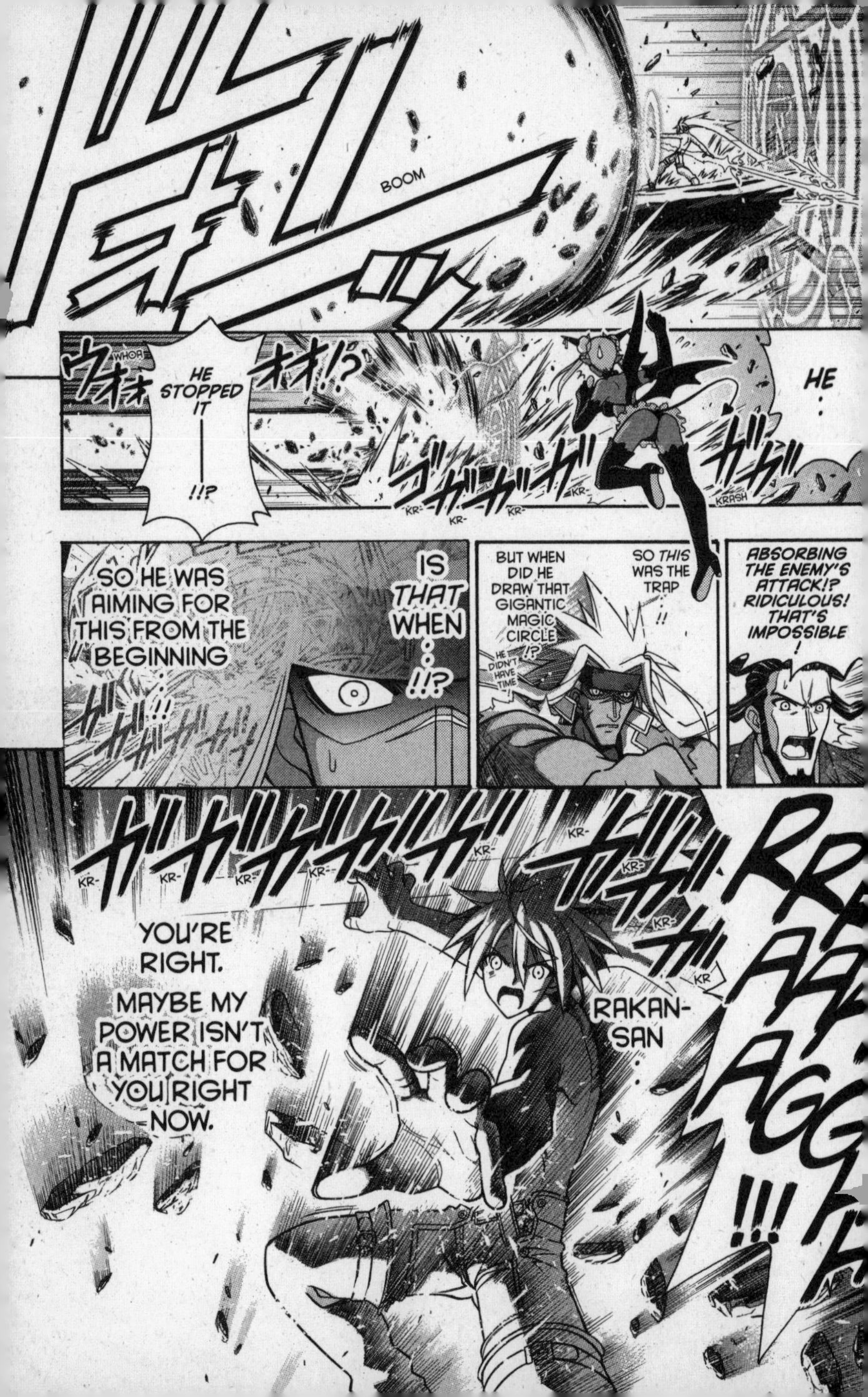

BOOM
HE...
KRASH
HE STOPPED IT——!!?
WHOA
KR-
ABSORBING THE ENEMY'S ATTACK!? RIDICULOUS! THAT'S IMPOSSIBLE!
SO THIS WAS THE TRAP...!!
BUT WHEN DID HE DRAW THAT GIGANTIC MAGIC CIRCLE!?
HE DIDN'T HAVE TIME
IS THAT WHEN...!!?
SO HE WAS AIMING FOR THIS FROM THE BEGINNING...!!
RRAAAAGG!!!
KR-
RAKAN-SAN...
YOU'RE RIGHT.
MAYBE MY POWER ISN'T A MATCH FOR YOU RIGHT NOW.

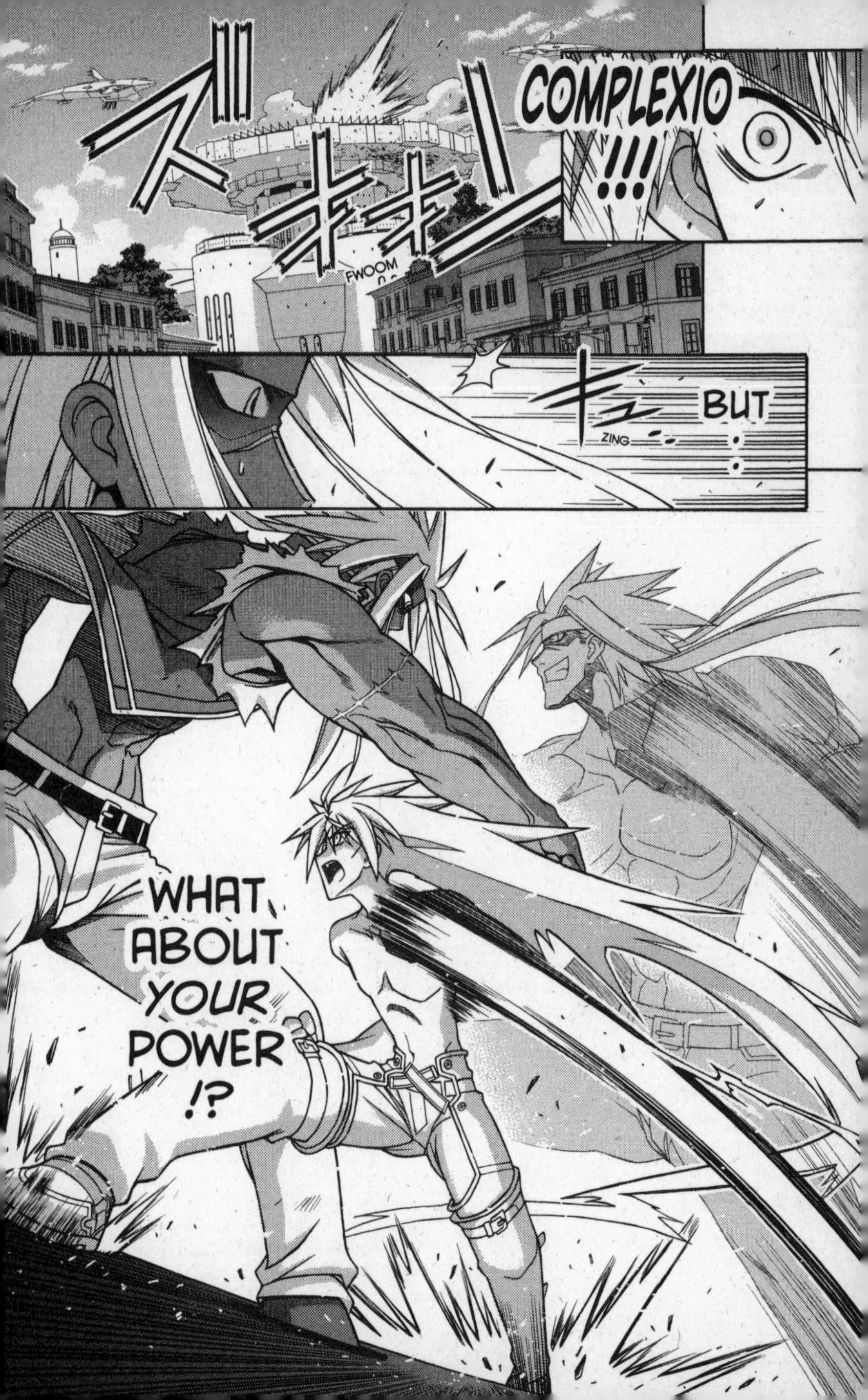
COMPLEXIO !!!
FWOOM
BUT . . .
ZING
WHAT ABOUT YOUR POWER !?

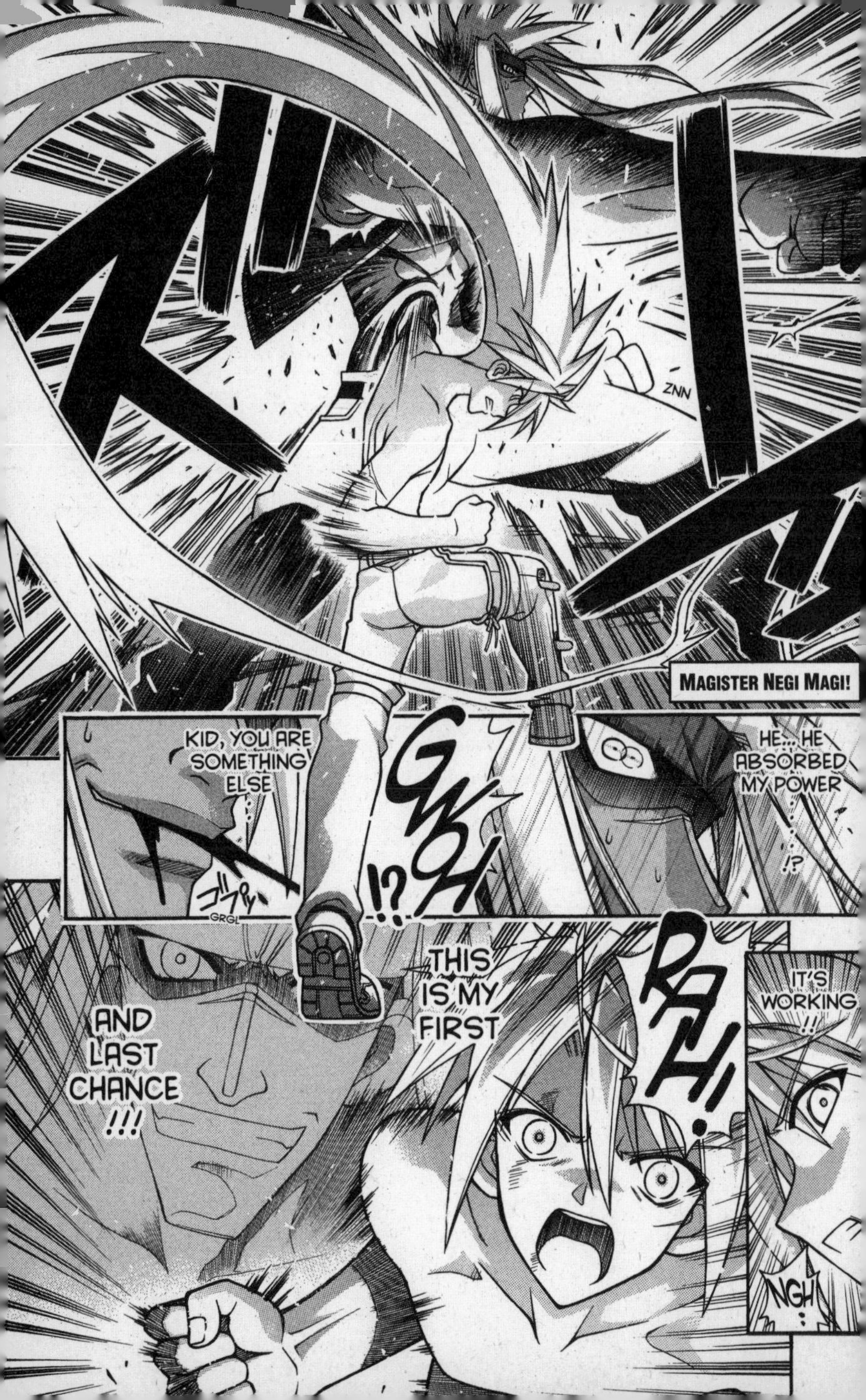
ZNN
MAGISTER NEGI MAGI!
HE... HE ABSORBED MY POWER...!?
GWOH!?
KID, YOU ARE SOMETHING ELSE...
GRGL
IT'S WORKING!!
NGH...
RAH!
THIS IS MY FIRST
AND LAST CHANCE!!!

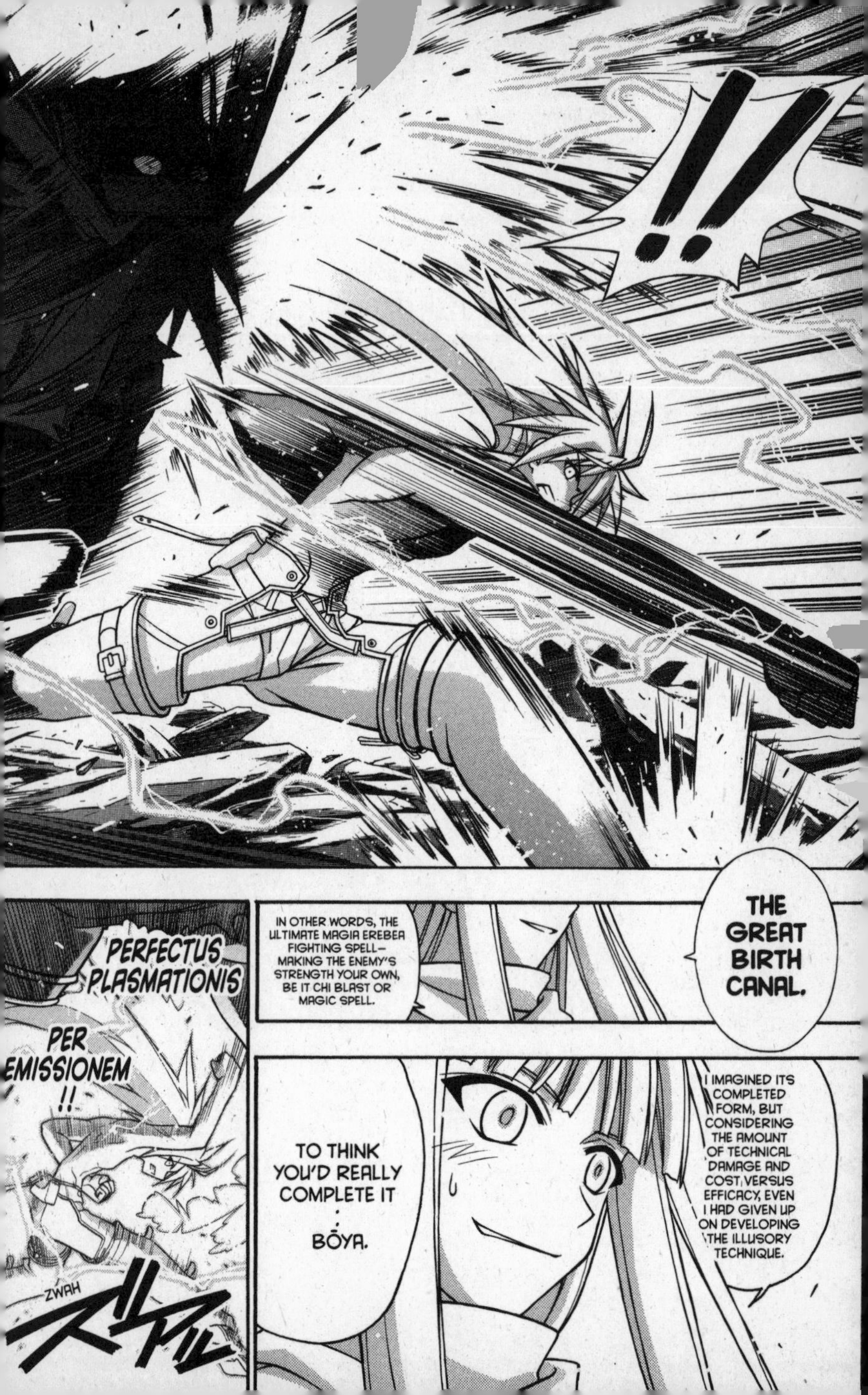
!!
THE GREAT BIRTH CANAL.
IN OTHER WORDS, THE ULTIMATE MAGIA EREBEA FIGHTING SPELL— MAKING THE ENEMY'S STRENGTH YOUR OWN, BE IT CHI BLAST OR MAGIC SPELL.
I IMAGINED ITS COMPLETED FORM, BUT CONSIDERING THE AMOUNT OF TECHNICAL DAMAGE AND COST VERSUS EFFICACY, EVEN I HAD GIVEN UP ON DEVELOPING THE ILLUSORY TECHNIQUE.
TO THINK YOU'D REALLY COMPLETE IT
...
BŌYA.
PERFECTUS PLASMATIONIS
PER EMISSIONEM !!
ZWAH

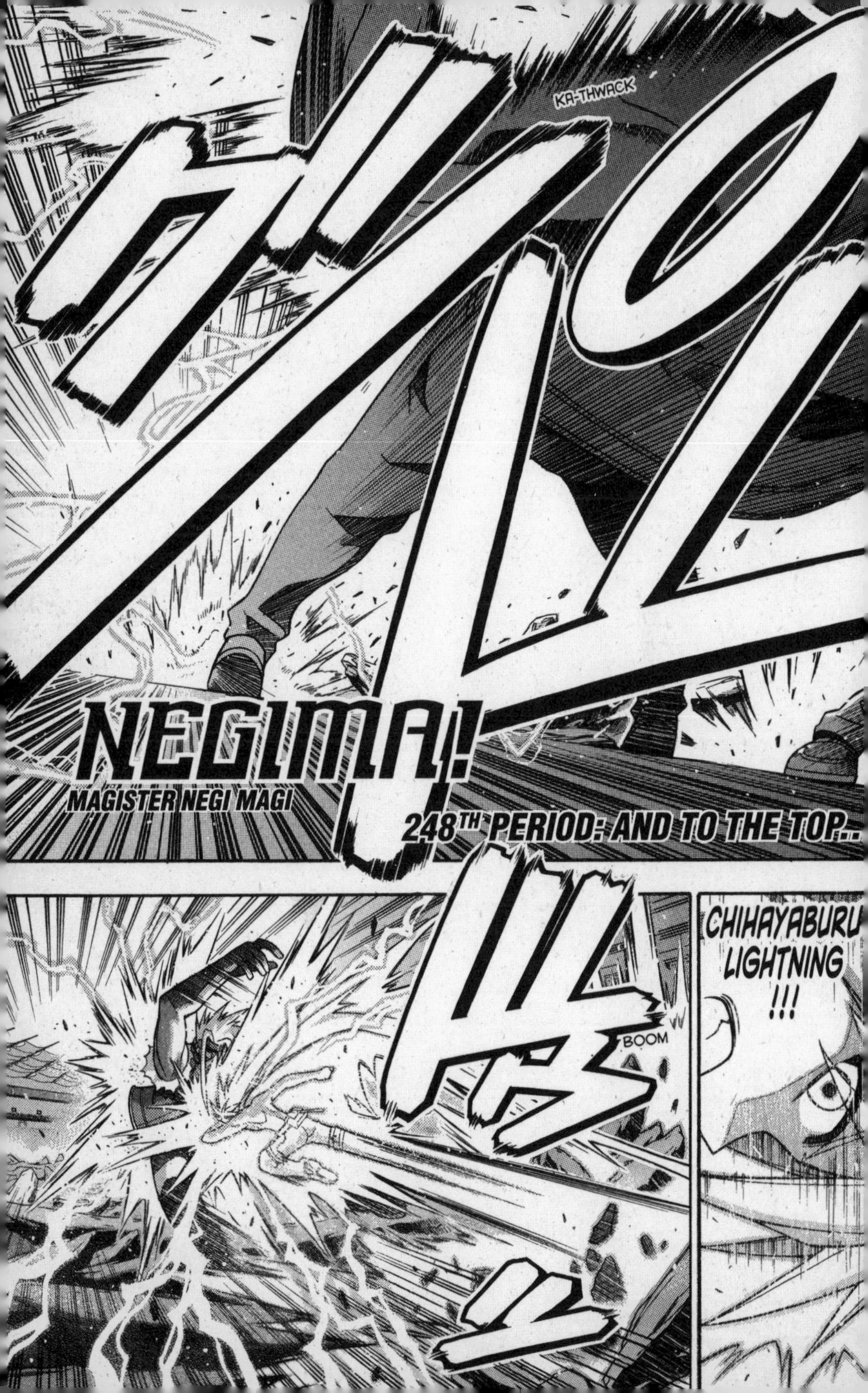
KA-THWACK
NEGIMA!
MAGISTER NEGI MAGI
248TH PERIOD: AND TO THE TOP..
CHIHAYABURU LIGHTNING !!!
BOOM

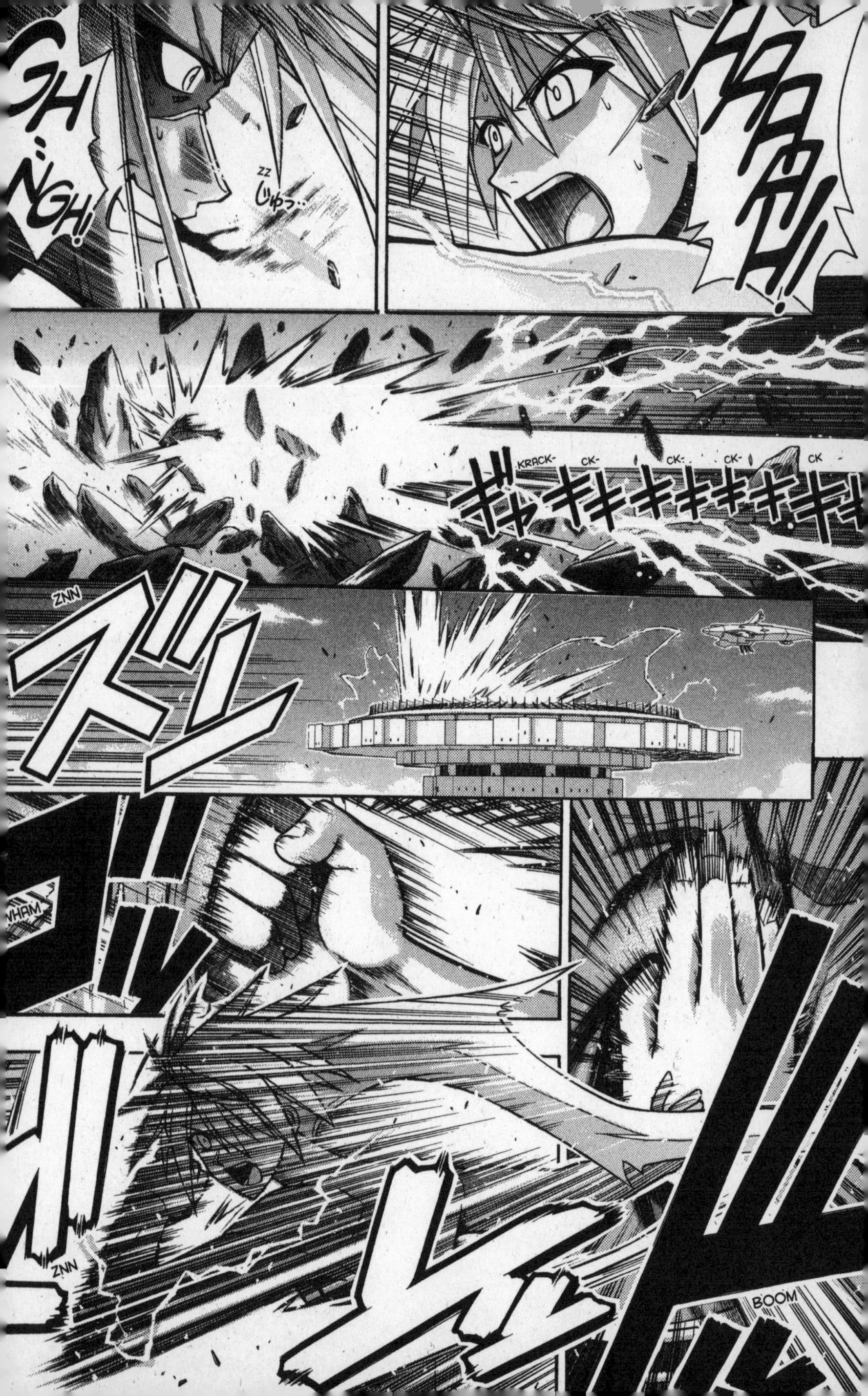
HAAAH!!
GH...NGH!
ZZ
じゅっ…
KRACK- CK- CK- CK- CK
ZNN
ズン
WHAM
ZNN
BOOM

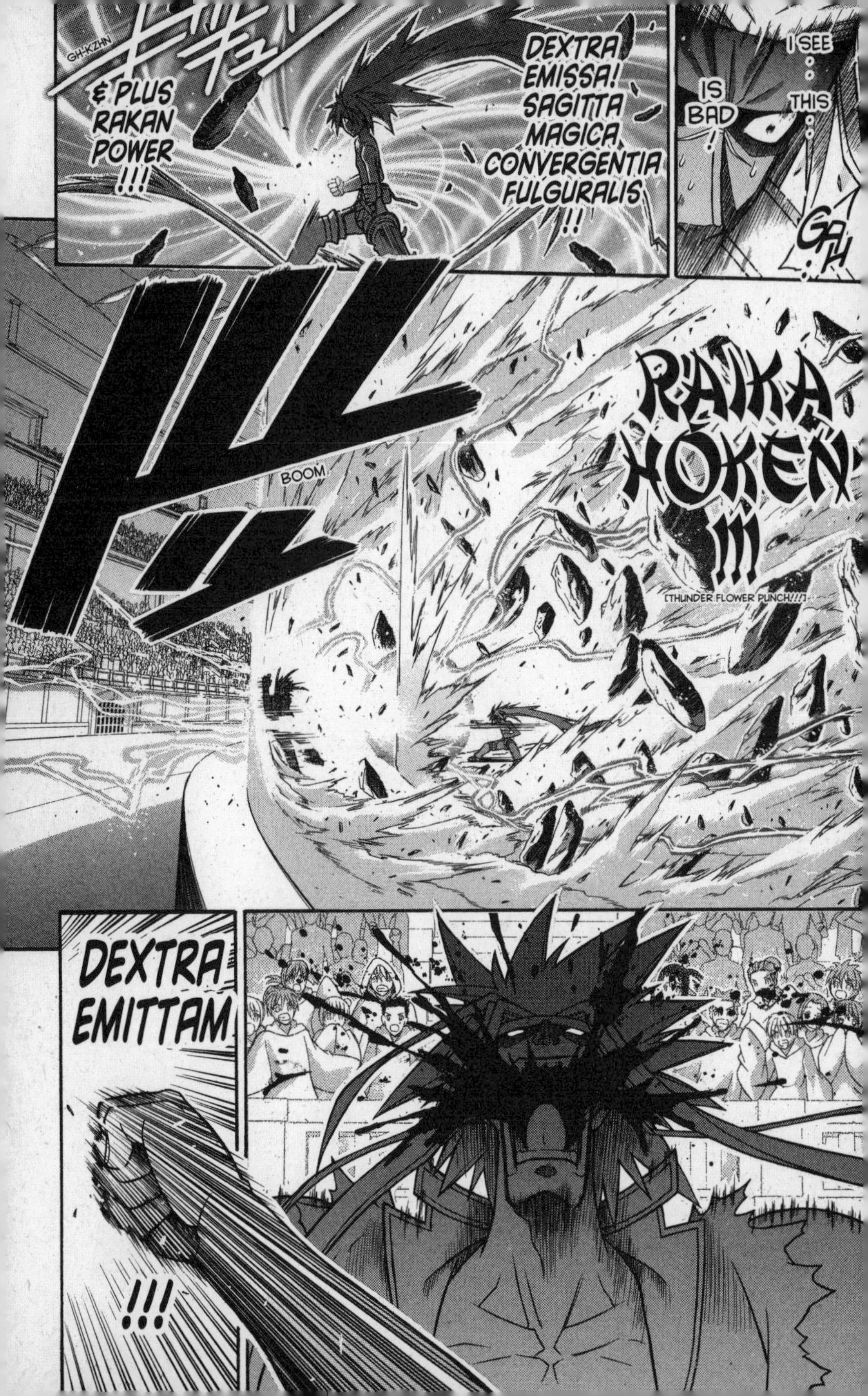
I SEE... THIS... IS BAD!
GAH
DEXTRA EMISSA! SAGITTA MAGICA, CONVERGENTIA FULGURALIS!!
& PLUS RAKAN POWER!!!
GH-KZHN
RAIKA HOKEN!!!
[THUNDER FLOWER PUNCH!!!]
BOOM
DEXTRA EMITTAM
!!!

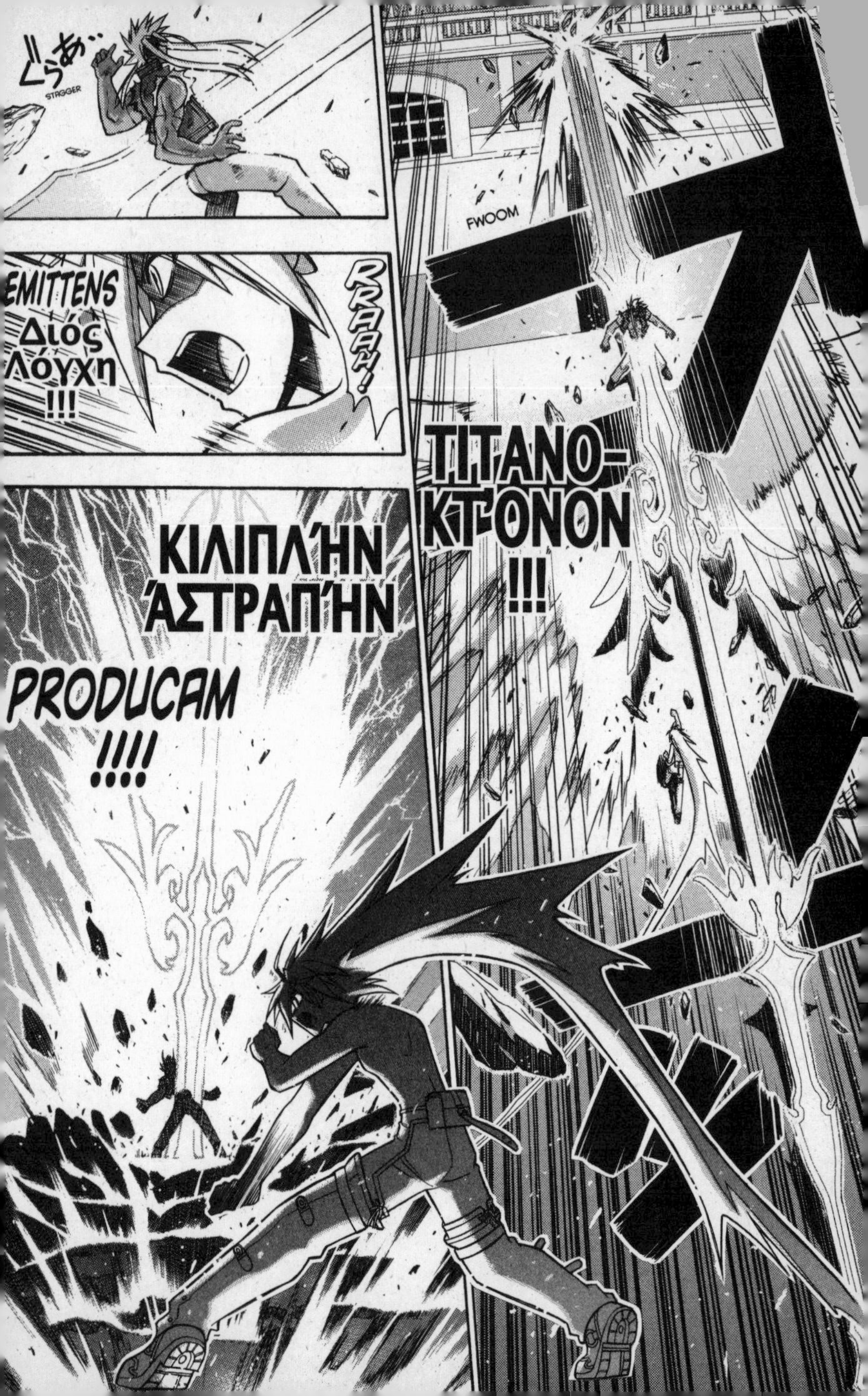
FWOOM
ΤΙΤΑΝΟ-
ΚΤΌΝΟΝ
!!!
くらあ…
STAGGER
EMITTENS
Διός
Λόγχη
!!!
RRAAH!
ΚΙΛΙΠΛΉΝ
ΆΣΤΡΑΠΉΝ
PRODUCAM
!!!!

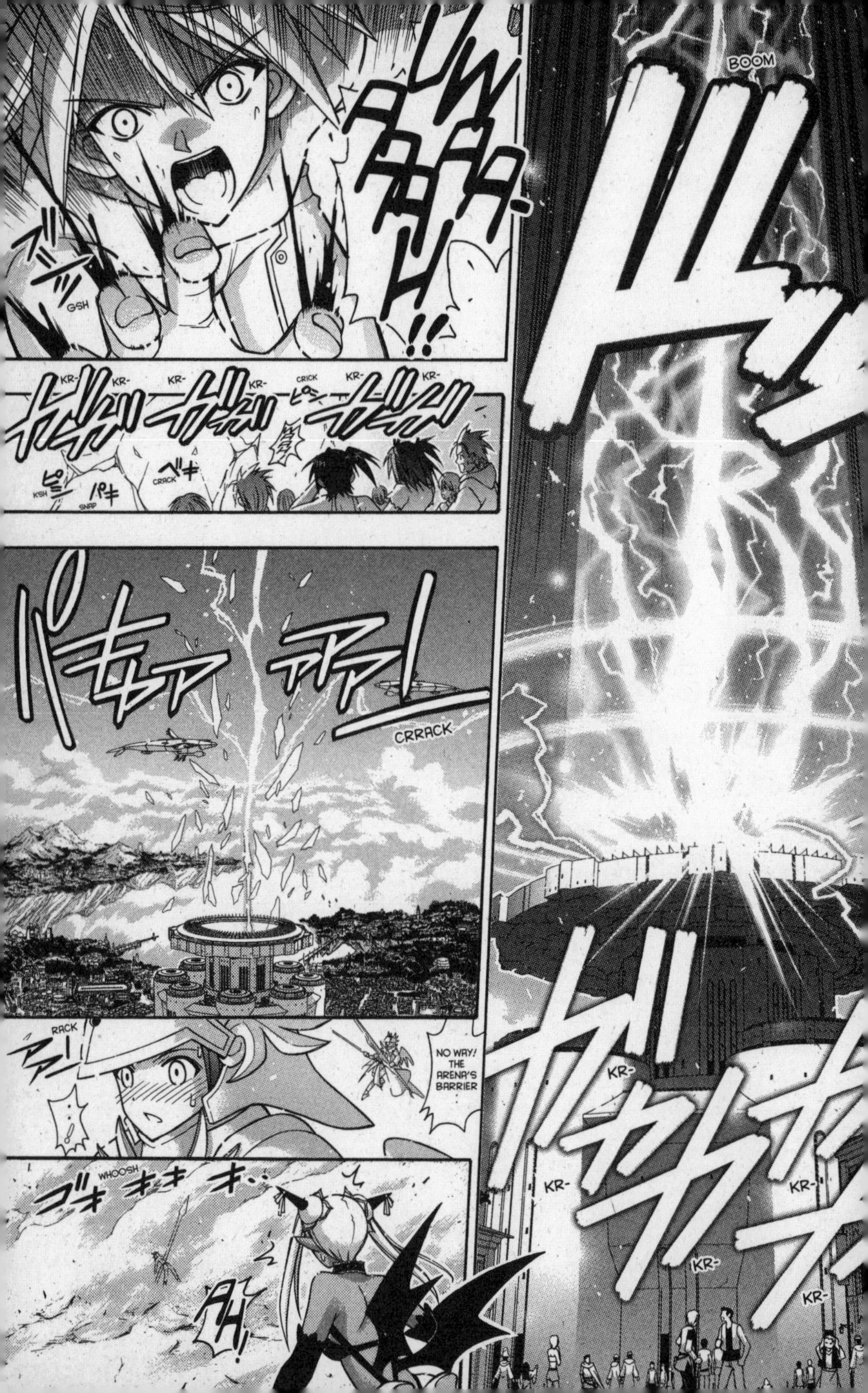
BOOM
KR-
KR-
KR-
KR-
GSH
KR- KR- KR- KR- CRICK KR- KR-
CRACK
KSH
SNAP
CRRACK
RACK
NO WAY! THE ARENA'S BARRIER
WHOOSH

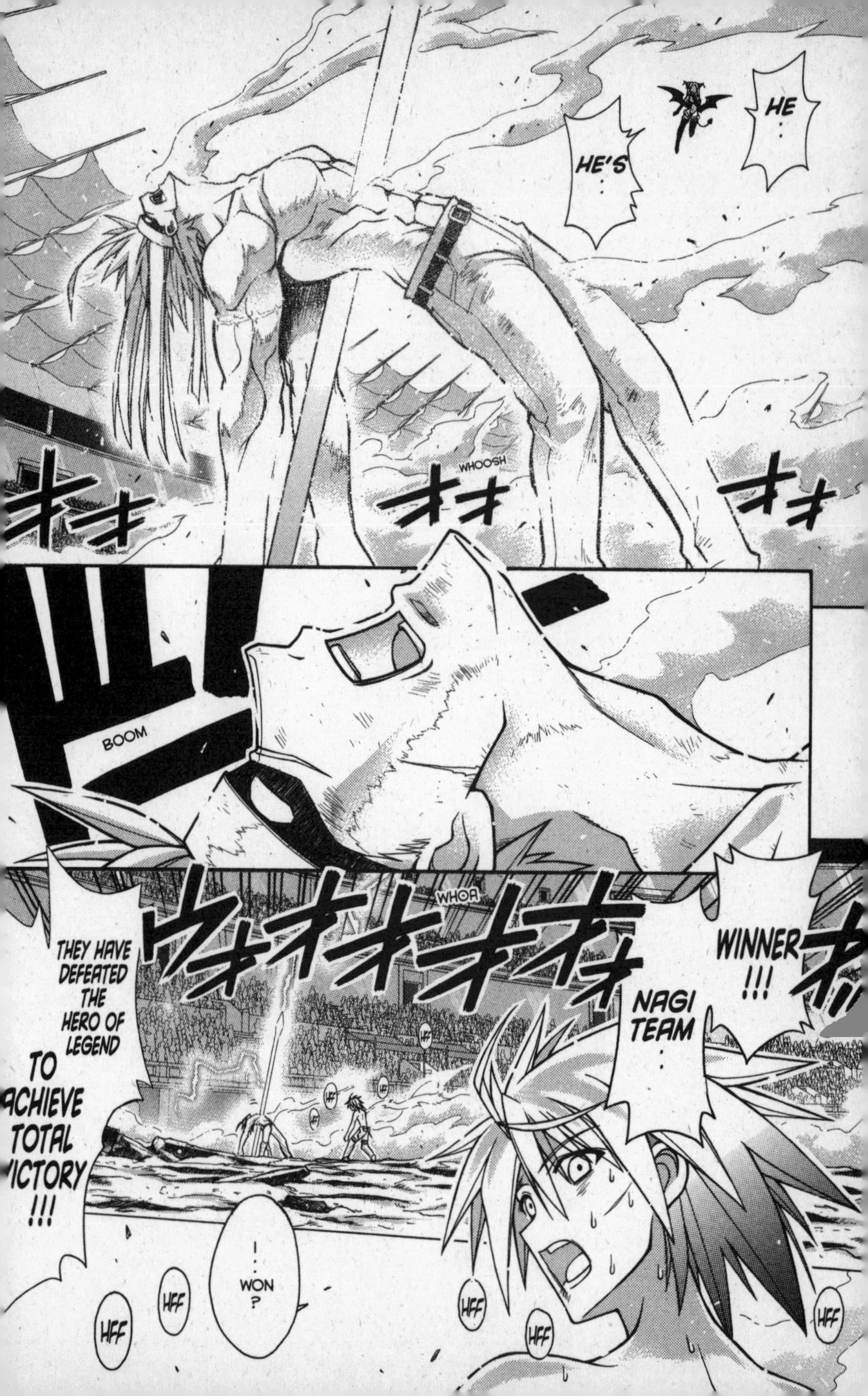
HE
HE'S
WHOOSH
BOOM
WINNER !!!
NAGI TEAM
WHOA
THEY HAVE DEFEATED THE HERO OF LEGEND
TO ACHIEVE TOTAL VICTORY !!!
HFF
HFF
HFF
! ... WON ?
HFF
HFF
HFF
HFF
HFF
HFF
HFF

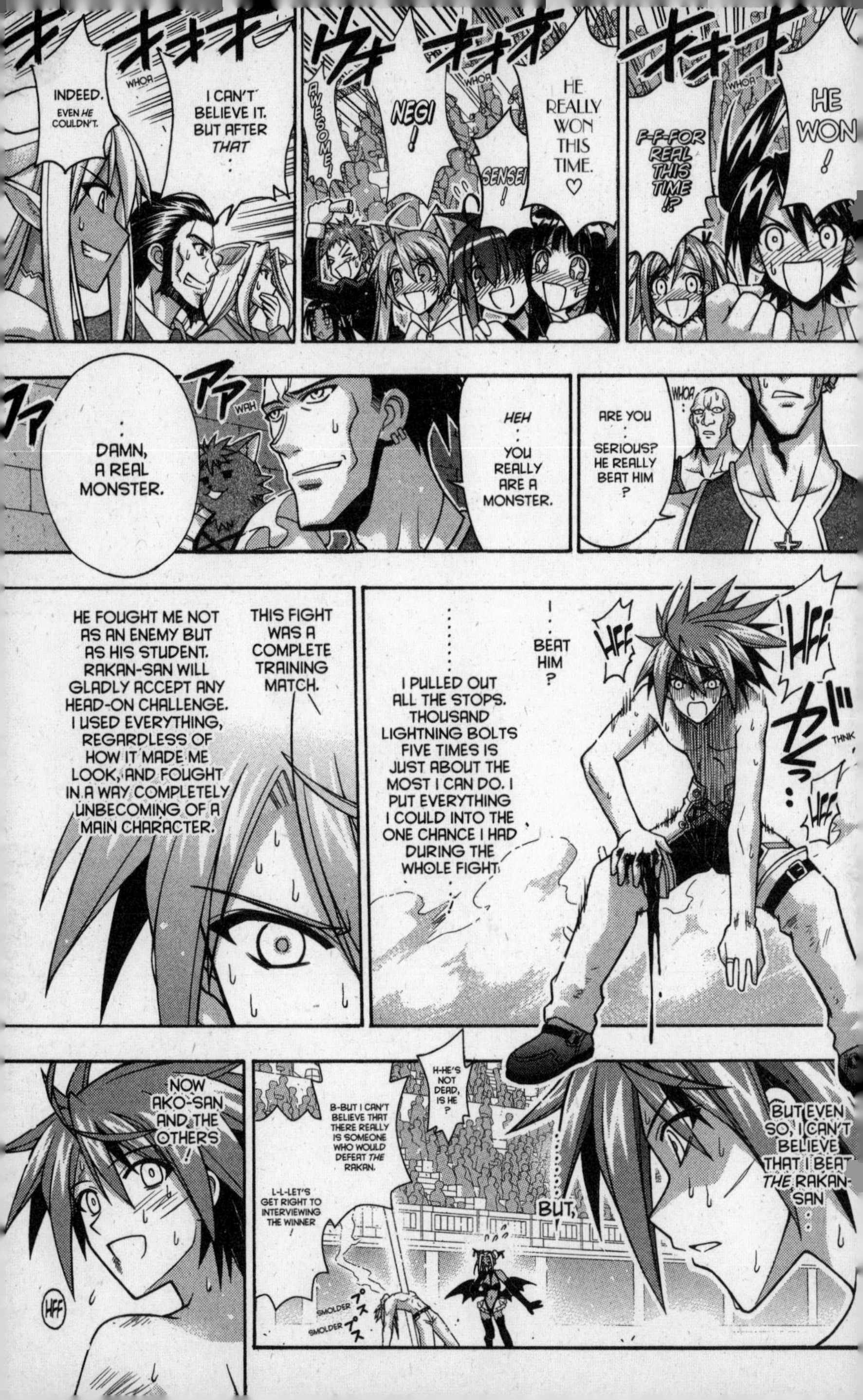
WHOA
HE WON!
F-F-FOR REAL THIS TIME!?
WHOA
HE REALLY WON THIS TIME. ♡
SENSEI!
NEGI!
AWESOME!
I CAN'T BELIEVE IT. BUT AFTER THAT...
WHOA
INDEED. EVEN HE COULDN'T.
WHOA
ARE YOU... SERIOUS? HE REALLY BEAT HIM?
HEH... YOU REALLY ARE A MONSTER.
WAH
...DAMN, A REAL MONSTER.
HFF
HFF
THNK
HFF
...BEAT HIM?
...... I PULLED OUT ALL THE STOPS. THOUSAND LIGHTNING BOLTS FIVE TIMES IS JUST ABOUT THE MOST I CAN DO. I PUT EVERYTHING I COULD INTO THE ONE CHANCE I HAD DURING THE WHOLE FIGHT...!
THIS FIGHT WAS A COMPLETE TRAINING MATCH.
HE FOUGHT ME NOT AS AN ENEMY BUT AS HIS STUDENT. RAKAN-SAN WILL GLADLY ACCEPT ANY HEAD-ON CHALLENGE. I USED EVERYTHING, REGARDLESS OF HOW IT MADE ME LOOK, AND FOUGHT IN A WAY COMPLETELY UNBECOMING OF A MAIN CHARACTER.
BUT EVEN SO, I CAN'T BELIEVE THAT I BEAT THE RAKAN-SAN...
BUT,
H-HE'S NOT DEAD, IS HE?
B-BUT I CAN'T BELIEVE THAT THERE REALLY IS SOMEONE WHO WOULD DEFEAT THE RAKAN.
L-L-LET'S GET RIGHT TO INTERVIEWING THE WINNER!
SMOLDER
SMOLDER
NOW AKO-SAN AND THE OTHERS!
HFF

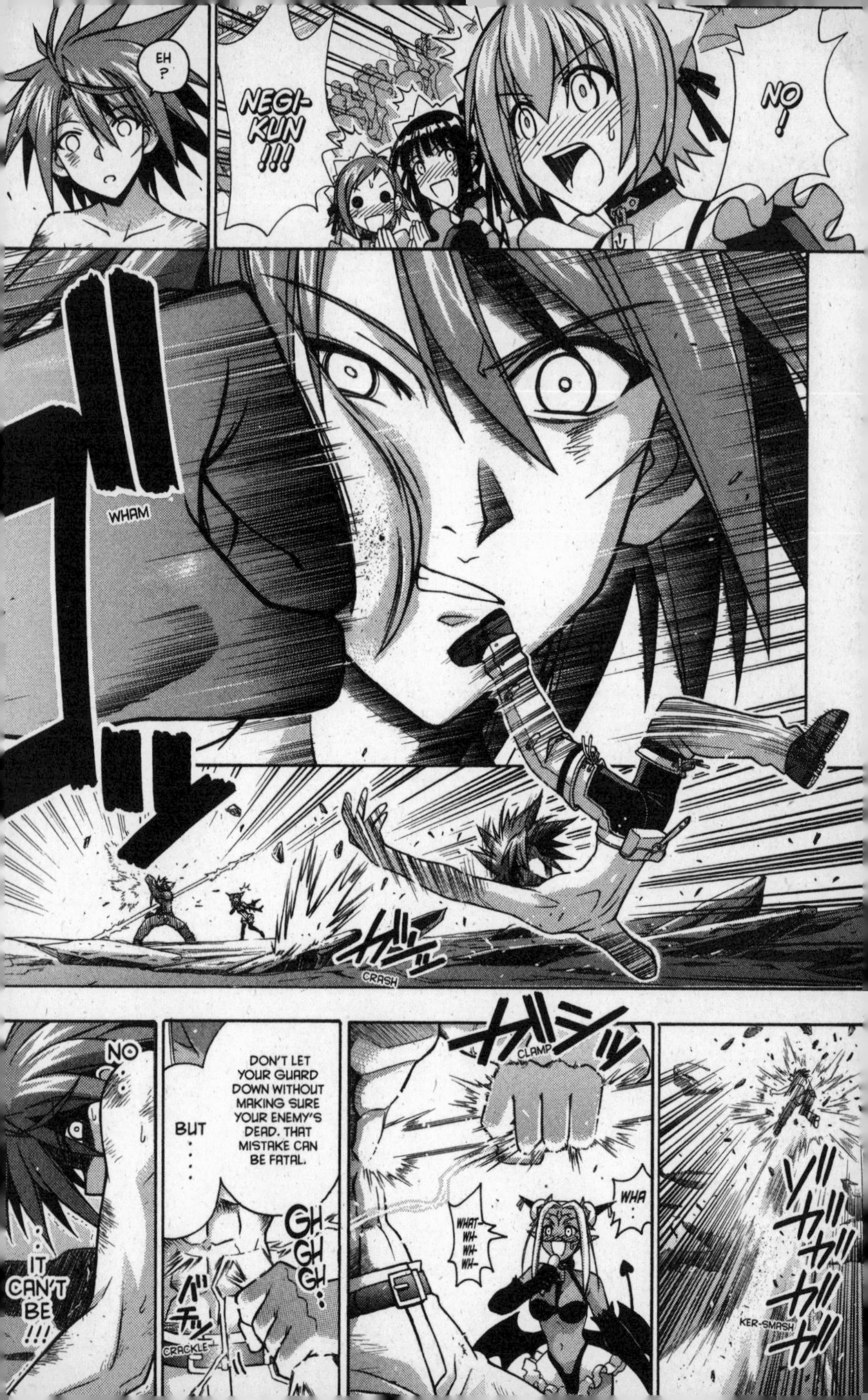
NO!
NEGI-KUN!!!
EH?
WHAM
CRASH
KER-SMASH
CLAMP
WHA
WHAT- WH- WH- WH-
DON'T LET YOUR GUARD DOWN WITHOUT MAKING SURE YOUR ENEMY'S DEAD. THAT MISTAKE CAN BE FATAL.
BUT...
GH GH GH...
CRACKLE
NO...
IT CAN'T BE!!!

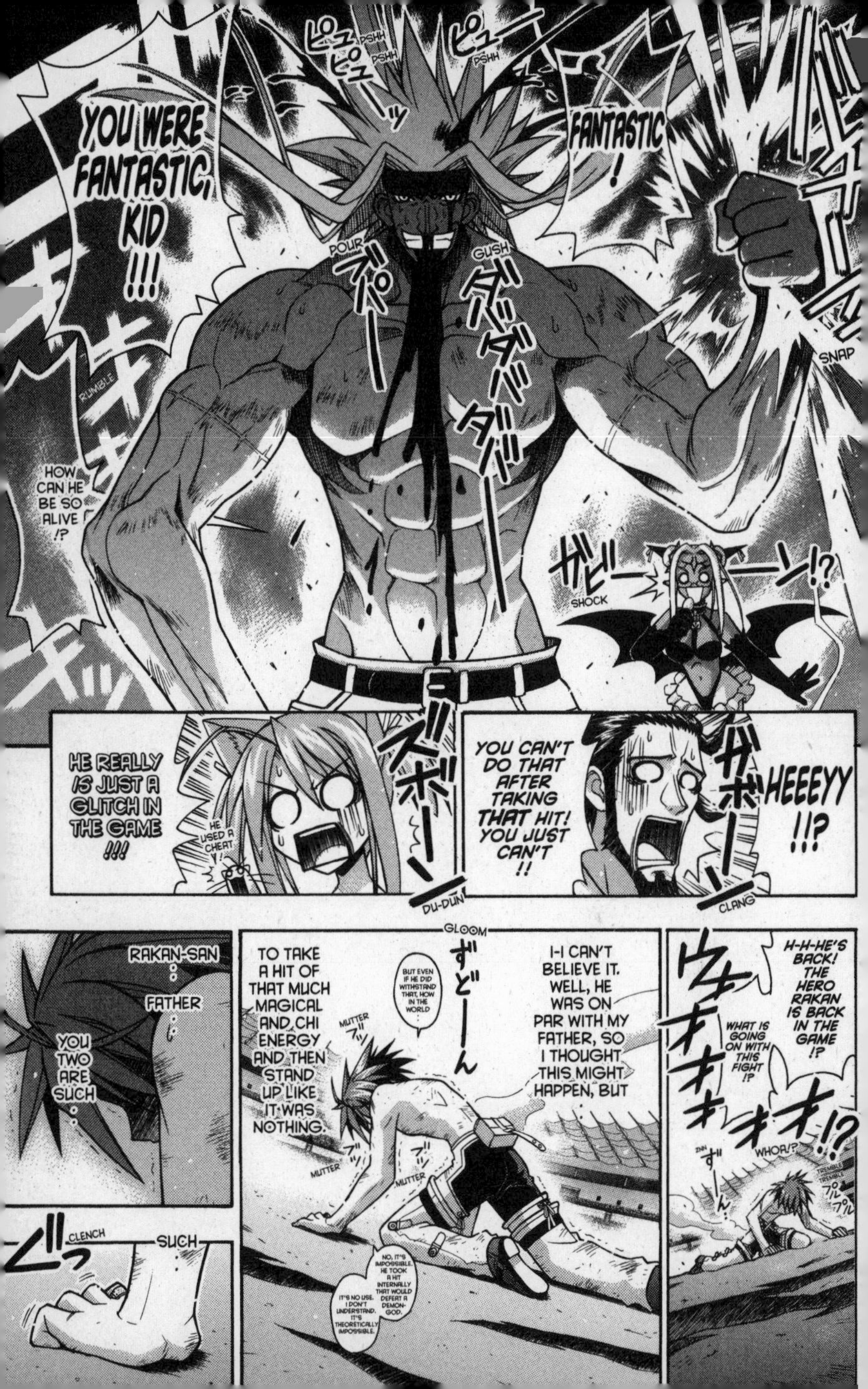
PSHH
PSHH
PSHH
FANTASTIC!
YOU WERE FANTASTIC, KID!!!
POUR
GUSH
SNAP
RUMBLE
HOW CAN HE BE SO ALIVE!?
SHOCK
YOU CAN'T DO THAT AFTER TAKING THAT HIT! YOU JUST CAN'T!!
HEEEYY!!?
CLANG
HE REALLY IS JUST A GLITCH IN THE GAME!!!
HE USED A CHEAT
DU-DUN
H-H-HE'S BACK! THE HERO RAKAN IS BACK IN THE GAME!?
WHAT IS GOING ON WITH THIS FIGHT!?
WHOA!?
TREMBLE TREMBLE
INN
I-I CAN'T BELIEVE IT. WELL, HE WAS ON PAR WITH MY FATHER, SO I THOUGHT THIS MIGHT HAPPEN, BUT
GLOOM
TO TAKE A HIT OF THAT MUCH MAGICAL AND CHI ENERGY AND THEN STAND UP LIKE IT WAS NOTHING.
BUT EVEN IF HE DID WITHSTAND THAT, HOW IN THE WORLD...
MUTTER
MUTTER
MUTTER
NO, IT'S IMPOSSIBLE. HE TOOK A HIT INTERNALLY THAT WOULD DEFEAT A DEMON-GOD.
IT'S NO USE. I DON'T UNDERSTAND. IT'S THEORETICALLY IMPOSSIBLE.
RAKAN-SAN...
FATHER...
YOU TWO ARE SUCH...
CLENCH
SUCH

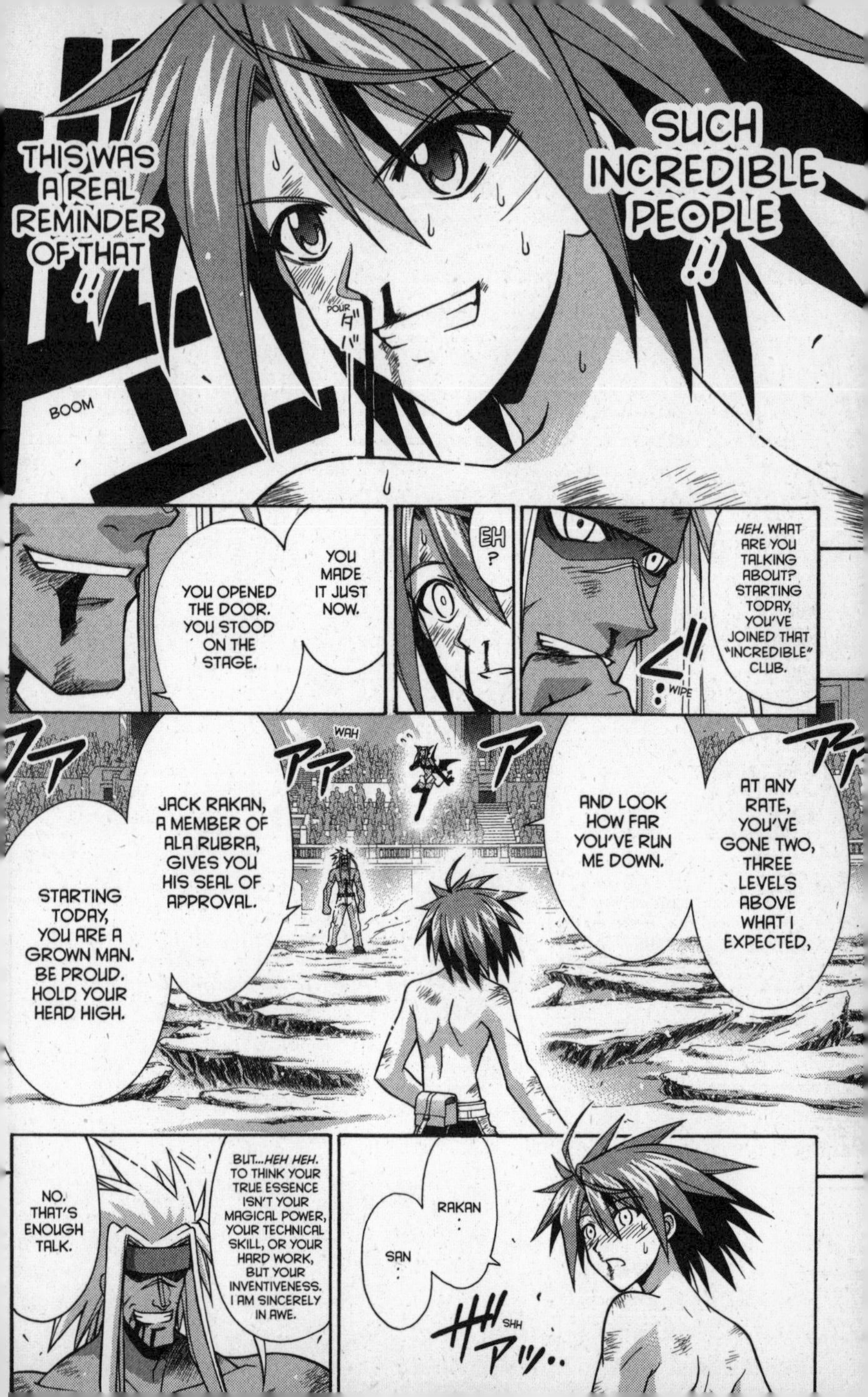
SUCH INCREDIBLE PEOPLE !!
THIS WAS A REAL REMINDER OF THAT !!
POUR
BOOM
HEH. WHAT ARE YOU TALKING ABOUT? STARTING TODAY, YOU'VE JOINED THAT "INCREDIBLE" CLUB.
WIPE
EH ?
YOU MADE IT JUST NOW.
YOU OPENED THE DOOR. YOU STOOD ON THE STAGE.
AT ANY RATE, YOU'VE GONE TWO, THREE LEVELS ABOVE WHAT I EXPECTED,
AND LOOK HOW FAR YOU'VE RUN ME DOWN.
WAH
JACK RAKAN, A MEMBER OF ALA RUBRA, GIVES YOU HIS SEAL OF APPROVAL.
STARTING TODAY, YOU ARE A GROWN MAN. BE PROUD. HOLD YOUR HEAD HIGH.
RAKAN : : SAN
SHH
BUT...*HEH HEH.* TO THINK YOUR TRUE ESSENCE ISN'T YOUR MAGICAL POWER, YOUR TECHNICAL SKILL, OR YOUR HARD WORK, BUT YOUR INVENTIVENESS. I AM SINCERELY IN AWE.
NO. THAT'S ENOUGH TALK.

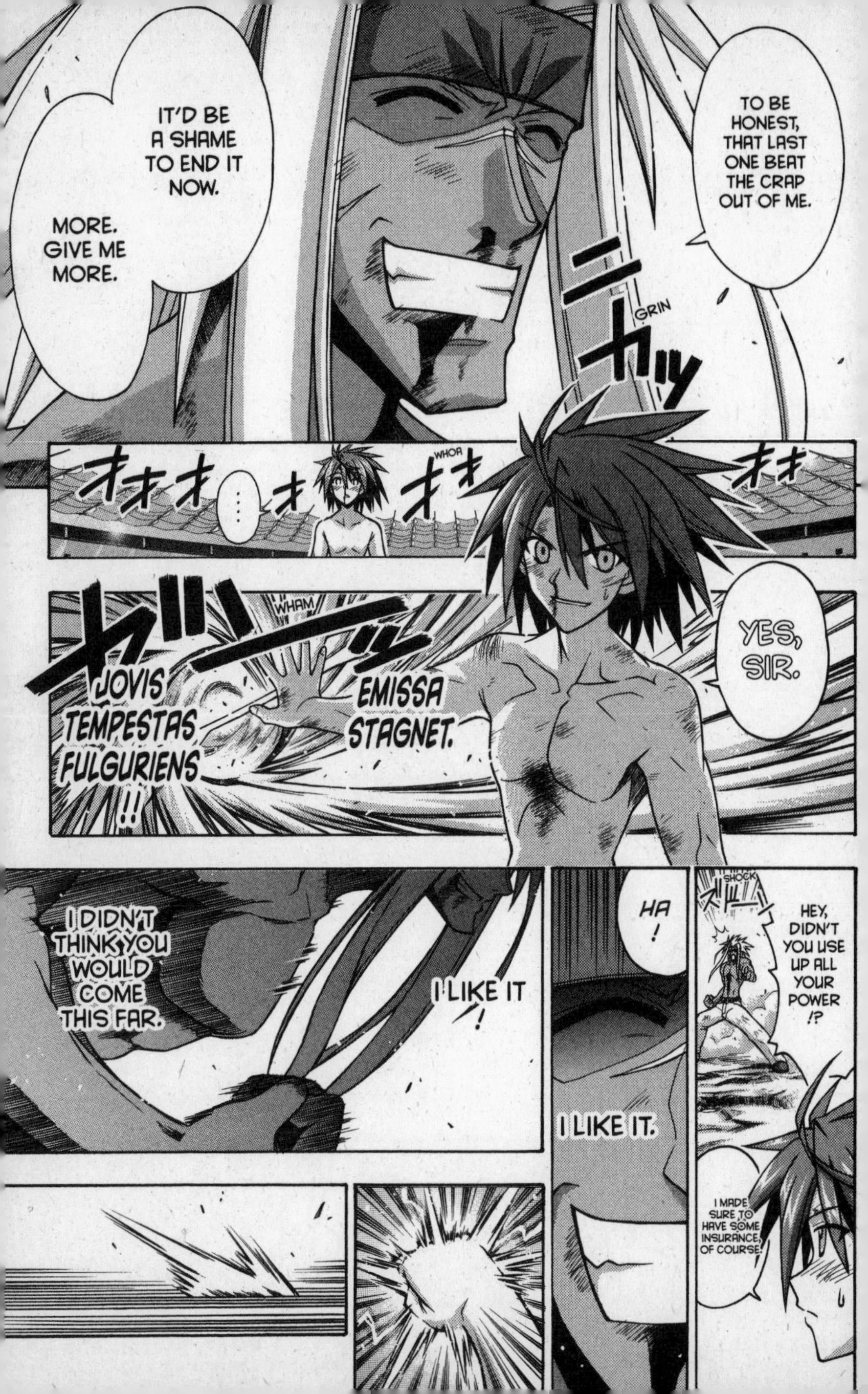
TO BE HONEST, THAT LAST ONE BEAT THE CRAP OUT OF ME.
GRIN
IT'D BE A SHAME TO END IT NOW.
MORE. GIVE ME MORE.
WHOA
...
YES, SIR.
WHAM
EMISSA STAGNET.
JOVIS TEMPESTAS FULGURIENS!!
SHOCK
HEY, DIDN'T YOU USE UP ALL YOUR POWER!?
I MADE SURE TO HAVE SOME INSURANCE, OF COURSE.
HA!
I LIKE IT.
I DIDN'T THINK YOU WOULD COME THIS FAR.
I LIKE IT!

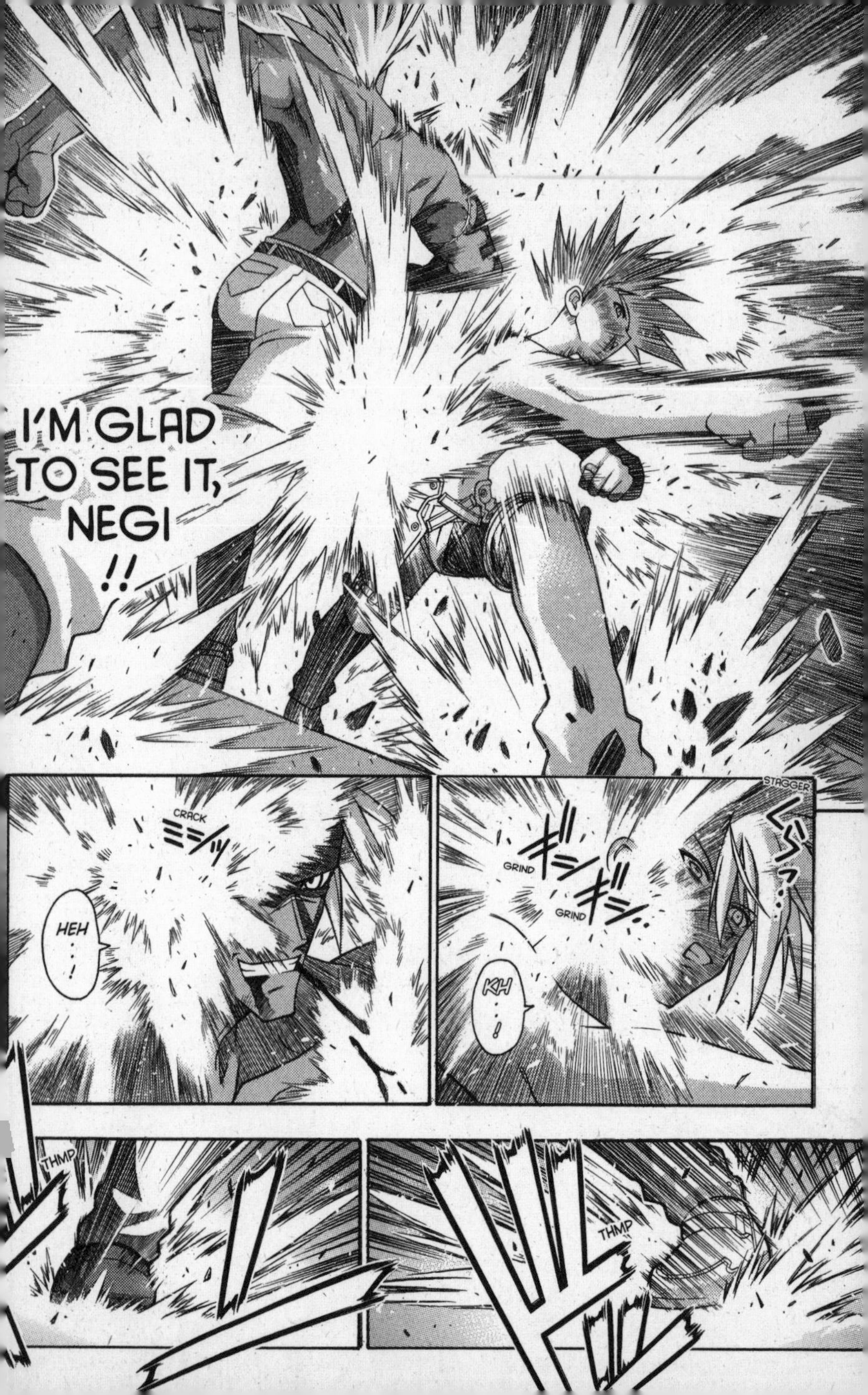
I'M GLAD TO SEE IT, NEGI !!
STAGGER
GRIND
GRIND
KH...!
CRACK
HEH...!
THMP
THMP

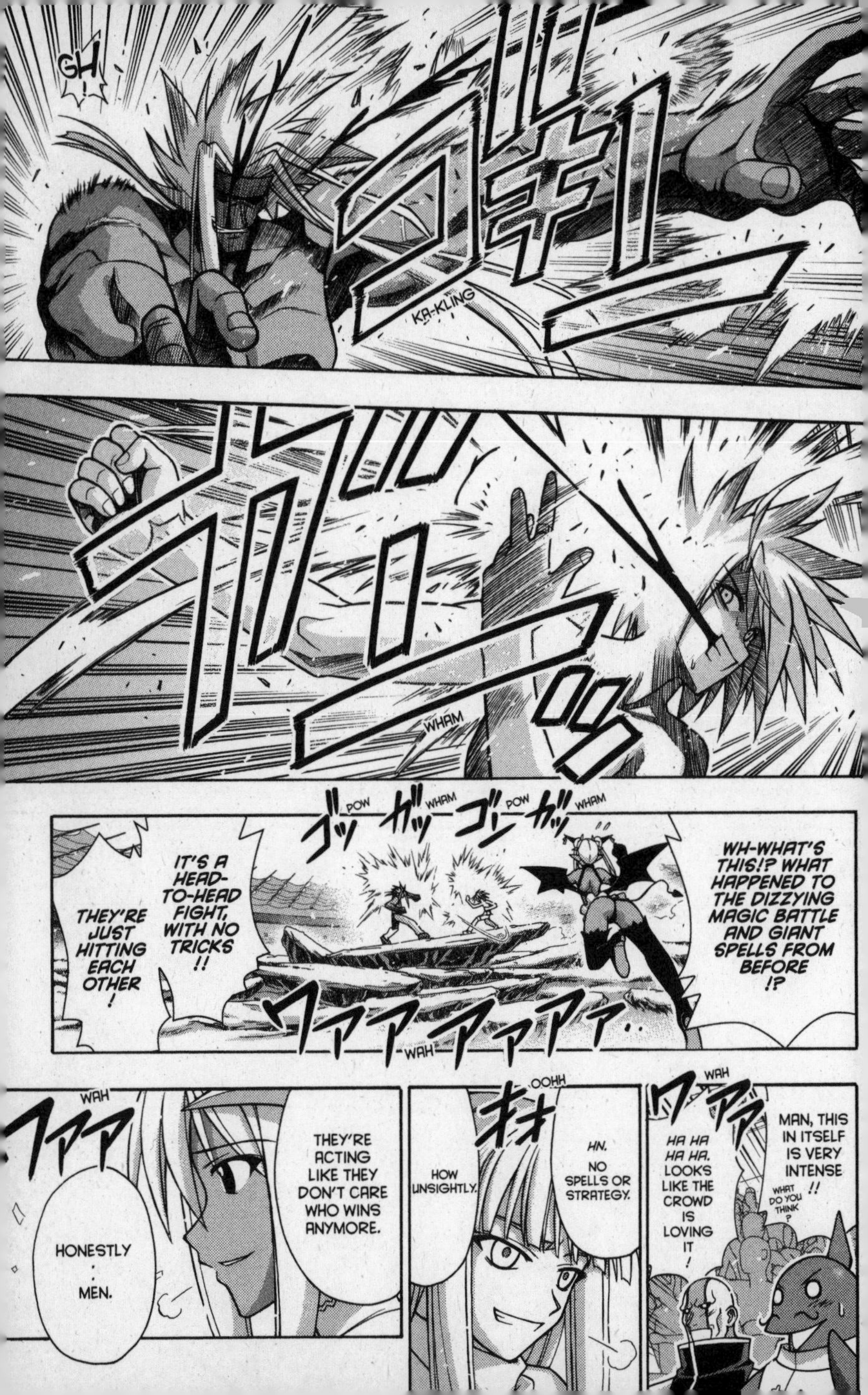
GH!
KA-KLING
WHAM
POW
WHAM
POW
WHAM
WH-WHAT'S THIS!? WHAT HAPPENED TO THE DIZZYING MAGIC BATTLE AND GIANT SPELLS FROM BEFORE !?
IT'S A HEAD-TO-HEAD FIGHT, WITH NO TRICKS !!
THEY'RE JUST HITTING EACH OTHER !
WAH
WAH
MAN, THIS IN ITSELF IS VERY INTENSE !!
WHAT DO YOU THINK ?
HA HA HA HA. LOOKS LIKE THE CROWD IS LOVING IT !
OOHH
HN. NO SPELLS OR STRATEGY.
HOW UNSIGHTLY.
WAH
THEY'RE ACTING LIKE THEY DON'T CARE WHO WINS ANYMORE.
HONESTLY ... MEN.

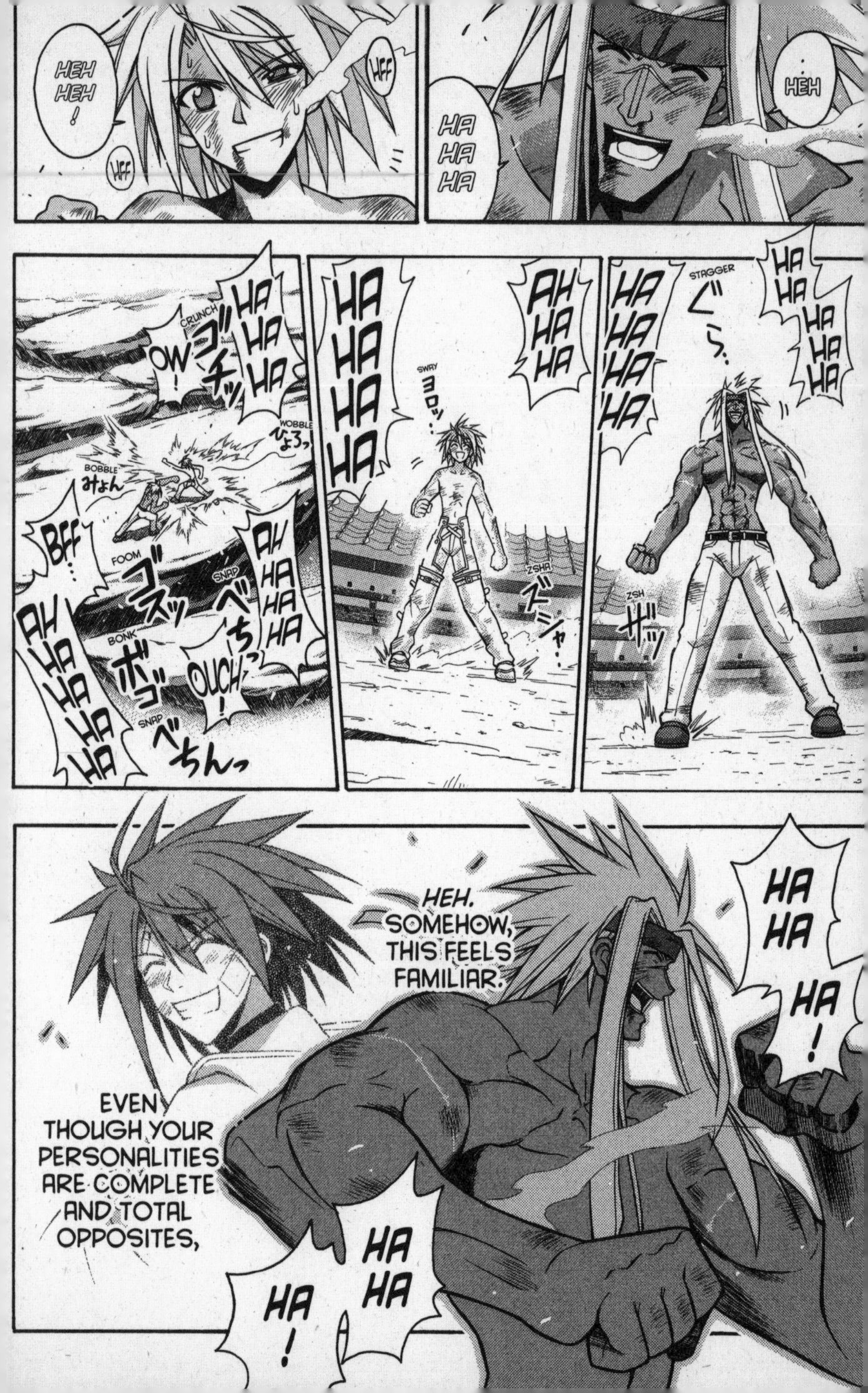
HEH
HA HA HA
HFF
HEH HEH !
HFF
HA HA HA HA HA
STAGGER ぐら…
HA HA HA HA HA
ZSH ザッ
AH HA HA
HA HA HA HA HA
SWAY ヨロッ…
ZSHA ズシャ…
HA HA HA
CRUNCH ゴチッ
OW!
WOBBLE ひょろっ
BOBBLE みょん
BFF…
FOOM ゴスッ
AH HA HA HA HA
SNAP べちっ
OUCH!
BONK ボゴ
SNAP べちんっ
AH HA HA HA HA HA
HA HA HA!
HEH. SOMEHOW, THIS FEELS FAMILIAR.
EVEN THOUGH YOUR PERSONALITIES ARE COMPLETE AND TOTAL OPPOSITES,
HA HA HA!

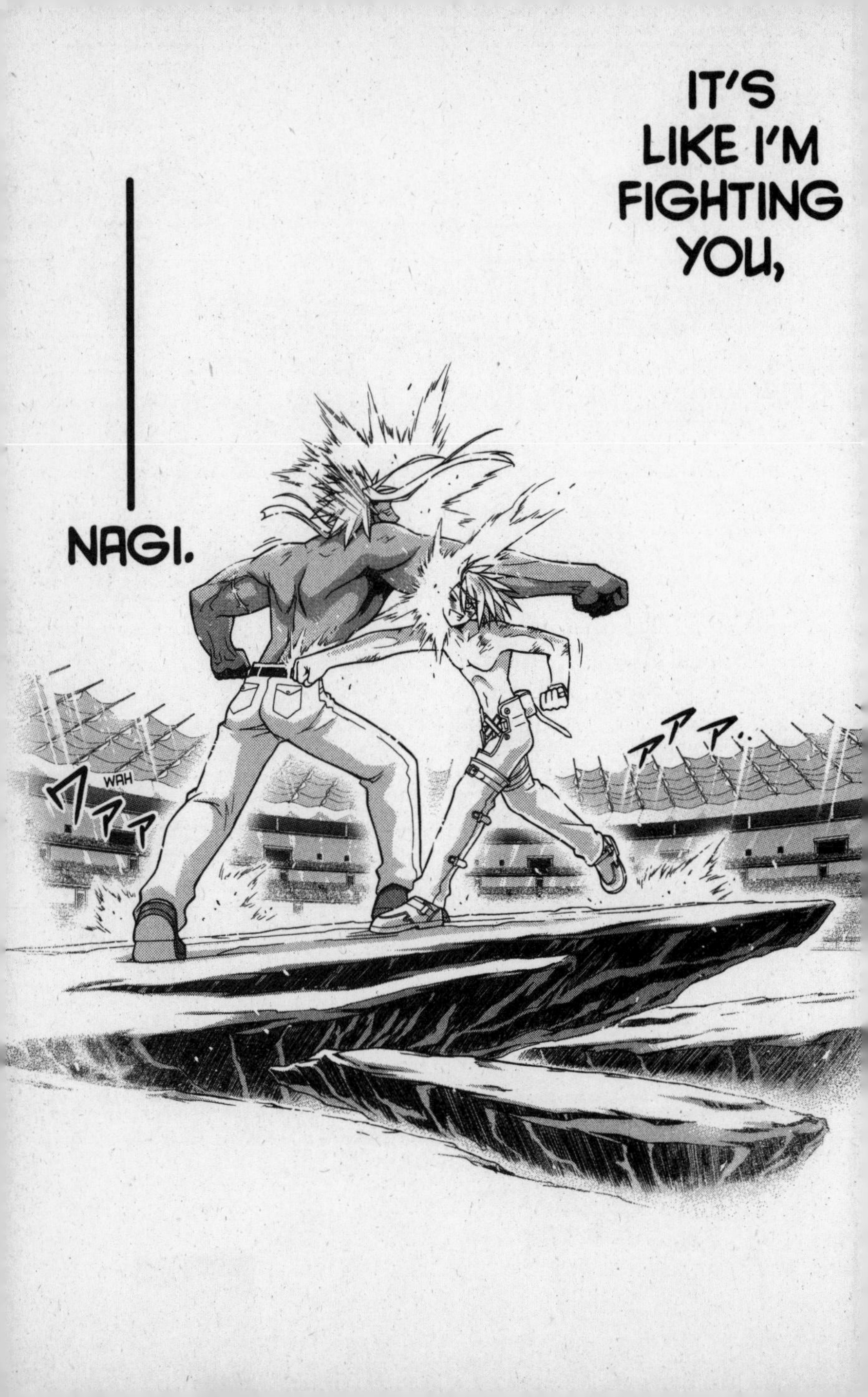
IT'S LIKE I'M FIGHTING YOU,
NAGI.
アアア‥
ワァァ
WAH

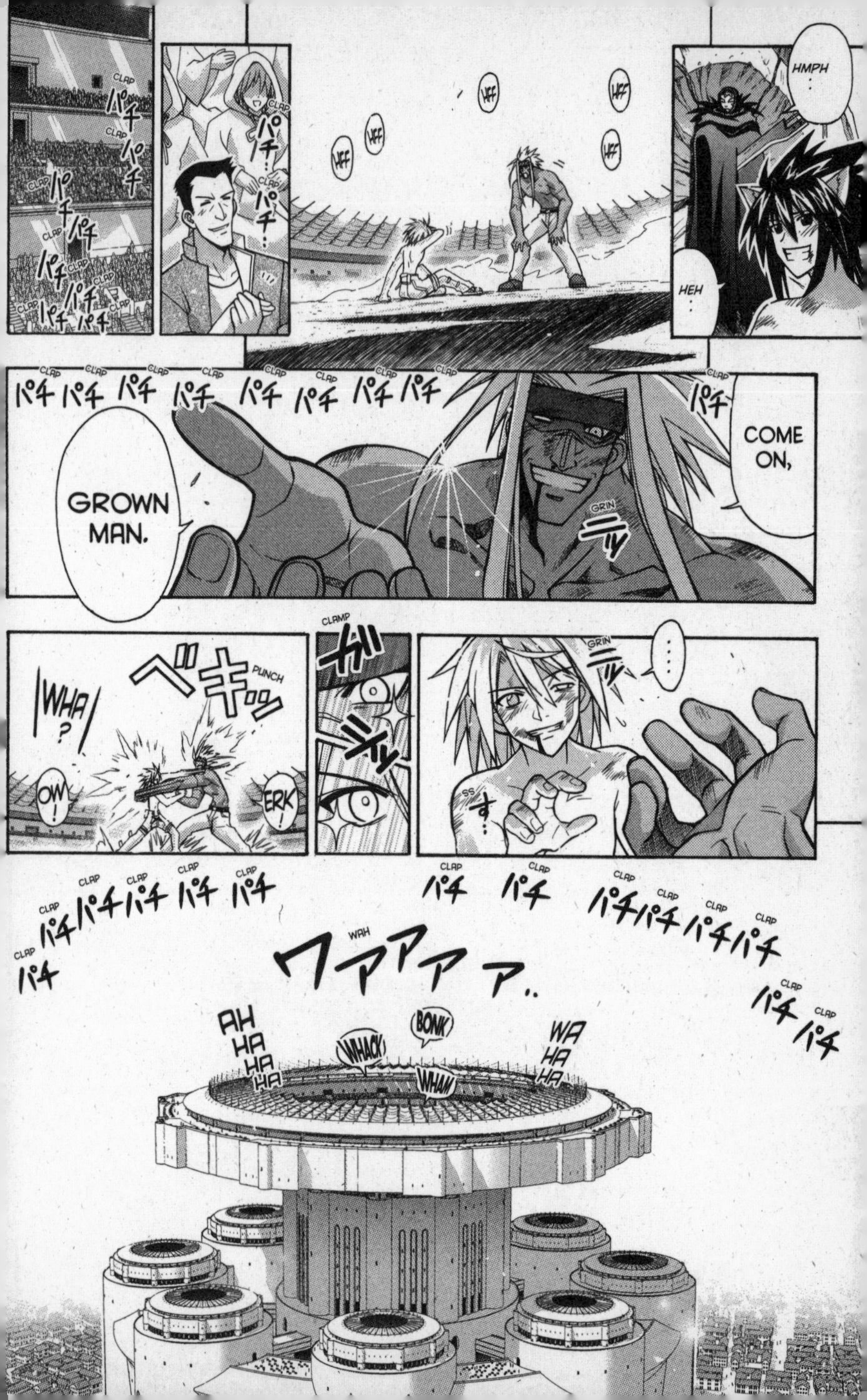
HMPH...
HEH...
HFF
HFF
HFF
HFF
HFF
CLAP パチ...
CLAP パチ...
CLAP パチ パチ
CLAP パチ パチ
CLAP パチ パチ
CLAP パチ パチ
CLAP パチ パチ
CLAP パチ パチ パチ パチ パチ パチ パチ パチ パチ
COME ON,
GRIN ニッ
GROWN MAN.
...
GRIN ニッ
SS す...
CLAMP ガッ
シッ
PUNCH ベキッ
WHA?
OW!
ERK!
CLAP パチ パチ パチ パチ パチ パチ
CLAP パチ パチ パチ パチ パチ パチ パチ パチ
WAH ワアアア..
AH HA HA HA
WHACK
BONK
WHAM
WA HA HA

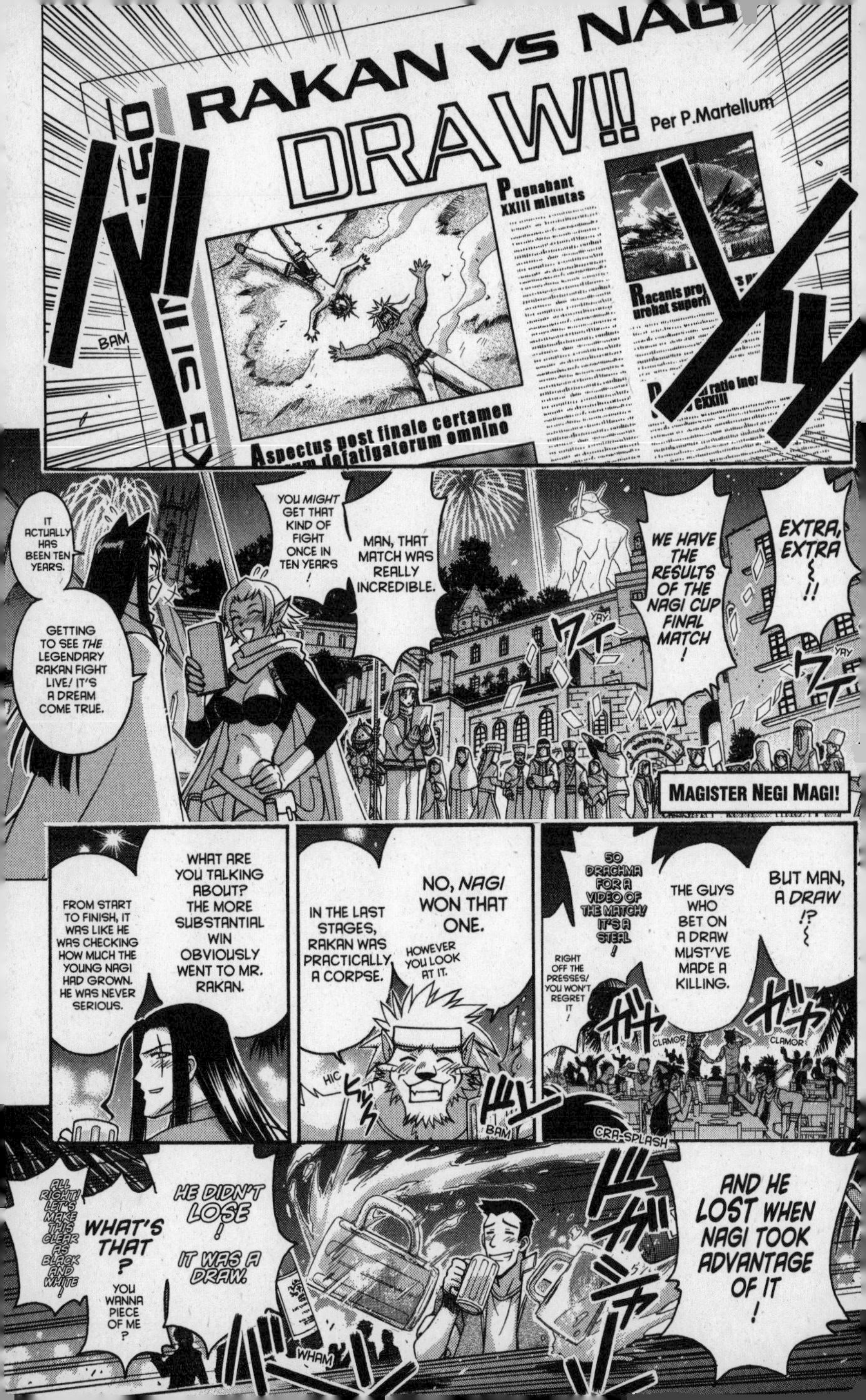
RAKAN VS NAG
DRAW!!
Per P.Martellum
Pugnabant XXIII minutas
Aspectus post finale certamen
defatigatorum omnino
BAM
EXTRA, EXTRA~!!
YAY
WE HAVE THE RESULTS OF THE NAGI CUP FINAL MATCH!
YAY
MAN, THAT MATCH WAS REALLY INCREDIBLE.
YOU MIGHT GET THAT KIND OF FIGHT ONCE IN TEN YEARS!
IT ACTUALLY HAS BEEN TEN YEARS.
GETTING TO SEE THE LEGENDARY RAKAN FIGHT LIVE! IT'S A DREAM COME TRUE.
MAGISTER NEGI MAGI!
BUT MAN, A DRAW!?~
THE GUYS WHO BET ON A DRAW MUST'VE MADE A KILLING.
50 DRACHMA FOR A VIDEO OF THE MATCH! IT'S A STEAL!
RIGHT OFF THE PRESSES! YOU WON'T REGRET IT!
CLAMOR
CLAMOR
NO, NAGI WON THAT ONE.
IN THE LAST STAGES, RAKAN WAS PRACTICALLY A CORPSE.
HOWEVER YOU LOOK AT IT.
HIC
BAM
WHAT ARE YOU TALKING ABOUT? THE MORE SUBSTANTIAL WIN OBVIOUSLY WENT TO MR. RAKAN.
FROM START TO FINISH, IT WAS LIKE HE WAS CHECKING HOW MUCH THE YOUNG NAGI HAD GROWN. HE WAS NEVER SERIOUS.
CRA-SPLASH
AND HE LOST WHEN NAGI TOOK ADVANTAGE OF IT!
HE DIDN'T LOSE! IT WAS A DRAW.
WHAT'S THAT?
YOU WANNA PIECE OF ME?
ALL RIGHT! LET'S MAKE THIS CLEAR AS BLACK AND WHITE
WHAM

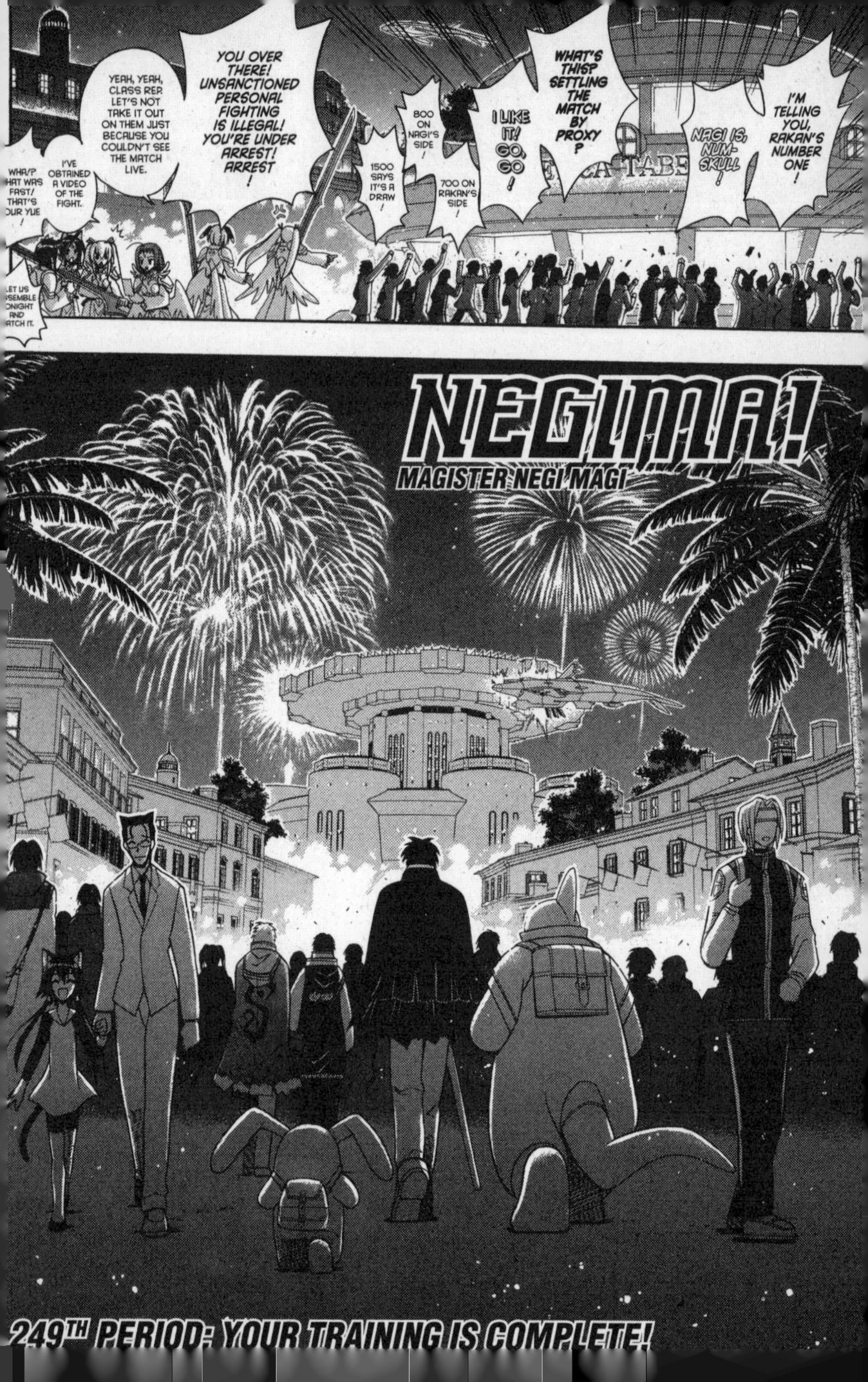
I'M TELLING YOU, RAKAN'S NUMBER ONE!
NAGI IS, NUM-SKULL!
WHAT'S THIS? SETTLING THE MATCH BY PROXY?
I LIKE IT! GO, GO!
700 ON RAKAN'S SIDE!
800 ON NAGI'S SIDE!
1500 SAYS IT'S A DRAW!
YOU OVER THERE! UNSANCTIONED PERSONAL FIGHTING IS ILLEGAL! YOU'RE UNDER ARREST! ARREST!
YEAH, YEAH, CLASS REP. LET'S NOT TAKE IT OUT ON THEM JUST BECAUSE YOU COULDN'T SEE THE MATCH LIVE.
I'VE OBTAINED A VIDEO OF THE FIGHT.
WHA!? HAT WAS FAST! THAT'S OUR YUE!
LET US SSEMBLE ONIGHT AND ATCH IT.
NEGIMA!
MAGISTER NEGI MAGI
249TH PERIOD: YOUR TRAINING IS COMPLETE!

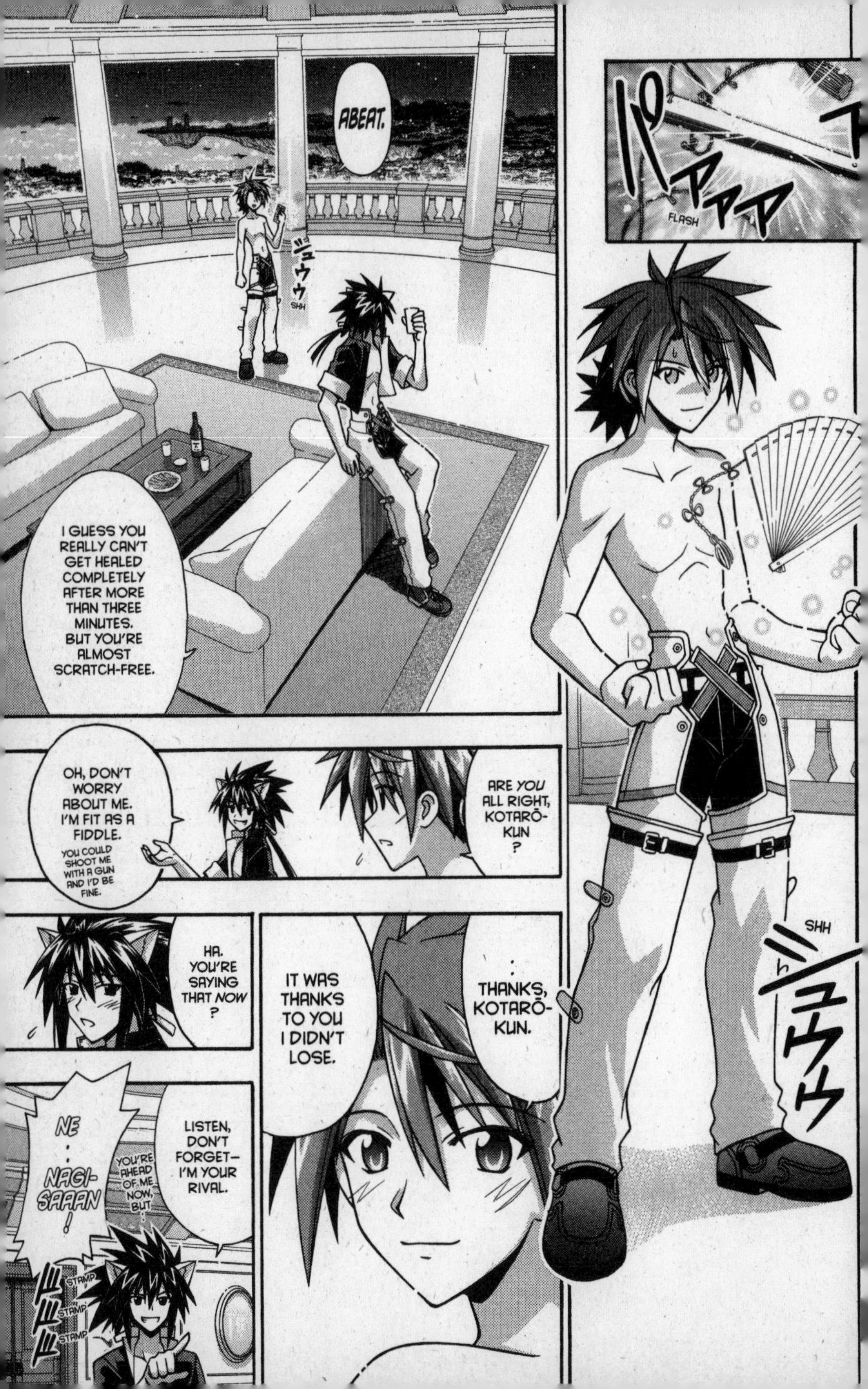
FLASH
SHH
ABEAT.
SHH
I GUESS YOU REALLY CAN'T GET HEALED COMPLETELY AFTER MORE THAN THREE MINUTES. BUT YOU'RE ALMOST SCRATCH-FREE.
ARE *YOU* ALL RIGHT, KOTARŌ-KUN?
OH, DON'T WORRY ABOUT ME. I'M FIT AS A FIDDLE.
YOU COULD SHOOT ME WITH A GUN AND I'D BE FINE.
: THANKS, KOTARŌ-KUN.
IT WAS THANKS TO YOU I DIDN'T LOSE.
HA. YOU'RE SAYING THAT *NOW*?
LISTEN, DON'T FORGET— I'M YOUR RIVAL.
YOU'RE AHEAD OF ME NOW, BUT...
NE : NAGI-SAAAN!
STAMP
STAMP
STAMP

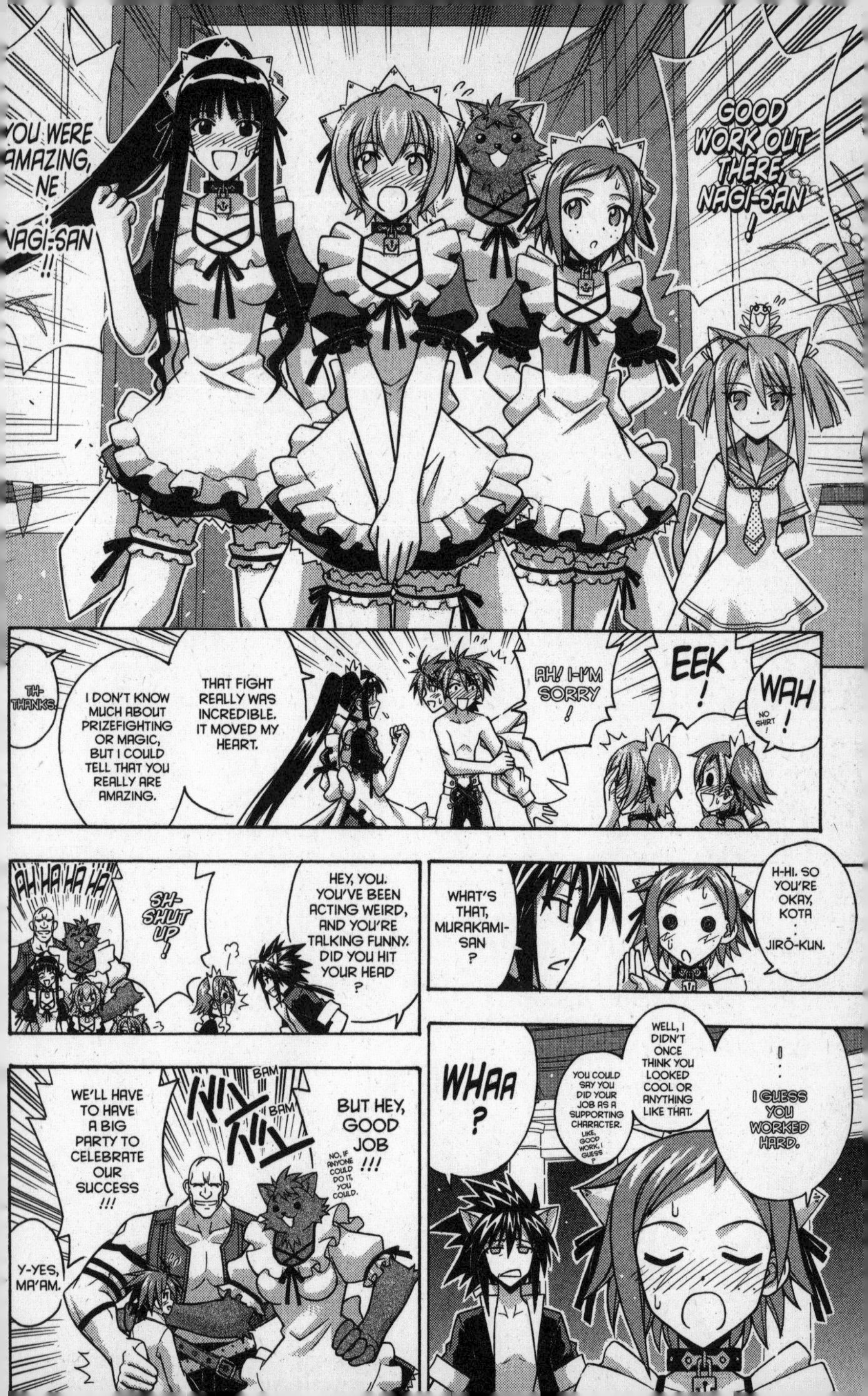

GOOD WORK OUT THERE, NAGI-SAN!
YOU WERE AMAZING, NE... NAGI-SAN!!
WAH
NO SHIRT!
EEK!
AH! I-I'M SORRY!
THAT FIGHT REALLY WAS INCREDIBLE. IT MOVED MY HEART.
I DON'T KNOW MUCH ABOUT PRIZEFIGHTING OR MAGIC, BUT I COULD TELL THAT YOU REALLY ARE AMAZING.
TH-THANKS.
H-HI. SO YOU'RE OKAY, KOTA... JIRŌ-KUN.
WHAT'S THAT, MURAKAMI-SAN?
HEY, YOU. YOU'VE BEEN ACTING WEIRD, AND YOU'RE TALKING FUNNY. DID YOU HIT YOUR HEAD?
SH-SHUT UP!
AH HA HA HA
I... I GUESS YOU WORKED HARD.
WELL, I DIDN'T ONCE THINK YOU LOOKED COOL OR ANYTHING LIKE THAT.
YOU COULD SAY YOU DID YOUR JOB AS A SUPPORTING CHARACTER.
LIKE, GOOD WORK, I GUESS?
WHAA?
BUT HEY, GOOD JOB!!!
NO, IF ANYONE COULD DO IT, YOU COULD.
BAM
BAM
WE'LL HAVE TO HAVE A BIG PARTY TO CELEBRATE OUR SUCCESS!!!
Y-YES, MA'AM.

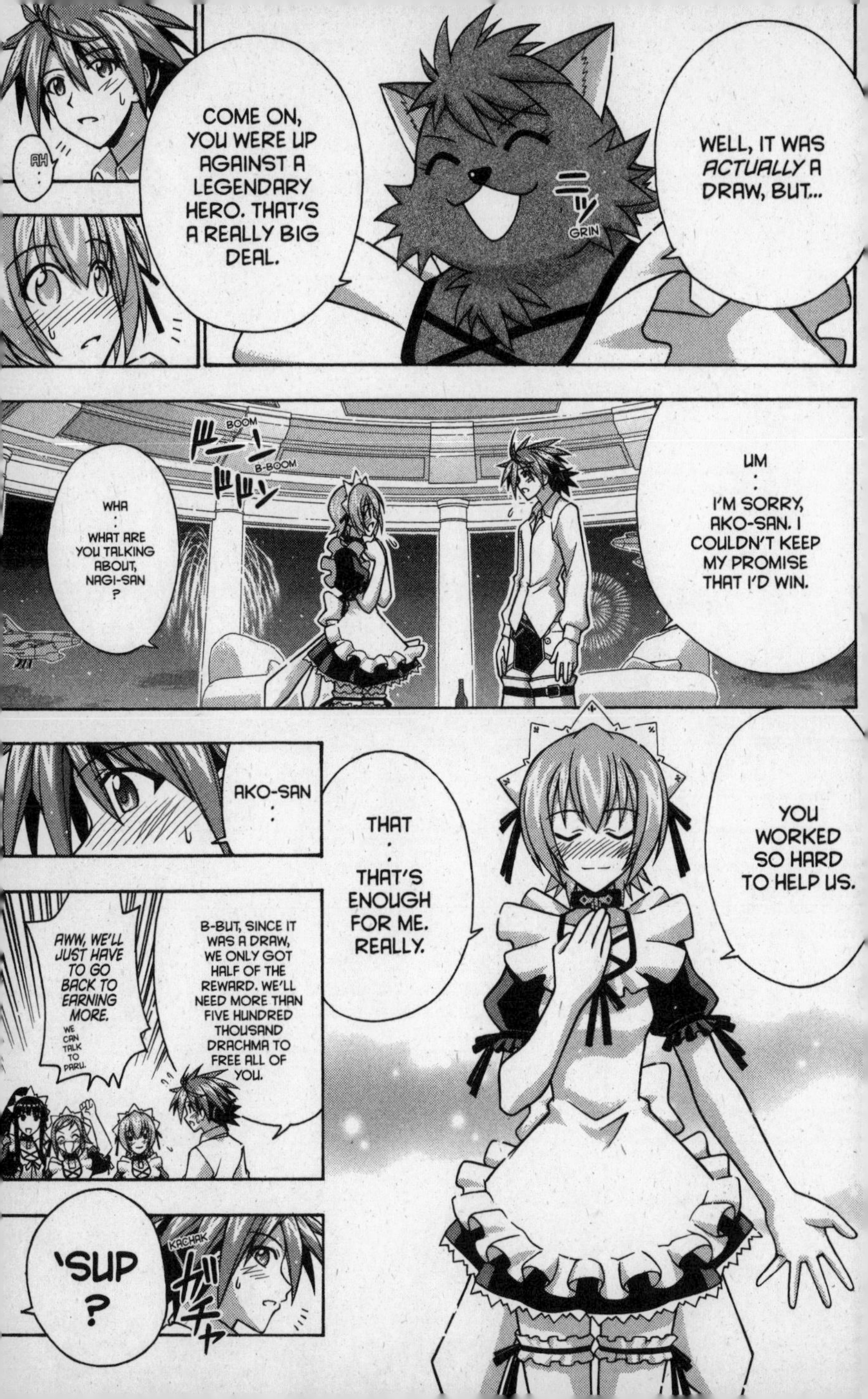
WELL, IT WAS ACTUALLY A DRAW, BUT...
GRIN
COME ON, YOU WERE UP AGAINST A LEGENDARY HERO. THAT'S A REALLY BIG DEAL.
AH :
UM : I'M SORRY, AKO-SAN. I COULDN'T KEEP MY PROMISE THAT I'D WIN.
BOOM
B-BOOM
WHA : WHAT ARE YOU TALKING ABOUT, NAGI-SAN ?
YOU WORKED SO HARD TO HELP US.
THAT : THAT'S ENOUGH FOR ME. REALLY.
AKO-SAN :
B-BUT, SINCE IT WAS A DRAW, WE ONLY GOT HALF OF THE REWARD. WE'LL NEED MORE THAN FIVE HUNDRED THOUSAND DRACHMA TO FREE ALL OF YOU.
AWW, WE'LL JUST HAVE TO GO BACK TO EARNING MORE.
WE CAN TALK TO PARU.
KACHAK
'SUP ?

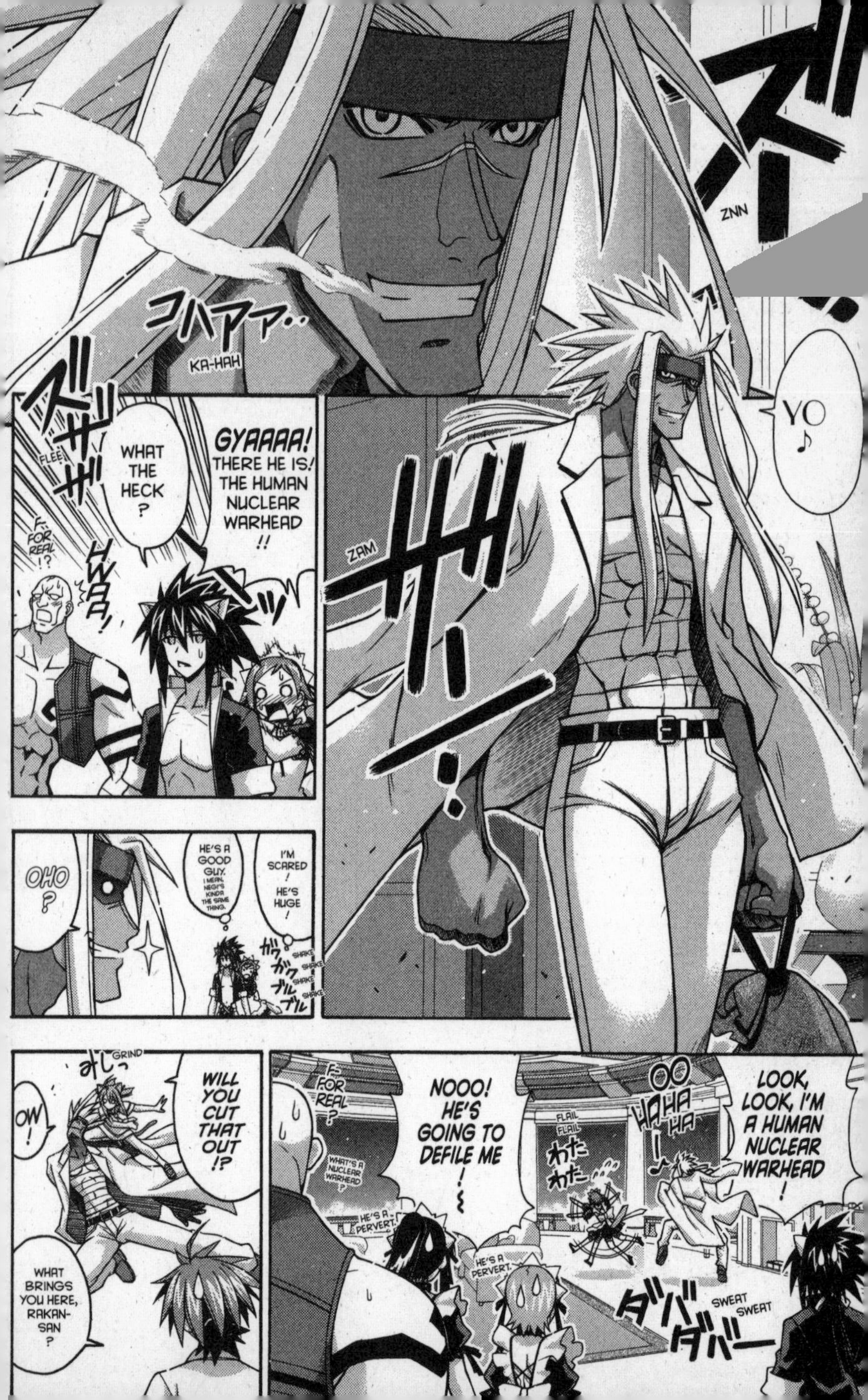ZNN
コハァァ..
KA-HAH
YO ♪
ZAM
GYAAAA! THERE HE IS! THE HUMAN NUCLEAR WARHEAD!!
WHAT THE HECK?
FLEE
F-FOR REAL!?
HWAA!
I'M SCARED! HE'S HUGE
HE'S A GOOD GUY. I MEAN, NEGI'S KINDA THE SAME THING.
OHO?
SHAKE SHAKE SHAKE SHAKE
LOOK, LOOK, I'M A HUMAN NUCLEAR WARHEAD!
HAHAHA!
FLAIL FLAIL
わたわた
NOOO! HE'S GOING TO DEFILE ME!~
F-FOR REAL?
WHAT'S A NUCLEAR WARHEAD?
HE'S A PERVERT.
HE'S A PERVERT.
SWEAT SWEAT
WILL YOU CUT THAT OUT!?
GRIND
OW!
WHAT BRINGS YOU HERE, RAKAN-SAN?

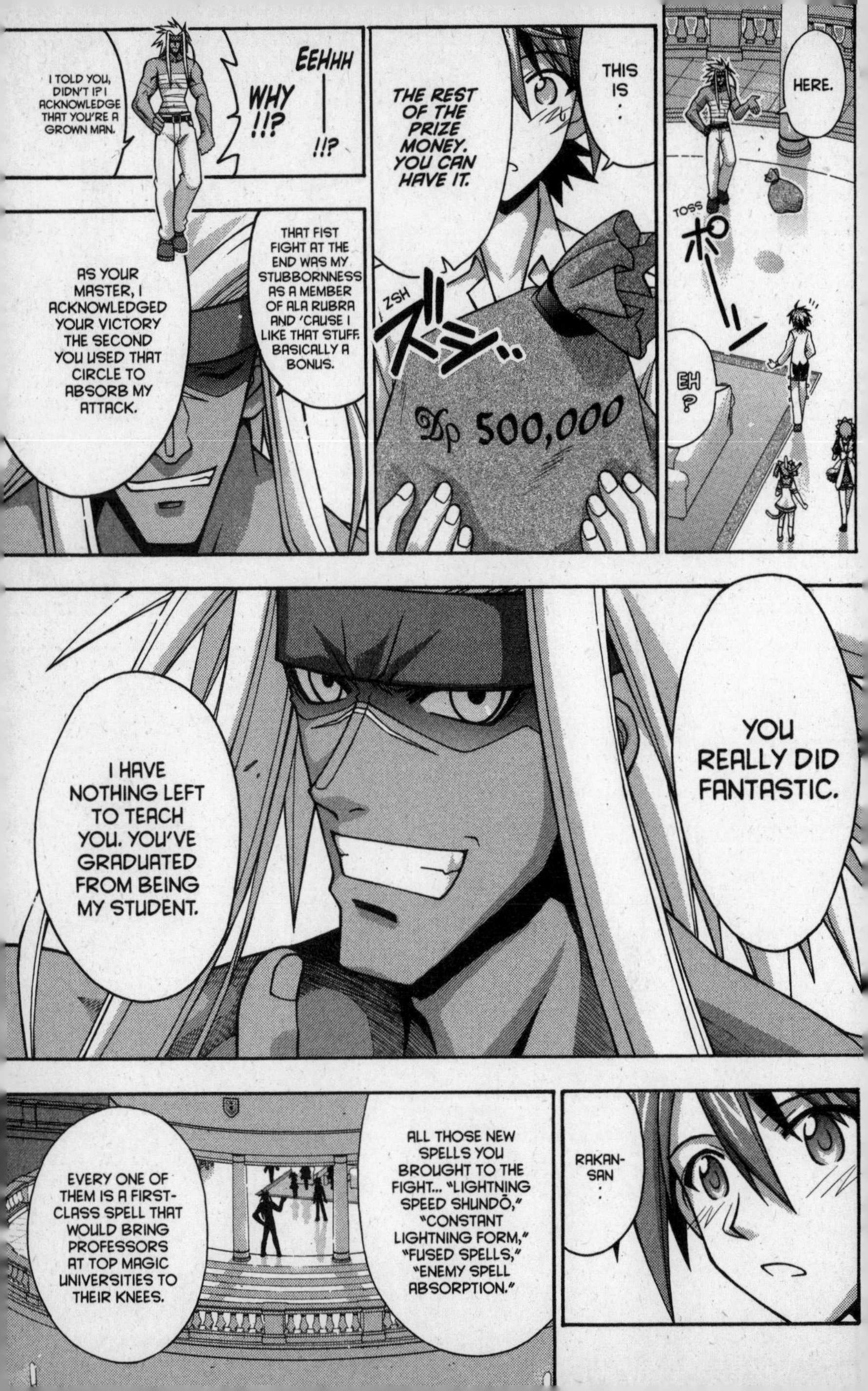
HERE.
TOSS
EH?
THIS IS . . .
THE REST OF THE PRIZE MONEY. YOU CAN HAVE IT.
ZSH
Dp 500,000
EEHHH —!!?
WHY!!?
I TOLD YOU, DIDN'T I? I ACKNOWLEDGE THAT YOU'RE A GROWN MAN.
THAT FIST FIGHT AT THE END WAS MY STUBBORNNESS AS A MEMBER OF ALA RUBRA AND 'CAUSE I LIKE THAT STUFF. BASICALLY A BONUS.
AS YOUR MASTER, I ACKNOWLEDGED YOUR VICTORY THE SECOND YOU USED THAT CIRCLE TO ABSORB MY ATTACK.
YOU REALLY DID FANTASTIC.
I HAVE NOTHING LEFT TO TEACH YOU. YOU'VE GRADUATED FROM BEING MY STUDENT.
RAKAN-SAN . . .
ALL THOSE NEW SPELLS YOU BROUGHT TO THE FIGHT... "LIGHTNING SPEED SHUNDŌ," "CONSTANT LIGHTNING FORM," "FUSED SPELLS," "ENEMY SPELL ABSORPTION."
EVERY ONE OF THEM IS A FIRST-CLASS SPELL THAT WOULD BRING PROFESSORS AT TOP MAGIC UNIVERSITIES TO THEIR KNEES.

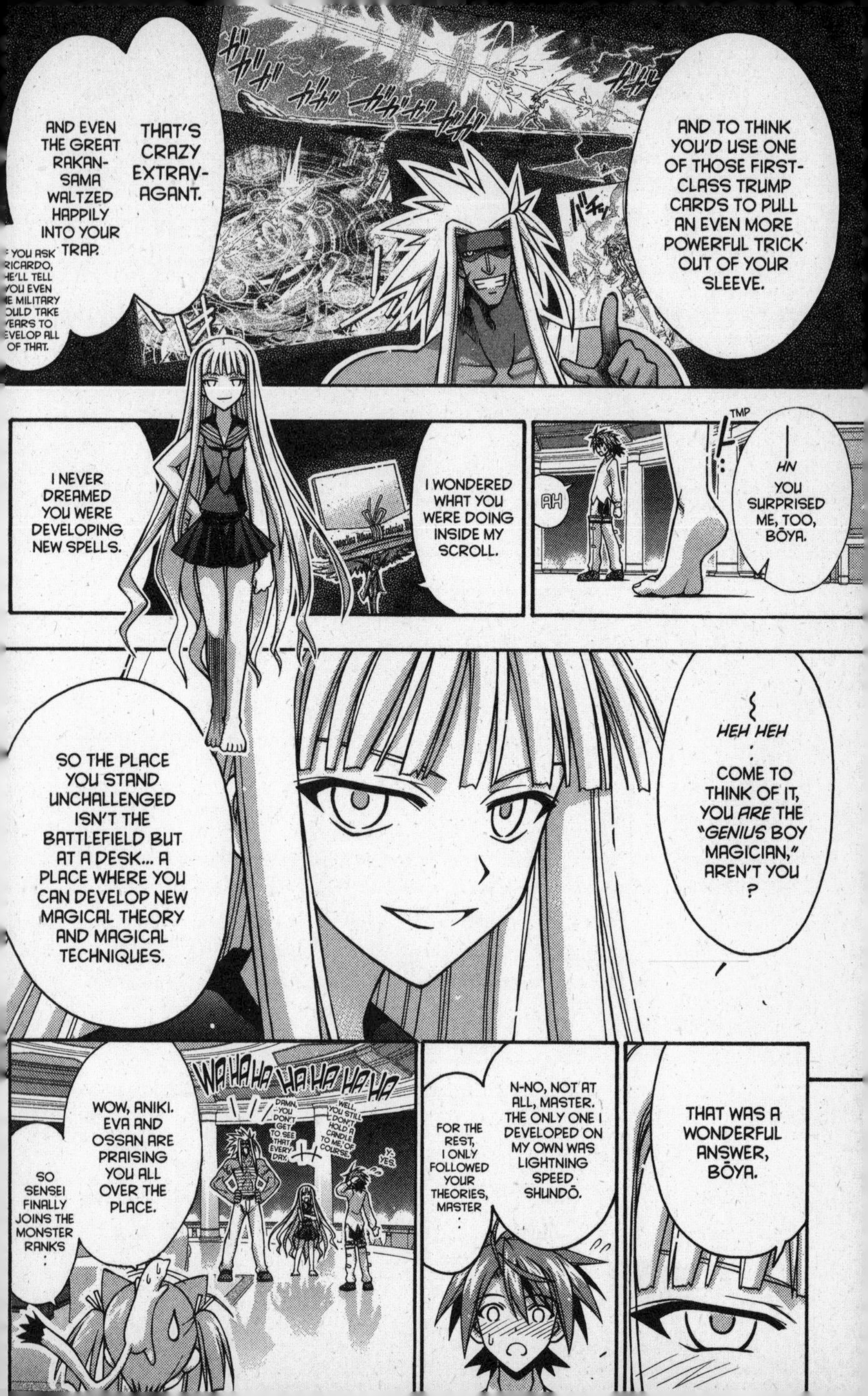
AND TO THINK YOU'D USE ONE OF THOSE FIRST-CLASS TRUMP CARDS TO PULL AN EVEN MORE POWERFUL TRICK OUT OF YOUR SLEEVE.
THAT'S CRAZY EXTRAV-AGANT.
AND EVEN THE GREAT RAKAN-SAMA WALTZED HAPPILY INTO YOUR TRAP.
F YOU ASK RICARDO, HE'LL TELL YOU EVEN E MILITARY OULD TAKE YEARS TO EVELOP ALL OF THAT.
TMP
HN YOU SURPRISED ME, TOO, BŌYA.
AH
I WONDERED WHAT YOU WERE DOING INSIDE MY SCROLL.
I NEVER DREAMED YOU WERE DEVELOPING NEW SPELLS.
HEH HEH... COME TO THINK OF IT, YOU *ARE* THE "*GENIUS* BOY MAGICIAN," AREN'T YOU?
SO THE PLACE YOU STAND UNCHALLENGED ISN'T THE BATTLEFIELD BUT AT A DESK... A PLACE WHERE YOU CAN DEVELOP NEW MAGICAL THEORY AND MAGICAL TECHNIQUES.
THAT WAS A WONDERFUL ANSWER, BŌYA.
N-NO, NOT AT ALL, MASTER. THE ONLY ONE I DEVELOPED ON MY OWN WAS LIGHTNING SPEED SHUNDŌ.
FOR THE REST, I ONLY FOLLOWED YOUR THEORIES, MASTER...
WA HA HA HA HA HA HA
DAMN, YOU DON'T GET TO SEE THAT EVERY DAY.
WELL, YOU STILL DON'T HOLD A CANDLE TO ME, OF COURSE.
Y-YES.
WOW, ANIKI. EVA AND OSSAN ARE PRAISING YOU ALL OVER THE PLACE.
SO SENSEI FINALLY JOINS THE MONSTER RANKS...

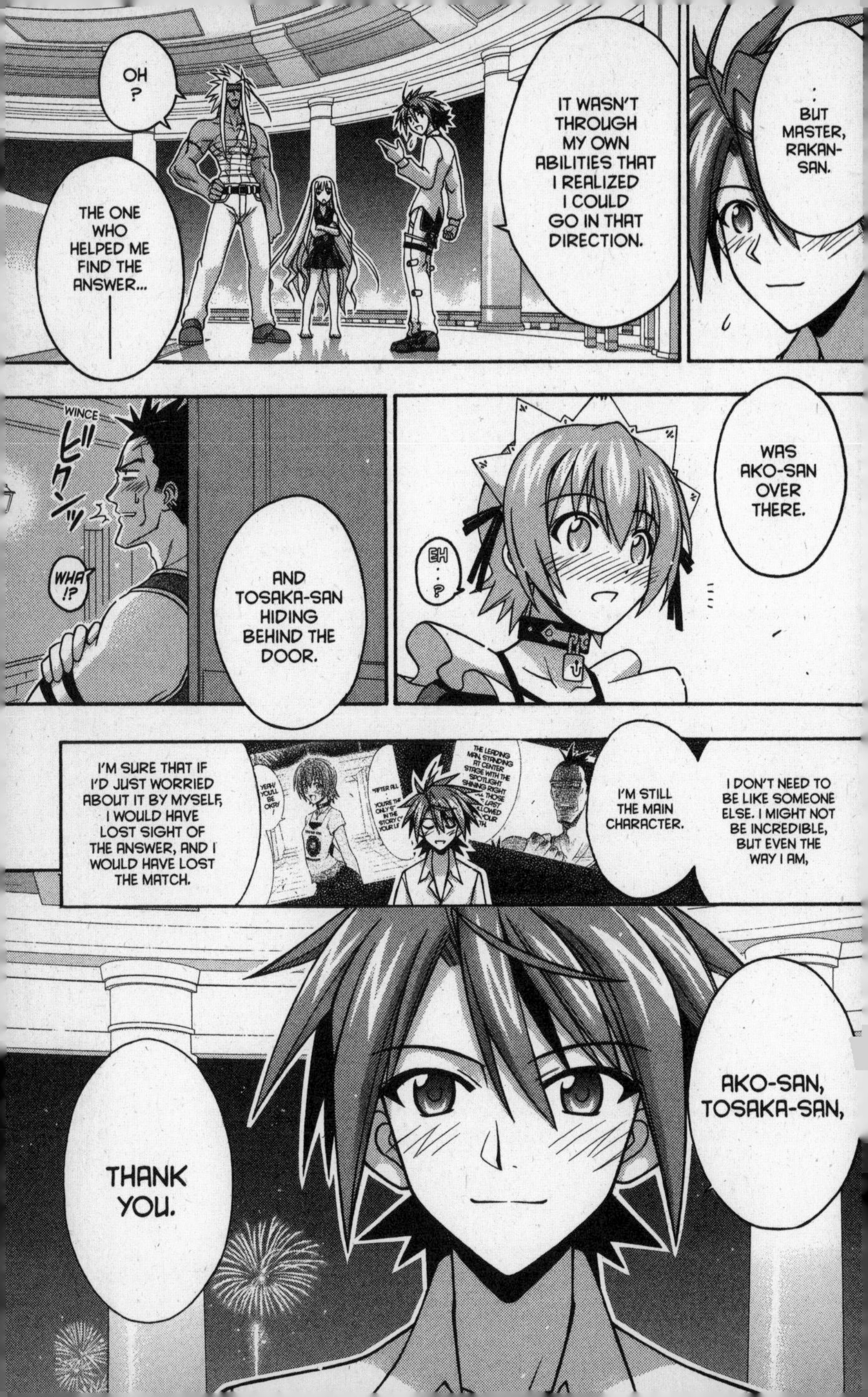
... BUT MASTER, RAKAN-SAN.
IT WASN'T THROUGH MY OWN ABILITIES THAT I REALIZED I COULD GO IN THAT DIRECTION.
OH?
THE ONE WHO HELPED ME FIND THE ANSWER... —
WAS AKO-SAN OVER THERE.
EH...?
AND TOSAKA-SAN HIDING BEHIND THE DOOR.
WINCE
WHA!?
I DON'T NEED TO BE LIKE SOMEONE ELSE. I MIGHT NOT BE INCREDIBLE, BUT EVEN THE WAY I AM,
I'M STILL THE MAIN CHARACTER.
YEAH YOU'LL BE OKAY!
I'M SURE THAT IF I'D JUST WORRIED ABOUT IT BY MYSELF, I WOULD HAVE LOST SIGHT OF THE ANSWER, AND I WOULD HAVE LOST THE MATCH.
AKO-SAN, TOSAKA-SAN,
THANK YOU.

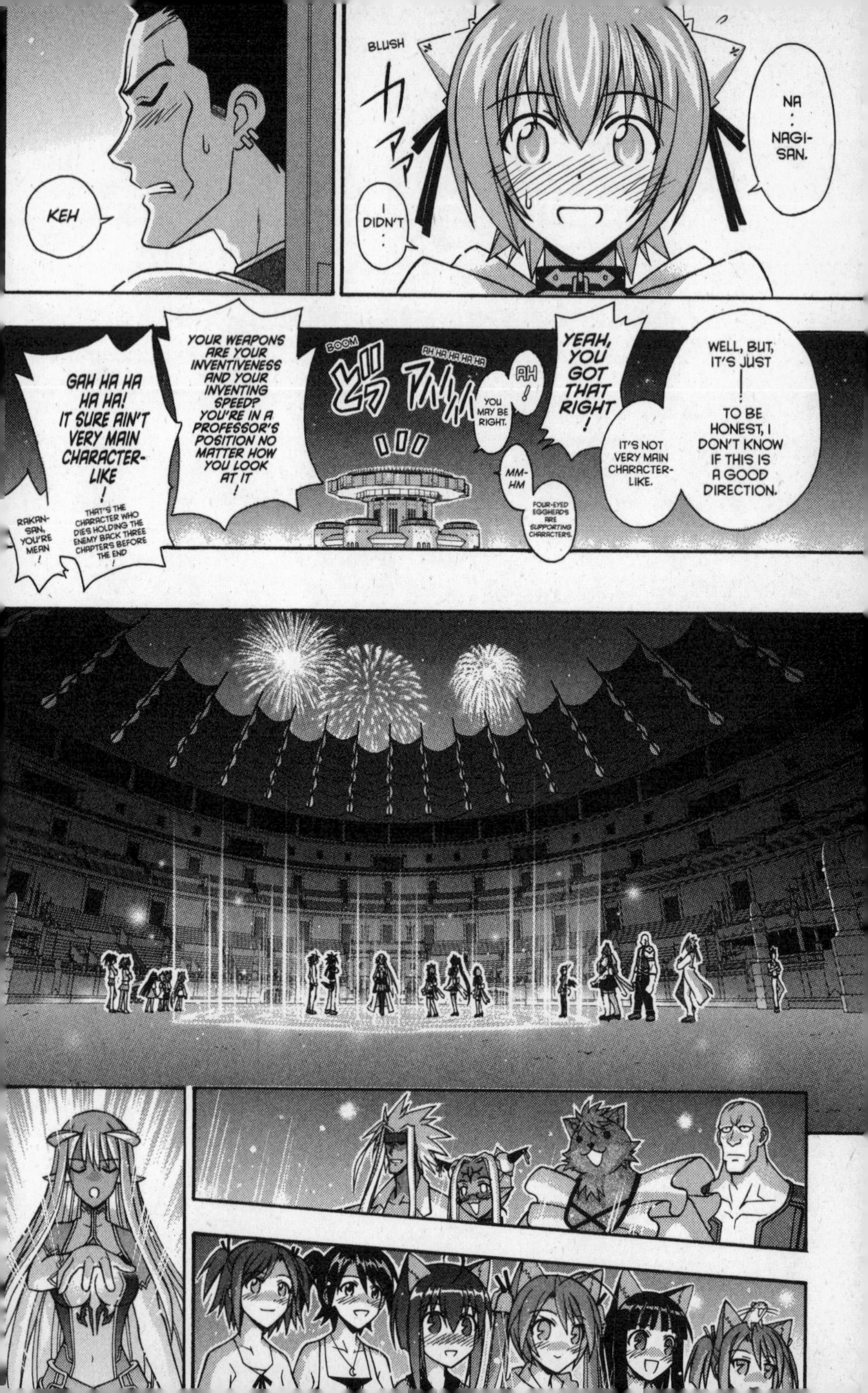
BLUSH
カァァ
NA... NAGI-SAN.
I DIDN'T...
KEH
WELL, BUT, IT'S JUST— TO BE HONEST, I DON'T KNOW IF THIS IS A GOOD DIRECTION.
YEAH, YOU GOT THAT RIGHT!
IT'S NOT VERY MAIN CHARACTER-LIKE.
AH!
YOU MAY BE RIGHT.
MM-HM
FOUR-EYED EGGHEADS ARE SUPPORTING CHARACTERS.
AH HA HA HA HA
アハハハ
BOOM
どっ
YOUR WEAPONS ARE YOUR INVENTIVENESS AND YOUR INVENTING SPEED? YOU'RE IN A PROFESSOR'S POSITION NO MATTER HOW YOU LOOK AT IT!
GAH HA HA HA HA! IT SURE AIN'T VERY MAIN CHARACTER-LIKE!
THAT'S THE CHARACTER WHO DIES HOLDING THE ENEMY BACK THREE CHAPTERS BEFORE THE END!
RAKAN-SAN, YOU'RE MEAN!

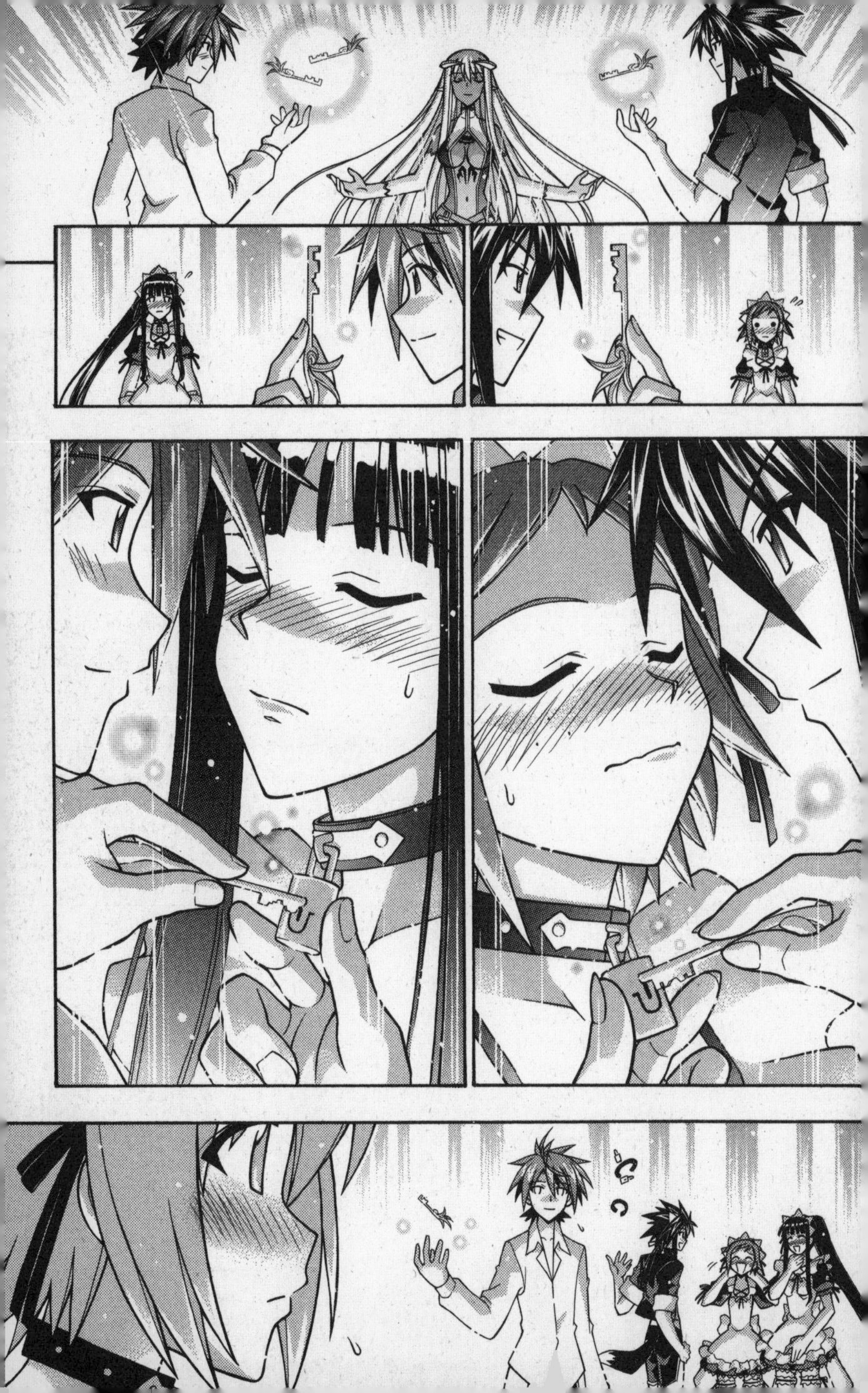

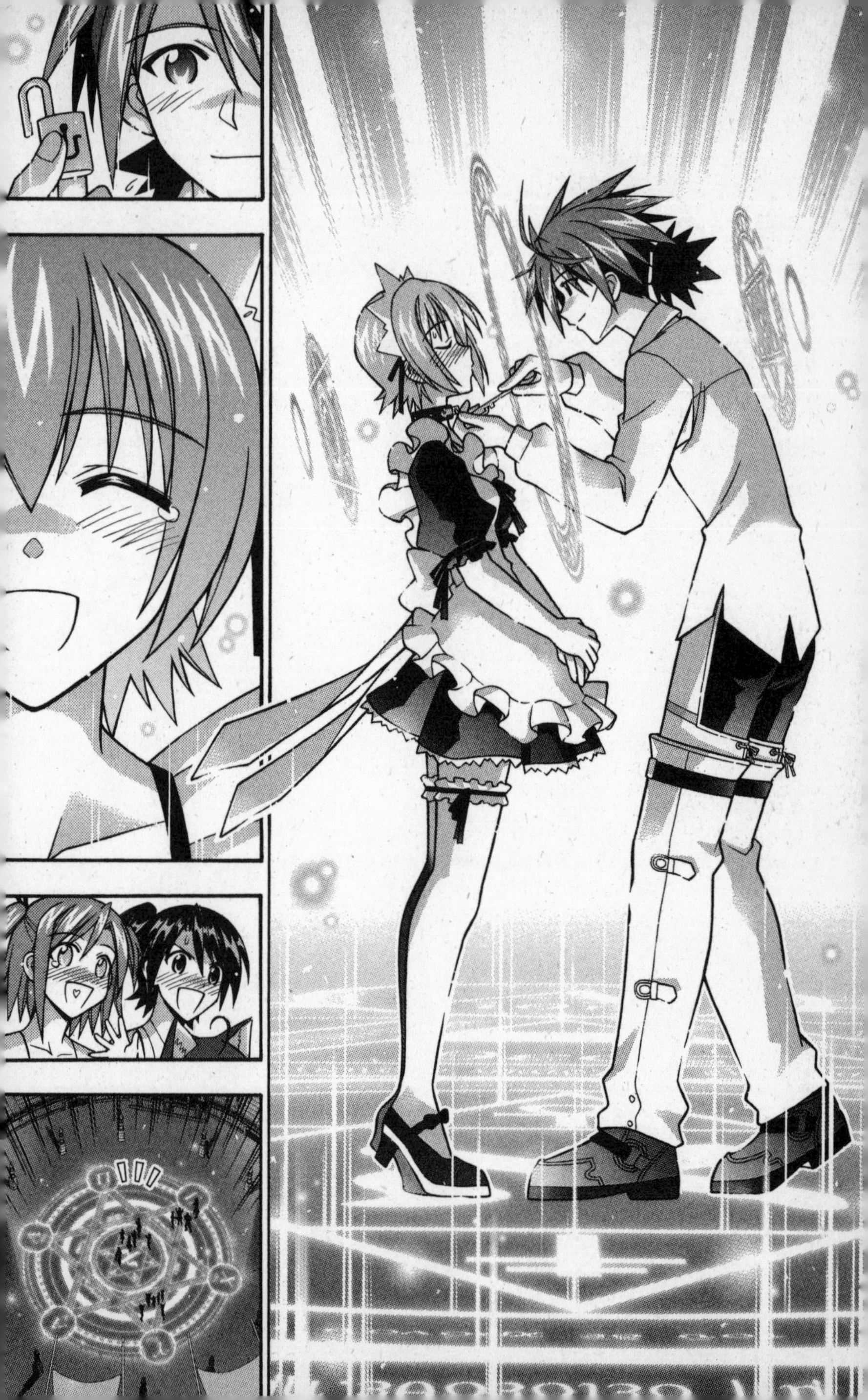

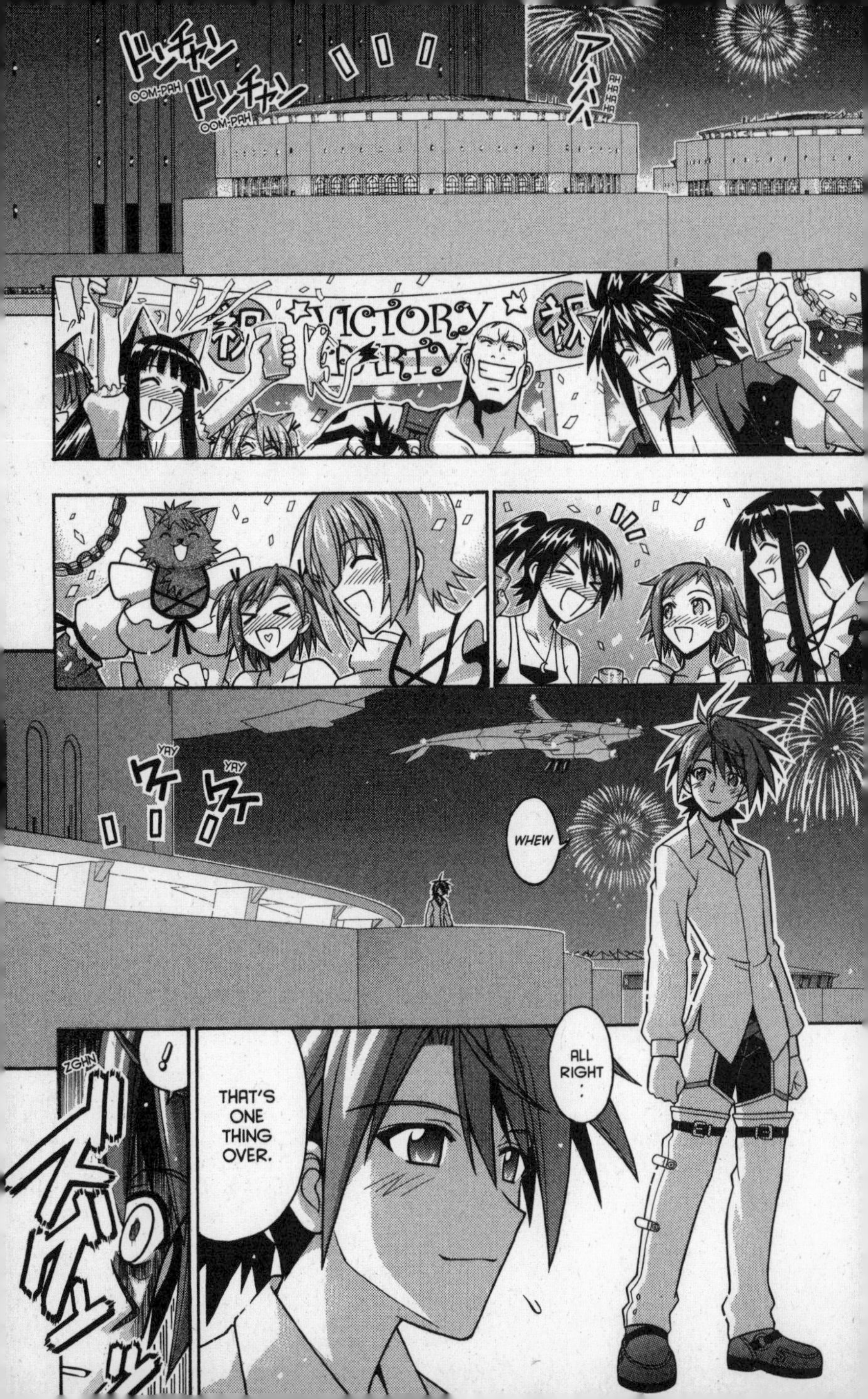
AH HA HA HA
OOM-PAH
OOM-PAH
VICTORY PARTY
YAY
YAY
WHEW
ALL RIGHT...
THAT'S ONE THING OVER.
!
ZGHN

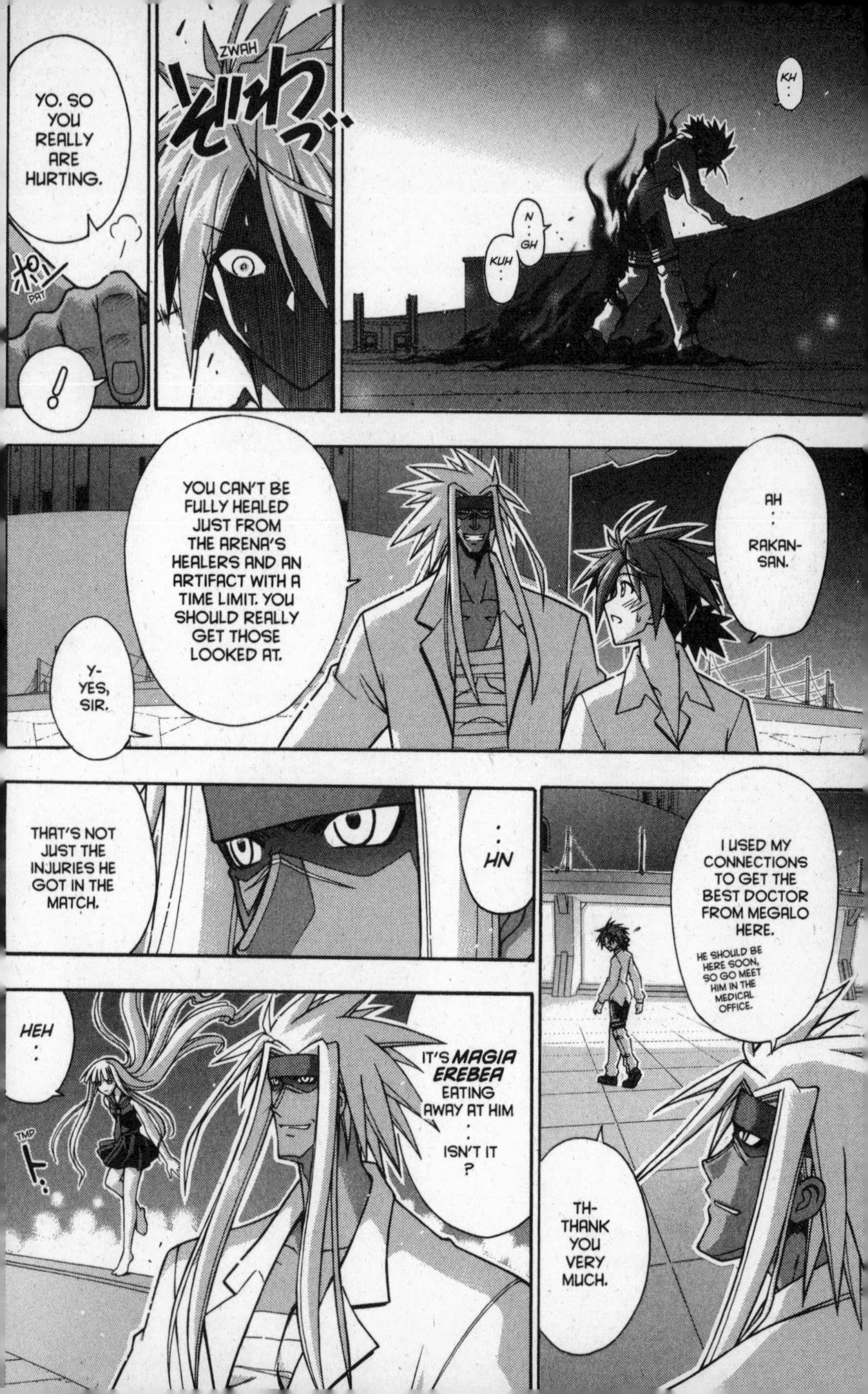
KH...
N...GH
KUH...
ZWAH
ぞわっ
YO. SO YOU REALLY ARE HURTING.
ポン
PAT
!
AH... RAKAN-SAN.
YOU CAN'T BE FULLY HEALED JUST FROM THE ARENA'S HEALERS AND AN ARTIFACT WITH A TIME LIMIT. YOU SHOULD REALLY GET THOSE LOOKED AT.
Y-YES, SIR.
I USED MY CONNECTIONS TO GET THE BEST DOCTOR FROM MEGALO HERE.
HE SHOULD BE HERE SOON, SO GO MEET HIM IN THE MEDICAL OFFICE.
TH-THANK YOU VERY MUCH.
...HN
THAT'S NOT JUST THE INJURIES HE GOT IN THE MATCH.
IT'S MAGIA EREBEA EATING AWAY AT HIM... ISN'T IT?
HEH...
TMP
ト

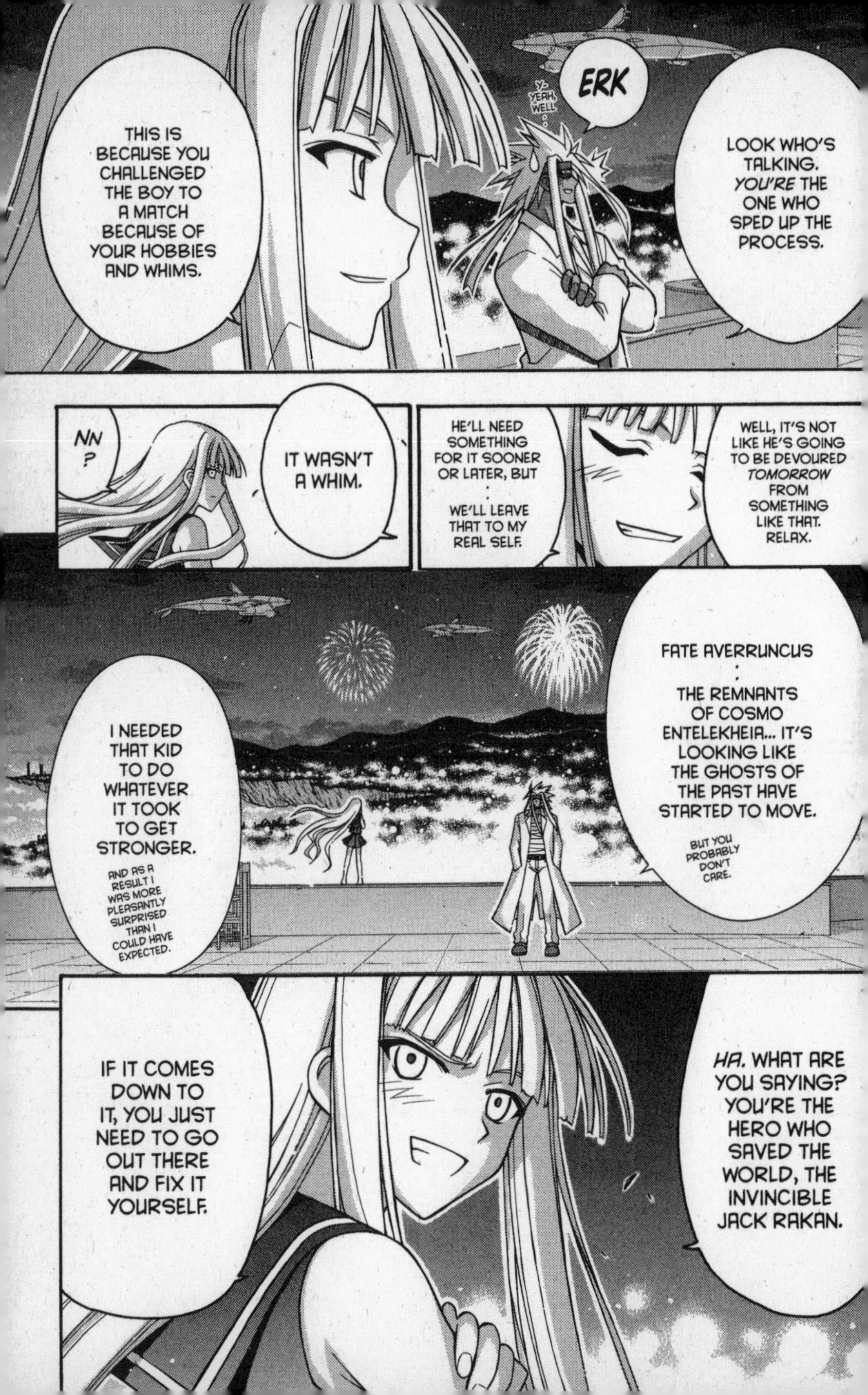
THIS IS BECAUSE YOU CHALLENGED THE BOY TO A MATCH BECAUSE OF YOUR HOBBIES AND WHIMS.
ERK
Y-YEAH, WELL...
LOOK WHO'S TALKING. *YOU'RE* THE ONE WHO SPED UP THE PROCESS.
WELL, IT'S NOT LIKE HE'S GOING TO BE DEVOURED *TOMORROW* FROM SOMETHING LIKE THAT. RELAX.
HE'LL NEED SOMETHING FOR IT SOONER OR LATER, BUT
:
WE'LL LEAVE THAT TO MY REAL SELF.
IT WASN'T A WHIM.
NN?
FATE AVERRUNCUS
:
THE REMNANTS OF COSMO ENTELEKHEIA... IT'S LOOKING LIKE THE GHOSTS OF THE PAST HAVE STARTED TO MOVE.
BUT YOU PROBABLY DON'T CARE.
I NEEDED THAT KID TO DO WHATEVER IT TOOK TO GET STRONGER.
AND AS A RESULT I WAS MORE PLEASANTLY SURPRISED THAN I COULD HAVE EXPECTED.
HA. WHAT ARE YOU SAYING? YOU'RE THE HERO WHO SAVED THE WORLD, THE INVINCIBLE JACK RAKAN.
IF IT COMES DOWN TO IT, YOU JUST NEED TO GO OUT THERE AND FIX IT YOURSELF.

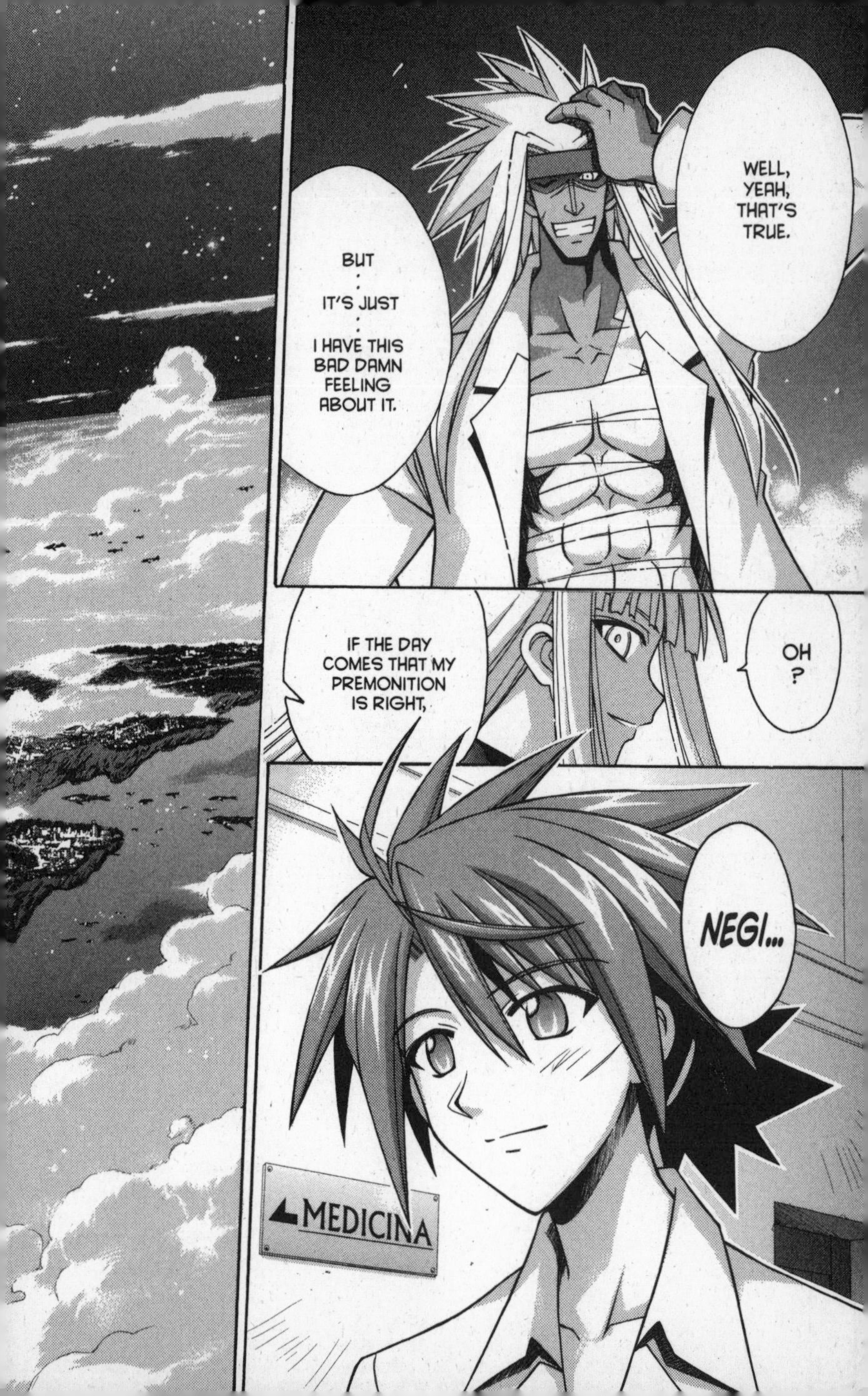
WELL, YEAH, THAT'S TRUE.
BUT . . . IT'S JUST . . . I HAVE THIS BAD DAMN FEELING ABOUT IT.
OH ?
IF THE DAY COMES THAT MY PREMONITION IS RIGHT,
NEGI...
MEDICINA

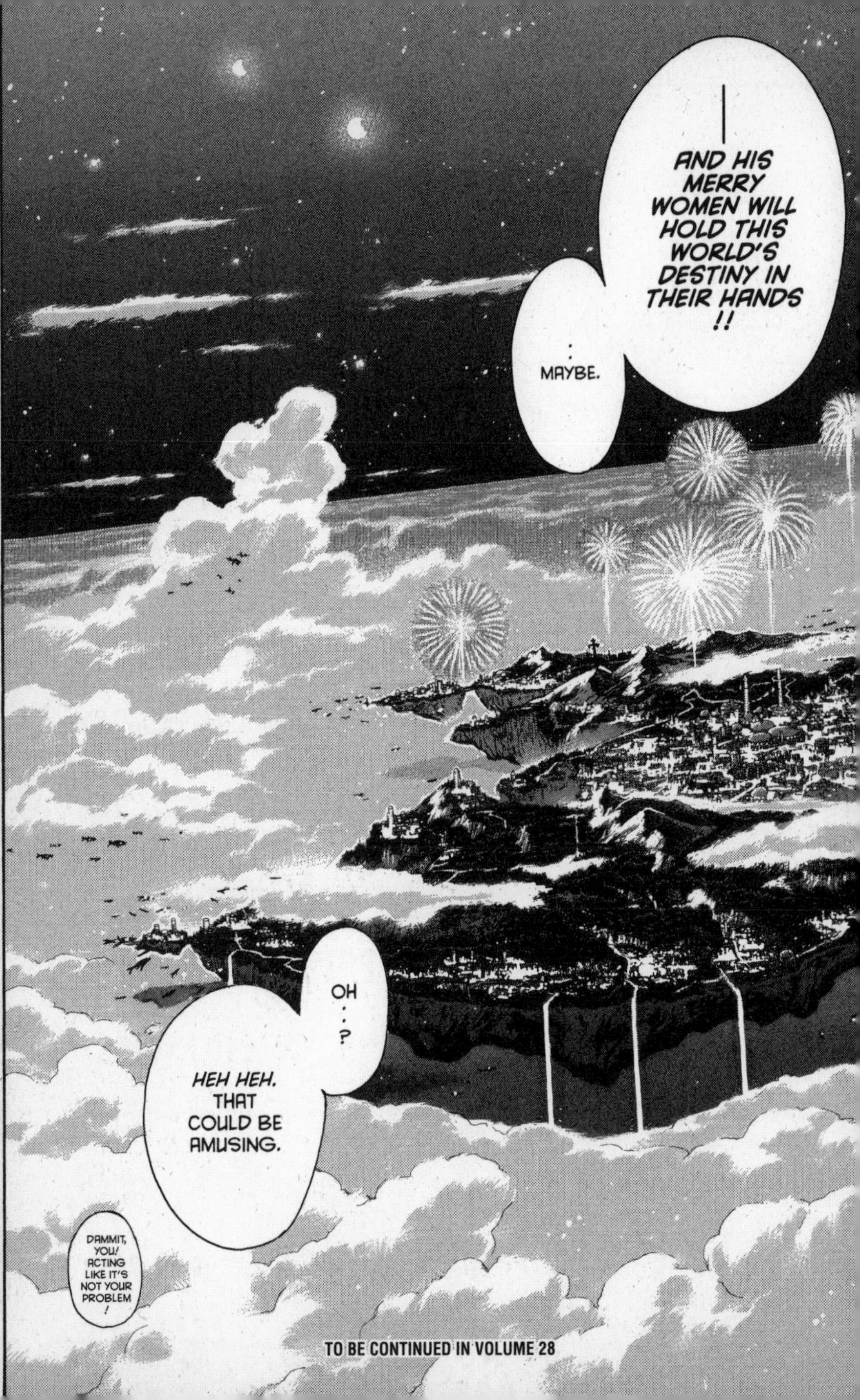
—AND HIS MERRY WOMEN WILL HOLD THIS WORLD'S DESTINY IN THEIR HANDS!!
: MAYBE.
OH..?
HEH HEH. THAT COULD BE AMUSING.
DAMMIT, YOU! ACTING LIKE IT'S NOT YOUR PROBLEM!

TO BE CONTINUED IN VOLUME 28

-STAFF-

Ken Akamatsu
Takashi Takemoto
Kenichi Nakamura
Masaki Ohyama
Keiichi Yamashita
Tohru Mitsuhashi
Yuichi Yoshida

Thanks to
Ran Ayanaga

LEXICON NEGIMARIUM

■ "Thunder in Heaven, Great Vigor"
Ê ASTRAPÊ UPER OURANOU MEGA DUNAMENÊ
(ʹΗ ʹΑΣΤΡΑΠΗʹ ʹΥΠΕʹΡ ΟΥʹΡΑΝΟʹΥ ΜΕʹΓΑ ΔΥΝΑʹΜΕΝΗ)

One of the practical uses of dark magic, it takes the magic power from "Thousand Lightning Bolts (Kilipl Astrapê)" into one's flesh and fuses it with the spirit. In doing so, the caster becomes a mass of electrically charged particles.

"Thunder in Heaven, Great Vigor" is the aesthetic name of "Great Vigor," one of the hexagrams of I Ching divination. It gets the name because the zhèn (shake) trigram, symbolizing thunder, is placed above the qián (force) trigram, symbolizing heaven. The "Great Vigor" *Hsiang Chuan* of I Ching states, "Thunder is above the heavens, there will be great vigor," and the *T'uan Chuan* states, "Great vigor, greatness is vigor. It moves by means of strength, therefore it is vigor." Thus, the "Great Vigor" hexagram signifies strong, fierce mobility. In keeping with that, ʹΗ ΑΣΤΡΑΠΗʹΥΠΕʹΡ ΟΥʹΡΑΝΟʹΥ ΜΕΓΑ ΔΥΝΑʹΜΕΝΗ [ΕΣΤΙʹΝ] (Ê ASTRAPÊ UPER OURANOU MEGA DUNAMENÊ [ESTIN]) is ancient Greek meaning, "the lightning above heaven is greatly powerful."

Once the caster has become a mass of charged particles, he separates positively charged particles from his body and positions them to create a certain extent of an electrical field. The charged particles and electrical field can be changed at will from a latent state to an active one, and vice versa, by the caster, who has taken the lightning magic into himself. When the electrical field becomes active, its powerful electric potential difference draws the negatively charged particles that make up the caster's body toward the positively charged particles of the field with tremendous force. Thus, the caster can move at high speeds via the electrical discharge (In the story, Chamo says that he travels at 150km per second, because that is the average progression velocity of the advance discharge when lightning strikes. The main lightning strike occurs after the electrical path is opened, so it is even faster. For example, in a simple calculation, to ionize a nitrogen atom, a single electrical particle flying inside a discharge path needs to go at a speed greater than 2,260km/s. Either way, electrical discharge in the atmosphere is controlled by outside conditions such as temperature, pressure, and medium, so we can't expect an accurate figure).

During this time, the negatively charged particles of the caster's body collide with various molecules and atoms in the air, bringing with them tremendous kinetic energy. Because this kinetic energy becomes ionization energy, impact ionization occurs repeatedly along the discharge path followed by the caster, creating an enormous amount of charged particles and sending out giant flashes of lightning.

However, due to the repeated impact ionization, almost all of the negatively charged particles that made up the caster's body combine with the newly generated positively charged particles inside the discharge path. Therefore, the negatively charged particles making up the caster's body can't simply continue to move at high speeds in the direction of the positioned positively charged particles. This magic is not as simple as merely moving with the speed of lightning.

It was first proven that lightning is an electrical discharge in the air by an experiment conducted in 1752 by the American statesman B. Franklin (1706–90), using a kite and an electric condenser.

However, before modern times, lightning was considered to be *fire* in the sky. The ancient Greek philosopher Aristotle (384 BC–322 BC) states: "The compressed breath is frequently burnt by weak, small fire. This is what we call lightning. At the origin of this lightning, it appears just as though the breath has taken on color." (*Meteorologica*, 369B) In the age of mythology, too, lightning was fire. Hesiod (eighth century BC) states, "From his powerful arms sprang several bolts, bringing with them thunder and lightning. Whirling up the sacred flame (ιερή φλόξ, ieri flox)." (*Theogony*, 690–693) In that case, to put it in magical terms, "becoming a mass of electrically charged particles" means "turning one's body into fire."

Based on this, the spell "Thunder in Heaven, Great Vigor" would be magic that re-creates the caster's body of flesh and blood into a body of fire, changing him into a genie (جنّي). We can say this because a genie is an entity that has been given a body of fire. For example, in the *Qur'an*, it is stated, "Which of the blessings of your Lord will you decline? The Lord created man from the dry earth. Just as one creates earthen vessels. And the Lord created the genies from fire." (55:13–15).

Genies are a paranormal life-form famous in Middle Eastern folklore, such as the spirit in the lamp in *Aladdin*. While their bodies are made of burning fire, they never burn out (this is similar to how living things are not injured by their metabolism). By changing into a genie's body like this, even after losing the charged particles (his fire element) from the early stages of the spell, he regenerates by absorbing the charged particles in the discharge path, thus maintaining his body and continuing to exist.

■ "Spell Emission, Complete Lightning Form"
(perfectus plasmationis per emissionem)

A spell that uses all of the electric attacks taken inside the caster to expand the electrical field that was made active through "Thunder in Heaven, Great Vigor (È Astrapê Uper Ouranou Mega Dunamenê)." The electric potential difference expanded through this spell becomes extremely large, and the impact ionization generated in the discharge path becomes enormous. The electrical attack from this enormous impact ionization is "Chihayaburu Lightning." "*Chihayaburu*" is an ancient Japanese adjective describing forceful strength. It has been represented in ancient Japanese text with characters such as "千早振 (thousand fast tremors)," "知波夜夫流 (waves of knowledge, night man flow)," etc., but the ones used here, "千磐破 (thousand boulder smash)," are believed to give it the meaning "crushing as many as a thousand boulders."

[*Negima!* 246th Period Lexicon Negimarium]

■ "Shadow Cloth Sevenfold, Anti-Physical Wall"
(umbrae septemplex paries anti-corporalis)

A spell that sets up multiple layers of magical barriers made of shadow to defend against physical attacks.

[*Negima!* 247th Period Lexicon Negimarium]

■ "Left Arm Release Stabilize 'Thousand Thunder Bolts.' Right Arm Release Stabilize 'Thousand Thunder Bolts.' Double Load Magic."
(sinistra emissa stagnet KILIPL ASTRAPÊ. dextra emissa stagnet KILIPL ASTRAPÊ. DUPLEX COMPLEXIO)

A spell that first releases two delayed spells of Thousand Lightning Bolts, then takes them into one's flesh and fuses them with the spirit. It exercises double the power of "Thunder in Heaven, Great Vigor." When "Thunder in Heaven, Great Vigor" is only used once, the caster cannot travel at high speeds via the discharge path until after he has separated the positively charged particles from himself and formed the electrical field. But when exercising two "Thunder in Heaven, Great Vigor" spells, the caster can position a new set of positively charged particles while traveling at high speeds, so he can create his next discharge path while in transit. As he repeatedly secures a discharge path mid-motion, it becomes possible for the caster to constantly travel at high speeds.

■ "Dual Arm Release, Right Arm Stabilize 'Thousand Lightning Bolts,' Left Arm Stabilize 'Throwing Thunder,' Spells Unite. Thunder Deity Spear, 'Titan Slayer.'"

(duabus emissae, dextra stagnans *ΚΙΛΙΠΛ΄ ΄ΑΣΤΡΑΠ΄Η*, sinistra stagnans JACULATIO FULGORIS, unisonent. *Διὸς Λόγχη. ΤΙΤΑΝΟ-ΚΤ΄ΟΝΟΝ.*)

A spell that releases the delayed spells, "Thousand Lightning Bolts" and "Throwing Thunder," and breathes the enormous magical power from "Thousand Lightning Bolts" into the magic spear created by "Throwing Thunder," creating a gigantic thunder spear. Because it focuses the power of super-wide-range extermination lightning magic into a single point, the sparks created by a direct attack from the spear are limitlessly intense.

■ "Spell Thaw. Negi-style Dark Magic. 'Enemy Spell Absorption Circle.'"

(agite extractio. Negica Magia Erebea. CIRCULI ABSOPTIONES.)

A spell that draws out a magical-power-absorbing circle that had been drawn and hidden beforehand. The circle that absorbs the magical power is joined directly to Negi's body and soul. For that reason, the magic (or chi energy) absorbed by the circle is activated by dark magic.

[*Negima!* 248th Period Lexicon Negimarium]

■ "The Great Birth Canal"

(sinus magnus)

In Latin, "sinus magnus" means "great birth canal." The birth canal is the path to the great womb, through which life is born and to which life returns. Like the dolmens in Ireland and the tortoise-shell tombs in Okinawa, the tombs seen in various regions are modeled after the womb and birth canal. This is because they were considered to be part of the refrain in which one returns to the source of life through death and is born again. The process of death and rebirth, in which the caster takes the phenomena before his eyes into the bosom of death and gives new life to them is the deepest secret of dark magic.

■ "Release, Thunder Deity Spear, Bring Thousand Thunder Bolts"

(emittens, dios lonchi, KILIPLĒN ASTRAPĒN producam)

The spell that releases the "Thousand Lightning Bolts" electrical attack breathed into the magic spear created by the fusion of "Throwing Thunder" and "Thousand Lightning Bolts."

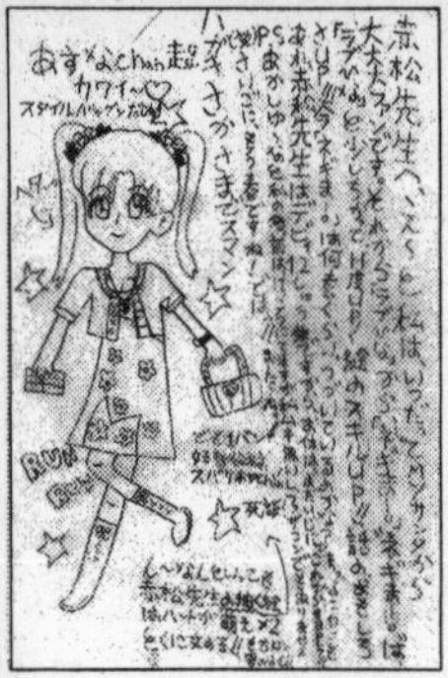

▲ ASUNA'S ALL DRESSED UP.☆

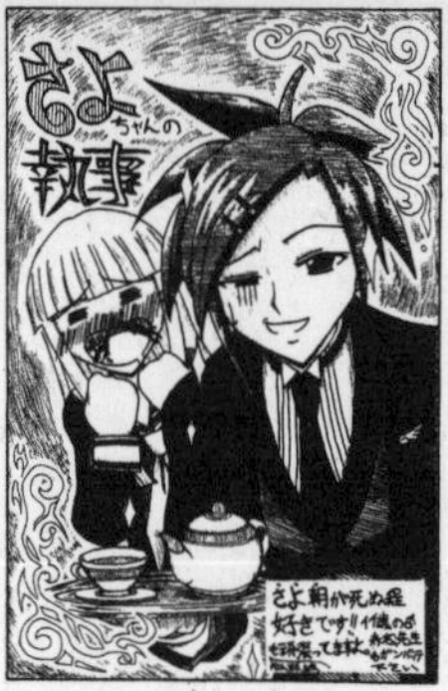

▲ HANDSOME! KAZUMI☆

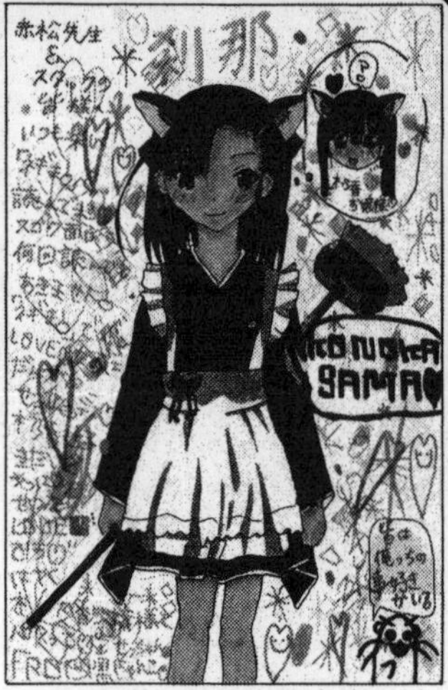
KONOKA SAMA

I FEEL HOW OVERFLOWING WITH LOVE IT IS. ▶

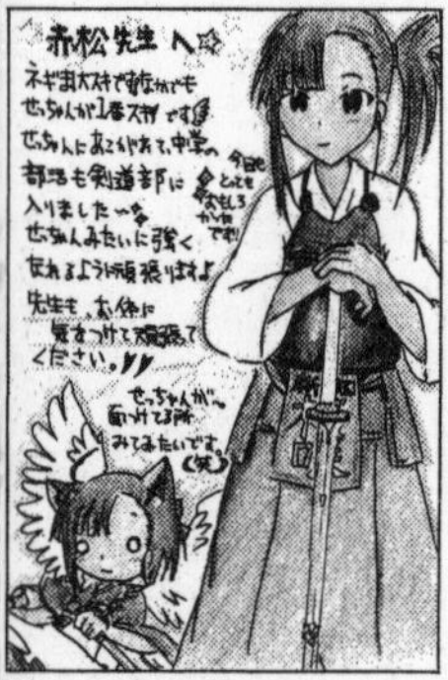

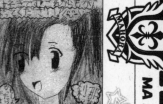

▲ SHE LOOKS SO GALLANT.☆

NEGIMA!
FAN ART CORNER

HELLO, HELLO! I FEEL LIKE THERE WERE A LOT OF KIND OF INTENSE DRAWINGS THIS TIME (IMPRESSED). (^^)♪ OF COURSE I MEAN THAT IN A GOOD WAY (LAUGH). STILL, SETSUNA SURE IS POPULAR, HUH? (LAUGH) WELL, LET'S TAKE A LOOK. ☆

TEXT BY MAX

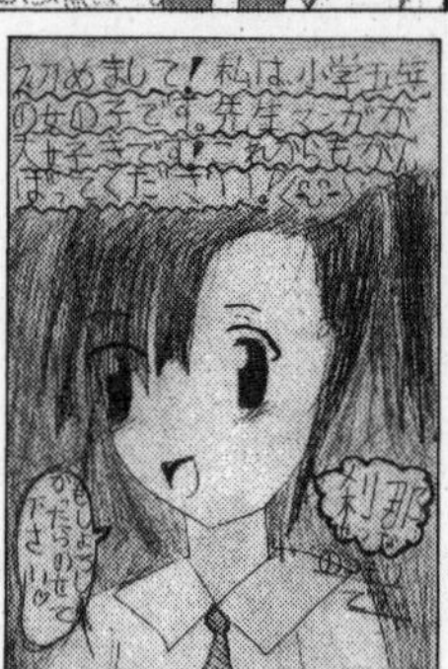

▶ SUCH A KIND-LOOKING SETSUNA.

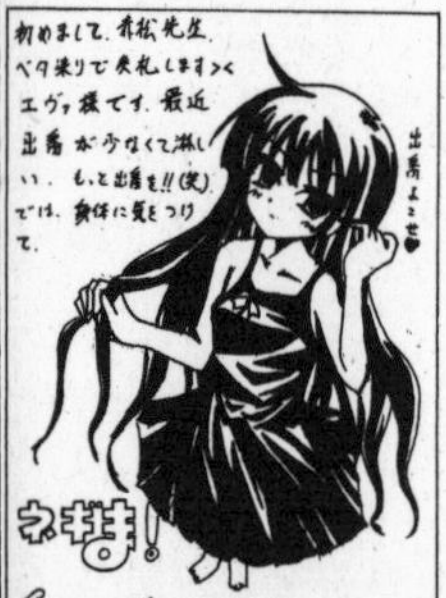
ネギま!
Evangeline. A.K. McDowell

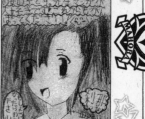

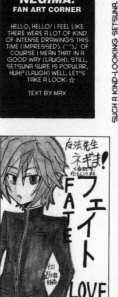

▲ IT MIGHT BE A NICE CHANGE TO SEE EVA WITH BLACK HAIR.

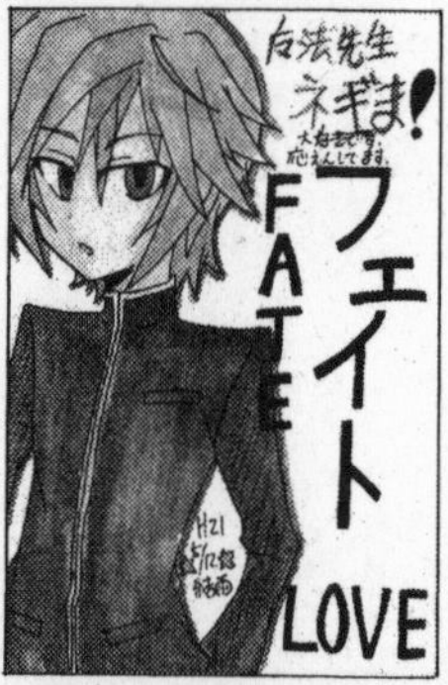
ネギま!
フェイト
FATE
LOVE

▲ HE LOOKS SO GOOD, I'M SURE THE GIRLS WILL LOVE HIM.

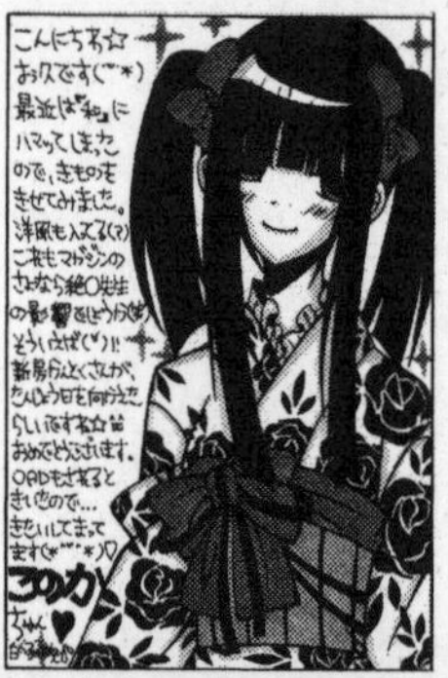

▶ SO REFRESHING.

NEGI MAGI

MAGISTER

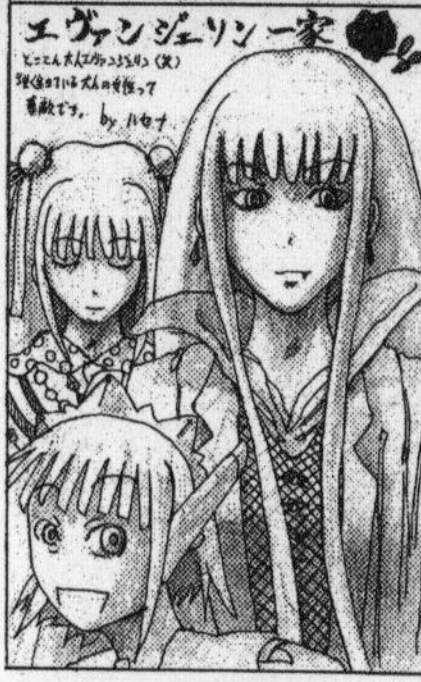

エヴァンジェリン一家

▲ THEY MAKE A DIGNIFIED FAMILY, DON'T THEY?

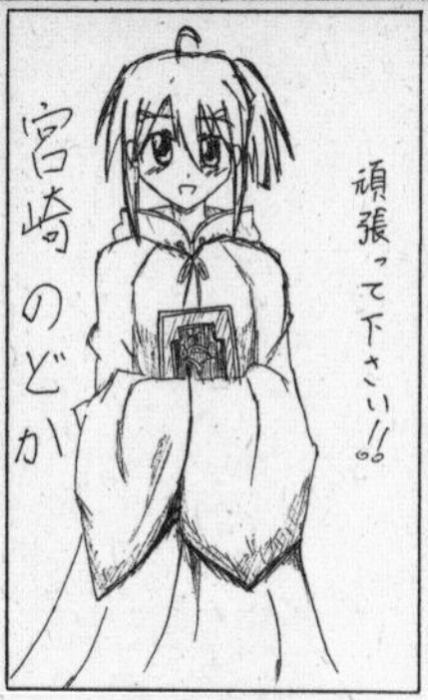

宮崎のどか
頑張って下さい!!

▲ BOOKSTORE'S PERSONALITY FILLS THIS DRAWING.

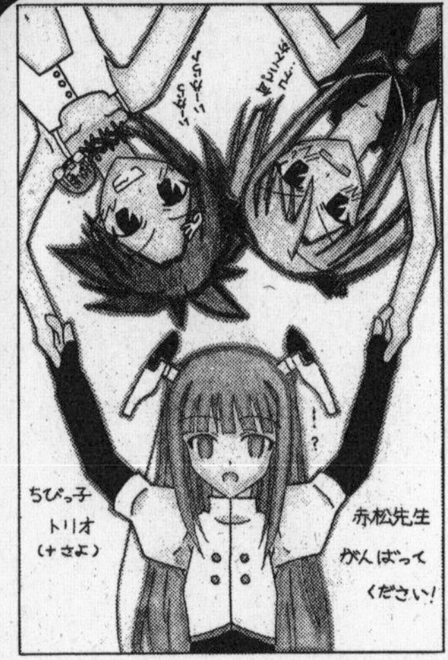

!…?
ちびっ子 トリオ (+さよ)
赤松先生 がんばって ください!

◀ KIND OF A NICE TRIO.

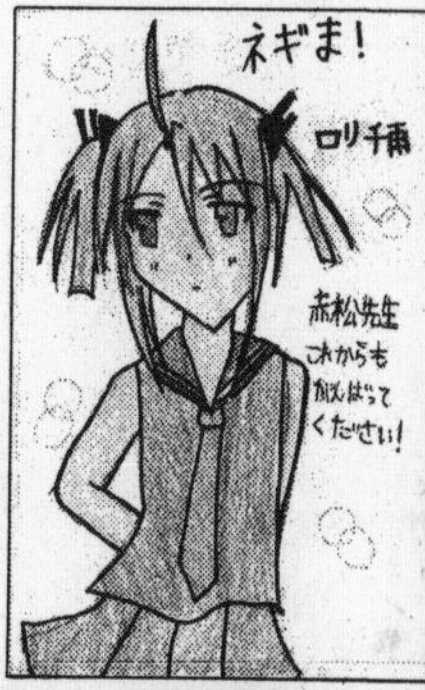

ネギま!
ロリ千雨
赤松先生 これからも がんばって ください!

CHISAME WITH A MELANCHOLY EXPRESSION.

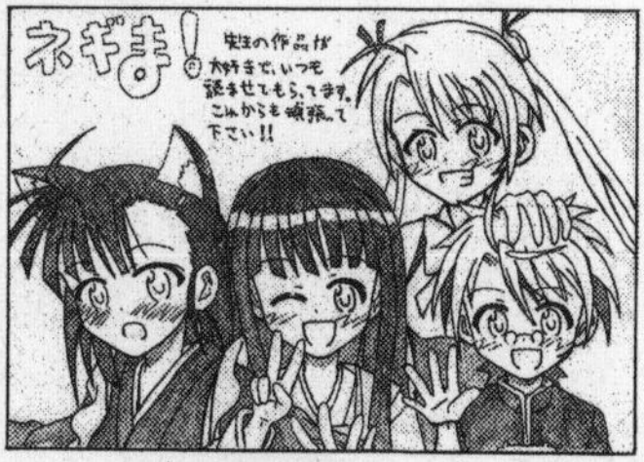

ネギま!
先生の作品が大好きで、いつも読ませてもらってます。これからも頑張って下さい!!

THEIR EYES ARE SO ROUND AND CUTE.☆

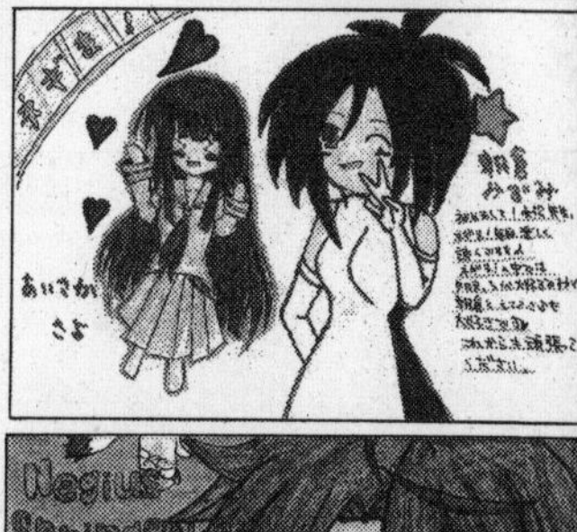

あいさかさよ

SAYO LOOKS SO HAPPY.

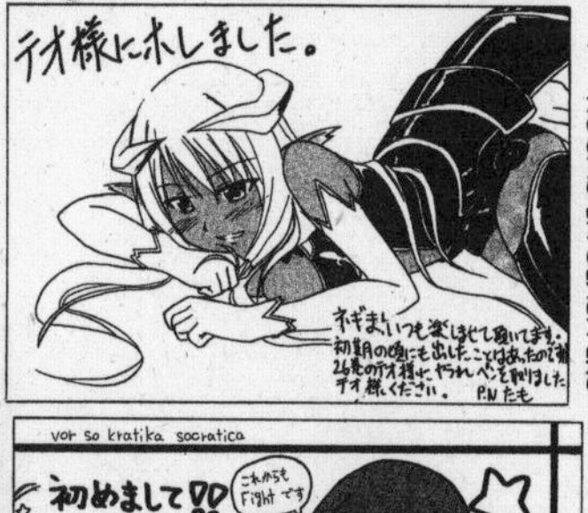

テオ様にホレました。
P.N たも

SHE MAKES ME SWOON. (LAUGH)

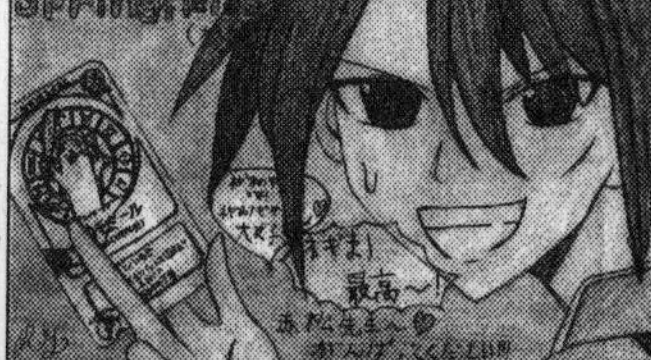

Negius Springfield

THAT CHAMO CARD IS EXCELLENT.☆

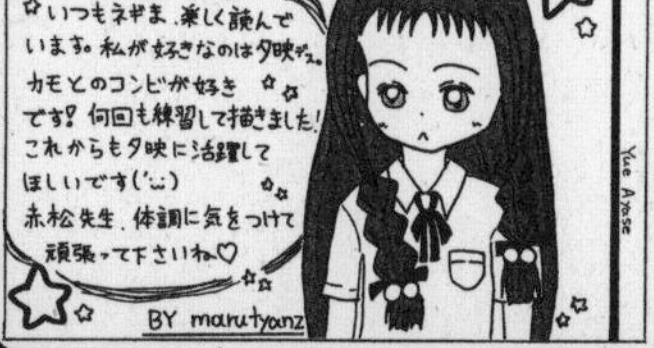

vor so kratika socratica
初めまして!!
これからもFight です
いつもネギま、楽しく読んでいます。私が好きなのは夕映です。カモとのコンビが好きです! 何回も練習して描きました! これからも夕映に活躍してほしいです(;ω;)
赤松先生、体調に気をつけて頑張って下さいね。♡
Yue Ayase
BY marutyanz

I LIKE HER SERIOUS ATMOSPHERE.

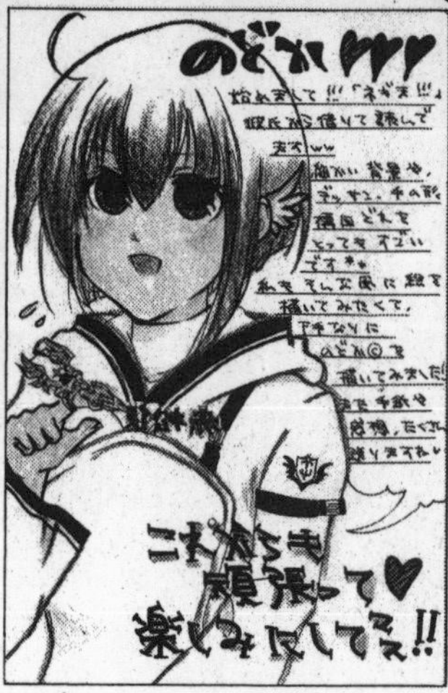
のどか
赤松先生頑張って♥
楽しみにしてま!!

▲ A VERY CALM NODOKA.

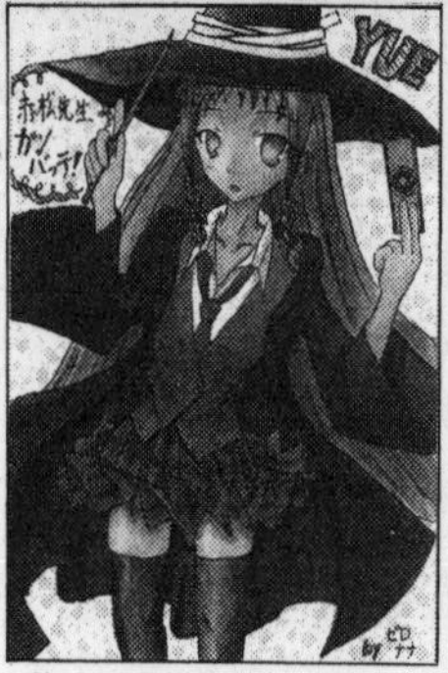
YUE

▲ A SLENDER AND BEAUTIFUL YUECCHI.

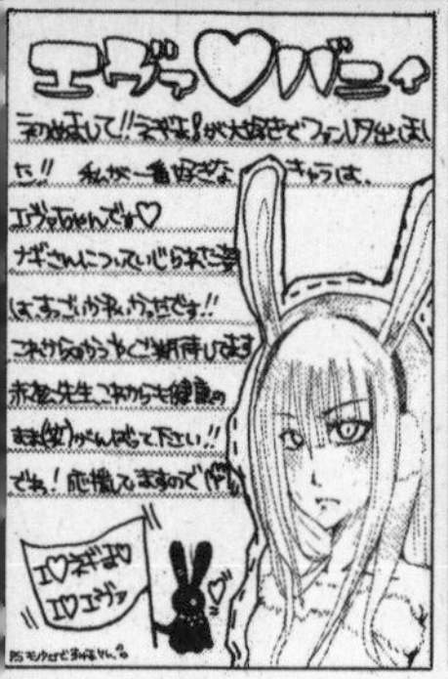
エヴァ♡バニィ

▲ COOL BUNNY EARS.

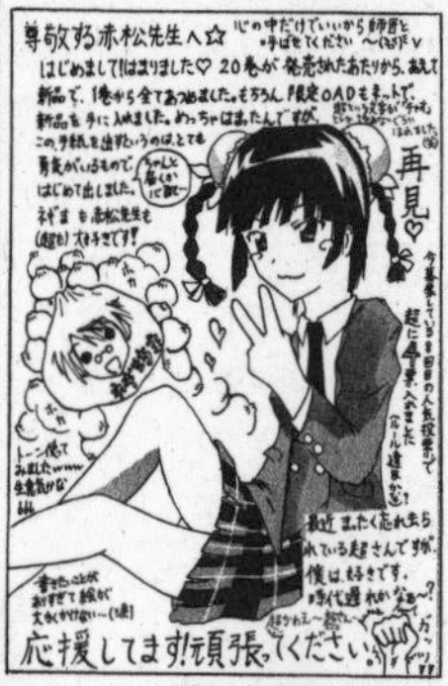
再見
応援してます!頑張ってください。

▲ THIS IS A NICE CHAO.♪

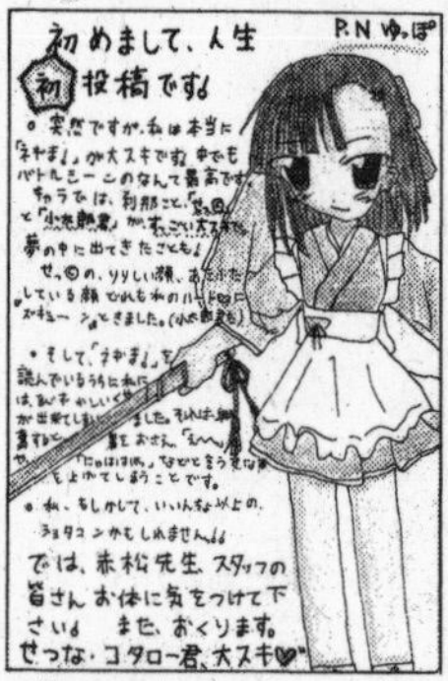
P.N ゆぽ
初めまして、人生初投稿です。

▲ THIS MADE MY HEART SKIP A BEAT.

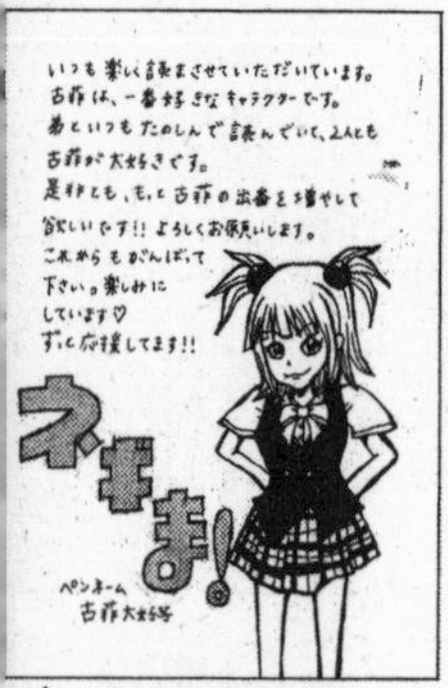
いつも楽しく読ませていただいています。
古菲は、一番好きなキャラクターです。
これからもがんばって下さい。楽しみにしています♡
ずっと応援してます!!
ネギま!

▲ KŪ FEI IN A UNIFORM. THAT'S ALMOST A NOSTALGIA TRIP.

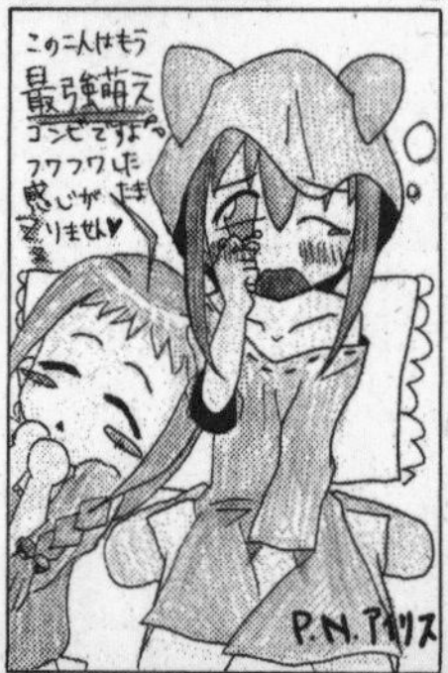
P.N. アイリス

▲ THEY SHARE A PILLOW.☆

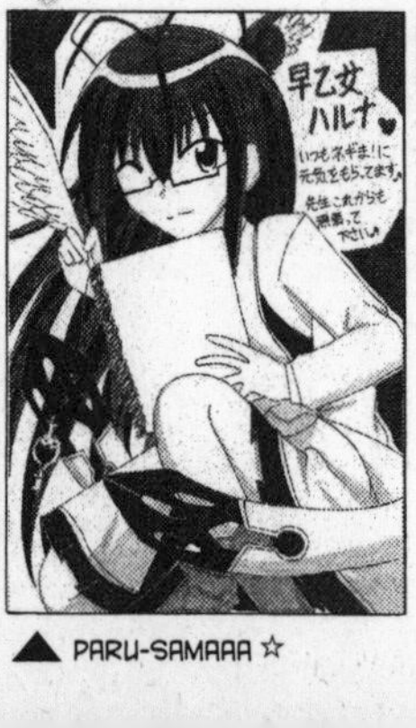
早乙女ハルナ

▲ PARU-SAMAAA ☆

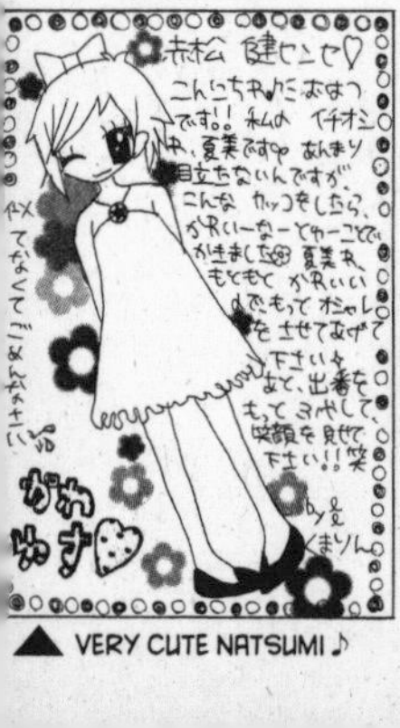
赤松健センセ♡

▲ VERY CUTE NATSUMI ♪

THIS VOLUME'S

FEATURED CHARACTER

MAKIE SASAKI

RANKING

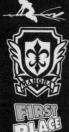

MAGISTER NEGI MAGI

MAHORA

FIRST PLACE

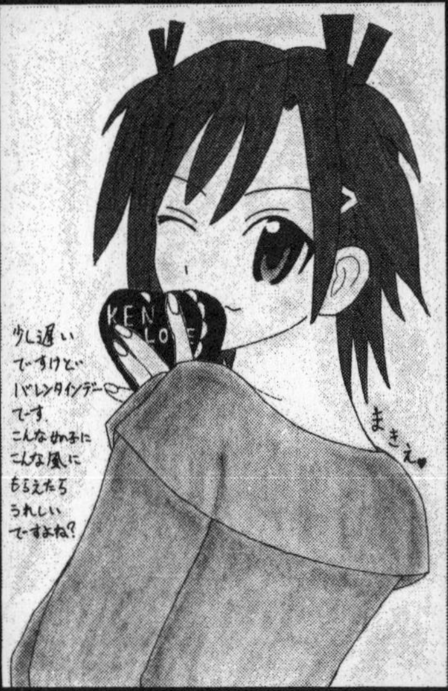
KEN LOVE
少し遅いですけどバレンタインデーです。こんな女の子にこんな風にもらえたらうれしいですよね？
まきえ♥

I'VE NEVER GOTTEN ONE LIKE THIS. (LAUGH) THE CHOCOLATE SAYS "KEN LOVE" ON IT, SO IS SHE GONNA GIVE IT TO ME!? THANK YOU ♡

(AKAMATSU)

SECOND PLACE

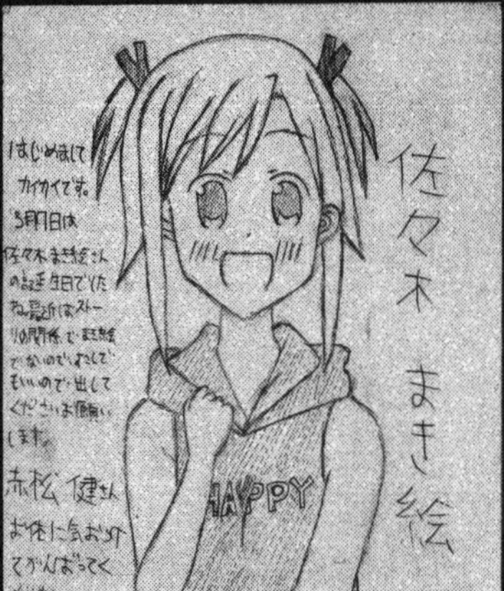
はじめましてカイカイです。3月7日は佐々木まき絵さんの誕生日でしたね。最近はストーリ的関係でまき絵でないのでちょっとでもいいので出してくださいお願いします。
赤松健さんお体に気をつけてがんばってください。
佐々木まき絵
HAPPY
だしてください♡

SHE'LL BE IN THE NEXT VOLUME A LOT. PLEASE BE PATIENT! ~

THIRD PLACE

YOUR SISTER GETS A NOSEBLEED WHEN SHE SEES SETSUNA? WHAT IN THE WORLD? (LAUGH) I'VE ALREADY DONE THE DESIGN FOR MAKIE'S CARD, AND I WANT TO BRING IT OUT SOON, BUT... SO MANY REASONS...

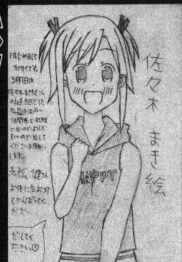

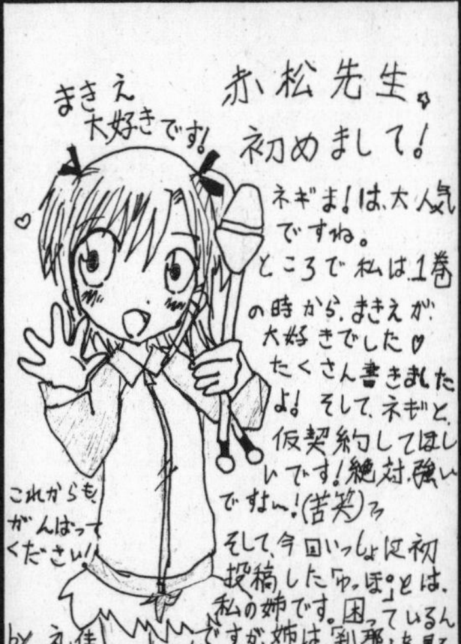
まきえ大好きです！
赤松先生。初めまして！
ネギま！は、大人気ですね。ところで私は1巻の時から、まきえが大好きでした♥ たくさん書きましたよ！そして、ネギと仮契約してほしいです！絶対強いですよ～！(苦笑) そして、今回いっしょに初投稿した「ゆっぽ」とは、私の姉です。困っているんですが、姉は「刹那」を見ると鼻血を出す。すんません なんです。まったく…。
これからもがんばってください！
by. 礼佳

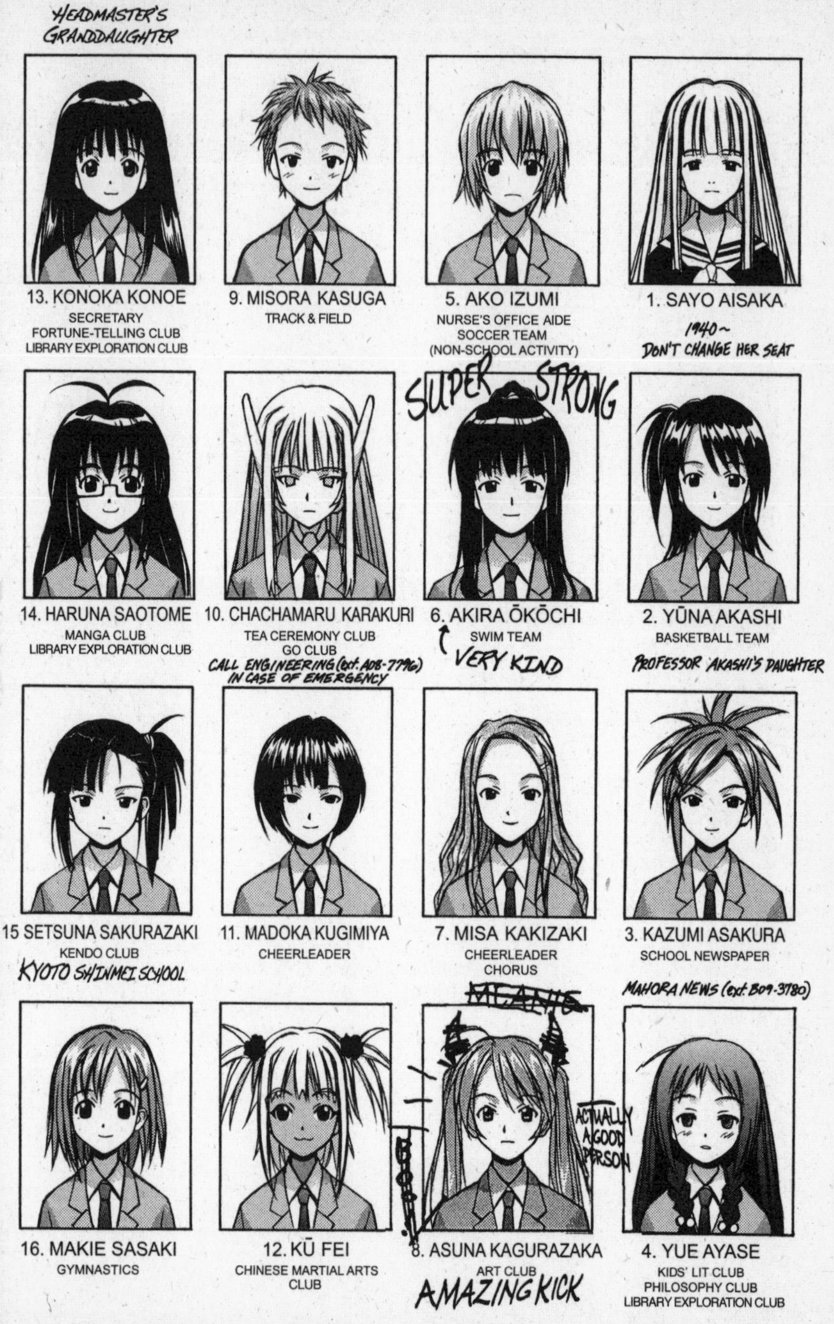

1. SAYO AISAKA
1940~
DON'T CHANGE HER SEAT
5. AKO IZUMI
NURSE'S OFFICE AIDE
SOCCER TEAM
(NON-SCHOOL ACTIVITY)
9. MISORA KASUGA
TRACK & FIELD
HEADMASTER'S GRANDDAUGHTER
13. KONOKA KONOE
SECRETARY
FORTUNE-TELLING CLUB
LIBRARY EXPLORATION CLUB
2. YŪNA AKASHI
BASKETBALL TEAM
PROFESSOR AKASHI'S DAUGHTER
SUPER STRONG
6. AKIRA ŌKŌCHI
SWIM TEAM
VERY KIND
10. CHACHAMARU KARAKURI
TEA CEREMONY CLUB
GO CLUB
CALL ENGINEERING (ext. A08-7796) IN CASE OF EMERGENCY
14. HARUNA SAOTOME
MANGA CLUB
LIBRARY EXPLORATION CLUB
3. KAZUMI ASAKURA
SCHOOL NEWSPAPER
MAHORA NEWS (ext. B09-3780)
7. MISA KAKIZAKI
CHEERLEADER
CHORUS
11. MADOKA KUGIMIYA
CHEERLEADER
15 SETSUNA SAKURAZAKI
KENDO CLUB
KYOTO SHINMEI SCHOOL
4. YUE AYASE
KIDS' LIT CLUB
PHILOSOPHY CLUB
LIBRARY EXPLORATION CLUB
ACTUALLY A GOOD PERSON
8. ASUNA KAGURAZAKA
ART CLUB
AMAZING KICK
12. KŪ FEI
CHINESE MARTIAL ARTS CLUB
16. MAKIE SASAKI
GYMNASTICS

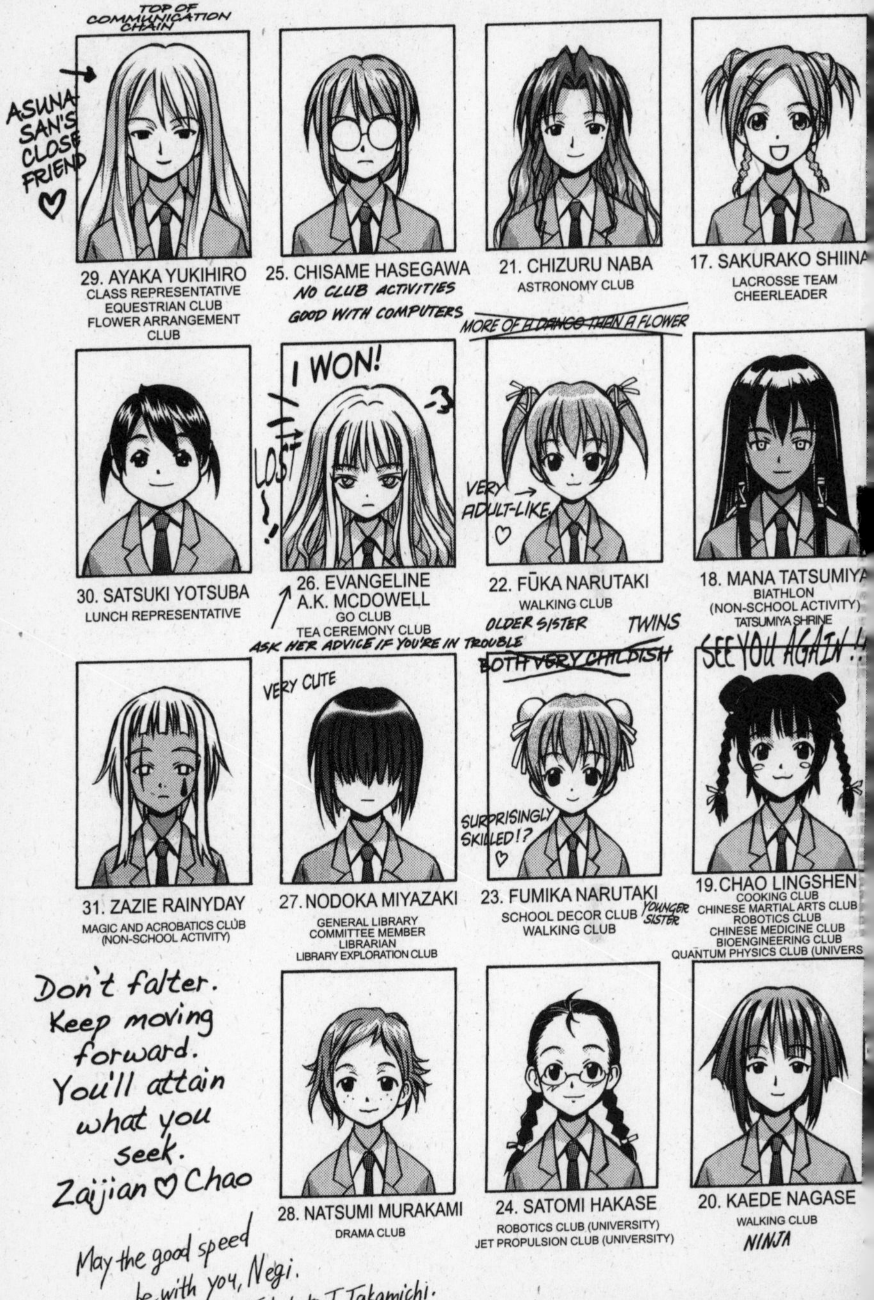

17. SAKURAKO SHIINA
LACROSSE TEAM
CHEERLEADER
21. CHIZURU NABA
ASTRONOMY CLUB
~~MORE OF A DANGO THAN A FLOWER~~
25. CHISAME HASEGAWA
NO CLUB ACTIVITIES
GOOD WITH COMPUTERS
TOP OF COMMUNICATION CHAIN
ASUNA-SAN'S CLOSE FRIEND ♥
29. AYAKA YUKIHIRO
CLASS REPRESENTATIVE
EQUESTRIAN CLUB
FLOWER ARRANGEMENT CLUB
18. MANA TATSUMIYA
BIATHLON
(NON-SCHOOL ACTIVITY)
TATSUMIYA SHRINE
VERY ADULT-LIKE ♥
22. FŪKA NARUTAKI
WALKING CLUB
OLDER SISTER
TWINS
~~BOTH VERY CHILDISH~~
I WON!
-3
LOST...!
26. EVANGELINE A.K. MCDOWELL
GO CLUB
TEA CEREMONY CLUB
ASK HER ADVICE IF YOU'RE IN TROUBLE
30. SATSUKI YOTSUBA
LUNCH REPRESENTATIVE
SEE YOU AGAIN!!
19. CHAO LINGSHEN
COOKING CLUB
CHINESE MARTIAL ARTS CLUB
ROBOTICS CLUB
CHINESE MEDICINE CLUB
BIOENGINEERING CLUB
QUANTUM PHYSICS CLUB (UNIVERS
SURPRISINGLY SKILLED!? ♥
23. FUMIKA NARUTAKI
YOUNGER SISTER
SCHOOL DECOR CLUB
WALKING CLUB
VERY CUTE
27. NODOKA MIYAZAKI
GENERAL LIBRARY
COMMITTEE MEMBER
LIBRARIAN
LIBRARY EXPLORATION CLUB
31. ZAZIE RAINYDAY
MAGIC AND ACROBATICS CLUB
(NON-SCHOOL ACTIVITY)
20. KAEDE NAGASE
WALKING CLUB
NINJA
24. SATOMI HAKASE
ROBOTICS CLUB (UNIVERSITY)
JET PROPULSION CLUB (UNIVERSITY)
28. NATSUMI MURAKAMI
DRAMA CLUB
Don't falter. Keep moving forward. You'll attain what you seek. Zaijian ♥ Chao
May the good speed be with you, Negi. Takahata T. Takamichi.

魔法先生ネギま!
MAGISTER NEGI MAGI

赤松健 SHONEN MAGAZINE COMICS
KEN AKAMATSU

27

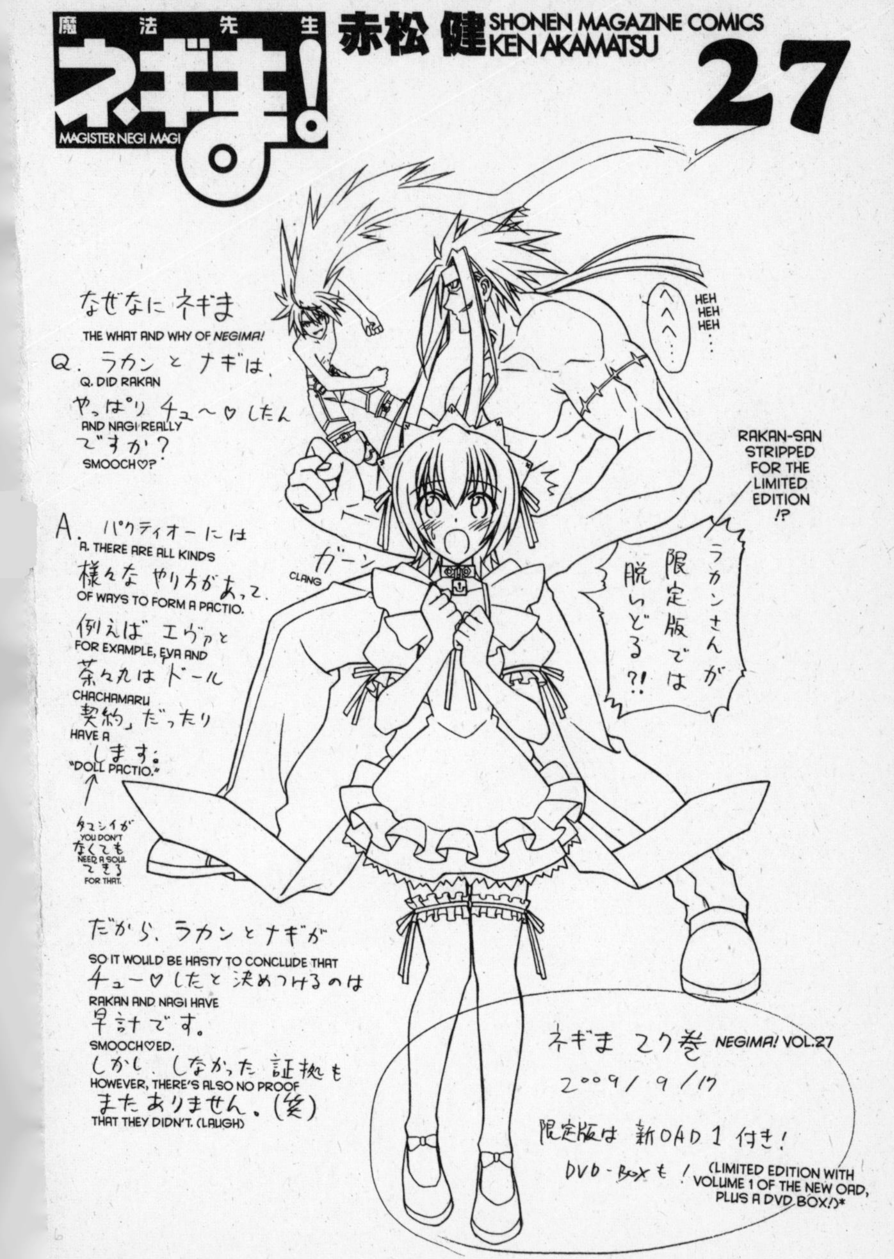

なぜなにネギま
THE WHAT AND WHY OF NEGIMA!
Q. ラカンとナギは、やっぱりチュ～♡したんですか?
Q. DID RAKAN AND NAGI REALLY SMOOCH♡?
へへへ…
HEH HEH HEH...
ラカンさんが限定版では脱ぐどる?!
RAKAN-SAN STRIPPED FOR THE LIMITED EDITION!?
A. パクティオーには様々なやり方があって、例えばエヴァと茶々丸はドール契約」だったりします。
A. THERE ARE ALL KINDS OF WAYS TO FORM A PACTIO. FOR EXAMPLE, EVA AND CHACHAMARU HAVE A "DOLL PACTIO."
ガーン
CLANG
タマシイがなくてもできる
YOU DON'T NEED A SOUL FOR THAT.
だから、ラカンとナギがチュ～♡したと決めつけるのは早計です。
SO IT WOULD BE HASTY TO CONCLUDE THAT RAKAN AND NAGI HAVE SMOOCH♡ED.
しかし、しなかった証拠もまたありません。(笑)
HOWEVER, THERE'S ALSO NO PROOF THAT THEY DIDN'T. (LAUGH)
ネギま 27巻 NEGIMA! VOL.27
2009/9/17
限定版は新OAD1付き! DVD-BOXも!
(LIMITED EDITION WITH VOLUME 1 OF THE NEW OAD, PLUS A DVD BOX!)*

*OFFER AVAILABLE ONLY IN JAPAN

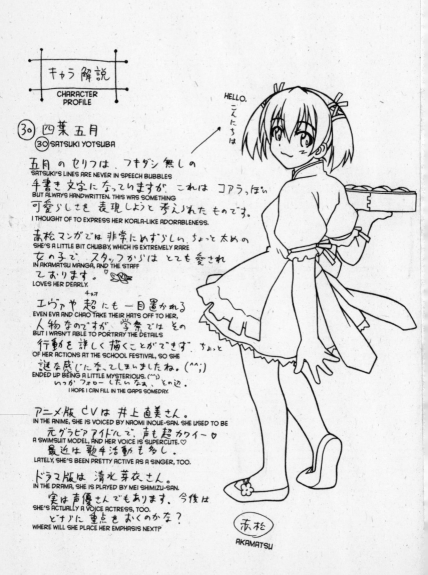

キャラ解説
CHARACTER PROFILE

㉚ 四葉五月
㉚ SATSUKI YOTSUBA

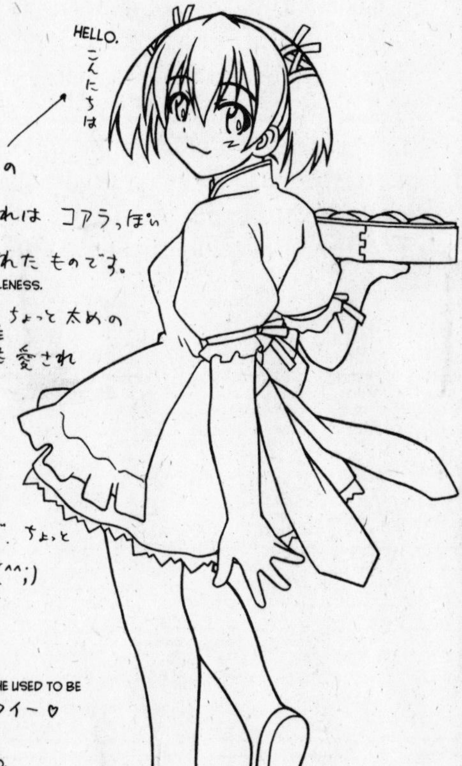
HELLO.
こんにちは

五月のセリフは、フキダシ無しの
SATSUKI'S LINES ARE NEVER IN SPEECH BUBBLES
手書き文字になっていますが、これはコアラっぽい
BUT ALWAYS HANDWRITTEN. THIS WAS SOMETHING
可愛らしさを表現しようと考えられたものです。
I THOUGHT OF TO EXPRESS HER KOALA-LIKE ADORABLENESS.

赤松マンガでは非常にめずらしい、ちょっと太めの
SHE'S A LITTLE BIT CHUBBY, WHICH IS EXTREMELY RARE
女の子で、スタッフからはとても愛され
IN AKAMATSU MANGA, AND THE STAFF
ております。♡
LOVES HER DEARLY.

エヴァや超（チャオ）にも一目置かれる
EVEN EVA AND CHAO TAKE THEIR HATS OFF TO HER,
人物なのですが、学祭ではその
BUT I WASN'T ABLE TO PORTRAY THE DETAILS
行動を詳しく描くことができず、ちょっと
OF HER ACTIONS AT THE SCHOOL FESTIVAL, SO SHE
謎な感じになってしまいましたね。(^^;)
ENDED UP BEING A LITTLE MYSTERIOUS. (^^;)
いつかフォローしたいなあ、その辺。
I HOPE I CAN FILL IN THE GAPS SOMEDAY.

アニメ版CVは井上直美さん。
IN THE ANIME, SHE IS VOICED BY NAOMI INOUE-SAN. SHE USED TO BE
元グラビアアイドルで、声も超カワイー♡
A SWIMSUIT MODEL, AND HER VOICE IS SUPERCUTE.♡
最近は歌手活動も多し。
LATELY, SHE'S BEEN PRETTY ACTIVE AS A SINGER, TOO.
ドラマ版は清水芽衣さん。
IN THE DRAMA, SHE IS PLAYED BY MEI SHIMIZU-SAN.
実は声優さんでもあります、今後は
SHE'S ACTUALLY A VOICE ACTRESS, TOO.
どちらに重点をおくのかな？
WHERE WILL SHE PLACE HER EMPHASIS NEXT?

赤松
AKAMATSU

About the Creator

Negima! is only Ken Akamatsu's third manga, although he started working in the field in 1994 with *AI Ga Tomaranai* (released in the United States with the title *A.I. Love You*). Like all of Akamatsu's work to date, it was published in Kodansha's *Shonen Magazine*. *AI Ga Tomaranai* ran for five years before concluding in 1999. In 1998, however, Akamatsu began the work that would make him one of the most popular manga artists in Japan: *Love Hina*. *Love Hina* ran for four years, and before its conclusion in 2002, it would cause Akamatsu to be granted the prestigious Manga of the Year award from Kodansha, as well as going on to become one of the bestselling manga in the United States.

Translation Notes

Japanese is a tricky language for most Westerners, and translation is often more art than science. For your edification and reading pleasure, here are notes on some of the places where we could have gone in a different direction with our translation of the work, or where a Japanese cultural reference is used.

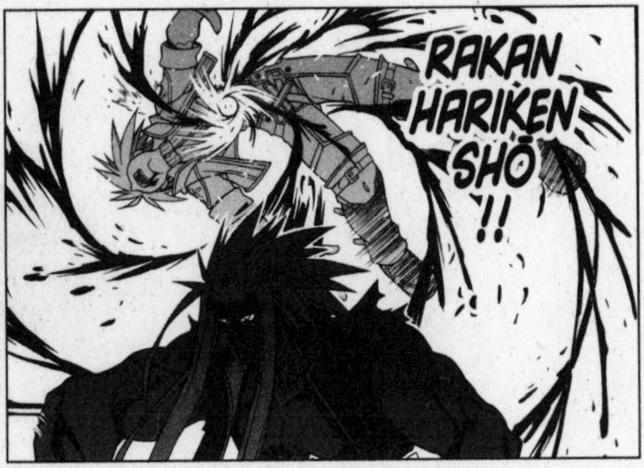
RAKAN HARIKEN SHŌ!!

Rakan Hariken Shō, page 56

The name of this attack is packed with meaning. Of course, Rakan also refers to Jack Rakan himself, but when he puts his name in an attack, he gives it *kanji* meaning "achiever of Nirvana." In English, it could be translated as "enlightened destructive reverse sword palm." And "*hariken*" can also be the English word "hurricane," which, based on the shower of blood from Negi, is also very appropriate, and the attack could also be "Rakan Hurricane Palm."

Complete training match, page 137

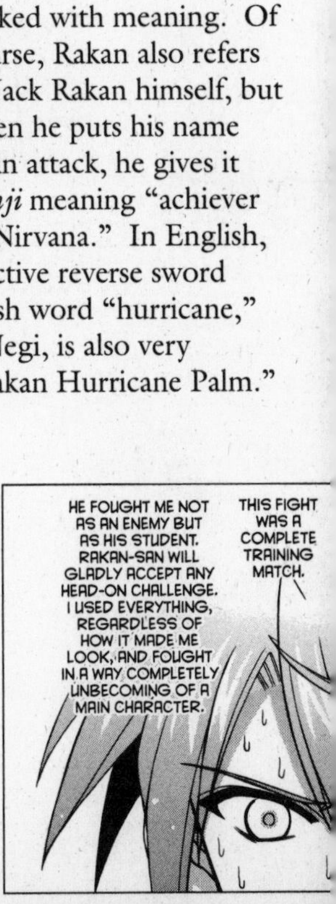
THIS FIGHT WAS A COMPLETE TRAINING MATCH.
HE FOUGHT ME NOT AS AN ENEMY BUT AS HIS STUDENT. RAKAN-SAN WILL GLADLY ACCEPT ANY HEAD-ON CHALLENGE. I USED EVERYTHING, REGARDLESS OF HOW IT MADE ME LOOK, AND FOUGHT IN A WAY COMPLETELY UNBECOMING OF A MAIN CHARACTER.

More literally, Negi says, "This was a complete chest-borrowing match." The phrase comes from sumo, when a lower-level wrestler will "borrow the chest" of a higher-level, stronger wrestler to practice his fighting skills and techniques.

Preview of *Negima!* Volume 28

We're pleased to present you a preview from volume 28. Please check our website, www.delreymanga.com, to see when this volume will be available in English. For now you'll have to make do with Japanese!

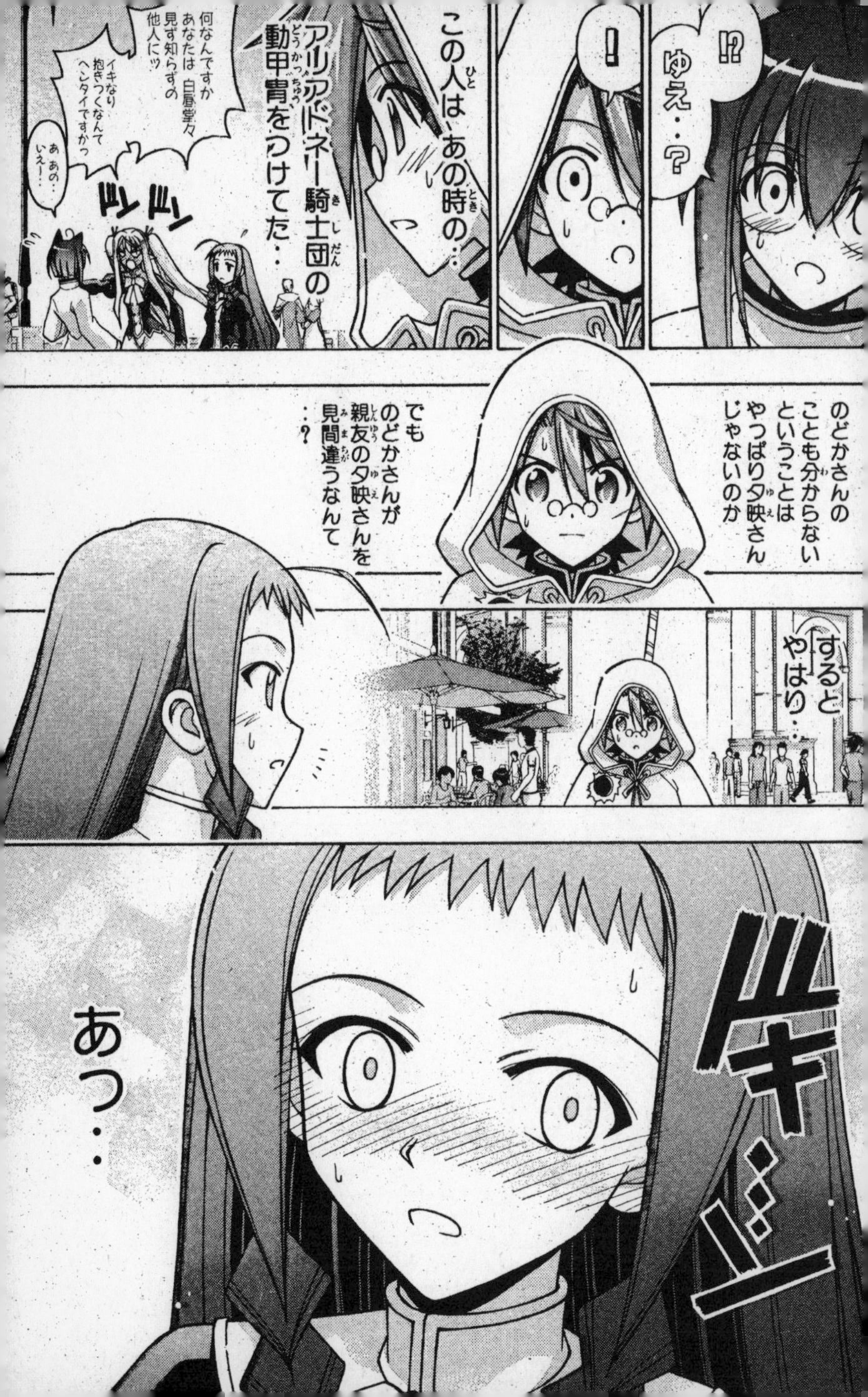
!?
ゆえ・・・?
!
この人は、あの時の・・・
アリアドネー騎士団の
動甲冑をつけてた・・・
何なんですか あなたは 白昼堂々 見ず知らずの他人にッ
イキなり抱きつくなんてヘンタイですかっ
ドン ドン
あ あの・・・ いえ――・・・
のどかさんのことも分からないということはやっぱり夕映さんじゃないのか
でものどかさんが親友の夕映さんを見間違うなんて・・・?
するとやはり・・・
ドキッ
あっ・・・

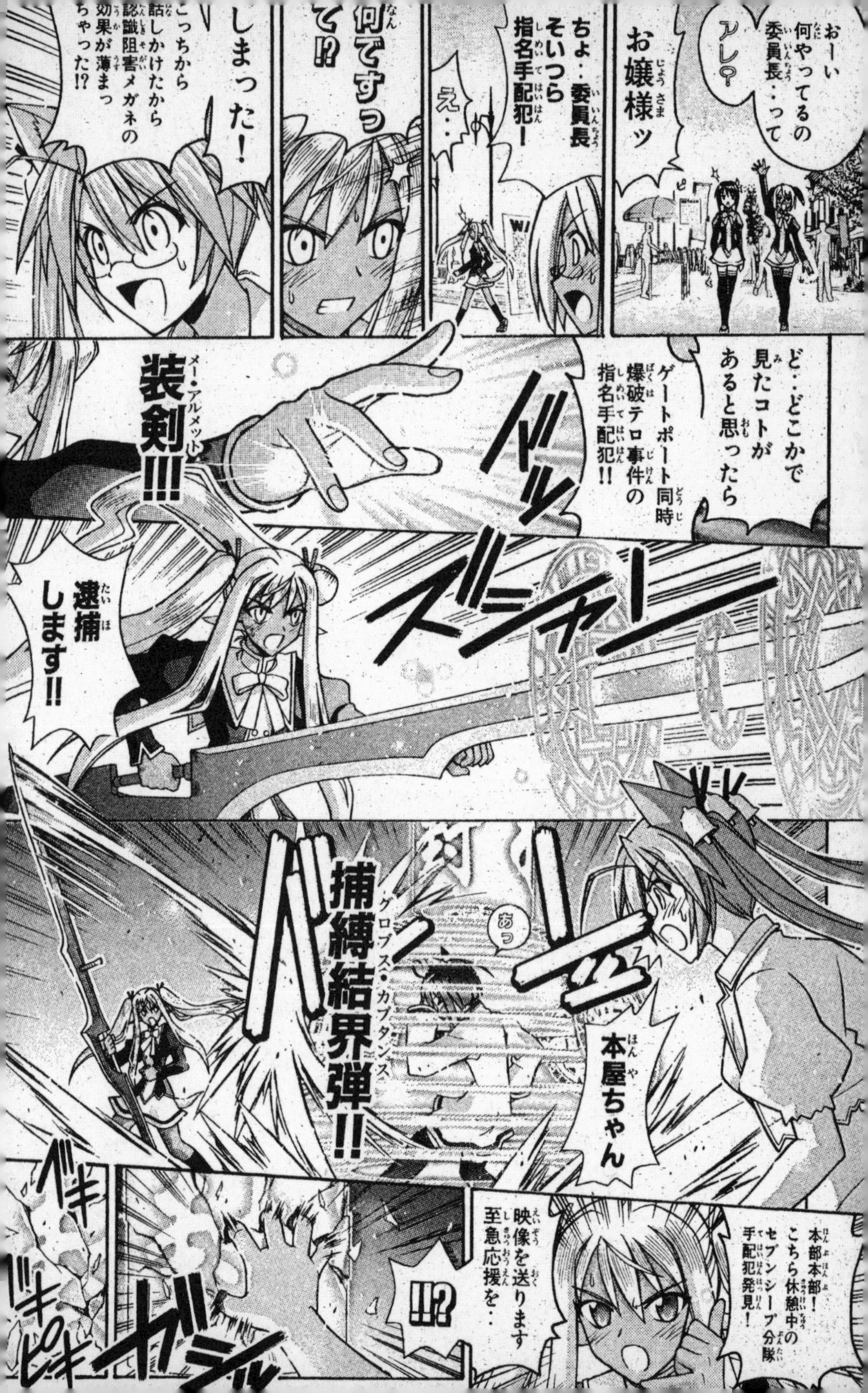
おーい
何やってるの
委員長・・・って
アレ？
お嬢様ッ
ピ
え・・・
ちょ・・委員長
そいつら
指名手配犯ー
何ですって!?
しまった！
こっちから
話しかけたから
認識阻害メガネの
効果が薄まっ
ちゃった!?
ど・・どこかで
見たコトが
あると思ったら
ゲートポート同時
爆破テロ事件の
指名手配犯!!
ドッ
装剣!!!
ズシャー
逮捕
します!!
本屋ちゃん
あっ
捕縛結界弾!!
本部本部！
こちら休憩中の
セブンシープ分隊
手配犯発見！
映像を送ります
至急応援を・・・
!!?
ビキ
ビキピキ

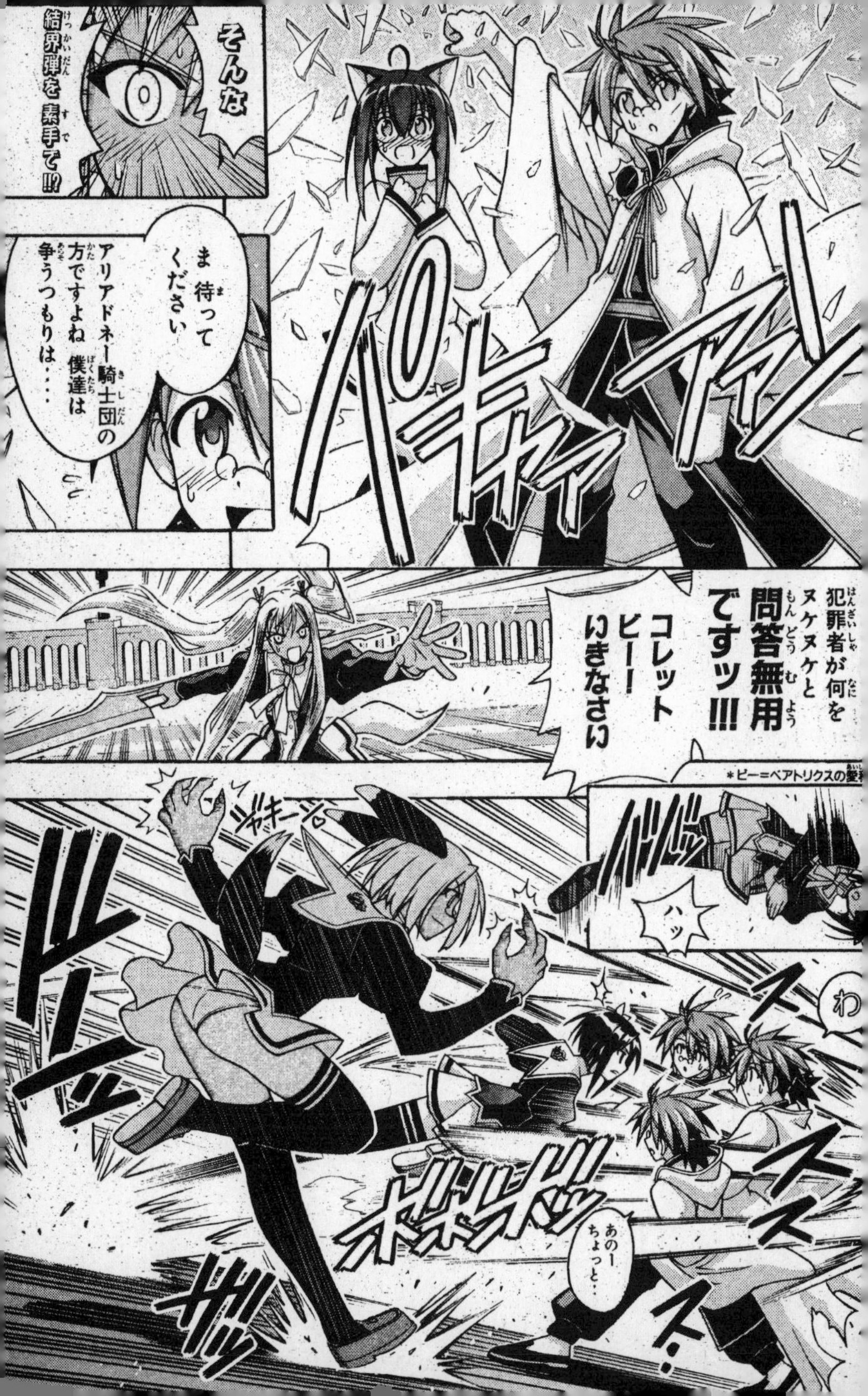
パキャァァン
そんな
結界弾を素手で!!?
ま待ってください
アリアドネー騎士団の方ですよね 僕達は争うつもりは‥‥
犯罪者が何をヌケヌケと
問答無用ですッ!!!
コレットビー!! いきなさい
＊ビー＝ベアトリクスの愛称
バッ
ハッ
ジャキーン♡
ドドンッ
わ
ドドドドッ
ザッ
あのーちょっと‥

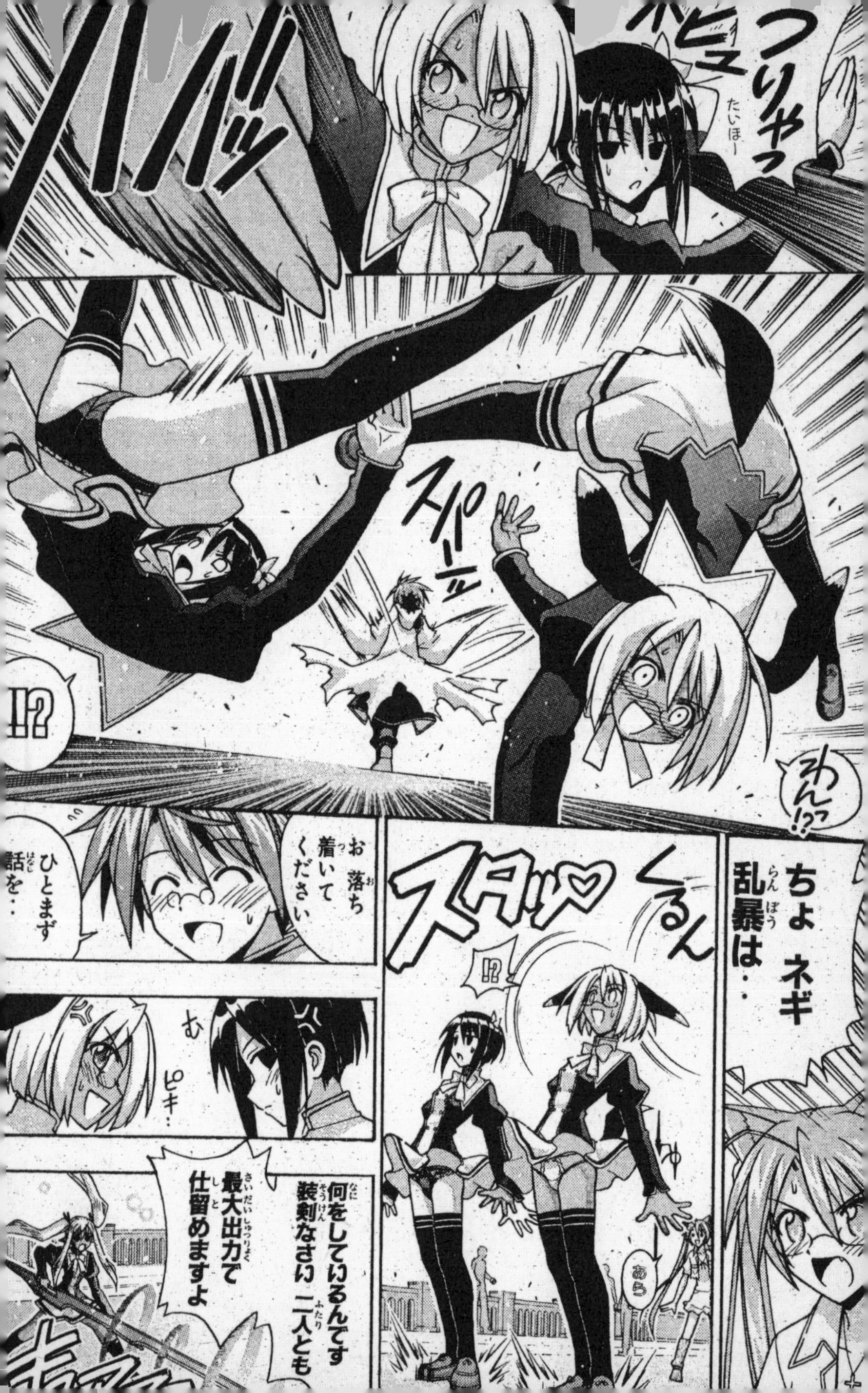
ヒュ
つりゃっ
たいほー
バババッ
わんっ!?
スパーッ
!?
ちょ ネギ 乱暴は・・
くるん
スルッ♡
!?
あら
お落ち着いてください
ひとまず話を・・
む
ピキ…
何をしているんです 装剣なさい 二人とも
最大出力で仕留めますよ

STORY BY KEN AKAMATSU
ART BY TAKUYA FUJIMA

BASED ON THE POPULAR ANIME!

Negi Springfield is only ten years old, but he's already a powerful wizard. After graduating from his magic school in England, the prodigy is given an unusual assignment: teach English at an all-girl school in Japan. Now Negi has to find a way to deal with his thirty-one totally gorgeous (and completely overaffectionate) students—without using magic! Based on the *Negima!* anime, this is a fresh take on the beloved *Negima!* story.

Available anywhere books or comics are sold!

VISIT WWW.DELREYMANGA.COM TO:
- Read sample pages
- View release date calendars for upcoming volumes
- Sign up for Del Rey's free manga e-newsletter
- Find out the latest about new Del Rey Manga series

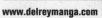

TOMARE!

[STOP!]

You're going the wrong way!

Manga is a completely different type of reading experience.

To start at the *beginning*, go to the *end*!

That's right! Authentic manga is read the traditional Japanese way—from right to left, exactly the *opposite* of how American books are read. It's easy to follow: Just go to the other end of the book, and read each page—and each panel—from right side to left side, starting at the top right. Now you're experiencing manga as it was meant to be.